Flexible Learning in an Information Society

Badrul H. Khan
The George Washington University, USA

 Information Science Publishing

Hershey • London • Melbourne • Singapore

Acquisitions Editor:	Michelle Potter
Development Editor:	Kristin Roth
Senior Managing Editor:	Jennifer Neidig
Managing Editor:	Sara Reed
Copy Editor:	Maria Boyer
Typesetter:	Jessie Weik
Cover Design:	Lisa Tosheff
Printed at:	Integrated Book Technology

Published in the United States of America by
    Information Science Publishing (an imprint of Idea Group Inc.)
    701 E. Chocolate Avenue
    Hershey PA 17033
    Tel: 717-533-8845
    Fax: 717-533-8661
    E-mail: cust@idea-group.com
    Web site: http://www.idea-group.com

and in the United Kingdom by
    Information Science Publishing (an imprint of Idea Group Inc.)
    3 Henrietta Street
    Covent Garden
    London WC2E 8LU
    Tel: 44 20 7240 0856
    Fax: 44 20 7379 0609
    Web site: http://www.eurospanonline.com

Library of Congress Cataloging-in-Publication Data

Flexible learning in an information society / Badrul H. Khan, editor.
    p. cm.
  Summary: "This book uses a flexible learning framework to explain the best ways of creating a meaningful learning environment. This framework consists of eight factors - institutional, management, technological, pedagogical, ethical, interface design, resource support, and evaluation;a systematic understanding of these factors creates successful flexible learning environments"--Provided by publisher.
  Includes bibliographical references and index.
  ISBN 1-59904-325-4 (hardcover : alk. paper) -- ISBN 1-59904-326-2 (softcover : alk. paper) -- ISBN 1-59904-327-0 (ebook : alk. paper)
  1. Distance education. 2. Instructional systems--Design. 3. Educational technology. 4. Effective teaching. 5. Open learning. 6. Effective teaching--Evaluation. I. Khan, Badrul H., 1958-
  LC5800.F55 2006
  371.35'8--dc22
                              2006015054

British Cataloguing in Publication Data
A Cataloguing in Publication record for this book is available from the British Library.

All work contributed to this book is new, previously-unpublished material. The views expressed in this book are those of the authors, but not necessarily of the publisher.

Dedication

This book is dedicated to my late parents—Mr. Lokman Khan Sherwani & Mrs. Shabnom Khanam Sherwani of Khan Manzil, Pathantooly, Chittagong, Bangladesh.

Flexible Learning in an Information Society

Table of Contents

Foreword

It is a pleasure to have the opportunity of "saying" a few words as a foreword to Badrul Khan's book. Frankly, I was not very enthusiastic when he first invited me; with a second edition of a book of my own under way, an issue of *The American Journal of Distance Education* to hand over, and a full teaching schedule, among other things, one more writing assignment was not what I wanted. However, a quick look at Dr. Khan's Preface to the book resulted in an immediate change of mood, from reluctance to excitement. What caused this was the following, the first thing I read: " In the information age ... Learners expect on-demand, anytime/anywhere high-quality learning environments ... They want increased flexibility in learning—they want to have more say in what they learn, when they learn, and where and how they learn." This is what I found irresistible. How could I resist a new book that seems to validate a position formulated in earlier times, regarded by one's colleagues as marginal, if not bizarre, that now seems to be entering the mainstream. Well, such was my reaction when I read those opening sentences of *Flexible Learning in an Information Society*—seducing me into reading on through the following chapters, and then gladly letting Dr. Khan know I would write what I hope will be interpreted as a warm endorsement of his publication.

It would be unfairly enigmatic to leave the above reference to the position "formulated in earlier times" without a short explanation, so let me explain that flexibility is a subject that has preoccupied me since the first research that I reported in 1972, when I classified educational programs into a typology according to the extent to which they were more or less flexible. Programs offering greater flexibility were described as having less structure, greater opportunity for dialogue between teachers and learners, and giving more control of the teaching-learning process to the student. Here is exactly what I wrote at that time:

For every program, we seek to identify the relationship between learners and teachers, and where control of each instructional process lies, by asking: Is learning self-initiated and self-motivated? Who identifies goals and objectives, and selects problems for study? Who determines the pace, the sequence, and the methods of information gathering? What provision is there for the development of learners' ideas and for creative solutions to problems? Is emphasis on gathering information external to the learner? How flexible is each instructional process to the requirements of the learner? How is the usefulness and quality of learning judged? (Moore, 1972, p. 81)

I trust this reference will serve to explain my very positive response to *Flexible Learning in an Information Society*. To be offered a book of 30 chapters on a subject that has exercised me for so long at both micro-levels (course design and instruction) and more recently at macro-levels (institutional organization and policy, of which more later), this is exciting indeed.

In the 1972 report, the term I used to define the learner's flexibility in deciding and directing what to learn, how, and to what extent was "learner autonomy." That term was derived from a sound tradition, a pedagogy referred to for several decades as independent study, which incorporated teaching through the technology of printed text. In spite of considerable evidence that flexible learning using older technologies could be very successful, the question of flexibility has remained on the margin of educators' attention until very recently. The promise of this new book is that now, in the Information Age, with leadership from academics like Badrul Khan, we might see a larger cadre of researchers with better institutional resources address some of the long-standing questions. What, we want to know, are the psychological and learning theory justifications for flexible learning? What are the ethical and philosophical justifications for allowing (or denying) the freedoms of flexible learning? What are the optimally flexible ways of structuring a curriculum and structuring the processes by which teachers and learners enter conversation, interaction, dialogue? The editor of *Flexible Learning in an Information Society* and the other authors in this book have provided a valuable contribution to our search for answers to these questions, the former by providing a structure that enables his contributors to focus on each of the several domains that will have to be mastered, and the latter by providing as rich a variety of topics as could be hoped for in a single volume—including a strong thematic concern with evaluation and assessment, chapters that deal directly with key pedagogical concepts such as "humanizing" (there's a concept with deep roots!), and more elusive core macro- issues such as those concerning intercultural collaboration and ethical challenges. Although there is so much here, one reaction to reading it all is to realize how much more remains to be done. This book indeed exposes the irony of our situation, showing on the one hand the importance of flexibility and progress being made towards achieving more flexibility, but at the same time showing how limited is the flexibility we enjoy, even in this Information Age.

What we are able to celebrate so far is primarily flexibility in use of new technologies. There is also a somewhat increased flexibility in teaching methods in our schools, colleges, and training departments—seen in more flexible course structures and the use of constructivist pedagogical techniques to enhance the frequency and quality of dialogue between learners and instructors. However, these technological and pedagogical flexibilities are limited, squeezed, and constrained by highly *inflexible institutional structures and almost totally inflexible national, state, and institutional policies.* The majority of teachers work in organizations that are governed by academic policies formulated when rigidity, not flexibility was the norm. It is these organizational structures and policies that are the hardest barriers to overcome as we look to extend

x

greater flexibility through new technology and new pedagogy. The kinds of problems I have in mind are restrictive admissions criteria (which includes tuition fees), rules about time to graduation, and the insistence by long-established institutions on an arbitrarily determined standard period of residence for every student, regardless of the subject of study, or the student's intellectual or personal attributes. Many older universities that are now sufficiently flexible to deliver courses online nevertheless insist that their professors must be resident on the campus, limiting the pool of teaching talent quite unnecessarily in the Information Age when the Internet makes geographic location irrelevant. The allocation of resources and inflexible budgetary procedures are heavily biased towards synchronous interactivity—that is, the classroom, leaving inadequate investment in the pre-active course design process that is at least as important for programs delivered by technology. Inflexible, traditional evaluation methods are often unsuitable for monitoring and evaluating the effectiveness of programs using distance teaching products and methods. I do not of course criticize restrictions and rules designed to protect the student or to support the quality of teaching and learning, but I do suggest there is a need to recognize and understand more about the effects of policies that are enforced only because of tradition and administrative inertia. Issues of policy that are most obvious in our educational institutions need examination at national and state levels too. The recent (2006) decision to amend the infamous 50% rule that withheld federal funding from some of the more flexible technology-based teaching institutions illustrates the kind of higher level policy issue that I refer to. I was among a group of educators who signed a petition to Congress on this issue—and that was some 10 years ago. Now we can hope that the pace of change is accelerating, and surely will move faster as we develop shared understanding among innovative stakeholders about the need to change the culture and practice of our educational organizations, and to effect change at the state and national levels. For those of us who are committed to the value of giving greater freedom and flexibility to learners, it is the direction we have to go in. Further progress will depend on our acquiring more knowledge as well as mutual, collegial support. Surely both of these needs will be met in some degree from reading the galaxy of global stars assembled by the editor of this book. I invite you to proceed, and hope you enjoy the adventure!

M.G. Moore

References

Mitchell, S. C. (1938). The Benton Harbour plan. *The American Journal of Distance Education, 16*(4), 204.

Moore, M. G. (1972). Learner autonomy: The second dimension of independent learning. *Convergence, 5*(2), 76-88. Retrieved from http://www.ajde.com/Documents/learner_autonomy.pdf

Moore, M. G. (1980). Independent study. In R. Boyd & J. Apps (Eds.), *Redefining the discipline of adult education* (pp. 16-31). San Francisco: Jossey-Bass. Retrieved from http://www.ajde.com/Documents/independent_study.pdf

Preface

With the increasing use of a variety of approaches for learning in the information age, learners' preferences are changing from wanting to be taught mostly in lectures or direct training sessions to wanting increased *flexibility*. Learners expect on-demand, anytime/anywhere high-quality learning environments with good support services. They want increased *flexibility* in learning—they want to have more say in what they learn, when they learn, and where and how they learn.

Since 1997 I have studied the critical issues of flexible learning. I have communicated with learners, instructors, administrators, and technical and other support services staff involved in flexible learning, in both academic and corporate settings, all over the world. I have researched flexible learning issues discussed in professional discussion forums, newspapers, magazines, and journals, and I have designed and taught online courses. Also, as the editor of *Web-Based Instruction* (Educational Technology Publications, 1997) and *Web-Based Training* (Educational Technology Publications, 2001), I had the opportunity to work closely on critical flexible learning issues with more than 100 authors worldwide who contributed chapters to these books.

Through these activities, I found that numerous factors help to create a meaningful learning environment, and many of these factors are systemically interrelated and interdependent. A systemic understanding of these factors can help us create meaningful flexible learning environments. I clustered these factors into eight categories: institutional, management, technological, pedagogical, ethical, interface design, resource support, and evaluation. I found these eight categories to be logically comprehensive and empirically the most useful dimensions for a flexible learning environment. With these eight dimensions, I developed *A Framework for Flexible Learning*. The framework is reviewed by researchers and practitioners from various countries: Betty Collis, University of Twente, The Netherlands; Som Naidu, University of Melbourne, Australia; Robin Mason, Open University, England; Ali Ekrem Ozkul, Anadolu University, Turkey; Jianwei Zhang, Tsinghua University, China; Myunghee Kang, Ewha Womans University, Korea; Sanjaya Mishra, Commonwealth Educational Media Center for Asia, India; Alex and Lani Romiszowsky, Brazil; Reynold Macpherson, University of Auckland, New Zealand; Herman Van Der Merwe, South Africa; Jeroen van Merrienboer, Open University of The Netherlands; Charlotte N. (Lani) Gunawardena, University of New Mexico, USA; Walter Wager, Florida State University, USA; Amy Holloway, World Bank, USA; Thomas Reeves, University of Georgia, USA; Janette Hill, University of Georgia, USA; Philip Doughty, Syracuse University, USA; Nada Dabbagh, George Mason University,

USA; Joanne Williams, University of Texas, USA; Zane Berge, University of Maryland, USA; and David Peal, Harvey Singh, and Greg Kearsley in the U.S. I am indebted to them for their insightful comments that truly improved the framework.

I use the *flexible learning framework* as a guide to solicit contributions for this book. I am very fortunate to have researchers and practitioners involved in flexible learning as contributors of this book. As the editor of this book, I took an open and democratic approach to solicit contributions. I sent e-mail messages to potential authors and also cross-posted a message to several listservs soliciting contributions for the book. As a result, I put together this book by incorporating works of talented individuals with unique backgrounds from around the globe. It should also be noted that there may be many significant people involved in doing research in flexible learning who are not included in this book.

The *purpose of this book* is to provide you with a broad understanding of the emerging field of flexible learning from the perspectives of the eight categories of the *flexible learning framework.* Chapters included in this book encompass various critical issues dealing with one or more categories of the flexible learning framework and offer a variety of points of view on these issues. Below, I briefly present each chapter of the book.

In **Chapter I**, entitled *Flexible Learning in an Open and Distributed Environment*, Khan argues for the importance of increased flexibility in learning, and introduce *A Framework for Flexible Learning* to help us think through every aspect of what we are doing during the steps of the planning, designing, developing, implementing, managing, and evaluating of flexible learning materials.

Spiro, Collins, and Ramchandran (**Chapter II**, *Modes of Openness and Flexibility in Cognitive Flexibility Hypertext Learning Environments*) talk about characteristics of cognitive flexibility hypertext learning environments (CFHs) and present various modes of openness in CFHs based on cognitive flexibility theory (CFT). They believe that all kinds of openness built into CFHs are intended to shift habits of mind from the relatively closed to the more open, as well as to build specific content knowledge that has various forms of openness.

Herrington, Oliver and Herrington (**Chapter III**, *Authentic Learning on the Web: Guidelines for Course Design*) propose nine critical characteristics of learning as a framework for the design of more authentic learning environments on the Web. The elements are based on situated learning theory and other compatible research, with particular emphasis on computer and Web-based applications.

Fisher, Coleman, Sparks, and Plett (**Chapter IV**, *Designing Community Learning in Web-Based Environments*) review several strategies for creating effective collaboration and community in online environments. They provide examples and models with the goal of preparing others to design and teach effectively in collaborative Web-based environments.

Murphy, Gazi, and Cifuentes (**Chapter V**, *Intercultural Collaborative Project-Based Learning in Online Environments*) address the question, "How can we overcome potential cultural discontinuities in online collaborative project-based learning environments?" They identify differing worldviews, communication practices, and technological issues that can present barriers that frequently arise in intercultural online courses. In this chapter, they present a model for a polycentric culture that minimizes differences among individuals in terms of their worldviews, communication practices, and technological issues.

Dennen and Bonk (**Chapter VI**, *We'll Leave the Light on for You: Keeping Learners Motivated in Online Courses*) focus on 10 key elements for motivating online learners. Each element is discussed separately, along with corresponding course activities that can be used to address that element. They also provide a few useful examples and ideas that can be adopted and adapted by online instructors in higher education as well as business learning environments.

Barclay (**Chapter VII**, *Humanizing Learning-at-Distance: Best Practice Guidelines for Synchronous Instructors*) presents a set of guidelines that raises awareness of best-practices that novice and seasoned synchronous instructors may use to foster successful live online learning environments.

Nissley (**Chapter VIII**, *Storytelling as a Web-Based Workplace Learning Pedagogy*) describes the evolution of storytelling in the workplace—from a face-to-face learning pedagogy to the use of storytelling as a flexible learning pedagogy.

Tan and Subramaniam (**Chapter IX**, *Use of Virtual Exhibits for Promoting Science Learning on the Webs of Science Centers*) discuss how virtual exhibits provide useful instructional support for exploring scientific concepts through inquiry. The creation of dynamic learning environments for experimentation through technological mediation as well as the fostering of endogenous play elements in the learning process are effective strategies for engaging visitors. They stress that this motivates visitors to strive towards acquisition of new skills and knowledge, thus opening up enhanced possibilities for knowledge transfer in cyberspace.

Witfelt (**Chapter X**, *Flexible Learning—Onsite!*) takes a different approach to flexible learning and how technologies from distributed, flexible learning can be used in everyday university teaching and learning—onsite learning. Onsite learning is characterized not by virtual and distributed processes, but by actual presence of the students.

Kurubacak and Yuzer (**Chapter XI**, *Asynchronous Content Design for Flexible Learning: The Macro and Micro Level of Frameworks to Share Knowledge Online Between Professionals and Community*) discuss design principles, ethics, and pitfalls of asynchronous content in e-learning systems. They introduce macro- and micro-level frameworks that provide useful assessment methods and techniques for e-learning providers and producers to improve their understandings about the cutting-edge technology applications into asynchronous milieu.

Baker and Tonkin (**Chapter XII**, *Online Faculty Proficiency and Peer Coaching*) share a case study of peer observation and coaching activities in their institution as an accepted means of generating data for assessing teaching for online instruction. The peer coaching cycle used consists of three stages: a planning conference, instructional observation, and a reflecting conference.

Payne (**Chapter XIII**, *What Do They Learn?*) stresses that the results of transcript analysis can be the recognition of the impacts of the various "inputs" on learning outcomes and can be a useful tool for achieving greater teaching effectiveness.

Gayeski (**Chapter XIV**, *Mobile Learning Technologies*) rationalizes the need and significance of mobile technologies in flexible learning. She discusses how college campuses are quickly adopting wireless networks to make instruction, collaboration, and scheduling available at a lower cost per delivery medium and networking than conventional desktop computers and wired campuses.

Caladine and Yecies (**Chapter XV**, *Strategies for Sharing the ReMoTe: Changing the Nature of Online Collaboration*) offer a rich case study of a project that takes online interactions beyond the limits imposed by recent Web technology. They discuss the delivery and evaluation of ReMoTe, a Web-based virtual group workspace that facilitates learning activities between learners at a distance.

Mittal, Pagalthivarthi, and Altman (**Chapter XVI**, *Integrating Multimedia Cues in E-learning Documents for Enhanced Learning*) present a user-centric approach to e-learning where students can organize, analyze, share, and discuss their insights, experiments, and results more easily and in a more effective manner. The approach presented in the chapter utilizes the lecture slides and video content to index the lecture material into semantic labels, such as Discussion, Example, and Definition.

Uden (**Chapter XVII**, *Interface Design for Web Learning*) promotes that high usability in Web based learning help users to use the interface more intuitively. She discusses the Web user object modeling method to guide designers to develop Web learning applications that have high usability.

Lohr, Falvo, Hunt, and Johnson (**Chapter XVIII**, *Improving the Usability of Distance Learning Through Template Modification*) examine the interactions of instructors and students with a widely used distance learning authoring system. She reports that the instructors identified the authoring system's potential to be modified to improve student navigation and access to instructional content.

Powers and Salmon (**Chapter XIX**, *Management of the Learning Space*) argue that the key to a successful distance education experience for both faculty and students is to effectively manage the learning space. They discuss workload management, student management, and time management as three principal issues involved in effective learning space management.

McMahon (**Chapter XX**, *Ethical Issues in Web-Based Learning*) tackles the important issue of ethical issues that arise with online education. She suggests that departments, curriculum committees, and other approval bodies will need to reexamine values, rights, and professional responsibilities specifically in curricular quality control, advising, intellectual property rights, and succession planning.

Kähkönen and Sutinen (**Chapter XXI**, *Moving Toward the Implementation of Contextualized Educational Technology*) argue for various methods and processes related to the design issues, contents, or applied technologies when developing contextual and culturally sensitive e-learning materials. They discuss key areas in the implementation of contextualization, including dialogical learning, community building, and the concept of "ethnocomputing".

Reeves and Hedberg (**Chapter XXII**, *Evaluation Strategies for Open and Distributed Learning Environments*) present a pragmatic philosophy of evaluation that maintains that we should evaluate in order to provide the information that we and other decision makers need to make better decisions about the design and implementation of open and distributed learning environments.

Terrell (**Chapter XXIII**, *Components of Effective Evaluation in Online Learning Environments*) explores evaluation as a critical element to the success of online learning by focusing on four distinct components of effective evaluation: course content, the instructional process, learners, and the online learning environments as an entity unto itself. He provides a model to address the notion that evaluation and assessment should be included as an integral, ongoing part of an online learning management system.

Morgan and Bird (**Chapter XXIV**, *Flexible Assessment: Some Tensions and Solutions*) argue that although flexible teaching and assessment methods offer some alternatives for teachers and students, they clearly require considerable thought and planning. There is a range of tensions operating in both the purposes and processes of flexible assessment that deserve some closer examination. They discuss how many of these tensions arise in our efforts to adopt a flexible approach to assessment, yet deal with the competing interests of institutional policies and culture, and ever increasing workloads.

Bonk, Wisher, and Champagne (**Chapter XXV**, *Toward a Comprehensive Model of E-Learning Evaluation: The Components*) note that evaluating e-learning, or any learning for that matter, is a difficult and highly complex endeavor. They provide eight evaluation considerations that can assist in understanding the impact and effectiveness of an e-learning effort.

Collis and Margaryan (**Chapter XXVI**, *Evaluating Flexible Learning in Terms of Course Quality*) present a model for evaluating the quality of blended courses in the corporate setting. They share the results of the use of the evaluation approach with over 60 blended courses, and discuss the implications and transferability of the evaluation approach.

Harasim (**Chapter XXVII**, *Assessing Online Collaborative Learning: A Theory, Methodology, and Toolset*) focuses especially on the unique opportunities whereby instructors, educators, researchers, and students can analyze and assess learning (conceptual change) in OCL environments and applications—that is, online discussion that progresses from divergent (brainstorming) to convergent (conclusive statements) in such educational activities as group seminars, discussions, debates, case analyses, and/or team projects.

Dimitrova (**Chapter XXVIII**, *Evaluating the Flexibility of Learning Processes in E-Learning Environments*) describes the three main dimensions of flexible learning in online learning environments: location, time, and method flexibility. She presents a checklist outlining evaluation criteria for each dimension for assessing the flexibility of learning processes in e-learning environments.

Khan, Cataldo, Bennett, and Paratore (**Chapter XXIX**, *Obstacles Encountered by Learners, Instructors, Technical Support, and Librarians*) present a compilation of major obstacles encountered by learners, instructors, technical support, and librarians during online learning. In compiling these lists, they communicated with learners, instructors, and technical and library support services staff actively involved in flexible learning all over the world.

Finally, Smith and Khan (**Chapter XXX**, *A Program Satisfaction Survey Instrument for Online Students*) use a program evaluation survey based on the eight dimensions of the *flexible learning framework* to understand the attitudes of online education students in a particular graduate program and the issues they encounter in online learning implementations. We found that students are capable of evaluating the factors that they have encountered, expressing their level of satisfaction with those factors, and estimating how those factors have impacted their online learning experience.

As you know, like any emerging field, the world of flexible learning is constantly changing and evolving. To keep you up to date with resources, FAQs, strategies, best practice examples, and any change of addresses for chapter-related Web sites and other corrections, I maintain a Web site at http://BooksToRead.com/flexible-learning.

Hopefully, this collection of ideas and issues discussed by international authors will help you understand various aspects of the flexible learning environment and provide valuable guidance in creating flexible learning experiences for your target audience. I would appreciate hearing your comments regarding this book.

Badrul H. Khan
bhk@BooksToRead.com
http://BadrulKhan.com/khan

Acknowledgments

This book owes much to the encouragement and assistance of many people. First of all, I would like to thank Ruth Bennett for her critical review and helpful feedback. I would also like to thank my well-wishers who believed in me and were very supportive of my ideas and visions: Larry Lipsitz and Howard Lipsitz of Educational Technology Publications, and Laura Granato of The Federal Leadership Institute.

Finally, and most important, I thank my wife Komar Khan and my sons Intisar Sherwani Khan and Inshat Sherwani Khan; my brothers Kamrul Huda Khan, Manzurul Huda Khan, and Nazrul Huda Khan; and my sisters Nasima Zaman and Akhtar Janhan Khanam—all for their continued support and encouragement. I would also like to thank all my nieces and nephews for their encouragement.

Chapter I

Flexible Learning in an Open and Distributed Environment

Badrul H. Khan, The George Washington University, USA

Introduction

Advances in information technology, coupled with changes in society, have had a tremendous impact on our educational and training systems. Participants in this educational and training paradigm require rich learning environments supported by well designed resources. They expect on-demand, anytime/anywhere high-quality learning environments with good support services. In other words, they want increased *flexibility* in learning—they want to have more say in what they learn, when they learn, and where and how they learn. They may choose a mix of traditional and new learning approaches and technology; they may want to study at their chosen time and location and at their own pace. Therefore, *flexible learning can be defined as an innovative approach for delivering well-designed, learner-centered, and interactive learning environments to anyone, anyplace, anytime by utilizing the attributes and resources of the Internet, digital technologies, and other modes of learning in concert with instructional design principles. Can we do what learners want?* Nunan (1996) stated:

Teaching and learning may be created through exploring different ways of delivering education. When 'delivery' or 'learning' is coupled with the word flexible, the intention to increase for learners both their access to, and their control over, particular teaching and learning environments is implied.

New developments in learning science and technology provide opportunities to develop learning environments that suit students' needs and interests by offering them the choice of increased flexibility. A mix of traditional and new learning approaches and technologies is instrumental in creating innovative learning environments with increased flexibility.

Meaning of Flexibility in Learning

In any educational system there are several stakeholder groups, including learners, instructors, support services staff, and the institution. The term *flexibility* can mean different things to different stakeholder groups. Nunan (1996) noted:

Flexibility is a characteristic which satisfies many stakeholders in education. It can serve the interests of managers and politicians who focus on effectiveness and efficiency and cut-price solutions to the delivery of a service. For students and teachers it can suggest a student-centered approach to learning and the democratization of processes of learning and teaching. For curriculum developers it may mean the availability of a range of approaches to suit student diversity. For those marketing educational services it can mean the production of commodities which can be used competitively in a global educational market. (p. 2)

No matter how each stakeholder group feels about or views flexibility in learning, they are all in favor of meaningful learning that is suitable for a diverse population.

Learner-Focused
Flexible Learning System

A leading theorist of educational systems, Banathy (1991) makes a strong case for learning-focused educational and training systems where "the learner is the key entity and occupies the nucleus of the systems complex of education" (p. 96). For Banathy, "*when learning is in focus*, arrangements are made in the environment of the learner that communicate the learning task, and learning resources are made available to learners so that they can explore and master learning tasks" (p. 101). A distributed learning environment that can effectively support learning-on-demand must be designed by placing the learners at the center. In support of a learner-centered approach, Moore (1998) states:

Our aim as faculty should be to focus our attention on making courses and other learning experiences that will best empower our students to learn, to learn fully, effectively, efficiently, and with rewarding satisfaction. It is the responsibility of our profession to study ways of maximizing the potential of our environments to support their learning and to minimize those elements in their environments that may impede it. (p. 4)

A successful flexible learning system involves a systematic process of planning, design, development, evaluation, and implementation to create an environment where learning is actively fostered and supported. Therefore, a flexible learning system should be meaningful not only to learners, but also to all stakeholder groups. For example, a flexible learning system is meaningful to *learners* when it is easily accessible, well designed, learner centered, affordable, efficient, flexible, and has a facilitated learning environment. When learners display a high level of participation and success in meeting a course's goals and objectives, this can make learning meaningful to *instructors.* In turn, when learners enjoy all available support services provided in the course without any interruptions, it makes *support services staff* happy as they strive to provide easy-to-use, reliable services. Finally, a flexible learning system is meaningful to *institutions* when it has a sound return-on-investment (ROI), a moderate to high level of learner satisfaction with both the quality of instruction and all support services, and a low dropout rate (Morrison & Khan, 2003).

To stay viable in this global competitive market, providers of education and training must develop *well-designed, learner-centered, affordable, easily accessible, efficient,* and *effective* flexible learning systems to meet learners' needs. How do we develop flexible learning materials for diverse learners? The following is an outline for this chapter which I believe will help us understand how to plan, design, and implement flexible methods of delivering instruction to diverse learners:

- Traditional instruction and flexible learning
- Open and distributed learning environment
- Blending various learning approaches for flexibility
- A framework for flexible learning

Traditional Instruction and Flexible Learning

Traditional classrooms are space bound. Traditional instruction is for the most part a *closed system,* with learning taking place within the confines of a given classroom, school, textbook, field trip, and so forth. However, classroom-taught courses are not necessarily closed systems. When teachers assign students to do library-based research papers, interview members of a professional community, and engage in service-learning activities, they extend their learning initiatives far beyond the classroom itself. Unfortunately, many classes are bound by their four walls, involving only the thoughts of the instructor, the textbook writer, and occasional student comments. Classroom courses are also closed in the sense that they are limited to only those students who can physically come to the location.

On the other hand, flexible learning extends the boundaries of learning so that learning can occur in classrooms, from home, and in the workplace (Relan & Gillani, 1997). It is a flexible form of education because it creates options for learners in terms of where and when they can learn (Krauth, 1998). A well-designed flexible learning course allows learners to become actively involved in their learning processes. However, a poorly designed flexible learning course can be just as rigid and dogmatic and non-interactive as a poorly taught face-to-face course. The scope of openness and flexibility in learning is dependent upon how it is designed. "While having an open system has its appeal, it can make designing for it extremely difficult, because in an open system, the designer agrees to give up a certain amount of control to the user" (Jones & Farquhar, 1997, p. 240). The more open the learning environment, the more complex the planning, management, and evaluation of it (Land & Hannafin, 1996). For example, the instructor cannot monitor who helps the student on tests unless proctored. In this chapter, the term flexible learning is used in its broadest sense to include all aspects of open and distributed learning.

Open and Distributed Learning Environment

What is an open and distributed learning environment? According to Calder and McCollum (1998): "The common definition of open learning is learning in your own time, pace and place" (p. 13). Ellington (1997) notes that open and flexible learning allows learners to have some say in how, where, and when learning takes place. Saltzberg and Polyson (1995) noted that distributed learning is not synonymous with distance learning, but they stress its close relationship with the idea of distributed resources:

Distributed learning is an instructional model that allows instructor, students, and content to be located in different, non-centralized locations so that instruction and learning occur independent of time and place... The distributed learning model can be used in combination with traditional classroom-based courses, with traditional distance learning courses, or it can be used to create wholly virtual classrooms. (p. 10)

Janis Taylor of Clarke College in Iowa who teaches students coming from different places in the Midwest commented on open, distributed, and flexible learning:

Consider a student user who described her online education as open because she can sit out on her back deck supervising her children in the swimming pool while doing her homework. Now that's open-air and open learning. One of my pre service teachers works in a chemical lab in Cleveland, another is a court reporter three hours drive from

Figure 1. Open and distributed flexible learning

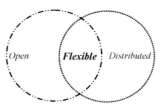

me and another is a nurse in rural western Iowa. I, their teacher, am sitting in a small liberal arts college in eastern Iowa, a state badly needing to tap new people to come into the teaching profession. How could I get them all here to my campus if e-learning weren't distributed? This open and distributed learning environment made learning flexible for a young traveling business woman who says 'I take my college course, my instructor, and all of my fellow students with me on every business trip. With my laptop in my hotel room, I can view my teacher's demonstration, discuss it with my classmates in the Chat Room, and turn in my assignment by e mail.' Now that's a flexible college program. (Taylor, 2004)

Flexibility in learning is, therefore, dependent on the openness of the system and the availability of learning resources distributed in various locations. A clear understanding of the *open and distributed* nature of learning environments will help us create meaningful learning environments with increased flexibility. Figure 1 graphically shows how an open and distributed educational system contributes to flexibility.

The Role of the Internet and Digital Technologies in Flexible Learning

Both human and technological resources are critical to support flexibility in learning. The advancement of information and communication technologies is a blessing for flexible learning. For example, as the Internet is fast emerging, the Web has become an increasingly powerful, global, interactive, and dynamic medium for sharing information. The Web provides an opportunity to develop new flexible learning experiences for students which have not been possible before (Alexander, 1995). The Internet supports *open* learning because it is device, platform, time, and place independent. It is designers who take advantage of the openness of the Internet to create learning environments that are *flexible* for learners. Therefore, openness is a technical matter; flexibility is a design matter (Khan, 2001a). The Internet, by its very nature, distributes resources and information, making it the tool of choice for those interested in delivering instruction using the distributed learning model (Saltzberg & Polyson, 1995). Thus, the Internet, supported by various digital technologies, is well suited as one of the delivery modes for flexible learning. However, we have to remember that no one single delivery mode is better than others in providing flexibility in learning. Singh (2003) states:

A single delivery mode inevitably limits the reach of a learning program or critical knowledge transfer in some form or fashion. For example, a physical classroom training program limits the access to only those who can participate at a fixed time and location, whereas a virtual classroom event is inclusive of remote audiences and, when followed up with recorded knowledge objects (ability to playback a recorded live event), can extend the reach to those who could not attend at a specific time. (p. 53)

Blending Various Learning Strategies and Approaches for Flexibility

With the increasing use of a variety of approaches in learning in the information age, learners are moving away from wanting to be taught mostly in lectures or direct training sessions. There is no doubt that they now expect more variety in the ways that they can learn, and flexible learning helps provide this variety (Race, 1996). Considering the difference in learning requirements and preferences of each learner, we can now provide a myriad of learning approaches and choices.

No one single learning delivery method is capable of supporting the kind of flexibility that learners need. Therefore, a mix of traditional and new learning approaches and technology should be appropriately utilized for flexible learning. Singh (2003) notes that we should use a blend of learning approaches in our strategies to get the right content in the right format to the right people at the right time. Blended learning combines multiple delivery media that are designed to complement each other and promote flexibility in learning. It mixes various event-based activities, including face-to-face classrooms, live e-learning, and self-paced learning.

Singh (2003) discusses several possible dimensions and ingredients (learning delivery methods) of blended learning programs in Table 1 and Table 2 respectively.[1] In Table 1, there are five ways or dimensions of blending identified. Based on our resource capabilities and learners' needs, we may create flexible blended learning programs by combining one or more of the dimensions in Table 1. Today, we have a myriad of learning approaches and choices (or ingredients). Table 2 lists some of the choices.

To foster increased flexibility in learning, now we have the option of choosing dimensions of the blend from Table 1 and ingredients to support the blend from Table 2. It is important to create the appropriate blend by ensuring that each ingredient, individually and collectively, adds to a meaningful learning experience.

For effective strategies for a meaningful learning experience for each ingredient or learning delivery method of the blend, we have to consider a variety of issues to ensure effective delivery of learning and thus a high return on investment.

Table 1. Dimensions of blended learning programs

Dimensions of the Blend

The original use of the phrase "blended learning" was often associated with simply linking traditional classroom training to e-learning activities, such as asynchronous work (typically accessed by learners outside the class at their own time and pace). However, the term has evolved to encompass a much richer set of learning strategies or "dimensions." Today a blended learning program may combine one or more of the following dimensions, although many of these have over-lapping attributes.

Blending Offline and Online Learning

At the simplest level, a blended learning experience combines offline and online forms of learning where the online learning usually means "over the Internet or intranet" and offline learning happens in a more traditional classroom setting. We assume that even the offline learning offerings are managed through an online learning system. An example of this type of blending may include a learning program that provides study materials and research resources over the Web, while providing instructor-led, classroom training sessions as the main medium of instruction.

Blending Self-Paced and Live, Collaborative Learning

Self-paced learning implies solitary, on-demand learning at a pace that is managed or controlled by the learner. Collaborative learning, on the other hand, implies a more dynamic communication among many learners that brings about knowledge sharing. The blending of self-paced and collaborative learning may include review of important literature on a regulatory change or new product followed by a moderated, live, online, peer-to-peer discussion of the material's application to the learner's job and customers.

Blending Structured and Unstructured Learning

Not all forms of learning imply a premeditated, structured, or formal learning program with organized content in specific sequence like chapters in a textbook. In fact, most learning in the workplace occurs in an unstructured form via meetings, hallway conversations, or e-mail. A blended program design may look to actively capture conversations and documents from unstructured learning events into knowledge repositories available on-demand, supporting the way knowledge-workers collaborate and work.

Blending Custom Content with Off-the-Shelf Content

Off-the-shelf content is by definition generic—unaware of an organization's unique context and requirements. However, generic content is much less expensive to buy and frequently has higher production values than custom content. Generic self-paced content can be customized today with a blend of live experiences (classroom or online) or with content customization. Industry standards such as SCORM (Shareable Content Object Reference Model) open the door to increasingly flexible blending of off-the-shelf and custom content, improving the user experience while minimizing cost.

Blending Learning, Practice, and Performance Support

Perhaps the finest form of blended learning is to supplement learning (organized prior to beginning a new job-task) with practice (using job-task or business process simulation models) and just-in-time performance support tools that facilitate the appropriate execution of job-tasks. Cutting-edge productivity tools provide 'workspace' environments that package together the computer based work, collaboration, and performance support tools.

A Framework for Flexible Learning, discussed in the next section, can serve as a guide to plan, develop, deliver, manage, and evaluate flexible blended learning programs. It can also enable one to select appropriate ingredients for blended learning (Singh, 2003).

A Framework for Flexible Learning

What does it take to provide flexible learning environments for learners worldwide? Since 1997, I have communicated with learners, instructors, administrators, and technical

Table 2. Learning approaches and choices

Synchronous physical formats	Instructor-led Classrooms & Lectures Hands-on Labs & Workshops Field Trips
Synchronous online formats (live e-learning)	Online Meetings Virtual Classrooms Web Seminars and Broadcasts Coaching Instant Messaging Conference Calls
Self-paced, asynchronous formats	Documents & Web Pages Web/Computer Based Training Modules Assessments/Tests & Surveys Simulations Job Aids & Electronic Performance Support Systems (EPSS) Recorded Live Events Online Learning Communities and Discussion Forums Distributed and Mobile Learning

and other support services staff involved in flexible learning (in both academic and corporate settings) all over the world. I have researched flexible learning issues discussed in professional discussion forums, and I have designed and taught online and blended learning courses. I have surveyed online educators and students (Khan & Vega, 1997; Khan & Smith, 2006; Khan, Cataldo, Bennett, & Paratore, 2006). Also, as the editor of *Web Based Instruction* (1997), *Web Based Training* (2001), and *Flexible Learning in an Information Society* (2006), I have had the opportunity to work closely on critical flexible learning issues with more than 200 authors worldwide who contributed chapters to these books.

Through these activities, I learned that flexible learning represents a paradigm shift not only for learners, but also for instructors, administrators, technical and other support services staff, and the institution. As we are accustomed to teaching and learning in a closed system, the openness of flexible learning is new to us. To create effective flexible learning environments for diverse learners, we need to jump out of our closed system mentality. We need to change our mindset. We need to be attentive to a variety of new and emerging issues of flexibility, and address them in the design of learning environments. That is the paradigm shift! In order to facilitate such a shift, and in response to the range of issues I saw in my research, I created a *Framework for Flexible Learning* (Figure 2).

Through my research I found that numerous factors help to create a meaningful flexible learning environment, and many of these factors are systemically interrelated and interdependent. A systemic understanding of these factors can help us create meaningful learning environments. I clustered these factors into eight *categories:* institutional, management, technological, pedagogical, ethical, interface design, resource support, and evaluation (Table 3). Various issues within the eight categories of the framework were found to be useful in several studies that were conducted to review learning programs, resources, and tools (Khan et al., 2006; Khan & Smith, 2006; Romiszowski, 2004; Singh, 2003; Chin & Kon, 2003; Kuchi, Gardner, & Tipton, 2003; Mello, 2002; Barry, 2002;

Figure 2. A framework for flexible learning

Table 3. Eight categories of flexible learning

Categories	Descriptions
Institutional	The institutional category is concerned with issues of administrative affairs, academic affairs and student services related to e-learning.
Management	The management of e-learning refers to the maintenance of the learning environment and distribution of information.
Technological	The technological category examines issues of technology infrastructure in e-learning environments. This includes infrastructure planning, hardware and software.
Pedagogical	The pedagogical category refers to teaching and learning. This category addresses issues concerning content analysis, audience analysis, goal analysis, medium analysis, design approach, organization, and learning strategies.
Ethical	The ethical considerations of e-learning relate to social and political influences, cultural diversity, bias, geographical diversity, learner diversity, the digital divide, etiquette, and legal issues.
Interface design	Interface design refers to the overall look and feel of flexible learning programs. Interface design categories encompass page and site design, content design, navigation, accessibility and usability testing.
Resource support	The resource support category examines the online support and resources required to foster meaningful learning.
Evaluation	The evaluation of flexible learning includes both assessment of learners and evaluation of the instruction and learning environment.

Goodear, 2001; Khan, Waddill, & McDonald, 2001; Dabbagh, Bannan-Ritland, & Silc, 2001; Khan & Ealy, 2001; El-Tigi & Khan, 2001; Zhang, Khan, Gibbons, & Ni, 2001; Gilbert, 2002; Kao, Tousignant, & Wiebe, 2000).

The purpose of this framework is to help us think through every aspect of what we are doing during the steps of the flexible learning design process. Therefore I am going to look at each of the eight categories of this framework and show what questions we should ask about each category as we design a flexible learning segment, either a lesson, a course, or an entire program.

Table 4. Sub-categories of the Flexible Learning Framework

INSTITUTIONAL	ETHICAL
Administrative Affairs	Social and Cultural Diversity
Academic Affairs	Bias and Political Issues
Student Services	Geographical Diversity
MANAGEMENT	Learner Diversity
Managing Learning Content Development	Digital Divide
Managing Learning Delivery Environment	Etiquette
TECHNOLOGICAL	Legal Issues
Infrastructure Planning	INTERFACE DESIGN
Hardware	Page and Site Design
Software	Content Design
PEDAGOGICAL	Navigation
Content Analysis	Accessibility
Audience Analysis	Usability Testing
Goal Analysis	RESOURCE SUPPORT
Design Approach	Online Support
Instructional Strategies	Resources
Organization	EVALUATION
Blending Strategies	Evaluation of Content Development Process
	Evaluation of Learning Environment
	Evaluation of Leaning at the Program
	and Institutional Levels
	Assessment of Learners

Each category has several subcategories (Table 4). Each subcategory consists of items or issues focused on a specific aspect of a learning environment.

In this chapter, the issues within each subcategory of the framework are presented as questions that we can ask ourselves when planning flexible learning materials. Since each project is unique, I encourage you to identify as many issues (in the form of questions) as possible for your own flexible learning project by using the framework. One way to identify critical issues is by putting each stakeholder group (such as learner, instructor, support staff, etc.) at the center of the framework and raising issues along the eight categories of the flexible learning environment. This way you can identify many critical issues and answer questions that can help create a meaningful learning environment for your particular group. By repeating the same process for other stakeholder groups, you can generate a comprehensive list of issues for your flexible learning project. As examples, let me raise some issues within the eight categories:

Is the course sensitive to students from different time-zones (e.g., are synchronous communications such as chat discussions scheduled at reasonable times for all time zones represented)? This is an example of a question that a *learner* can ask in the *geographical diversity* section of the *ethical* category. As we know, synchronous online formats (see Table 2) such as scheduled chat discussions may not work for learners coming from different time zones. In the United States, there are six time zones. Therefore, you should be sensitive to diversity in geographical time zones (i.e., all courses where students can reasonably be expected to live in different time zones).

Would I be awarded the same credit for the development of an e-learning course as I would receive for the publication of an article in a professional journal or magazine? Developing a well-designed online course requires a great deal of time and effort. A nontenured faculty member would probably be more interested in publishing than developing an online course if the development of a course does not provide any impetus toward tenure and promotion. This is a type of question a *faculty member* would ask when focusing on issues relevant to the *academic affairs* section of the *institutional* category.

Does the course make an effort to reduce or avoid the use of jargon, idioms, ambiguous or cute humor, and acronyms? To improve cross-cultural verbal communication and avoid misunderstanding, we should refrain from icons, symbols, jokes, or comments that might be misinterpreted by others. In Bangladesh, the thumbs-up sign means to disregard someone, but in other cultures it means 'excellent' or 'job well done'. A pointing hand icon to indicate direction would violate a cultural taboo in certain African cultures because it represents a dismembered body part (this is also true for a pointing finger that indicates a hyperlink). A right arrow for the next page may instruct Arabic and Hebrew language speakers, as they read from left to right, to return to the previous page. This is a concern for *learners* with different cultural backgrounds. This is an issue relevant to the *page and site design* section of the *interface design* category.

How often is dynamic course content updated? In designing e-learning, we need to consider the stability of course content. Content that does not need to be updated can be categorized as static (e.g., historical events, grammar rules, etc.). Content that has the potential to change over time can be considered dynamic (e.g., laws, policies, etc.). Because dynamic content needs to be revised from time to time, it is necessary to identify such content in a course and establish an ongoing method for timely updating as needed. It would be very frustrating for learners if they would find outdated or obsolete information. This is a concern that a *student* might have. This is an example of an issue relevant to the *content analysis* section of the *pedagogical* category.

Are all learning objects created for the course reusable and shareable? If your institution creates learning objects by following the international interoperability standards (such as IEEE, SCORM, etc.), they can be reused and shared by various courses within your institution and beyond. Reusable and shareable learning objects not only save money, but also promote collaboration among e-learning partner institutions. This is a type of issue that an *administrator* would be interested in seeing included in the *infrastructure planning* section of the *technological* category.

Are students actually doing the work? How do we know we are assessing fairly and accurately? These are the types of questions that will always be in the minds of online *instructors* and *administrators*. Assessment of learners at a distance can be a challenge. Issues related to cheating are a major concern, and an institution offering e-learning should have a mechanism in which a learner can be truly measured and not cheat. This is an issue relevant to the *assessment of learners* section of the *evaluation* category.

Does the course have encryption (i.e., a secure coding system) available for students to send confidential information over the Internet? No institutions are immune from hackers. Academic networks can be targets of hackers if they lack security. This is a concern for *network managers* which falls under the *security measures* section of the *management* category.

Do technical and other support staff receive training on how to communicate with remote learners in difficult situations? When students encounter repeated technical difficulties with e-learning, they become very frustrated. It is not easy for technical support staff to deal with learners in such situations. Technical staff members need training to improve their human skills. This is a concern for *technical* or *help-line staff.* This is an issue relevant to the *online support* section of the *resource support* category.

The purpose of raising many questions within each category (Table 3) is to help us think through our projects thoroughly. Note that there might be other issues not yet known or not yet encountered. As more and more institutions offer flexible learning worldwide, we will become more knowledgeable about new issues within the eight categories of the framework.

The framework can be applied to flexible learning of any scope. This "scope" refers to a continuum defined by the extent to which instruction is delivered on the Internet and hence must be systematically planned for. The weight placed on any flexible learning category or subcategory, or on any set of flexible learning items, will vary with the scope of the instruction. This continuum is described below, with examples, to show the type and scope of flexible learning activities and how their design relates to various categories of the framework.

At the "micro" end of the continuum, flexible learning activities and information resources can be designed for face-to-face instruction in educational and training settings (e.g., blending off-line and online learning, see Table 1). In the high-school physics classroom, for example, a teacher can use Shockwave simulations to support the cognitive work of analyzing data, visualizing concepts, and manipulating models. See, for example, the simulations available at Explore Science (http://www.explorescience .com). The teacher would have to design activities that provide context for and elabo-ration of this highly visual, Web-mediated simulation. In a traditional course, the framework's *institutional* and *management* categories will matter much less than the *learning strategies* section of the *pedagogical* category (Table 2), which provides guidelines for integrating the simulation into the curriculum. However, the *interface design* category of the framework is very critical here. One needs to ensure that the user interface supports all the elements of the blend. The interface has to be sophisticated enough to integrate the different elements of the blend. This will enable the learner to use each delivery type and switch between the different types. For example, in a higher education course, students may study online and then attend a lecture with the professor. The blended learning course should allow students to assimilate both the online learning and the lecture equally well (Singh, 2003).

Further along the continuum, a more comprehensive design is required for the complete academic or training course, where content, activities, interaction, tutorials, project work, and assessment must all be delivered on the Internet. Petersons.com provides links to a large number of such courses that are exclusively or primarily distance based. (The Petersons database can be searched at http://www.lifelonglearning.com.) Additional categories of the framework will be useful in designing such courses.

Finally, at the "macro" end of the continuum, the framework can serve the design of complete distance-learning programs and virtual universities (Khan, 2001b) without a face-to-face component, such as continuing education programs for accountants or network engineers. Petersons.com, again, provides links to dozens of such programs as well as to institutions based on such programs. For example, designers of Web-based continuing education for accountants dispersed all around the world would have to plan for every category of the framework in considerable detail. They would have to work with computer programmers, testing specialists, security professionals, subject-matter experts, and accountants' professional organizations. These designers would have to do everything from planning a secure registration system to considering cultural and language differences among accountants seeking continuing education credit.

As the scope of flexible learning design expands, design projects change from one-person operations to complex team efforts. *The framework can be used to ensure that no important factor is omitted from the design of flexible learning, whatever its scope or complexity.* It also helps to create the appropriate blend by ensuring that each ingredient (Table 2), individually and collectively, adds to a meaningful flexible learning environment.

You might wonder: *Are all subcategories within the eight categories necessary for flexible learning?* You might also wonder: *There are a lot of questions here! Which ones do I need to address?* Again, it depends on the scope of your flexible learning initiative. To initiate a flexible learning degree program, for example, it is critical to start with the *institutional* category of the framework and also investigate all issues relevant to your project in other categories. In this case, a comprehensive readiness assessment should be conducted. However, to create a single flexible learning lesson, some institutional subcategories (such as *admissions*, *financial aid*, and others) may not be relevant.

Conclusion

Designing open and distributed flexible learning systems for globally diverse learners is challenging; however, as more and more institutions offer flexible learning to students worldwide, we will become more knowledgeable about what works and what does not work. We should try to accommodate the needs of diverse learners by asking critical questions along the eight categories of the framework. The questions may vary based on each flexible learning system. The more issues within the eight categories of the framework we explore, the more meaningful and supportive a learning environment we can create. Given our specific contexts, we may not be able to address all issues within the eight categories of the framework, but we should address as many as we can in order to provide increased flexibility for learners.

Future Work in Flexible Learning

Implementation of flexible learning is likely to increase. As I indicated earlier, flexible learning in an open and distributed environment is new to us. As more and more institutions offer flexible learning worldwide, we will become more knowledgeable about new issues within the eight categories of the framework. I believe issues within the eight dimensions of the framework can guide us to further inquiry in the field. There are a number of important areas which deserve further investigation. For example, a *geo-*

graphical diversity issue such as *"Is the course sensitive to students from different time-zones?"* can encourage us to examine the factors bearing on the success and failure of courses that have used synchronous communications for learning. An *interface design* issue such as *"Does the course make an effort to reduce or avoid the use of jargon, idioms, ambiguous or cute humor, and acronyms?"* can encourage us to examine the factors bearing on cross-cultural communication in the design of online courses for global audiences. Similarly, an *academic affairs* issue such as *"Would I be awarded the same credit for the development of an e-learning course as I would receive for the publication of an article in a professional journal or magazine?"* can prompt us to investigate the factors bearing on the motivation level of nontenure faculty in the development of online courses.

Acknowledgments

There are many individuals who I should thank for their comments and suggestions that helped improved the utility of the framework. I acknowledged their names at http://www.BooksToRead.com/framework/#acknowledgement. I would like to thank students at the University of Texas at Brownsville, George Washington University, George Mason University, and Towson University who used the framework as part of their coursework to review online courses and programs. Their comments and suggestions were very useful. I would also like to thank participants in my various keynote and invited addresses for their insightful comments and suggestions about the framework. Finally, I would like to thank Ruth Bennett for her helpful comments on an earlier draft of this chapter.

References

Alexander, S. (1995). *Teaching and learning on the World Wide Web.* Retrieved from http://www.scu.edu.au/ausweb95/papers/education2/alexander/

Banathy, B. H. (1991). *Systems designs of education: A journey to create the future.* Englewood Cliffs, NJ: Educational Technology Publications.

Barry, B. (2002). *ISD and the e-learning framework.* Retrieved January 24, 2003, from http://www.wit.ie/library/webct/isd.html

Calder, J., & McCollum, A. (1998). *Open and flexible learning in vocational education and training.* London: Kogan Page.

Chin, K. L., & Kon, P. N. (2003, December 7-10). Key factors for a fully online e-learning mode: A Delphi study. In G. Crisp, D. Thiele, I. Scholten, S. Barker, & J. Baron (Eds.), *Interact, Integrate, Impact: Proceedings of the 20th Annual Conference of the Australasian Society for Computers in Learning in Tertiary Education,* Adelaide, Australia.

Dabbagh, N. H., Bannan-Ritland, B., & Silc, K. (2000). Pedagogy and Web-based course authoring tools: Issues and implications. In B. H. Khan (Ed.), *Web-based training* (pp. 343-354). Englewood Cliffs, NJ: Educational Technology Publications.

Ellington, H. (1995). Flexible learning, your flexible friend. In C. Bell, M. Bowden, & A. Trott (Eds.), *Implementing flexible learning* (pp. 3-13). London: Kogan Page.

El-Tigi, M. A., & Khan, B. H. (2001). Web-based learning resources. In B.H. Khan (Ed.), *Web-based training* (pp. 59-72). Englewood Cliffs, NJ: Educational Technology Publications.

Gilbert, P. K. (2002). *The virtual university: An analysis of three advanced distributed leaning systems.* Retrieved February 24, 2004, from http://gseacademic.harvard.edu/~gilberpa/homepage/portfolio/research/pdf/edit611.pdf

Goodear, L. (2001). Cultural diversity and flexible learning. *Presentation of Findings of the 2001 Flexible Learning Leaders Professional Development Activity,* South West Institute of TAFE, Australia. Retrieved February 24, 2004, from http://www.flexiblelearning.net.au/leaders/events/pastevents/2001/statepres01/papers/l_goodear.pdf

Jones, M. G., & Farquhar, J. D. (1997). User interface design for Web-based instruction. In B.H. Khan (Ed.), *Web-based instruction* (pp. 239-244). Englewood Cliffs, NJ: Educational Technology Publications.

Kao, D., Tousignant, W., & Wiebe, N. (2000). A paradigm for selecting an institutional software. In D. Colton, J. Caouette, & B. Raggad (Eds.), *Proceedings of ISECON 2000,* Philadelphia (Vol. 17, p. 207). AITP Foundation for Information Technology Education.

Khan, B. H. (1997). Web-based instruction: What is it and why is it? In B. H. Khan (Ed.), *Web-based instruction* (pp. 5-18). Englewood Cliffs, NJ: Educational Technology Publications.

Khan, B. H. (2001a). A framework for Web-based learning. In B. H. Khan (Ed.), *Web-based training* (pp. 75-98). Englewood Cliffs, NJ: Educational Technology Publications.

Khan, B. H. (2001b). Virtual U: A hub for excellence in education, training and learning resources. In B. H. Khan (Ed.), *Web-based training* (pp. 491-506). Englewood Cliffs, NJ: Educational Technology Publications.

Khan, B. H. (2006). E-learning program evaluation instrument. In B. H. Khan (Ed.), *Flexible learning.* Englewood Cliffs, NJ: Educational Technology Publications.

Khan, B. H., & Ealy, D. (2001). A framework for Web-based authoring systems. In B. H. Khan (Ed.), *Web-based training* (pp. 355-364). Englewood Cliffs, NJ: Educational Technology Publications.

Khan, B. H., Cataldo, L., Bennett, R., & Paratore, S. (2006). Obstacles encountered during e learning. In B. H. Khan (Ed.), *Flexible learning in an information society* (pp. 307-320). Hershey, PA: Information Science Publishing.

Khan, B. H., & Smith, H. L. (2006). A program satisfaction survey instrument for online students. In B. H. Khan (Ed.), *Flexible learning in an information society* (pp. 321-338). Hershey, PA: Information Science Publishing.

Khan, B. H., & Vega, R. (1997). Factors to consider when evaluating a Web-based instruction course: A survey. In B. H. Khan (Ed.), *Web-based instruction* (pp. 375-380). Englewood Cliffs, NJ: Educational Technology Publications.

Khan, B. H., Waddill, D., & McDonald, J. (2001). Review of Web-based training sites. In B. H. Khan (Ed.), *Web-based training* (pp. 367-374). Englewood Cliffs, NJ: Educational Technology Publications.

Krauth, B. (1998). Distance learning: The instructional strategy of the decade. In G. P. Connick (Ed.), *The distance learner's guide.* Upper Saddle River, NJ: Prentice-Hall.

Kuchi, R., Gardner, R., & Tipton, R. (2003). *A learning framework for information literacy and library instruction programs at Rutgers University Libraries. Recommendations of the Learning Framework Study Group.* Rutgers University Libraries.

Land, S. M., & Hannafin, M. J. (1997). Patterns of understanding with open-ended learning environments: A qualitative study. *Educational Technology Research and Development, 45*(2), 47-73.

Mello, R. (2002, June). 100 pounds of potatoes in a 25-pound sack: Stress, frustration, and learning in the virtual classroom. *Teaching with Technology Today, 8*(9). Retrieved February 2004 from http://www.uwsa.edu/ttt/articles/mello.htm

Moore, M. G. (1998). Introduction. In C. C. Gibson (Ed.), *Distance learners in higher education.* Madison, WI: Atwood Publishing.

Morrison, J. L., & Khan, B. H. (2003). The global e-learning framework: An interview with Badrul Khan. *The Technology Source. A Publication of the Michigan Virtual University.* Retrieved December 8, 2005, from http://technologysource.org/article/global_elearning_framework/

Nunan, T. (1996, July 8-12). Flexible delivery—what is it and why is it a part of current educational debate? Different Approaches: Theory and Practice in Higher Education. In *Proceedings of the Higher Education Research and Development Society of Australia Conference (HERDSA 1996),* Perth, Western Australia. Retrieved from http://www.herdsa.org.au/confs/1996/nunan.html

Race, P. (1996). *Practical pointers to flexible learning.* Retrieved August 3, 2004, from http://www.city.londonmet.ac.uk/deliberations/flex.learning/race_fr.html

Relan, A., & Gillani, B. B. (1997). Web-based instruction and the traditional classrooms: Similarities and differences. In B. H. Khan (Ed.), *Web-based instruction* (pp. 41-46). Englewood Cliffs, NJ: Educational Technology Publications.

Romiszowski, A. J. (2004). How's the e learning baby? Factors leading to success or failure of an educational technology innovation. *Educational Technology, 44*(1), 5-27.

Saltzbert, S., & Polyson, S. (1995, September). Distributed learning on the World Wide Web. *Syllabus, 9*(1), 10-12.

Singh, H. (2003). Building effective blended learning programs. *Educational Technology, 44*(1), 5-27.

Taylor, J. (2004, June 22). Personal communication.

Zhang, J., Khan, B. H., Gibbons, A. S., & Ni, Y. (2001). Review of Web-based assessment tools. In B. H. Khan (Ed.), *Web-based training* (pp. 137-146). Englewood Cliffs, NJ: Educational Technology Publications.

Endnote

¹ [1]   Printed with permission from Educational Technology Publications, Inc. *Educational Technology, 43*(6), 52.

Chapter II

Modes of Openness and Flexibility in Cognitive Flexibility Hypertext Learning Environments

Rand J. Spiro, Michigan State University, USA

Brian P. Collins, Michigan State University, USA

Aparna R. Ramchandran, Michigan State University, USA

Introduction

The words openness and flexibility—the latter is the topic of this volume—are joined in the title of this chapter. We see them as two sides of the same coin—structure and process, as well as antecedent and consequent. Closed structures of *presentation* (how instructional materials are organized in delivery systems) and of *representation* (how knowledge is structured and operated upon in the mind) produce rigidity of thought and action. The antithesis of this rigidity is a kind of "openness-based" flexibility necessary for adaptive knowledge application, for transfer of knowledge to new situations, for situation-sensitive use of knowledge, and for the kind of world-fitting complexity of understanding that cognitive flexibility depends upon—and that the increasingly complex modern world of life and work needs now more than ever. Rigidity and oversimplification are rampant in learning and teaching (e.g., Feltovich, Coulson, & Spiro, 2001; Feltovich, Spiro, & Coulson, 1989, 1996; Spiro, Feltovich, & Coulson, 1996), but with the affordances of new media, we do not need to live complacently with this state of affairs (Spiro, in press).

The perspective of cognitive flexibility theory (CFT; Mishra, Spiro, & Feltovich, 1996; Spiro, Coulson, Feltovich, & Anderson, 1988, 2004; Spiro, Feltovich, Jacobson, & Coulson, 1992a, 1992b; Spiro & Jehng, 1990) enacts openness in many ways—in the theory itself and in the multimedia learning systems based on the theory (cognitive flexibility hypertext learning environments, CFHs). A recent overview of CFT can be found in Spiro, Collins, and Thota (2003).

A Non-Exhaustive Catalogue of Modes of Openness and Flexibility in Cognitive Flexibility Systems

Openness—and related flexibility—come into play in a wide variety of ways in learning systems based on CFT. Although we provide here the first *cataloguing* of a substantial sample of those ways that CFHs are characterized by forms of openness that promote flexibility, it is worth emphasizing that this is just a sample, that there are many more ways that each of the types listed below can be considered "open" and, in turn, create flexibility; and that there are more types than just these. It should also be noted that in this short chapter we will be talking only about characteristics of CFHs. We recognize that some of the features we discuss may be employed in other instructional design approaches in forms of varying similarity and difference to that used in CFHs.

Each of the following kinds of openness are found in *all* CFHs, with the exception of the ones that are specific to digital video cases, where the features are built into the subspecies of CFHs called EASEs (experience acceleration support environments). To see operative examples of many of the points that follow, see EASE-history (http://www.easehistory.org/), a system that uses presidential campaign ads, historical events, and core values to support the learning and teaching of U.S. history (Collins, Ramchandran, & Spiro, in preparation).[1]

The Foundation: Complex, Open, and Flexible Habits of Mind

Most important of all in fostering more flexible thinking is the establishment of appropriate habits of mind (ways of thinking, worldviews, mindsets, and so on that *prefigure* the *kinds* of knowledge that will be built by an individual). People too often adopt a knowledge stance that we have characterized as the reductive world view, made up of a number of Reductive Biases (Feltovich et al., 1989, 1996, 2001; Spiro et al., 1996, 1988, 2004). This is a tendency to see the world as made up of events and phenomena that are orderly, predictable, decomposable into additive elements, non-contingent, and well structured, and accordingly to have personal epistemologies that see learning as best accomplished by approaches that lead to representations that are simple and highly general (capturing a topic with a single schema, prototype example, set of general principles and definitions, etc.), compartmentalized or "chapterized," and so on. When these habits of mind are prevalent, the result is structures of knowledge that are relatively more closed and, as a result, inflexible in operation.

The alternative—necessary in complex and more ill-structured arenas of knowledge— counters the tendencies just described with approaches that foster the building of knowledge characterized by multiple representation, interconnectedness, contingency (context-dependence, a tendency to recognize when it is appropriate to say "it depends" and to acknowledge that many situations are not "either/or," but rather shades of gray in between). *All* of the kinds of openness built into CFHs, as outlined below, are intended to shift habits of mind from the relatively closed to the more open, as well as to build specific content knowledge that has various forms of openness.

Opening Up of Comparison and Contrast: Beyond Pairs

The latest versions of CFHs (EASE systems) permit video examples to be compared in pairs on the screen. However, an important innovation has been the ability to set up results from multiple theme searches in each of four quadrants. Four-way comparisons open up categories to reveal subtle but important differences (e.g., "example one is kind of like example two in one way, but like examples three and four in yet other ways, even though all are similarly categorized")—and these nuanced differences are a basis for flexible application of knowledge in situations that also differ from each other in subtle ways. (An even greater expansion of the notion of comparison and contrast is found in CFH/EASEs' use of as many as a dozen rapidly comparable short versions of larger, overlearned video cases to permit a many-times increase in the number of comparisons that can be made in a relatively short amount of time. This is a key feature promoting *experience acceleration* in these new systems).

Crossroads Cases

Instruction in CFHs begins with carefully chosen examples that are rich in the lessons they teach, and that we call "crossroads cases." The lesson for openness is that events in a knowledge domain are not just examples of *one* thing, but rather involve the intersection of multiple concepts and are amenable to a continuing process of making additional interpretations (all of which require justification, of course). Cases, occurrences, events, and examples are open, and therefore they are precedents/experiences that act as a basis for future knowledge assembly in a wider variety of ways—thus the openness of individual cases promotes *flexibility*.

Many Cases

CFHs employ large numbers of cases, opening up the space of possible precedents/ prototypes for greater *flexibility* in later knowledge application.

Furthermore, the fundamental organizing unit of CFHs is the *mini-case*. Larger cases are broken into several small segments so that coding of the CFH can be based on unique local properties rather than only those of the larger case they are drawn from, which would reduce the coding to a common denominator (which would miss much that is important) or, at the other extreme, include too much that applies only to a small region within a larger case and thus is misleading about the case as a whole. (Structuring in small segments also permits a *new incrementalism* of instructional sequencing in which one can begin learning with bite-size chunks of cognitively manageable complexity that establishes appropriately complex habits of mind from the beginning of instruction without over-whelming learners.) By breaking cases into a set of mini-cases, the number of examples worked with is greatly increased, further opening the space of possible prototypes for future action and providing many more opportunities for relating new instances to old ones—a many-fold increase in the bases for *flexibility*.

Conceptual Variability

One of the first instructional moves in any CFH is a conceptual-variability search. By clicking on a concept or theme, one finds a variety of real-world examples that illustrate that theme. The lesson that is immediately taught is that complex concepts do not have a denotative semantic core that *limits* their possibilities for application, but rather are governed by family resemblance relations. The conceptual-variability search illustrates the variety of ways the concept is *used*. This opening up of the range of possible uses of a concept in turn enables learners to use it in more different ways—that is, to employ the concept with greater *flexibility*.

Multiple Higher-Order Conceptual Themes

CFHs always employ multiple ideas "at the top." That is, we analyze the subject area to identify several different concepts that different experts have proposed as the "most important and central." And then we use them *all*. By opening up the topmost structure of a domain and providing learners with multiple entry points, each a candidate for "best superordinate concept," the chances of being able to optimize the prior knowledge activated to fit a new context is greatly increased—and situation-sensitive *flexibility* in applying knowledge is enhanced.

Multiple Theme Search:
Playgrounds for Combining Ideas

CFHs permit searches for examples that illustrate the *combination* of concepts or themes. This allows for learners to form increasingly more sophisticated hypotheses about the subject area they are studying, the problem they are trying to solve, or the essay they are trying to write. The CFH acts as a kind of Combinatorial Idea Playground, all the while tied to actual occurrences (to insure that the ideas do not end up in the clouds, unconnected to realities on the ground). This permits a many-times expansion of the ways material can be organized, and this opening up of the organizational space enables a great increase in the *flexibility* with which material can be conceptually captured and later deployed.

Multiple Interconnectedness

By having a large number of mini-cases coded with a large number of conceptual themes, CFHs automatically produce highly interconnected structures that intertwine along multiple dimensions. This produces a huge number of possible retrieval routes in memory and possibilities for *flexible* knowledge assembly in new contexts, as situational information 'carves out' alternative paths through the Web-like representation.

Nonlinear Juxtaposition

A basic feature of all CFHs is that they create juxtapositions, sometimes quite unexpected ones, of cases that diverge from ordinary conceptual category membership. These "jumps" are the result of an opening of the organizational space, and this flexibility of organization instills habits of mind of *flexibility,* showing learners that they need not be bound by preestablished "lines of thought."

Perceptual Overlays to Open Perception

Some CFHs for digital video cases (EASE systems) employ various kinds of perceptual overlays to open and deepen perception. For example, when learners tend to watch one part of a video scene to the exclusion of other parts, we show the scene again, this time perhaps in slow motion and with spotlights on the neglected parts. People quickly get the message that what they first see is not all they can and should see—and they develop the habit to look more closely, and then to look again to see more.

When we find that people accept what they see uncritically, we use editing effects to cause the appearance of the video image shattering into fragmented shards, accompanied by a sudden loud noise—dissonance is created and complacent viewers are shaken out of their too great ease with what they think they are seeing. Again, habits of mind are hard to change, and strong measures are required to capture their attention, make them realize they are seeing too simply, and show them that they are capable of seeing more if they look harder and with fewer blinders on.

Sometimes we have learners associate musical soundtracks that correspond to conceptual stances (as people naturally associate certain kinds of music in a film with suspense, for example), and then play the same video scene with different soundtracks. Learners quickly see that a scene, say from a classroom, is very much *open* to interpretation. (We do similar things with color filters, in much the same way as was done in the film, "Traffic.")

These are just a few of the ways that CFT uses perceptual enhancements to open up perception (and, incidentally, to reduce cognitive capacity demands). And the more one sees in a case, the more ways that case can be interpreted. As a result, there is a greater range of future uses to which the knowledge acquired from the case can be put—an important source of *flexibility*.

Opening Time

We are too often bound by temporal adjacency—events that occur near each other in time are easily related to each other, while those that are more temporally distant are less likely to be connected in our knowledge representations. CFH/EASE systems employ a convention for the placement of picture-in-picture videos to more organically connect events that have distant antecedents and consequents (with the former occurring in the lower left of the screen and the latter in the lower right of the screen, as an example of part of the time-representation scheme). By opening time, we increase the opportunity to form connections *flexibly*.

Conclusion

Various modes of openness in learning environments based on cognitive flexibility theory have been presented. The more ways that presentation formats and knowledge representations converge to promote open rather than closed thinking (though never in an "anything goes" manner—there must always be a warrant for any "opening" of representation), the greater the flexibility in future knowledge application that will result. This will be due in part to the greater opportunities for flexible knowledge assembly that open knowledge structures permit; but it will also be due to the more complex and flexible ways of thinking that will be formed and begin to become habitual. The result is the creation of mindsets that perpetuate the development of flexibly applicable knowledge and that eventually do not depend upon external support from computer learning environments—habits of mind that are the basis for independent, adaptive learning. And given the widespread bias toward rigid and oversimplified ways of thinking, the value of any learning approaches that combat that powerful trend cannot be underestimated—the reductive bias must be combated with all the resources that random access technologies can offer.

References

Collins, B. P., Ramchandran, A. R., & Spiro, R. J. (in preparation). *EASE history: A cognitive flexibility hypermedia system that supports history learning.*

Feltovich, P. J., Coulson, R. L., & Spiro, R. J. (2001). Learners' understanding of important and difficult concepts: A challenge to smart machines in education. In P. J. Feltovich & K. Forbus (Eds.), *Smart machines in education.* Cambridge, MA: MIT Press.

Feltovich, P. J., Spiro, R. J., & Coulson, R. L. (1989). The nature of conceptual understanding in biomedicine: The deep structure of complex ideas and the development of misconceptions. In D. Evans & V. Patel (Eds.), *The cognitive sciences in medicine* (pp. 113-172). Cambridge, MA: MIT Press.

Feltovich, P. J, Spiro, R. J., & Coulson, R. L. (1997). Issues of expert flexibility in contexts characterized by complexity and change. In P. J. Feltovich, K. M. Ford, & R. R. Hoffman (Eds.), *Expertise in context: Human and machine.* Cambridge, MA: MIT Press.

Mishra, P., Spiro, R. J., & Feltovich, P. J. (1996). Technology, representation, and cognition: The prefiguring of knowledge in Cognitive Flexibility Hypertexts. In H. van Oostendorp & A. de Mul (Eds.), *Cognitive aspects of electronic text processing* (pp. 287-305). Norwood, NJ: Ablex.

Spiro, R. J. (in press). The new Gutenberg revolution. *Educational Technology.*

Spiro, R. J., Collins, B. P. Thota, J. J., & Feltovich, P. J. (2003). Cognitive flexibility theory: Hypermedia for complex learning, adaptive knowledge application, and experience acceleration. *Educational Technology, 44*(5), 5-10.

Spiro, R. J., Coulson, R. L., Feltovich, P. J., & Anderson, D. (2004). Cognitive flexibility theory: Advanced knowledge acquisition in ill-structured domains. In R. B. Ruddell (Ed.), *Theoretical models and processes of reading* (5th ed., pp. 602-616). Newark, DE: International Reading Association. [*Reprinted from Proceedings of the 10th Annual Conference of the Cognitive Science Society* (1988). Hillsdale, NJ: Lawrence Erlbaum]

Spiro, R. J., Feltovich, P. J., & Coulson, R. L. (1996). Two epistemic world-views: Prefigurative schemas and learning in complex domains. *Applied Cognitive Psychology, 10,* 52-61.

Spiro, R. J., Feltovich, P. J., Jacobson, M. J., & Coulson, R. L. (1992a). Cognitive flexibility, constructivism, and hypertext: Random access instruction for advanced knowledge acquisition in ill-structured domains. In T. Duffy & D. Jonassen (Eds.),

Constructivism and the technology of instruction (pp. 57-75). Hillsdale, NJ: Lawrence Erlbaum. (Reprinted from a special issue of the journal *Educational Technology* on Constructivism.)

Spiro, R. J., Feltovich, P. J., Jacobson, M. J., & Coulson, R. L. (1992b). Knowledge representation, content specification, and the development of skill in situation-specific knowledge assembly: Some constructivist issues as they relate to cognitive flexibility theory and hypertext. In T. Duffy & D. Jonassen (Eds.), *Constructivism and the technology of instruction* (pp. 121-128). Hillsdale, NJ: Lawrence Erlbaum. (Reprinted from a special issue of the journal *Educational Technology* on Constructivism.)

Spiro, R. J., & Jehng, J. C. (1990). Cognitive flexibility and hypertext: Theory and technology for the nonlinear and multidimensional traversal of complex subject matter. In D. Nix & R. J. Spiro (Eds.), *Cognition, education, and multimedia: Explorations in high technology* (pp. 163-205). Hillsdale, NJ: Lawrence Erlbaum.

Spiro, R. J., Vispoel, W. L., Schmitz, J., Samarapungavan, A., & Boerger, A. (1987). Knowledge acquisition for application: Cognitive flexibility and transfer in complex content domains. In B. C. Britton & S. Glynn (Eds.), *Executive control processes.* Hillsdale, NJ: Lawrence Erlbaum.

Endnote

[1] For access to other systems that have a fuller set of features, send a note requesting URLs and a password to rspiro@msu.edu.

Chapter III

Authentic Learning on the Web:
Guidelines for Course Design

Jan Herrington, University of Wollongong, Australia

Ron Oliver, Edith Cowan University, Australia

Anthony Herrington, University of Wollongong, Australia

Introduction

In response to the growing influence of constructivism as a philosophical approach to learning, and a wide range of research studies investigating alternative models of teaching and learning over the last decade, many universities have experimented with the development of 'authentic' learning environments. How successful they have been in this quest is a subject of some debate. For instance, Gayeski (2005) has argued:

Many of today's programs are no better than those from the early days of interactive video—in fact, they are worse. We still see too many textbooks or PowerPoint slides 'ported' over to the Web with a few links or silly questions added to make them 'interactive' (p. 98)

The challenge instructors face is to align university teaching and learning more substantially with the way learning is achieved in real-life settings, and to base instructional methods on recent theories of learning which reflect this shift, such as situated learning (Brown, Collins, & Duguid, 1989; Collins, Brown, & Newman, 1989; McLellan, 1996; Choi & Hannafin, 1995). Authentic approaches, as well as requiring students to *apply theory*, also allow students to *create theories* by starting with a realistic problem, and then developing their own knowledge within the practical situations in which the need for learning was created.

This chapter proposes nine critical characteristics of learning as a framework for the design of more authentic learning environments on the Web. The elements are based on situated learning theory and other compatible research, with particular emphasis on computer and Web-based applications.

Design guidelines are presented below for teachers and designers as a framework for their instructional approach to course units on the Web (cf. Herrington & Oliver, 2000; Oliver & Herrington, 2000; Herrington & Herrington, 2006). Learning environments would provide:

1. **Authentic contexts that reflect the way the knowledge will be used in real life:** In designing online learning environments with authentic contexts, it is not sufficient to simply provide suitable examples from real-world situations to illustrate the concept or issue being taught. The context needs to be all-embracing, to provide the purpose and motivation for learning, and to provide a sustained and complex learning environment that can be explored at length. It needs to encompass a physical environment which reflects the way the knowledge will be used, and a large number of resources to sustain examination from different perspectives (Brown et al., 1989; Reeves & Reeves, 1997; Honebein, Duffy, & Fishman, 1993).

2. **Authentic activities:** The learning environment needs to provide ill-defined activities which have real-world relevance and present complex tasks to be completed over a sustained period of time, rather than a series of shorter disconnected examples (Bransford, Vye, Kinzer, & Risko, 1990; Brown et al., 1989; Lebow & Wager, 1994; Reeves & Reeves, 1997). Resources to support these activities should be sufficiently diverse and non-directed, to allow students the opportunity to discern relevant from irrelevant material (Young, 1993).

3. **Access to expert performances and the modelling of processes:** Access to expert performances and the modelling of processes has its origins in the apprenticeship system of learning, where students and craftspeople learned new skills under the guidance of an expert (Collins et al., 1989). Important elements of expert performances are found in modern applications of the apprenticeship model such as internships (Jonassen, Mayes, & McAleese, 1993) and case-based learning (Riesbeck, 1996). An important aspect of expert performances is that it enables the learner to compare his or her performance or understanding to an expert in the field (Candy, Harri-Augstein, & Thomas, 1985; Collins, Brown, & Holum, 1991) and with others at various levels of expertise (Collins et al., 1989).

4. **Multiple roles and perspectives:** In order for students to be able to investigate issues from more than a single perspective, it is important to enable and encourage

students to explore different perspectives, and to "crisscross" the learning environment repeatedly (Collins et al., 1989; Honebein et al., 1993).

5. **Collaborative construction of knowledge:** The opportunity for users to collaborate in a "community of learners" is an important design element, particularly for students who may be learning at a distance (Brown et al., 1989; Collins et al., 1989; Reeves & Reeves, 1997; Hooper, 1992). Collaboration has been defined as "the mutual engagement of participants in a coordinated effort to solve a problem together" (Roschelle & Behrend, 1995). Forman and Cazden (1985) have suggested that true collaboration is not simply working together, but also "solving a problem or creating a product which could not have been completed independently" (p. 329).

6. **Opportunities for reflection:** In order to provide opportunities for students to reflect on their learning, the online learning environment needs to provide an authentic context and task, as described earlier, to enable meaningful reflection. It also needs to provide nonlinear organisation to enable students to readily return to any element of the site if desired (Boud, Keogh, & Walker, 1985; Collins & Brown, 1988; Kemmis, 1985).

7. **Opportunities for articulation:** In order to produce a learning environment capable of providing opportunities for articulation, the tasks need to incorporate inherent—as opposed to constructed—opportunities for collaborative groups to engage in dialogue, and the public presentation of arguments to enable defence of a position (Collins et al., 1989; Edelson, Pea, & Gomez, 1996; Lave & Wenger, 1991). Baktin (1986) contends that "any true understanding is dialogic in nature" (cited in Brown & Campione, 1994, p. 267). The implication is that the very process of articulating enables formation, awareness, development, and refinement of thought.

8. **Coaching and scaffolding:** In order to accommodate a coaching and scaffolding role principally by the teacher (but also provided by other students), the online learning environment needs to provide collaborative learning, where more able partners can assist with scaffolding and coaching, as well as the means for the teacher to support learning via appropriate communication technologies (Collins et al., 1989; Greenfield, 1984).

9. **Authentic assessment:** In order to provide integrated and authentic assessment of student learning, the online learning environment needs to provide the opportunity for students to be effective performers with acquired knowledge, and to craft products or performances in collaboration with others. It also requires the assessment to be seamlessly integrated with the activity, and to provide appropriate criteria for scoring varied products (Duchastel, 1997; Reeves & Okey, 1996; Herrington & Herrington, 1998; Wiggins, 1993).

Applying the Model

How might a teacher designing an online course apply such principles? Imagine you are an instructor at a college or university, and as part of your teaching duties, you have been asked to design and teach an introductory online course on the Internet and the World Wide Web. The principal aim of the course is to introduce students to a wide range of online technologies and to promote understanding of how they are used.

One way to approach this challenge would be to list 12-15 different Web-based technologies (to correspond to the number of weeks in the semester), and create weekly online lectures, tasks, and readings on each. Topics and tasks would become progressively more complex as the course progressed, and three major assignments would be required at evenly spaced intervals throughout the semester. Such a course would fulfil your obligations as a teacher, and no doubt you would have a lot of fun and learn much while creating the course.

An alternative approach, based on the situated learning principles described above, would be more student centred, and designed around more authentic contexts and tasks.

The first crucial consideration is to create an *authentic context* that reflects the way the knowledge would be used in real life. This might involve the development of a story or scenario that is capable of carrying or instantiating all the concepts and skills associated with the course curriculum. Suppose you decide to focus your course on the creation of a Web page, how could you incorporate a range of Web technologies in a realistic and pedagogically appropriate way? You decide to create a scenario around a family reunion, due to take place in the near future. Capturing the "scene" will enable you to introduce students to Web technologies in a realistic and meaningful way. Suppose that the family is large, and a special Web site is required to mark the occasion and to focus all family members on the upcoming celebrations.

The next and possibly most important decision for the design of your learning environment is to create *authentic activities* or tasks for students to complete as they study the course. Because you have established a meaningful and authentic context, design of authentic tasks is usually readily achieved. Because of real-life university constraints that require you to set three assignments (rather than the one complex task that you are planning), you need to divide the creation of the family Web site into three stages, but you can incorporate this quite creatively into the scenario.

The three tasks you set are:

- **Task 1:** A distant cousin has written to you, telling you about a planned family reunion, and asking if you would be able to develop a family Web site. The first stage of the site is required for a family reunion to be held in five weeks time. At the reunion, you need to show a fully functioning Web site which includes an appropriate interface, 6-10 main menu items with pages, links to outside sites, and several family photographs. (Task due Week 5)

- **Task 2:** The family reunion was a huge success, and you and your cousin managed to acquire many useful resources to put onto the site. For example, people have sent old home movies on videotapes, audio recordings, recipes handed down from great-grandmother, war histories, information about famous and infamous ancestors, newspaper clippings, family trees, old letters, telegrams, slide transparencies, and many more relevant existing Internet links. Your next task is to include some of these items into your Web page. As a further consideration, the copyright of many of the items you receive is owned by outside parties (professional photographs, newspaper articles, television interviews, etc.), and you need to include a page on your Web site explaining copyright regulations and how you have satisfied them. (Task due Week 10)

- **Task 3:** The family is delighted at the progress of the Web site, and you are receiving many e-mails, phone calls, and letters almost on a daily basis. The family reunion has put many people in touch with each other after many years, and they are keen to keep contact. You decide to add some communication elements to the site. First, you decide to survey the family to find out how they would like to communicate (create an online feedback form), then based on that feedback, you establish discussion and chat boards, and other communicative elements as required. (Task due final week of semester)

To create a product such as the one that is required through fulfilment of these tasks, students need *access to expert performances and the modelling of processes*. Who are the experts in this situation? Because of the nature of the tasks, experts can be thought of as those people who have successfully completed this kind of task before. In creating the learning environment, you could give students access to other family Web sites and the methods that have been used to create such sites. As instructor, you can model the process of developing a Web site yourself in an online tutorial. Students have the capacity to compare themselves to others in varying stages of expertise.

In any complex learning environment, a single perspective such as that offered through a textbook or the instructor's online "lectures" is insufficient to reflect the authentic nature of the task. It is important to provide the kinds of *multiple roles and perspectives* that are available in real-life challenges. While a single textbook on creating Web pages would be useful and informative, it is insufficient. As noted by Spiro et al. (1991), instruction that puts forward a single, "correct" interpretation or method is not false, but inadequate. The affordances of the Web enable alternative perspectives to be readily accessed through directed resources or search engines, and online readings or specific databases can be targeted for particular tasks.

The authentic tasks in the learning environment lend themselves to individual endeavour, where students could use their own family histories to resource the site. The nature of university assessment also means that there is often a limiting of collaboration to a percentage of assessable tasks. Nevertheless, this learning environment allows *collaborative construction of knowledge* through construction of tools that could be used jointly, or through collaboration on the entire course through the creation of a fictitious or historical family site.

By allowing students to choose their own pathways through the tasks and resources, rather than providing a single step-by-step approach, the learning environment provides many *opportunities for reflection*. The social nature of the learning environment could be supported by discussion forums, Web conferences, and chats (e.g., on different aspects of the task, such as uploading, interface design, authoring tools, etc.), which not only allow active reflection, but also provide *opportunities for articulation* of students' growing understanding of their work. Lave and Wenger (1991) have argued that being able to speak the vocabulary and tell the stories of a culture of practice is fundamental to learning, but many Web-based learning environments allow the knowledge to remain tacit. Formulating arguments or questions and using the vocabulary of the discipline area strengthen students' professional role in their learning.

The role of the instructor changes in authentic learning environments *to coaching and scaffolding*—less the "sage on the stage" and more "guide on the side" (Laurel, 1993), or 'expert learner' along with novice learners in a community of learners (Carroll, 2000, cited in Sherry & Gibson, 2002). Rather than simplifying topics by breaking them down into their component parts, Perkins (1991) suggested temptation to oversimplify should be resisted, and instead instructors should search for new ways to provide appropriate scaffolding and support. There is no longer a need to focus on content and information, or on direct instruction about how to build a Web page, as these are available through rich resources and searching capacity within the learning environment, and the instructor is now able to focus on support for students at the metacognitive level.

Instead of essays, quizzes, or examinations, the tasks would be assessed using integrated and *authentic assessment*. The activities, and the Web site they produce, form the entire focus of the course, and it is on those activities and products that students would be assessed. Students working in this example learning environment would have a goal, and emerge with a real and tangible product. They would become, as noted by Wiggins (1993), effective performers with acquired knowledge, able to craft polished performances or products.

Conclusion

The alternative model described in this chapter draws widely upon the philosophy of constructivism, and on the extensive literature base on situated learning and other theory, and comprises a practical framework for teachers and designers to implement as they begin to work on their online courses. It reflects the growing trends in higher education towards pedagogy and curriculum that reflects vocational needs and develops students' lifelong learning skills (Tynjälä, Välimaa, & Sarja, 2003).

Many teachers, when faced with the task of creating an online course or adapting an existing course to an online format, are overwhelmed by both the affordances of the technology and by the need to create learning environments that do not simply replicate outmoded pedagogies in a new form. There are now growing numbers of online materials being developed based around the notions of authenticity and relevance to the workplace and real-world settings, such as in literature (Fitzsimmons, 2006), in business writing (Pennell, Durham, Orzog, & Spark, 1997), in physical activity fitness and health (Rice et al., 1999), in evaluation (Agostinho, 2006), in literacy education (Ferry et al., 2006), in mechanical engineering (Bullen & Karri, 2002), in transition from school to university (Hunt, Kershaw, & Seddon, 2002), in indigenous education (Marshall, Northcote, & Lenoy, 2001), in multimedia design (Bennett, Harper, & Hedberg, 2001), and in architecture (Challis, 2002). The model described here provides a useful framework for teachers and developers to guide the design of online courses in a way that may promote meaningful and transferable learning.

References

Agostinho, S. (2006). Using characters in online simulated environments to guide authentic tasks. In A. Herrington & J. Herrington (Eds.), *Authentic learning environments in higher education* (pp. 88-95). Hershey, PA: Information Science Publishing.

Bennett, S., Harper, B., & Hedberg, J. (2001). Designing real-life cases to support authentic design activities. In G. Kennedy, M. Keppell, C. McNaught, & T. Petrovic (Eds.), *Meeting at the Crossroads. Proceedings of the 18th Annual Conference of the Australian Society for Computers in Learning in Tertiary Education* (pp. 73-81). Melbourne: Biomedical Multimedia Unit, University of Melbourne.

Bullen, F., & Karri, V. (2002). Design and construction of a Formula SAE race car in a teaching and research framework. In A. Goody, J. Herrington, & M. Northcote (Eds.), *Quality conversations: Research and development in higher education* (Vol. 25, pp. 74-82). Jamison, ACT: HERDSA.

Challis, D. (2002). Integrating the conceptual and practice worlds: A case study from architecture. In A. Goody, J. Herrington, & M. Northcote (Eds.), *Quality conversations: Research and development in higher education* (Vol. 25, pp. 106-113). Jamison, ACT: HERDSA.

Boud, D., Keogh, R., & Walker, D. (1985). Promoting reflection in learning: A model. In D. Boud, R. Keogh, & D. Walker (Eds.), *Reflection: Turning experience into learning* (pp. 18-40). London: Kogan Page.

Bransford, J. D., Vye, N., Kinzer, C., & Risko, V. (1990). Teaching thinking and content knowledge: Toward an integrated approach. In B. F. Jones & L. Idol (Eds.), *Dimensions of thinking and cognitive instruction* (pp. 381-413). Hillsdale, NJ: Lawrence Erlbaum.

Brown, A. L., & Campione, J. C. (1994). Guided discovery in a community of learners. In K. McGilly (Ed.), *Classroom lessons: Integrating cognitive theory and classroom practice* (pp. 229-270). Cambridge, MA: MIT Press.

Brown, J. S., Collins, A., & Duguid, P. (1989). Situated cognition and the culture of learning. *Educational Researcher, 18*(1), 32-42.

Candy, P., Harri-Augstein, S., & Thomas, L. (1985). Reflection and the self-organized learner: A model for learning conversations. In D. Boud, R. Keogh, & D. Walker (Eds.), *Reflection: Turning experience into learning* (pp. 100-116). London: Kogan Page.

Choi, J., & Hannafin, M. (1995). Situated cognition and learning environments: Roles, structures and implications for design. *Educational Technology Research and Development, 43*(2), 53-69.

Collins, A., & Brown, J. S. (1988). The computer as a tool for learning through reflection. In H. Mandl & A. Lesgold (Eds.), *Learning issues for intelligent tutoring systems* (pp. 1-18). New York: Springer-Verlag.

Collins, A., Brown, J. S., & Holum, A. (1991). Cognitive apprenticeship: Making thinking visible. *American Educator, 15*(3), 6-11, 38-46.

Collins, A., Brown, J. S., & Newman, S. E. (1989). Cognitive apprenticeship: Teaching the crafts of reading, writing, and mathematics. In L. B. Resnick (Ed.), *Knowing, learning and instruction: Essays in honour of Robert Glaser* (pp. 453-494). Hillsdale, NJ: Lawrence Erlbaum.

Duchastel, P. C. (1997). A Web-based model for university instruction. *Journal of Educational Technology Systems, 25*(3), 221-228.

Edelson, D. C., Pea, R. D., & Gomez, L. (1996). Constructivism in the collaboratory. In B. G. Wilson (Ed.), *Constructivist learning environments: Case studies in instructional design* (pp. 151-164). Englewood Cliffs, NJ: Educational Technology Publications.

Ferry, B., Kervin, L., Puglisi, S., Cambourne, B., Turbill, J., Jonassen, D., & Hedberg, J. (2006). Online classroom simulation: Using a virtual classroom to support pre-service teacher thinking. In A. Herrington & J. Herrington (Eds.), *Authentic learning environments in higher education* (pp. 135-161). Hershey, PA: Information Science Publishing.

Fitzsimmons, J. (2006). Speaking snake: Authentic learning and the study of literature. In A. Herrington & J. Herrington (Eds.), *Authentic learning environments in higher education* (pp. 162-171). Hershey, PA: Information Science Publishing.

Forman, E. A., & Cazden, C. B. (1985). Exploring Vygotskyan perspectives in education: The cognitive value of peer interaction. In J. V. Wertsch (Ed.), *Culture, communication and cognition: Vygotskyan perspectives* (pp. 323-347). Cambridge: Cambridge University Press.

Gayeski, D. (2005). From stir fried circuit boards to streaming video: Perspectives from an interactive media pioneer. In G. Kearsley (Ed.), *Online learning: Personal reflections on the transformation of education* (pp. 92-100). Englewood Cliffs, NJ: Educational Technology Publications.

Greenfield, P. M. (1984). A theory of the teacher in the learning activities of everyday life. In B. Rogoff & J. Lave (Eds.), *Everyday cognition: Its development in social context* (pp. 117-138). Cambridge, MA: Harvard University Press.

Herrington, A., & Herrington, J., (2006). What is an authentic learning environment? In A. Herrington, & J. Herrington (Eds.), *Authentic learning environments in higher education* (pp. 1-13). Hershey, PA: Information Science Publishing.

Herrington, J., & Herrington, A. (1998). Authentic assessment and multimedia: How university students respond to a model of authentic assessment. *Higher Education Research and Development, 17*(3), 305-322.

Herrington, J., & Oliver, R. (2000). An instructional design framework for authentic learning environments. *Educational Technology Research and Development, 48*(3), 23-48.

Honebein, P. C., Duffy, T. M., & Fishman, B. J. (1993). Constructivism and the design of learning environments: Context and authentic activities for learning. In T. M. Duffy,

J. Lowyck, & D. H. Jonassen (Eds.), *Designing environments for constructive learning* (pp. 87-108). Heidelberg, Germany: Springer-Verlag.

Hooper, S. (1992). Cooperative learning and computer-based design. *Educational Technology Research and Development, 40*(3), 21-38.

Jonassen, D., Mayes, T., & McAleese, R. (1993). A manifesto for a constructivist approach to uses of technology in higher education. In T. M. Duffy, J. Lowyck, & D. H. Jonassen (Eds.), *Designing environments for constructive learning* (pp. 231-247). Heidelberg, Germany: Springer-Verlag.

Kemmis, S. (1985). Action research and the politics of reflection. In D. Boud, R. Keogh, & D. Walker (Eds.), *Reflection: Turning experience into learning* (pp. 139-163). London: Kogan Page.

Laurel, B. (1993). *Computers as theatre.* Reading, MA: Addison-Wesley.

Lave, J., & Wenger, E. (1991). *Situated learning: Legitimate peripheral participation.* Cambridge: Cambridge University Press.

Lebow, D., & Wager, W. W. (1994). Authentic activity as a model for appropriate learning activity: Implications for emerging instructional technologies. *Canadian Journal of Educational Communication, 23*(3), 231-144.

Marshall, L., Northcote, M., & Lenoy, M. (2001). Design influences in the creation of an online mathematics unit for indigenous adults. In G. Kennedy, M. Keppell, C. McNaught , & T. Petrovic (Eds.), *Meeting at the Crossroads. Proceedings of the 18th Annual Conference of the Australian Society for Computers in Learning in Tertiary Education* (pp. 113-116). Melbourne: University of Melbourne.

McLellan, H. (Ed.). (1996). *Situated learning perspectives.* Englewood Cliffs, NJ: Educational Technology Publications.

Oliver, R., & Herrington, J. (2000). Using situated learning as a design strategy for Web-based learning. In B. Abbey (Ed.), *Instructional and cognitive impacts of Web-based education* (pp. 178-191). Hershey, PA: Idea Group Publishing.

Pennell, R., Durham, M., Ozog, M., & Spark, A. (1997). Writing in context: Situated learning on the Web. In R. Kevill, R. Oliver, & R. Phillips (Eds.), *What Works and Why: Proceedings of the 14th Annual Conference of the Australian Society for Computers in Learning in Tertiary Education* (pp. 463-469). Perth, WA: Curtin University.

Perkins, D. N. (1991). What constructivism demands of the learner. *Educational Technology, 31*(8), 19-21.

Reeves, T. C., & Okey, J. R. (1996). Alternative assessment for constructivist learning environments. In B. G. Wilson (Ed.), *Constructivist learning environments: Case studies in instructional design* (pp. 191-202). Englewood Cliffs, NJ: Educational Technology Publications.

Reeves, T. C., & Reeves, P. M. (1997). Effective dimensions of interactive learning on the World Wide Web. In B. H. Khan (Ed.), *Web-based instruction* (pp. 59-66). Englewood Cliffs, NJ: Educational Technology Publications.

Rice, M., Owies, D., Campbell, A., Snow, R., Owen, N., & Holt, D. (1999). V-Lab: A virtual laboratory for teaching introductory concepts and methods of physical fitness and function. *Australian Journal of Educational Technology, 15*(2), 188-206.

Riesbeck, C. K. (1996). Case-based teaching and constructivism: Carpenters and tools. In B. G. Wilson (Ed.), *Constructivist learning environments: Case studies in instructional design* (pp. 49-61). Englewood Cliffs, NJ: Educational Technology Publications.

Roschelle, J., & Behrend, S. D. (1995). The construction of shared knowledge in collaborative problem solving. In C. O'Malley (Ed.), *Computer supported collaborative learning.* New York: Springer-Verlag.

Sherry, L., & Gibson, D. (2002). The path to teacher leadership in educational technology. *Contemporary Issues in Technology and Teacher Education* [Online serial], *2*(2), 178-203.

Spiro, R. J., Feltovich, P. J., Jacobson, M. J., & Coulson, R. L. (1991b). Knowledge representation, content specification, and the development of skill in situation-specific knowledge assembly: Some constructivist issues as they relate to cognitive flexibility theory and hypertext. *Educational Technology, 31*(9), 22-25.

Tynjälä, P., Välimaa, J., & Sarja, A. (2003). Pedagogical perspectives on the relationships between higher education and working life. *Higher Education, 46*(2), 147-166.

Wiggins, G. (1993). *Assessing student performance: Exploring the purpose and limits of testing.* San Francisco: Jossey-Bass.

Chapter IV

Designing Community Learning in Web-Based Environments

Mercedes Fisher, Pepperdine University, USA

Bonita Coleman, Valley Christian Schools, USA

Paul Sparks, Pepperdine University, USA

Cheryl Plett, Cerro Coso Community College, USA

A community can represent many things and be directed toward a definite goal, but community itself is the focus of a spiritual science that inspires universality. Day-to-day living in a community fosters a very practical concept of existence. Community life represents the frontier between the macro and micro in terms of human organization, making it possible to experience all levels of human existence. The community is, therefore, a vast landscape for a material realization whenever each person enters into contract with the gifts, virtues, and shortcomings of its members. It is also the immense spiritual and psychic laboratory that enables our spirits to develop.

~ Alex Polari de Alverga in *Forest of Vision: Ayahuasca, Amazonian Spirituality and the Santa Daime Tradition*

Community Learning Theory

... Learning is a fundamentally social phenomenon. (Wenger, 1998)

Current learning theory suggests that collaboration is a key to effective learning. Perhaps it is no coincidence that collaborative online tools have appeared as social theories of learning have become more widely accepted. Programs that embody the more traditional and linear teaching methods are slowly yielding to collaborative tools that more appropriately support our new understanding of social learning. As our tools become more powerful and sophisticated, so too will our ability to think and learn with them.

The design of successful Web-based learning environments is best when based on sound learning principles. Social learning theory, in which cognitive factors, environmental influences, and behavior work together to determine learning, suggests that knowledge is shared and that learning occurs when people interact with each other in meaningful ways (Wenger, 1998). The following principles help to define meaningful learning environments (IRL, 1990):

- People learn best socially, through collaboration.
- Knowledge relies heavily on context provided by the community.
- Communities of interest provide an ideal learning environment.
- Learning is gaining identity and confidence in the community.
- Knowing is participation in the practice of the community.
- Knowledge increases when new information makes a connection with prior knowledge.

The application of these principles to Web-based environments requires creativity and some courage, but has already proven to be effective (Fisher, 2003). One key to successful online learning is to create learning environments that promote sociability and encourage collaboration. Traditional distance learning courses provided almost no collaboration and were known to have abysmal completion rates, often less than 20%. Current online courses offering electronic collaboration capabilities often boast completion rates that approach 100% (Pepperdine University, 2002).

The collaborative design element of Web-based education involves interactivity. Effective collaboration in online environments provides the student the means of being actively involved in the learning activity. It results in learner-centered instruction, improves student attitude towards learning, and gives the student the opportunity of having personal interaction with both the instructor and other learners (Bills, 1997). According to Matthews (1997), active learning has been shown to be most effective when the learner is engaged. Technology, when used well, can tailor the instruction and learning experience. Interacting with virtual classmates and instructors makes learners creative and thoughtful. As reported in Song (1998), students assert that taking part in

Internet-based courses or programs engenders a higher set of skills, particularly the ability to communicate.

True education is naturally intended to promote learning in the highest degree, allowing learners to evaluate, assimilate, and associate facts with meaningful application. Learning cannot and should not be something rote. It is also not about distance or delivery, but about knowledge construction—the learner building his/her own knowledge as it is needed. Using collaborative pedagogy effectively in online courses can facilitate this higher level of learning.

Strategies for Designing Community Learning in Web-Based Environments

This chapter reviews several strategies for creating effective collaboration and community in online environments. Experienced online instructors provide examples and models with the goal of preparing others to design and teach effectively in collaborative Web-based environments. These strategies include the following:

- Allow groups to build a social identity
- Encourage meaningful interaction
- Establish a robust learning environment
- Relate learning to practice

Allow Groups to Build a Social Identity

Individuals perceive their identities in terms of their ability to contribute to a community. (Abbot, 1996)

There is a social identity within a learning community that is both individual and collective. It is important to allow community members the freedom to discover where they personally fit into the learning community. For example, there will be some members who naturally become the group organizers because of their ability to keep track of details. Those who have artistic abilities will find their personal identity as they offer creative input. Each group member also brings a unique set of experiences and sources of information. Community-building activities should be set up from the beginning, allowing instructors and students plenty of time to become well acquainted.

Facilitation of individual identity in the learning environment is a key component toward the interaction that is to take place during a course. In the case of a learning community, individuals within the group share their learning experiences, as they venture together. This exchange of knowledge and experience transforms a group of people into a community as members begin to appreciate the expertise and perspective of each member. As students interact, they develop relationships, shared values, and interests. In some cases these relationships will extend beyond the course environment.

In developing an online community for learning, groups must be given time to build an identity. Each learning group is unique because of the individuality of its members. Because of this distinctiveness learners within a group must have an opportunity to develop their group identity by interacting socially with one another. This sense of identity is a critical factor. Groups will naturally formulate their own patterns for interaction. Instructors should let this happen naturally to allow for the most meaningful communication to occur between peers. In order to encourage group identity, members can be encouraged to give their group a name. Some groups will even want to create a logo that expresses their group identity. The identity of the learning community will continue to grow as individuals see themselves as an important member within the community. Facilitation of social identity in the learning environment is a key component toward the interaction that is to take place during a course.

Encourage Meaningful Interaction

The heart and soul of the online course is the interaction between participants. (Draves, 2002)

Similar to what Bourdeau and Bates (1997) discovered regarding distance learning, collaboration between students is an essential component of the activities of participants involved in Web-based education. Participants have to join forces in order to learn more. Students will need to understand and demonstrate social skills required for working collaboratively on the Web, such as trust, acceptance, support, communication, and diplomacy. Instructors can encourage meaningful interaction by scheduling synchronous online discussions and planning small-group activities.

The purpose of synchronous discussions is to provide students with a structured place each week to share emerging thoughts and questions on learning and particularly on their role as a leader in their workplace. It is also a place to interact with other members of the group and the instructor around questions and issues that are raised in readings and course assignments. Each participant in class is expected to incorporate information and insights gained from assigned readings and personal experiences into discussions. In this environment, students create a dynamically evolving information base of ideas, facts, insights, goals, plans, and solutions to workplace-related issues. Introductory instructions in the process of online communication can be given to students to add clarity and deter frustration in synchronous discussion environments.

The initial meeting should provide time for the students to get to know one another, icebreaker elements, and a simple learning task. Instructors should plan regularly scheduled synchronous meetings, making sure to allow the first few minutes in these meetings each week for friendly dialogue. This helps relax students and make them more participative. An hour to an hour and fifteen minutes is usually appropriate. These meetings should be a required part of the course.

Because online communication is a new way of learning, many students are not aware of the level of interaction expected. Students tend to participate heavily in the early weeks of the course, but drop off towards the end. Others may participate in spurts. Students need to understand that consistent, well-paced interaction is necessary to support the online community-learning model. A natural tendency that some instructors face is trying to script the interaction to make sure all points are adequately covered. Collaborative learning suggests the more subtle approach of posing larger questions and allowing students the psychological learning space to develop frameworks of understanding and collaborative solutions. The instructor plays an influential role in determining who dominates the discussion. The instructor's response encourages or impedes collaboration in dialogue. Instructors should encourage silent members to contribute and tactfully redirect those who dominate.

Online learning and collaboration in a text-based environment has its own specific dialect and colloquialism; as students become more comfortable in the text-based conversation setting, they become increasingly able to express their thoughts, emotions, frustrations, and even gestures using symbolic or representative techniques. Since people generally speak faster than they type, students may find the synchronous discussion setting to be initially frustrating. Yet, students increase their speed as well as their ability to articulate (via text) the more they participate in this manner. Language can be more easily misinterpreted without the usual channels such as vocal inflection, gestures, facial expressions, and nonverbal cues to assist in our communications. Text alone is more than enough to convey an informed response, provided it is precise. Precise language, detailed descriptions, and other expressive elements become characteristic of learners working within this framework of communication. Learners become fluent in 'language' in order to convey or demonstrate their philosophies, ideals, emotions, undertakings, and outcomes. Learning to express their thoughts in precise ways helps learners to think critically.

Arranging for small-group interactions is another effective online strategy. Small groups force participants to take an active role in learning and provide the advantage of immediate feedback from peers. The variety of small-group interactions that can be implemented in Web-based environments includes, but is not limited to:

- Focused discussions
- Group writing activities
- Problem solving

Discussions are designed to fine tune understanding and should provide just enough focus to set the expectation and get the discussion started. Discussions can also occur asynchronously, but work best if given a relatively short timeframe for completion. Asking participants to take on specific roles also works well. For example, if the activity was discussing a chapter, one student might take the author's point of view, another student argues the opposite, and a third student observes and provides feedback. Online discussions allow students to set their own times and interact with many others regardless of location.

Group writing activities require the production of a joint document. This in turn requires the small group to share the same document and manage document versions as they pass it around for revisions. For instance, a small group of students could write a book review together to share with the rest of the class.

Small-group problem solving is yet another highly effective learning activity that can be accomplished online. Using whiteboard software, students can brainstorm in real time by drawing pictures that all members see and chatting to test their ideas with each other. Students can even interact with simulation software in various ways, testing their assumptions and developing solutions as they work together. Small-group problem solving is an effective way to encourage students to connect the concepts taught in a course to real-world situations.

Small-group interactions must be encouraged and supported by the instructor and the class culture. In online environments, interpersonal relations are sometimes more difficult to establish and maintain, so adequate time and clear expectations should be designed into the learning experience. Instructors can adapt most small-group activities for use in Web-based environments by understanding the capabilities of available collaboration tools. There should be a substantial component in the grading system for each group's performance. This can be done by giving both an individual grade and a group grade. When assessing group performance, peer evaluations will provide instructors with helpful insights.

Within the framework of a community structure with roles and protocols defined, interaction is more effective. It is within the community interactions that learning occurs.

Instructors need to let go and trust the process of collaborative learning. This means staying out of the way and encouraging learners to interact with each other. Instructors can then celebrate the interactions that create real meaning for students.

Establish a Robust Learning Environment

Supporting informed participation requires processes that integrate individual and group knowledge through collaborative constructions. (Arias, 1999)

Establishing the learning environment is initially the most critical factor. Because the learning environment is virtual, it requires additional care and effort to make sure it is ready for student interaction. Often this space has been set up in advance for the instructor as part of the infrastructure of the school or organization. Creating an effective learning space is more than just configuring the technology. It is also about the instructor setting a tone that invites collaboration. Students need to gain a comfort level with one another that allows them to effectively work together, debate issues without reprisal, and build a sense of team spirit. Forums may become stifling repositories of expected responses, or they can be alive with discussion, new solutions, and reflection.

After creating the learning space, the instructor must provide the framework for learning. These include communicating overall goals, adjusting for class personality, and delivering the expectations, which can be negotiated once students have been oriented to the course. Students should be given structured guidelines to begin the class, but once they are comfortable in this environment can begin to direct their own learning and utilize the environment to best meet their needs. Students are more engaged if they have the opportunity to set their own norms and standards, and negotiate the expectations. When possible, assignments should be open-ended. This increases the potential of eliciting a participant's real thinking on a topic (Haavind, 2001).

Another technique for creating a robust learning environment is to have students comment on each others' assignments. The benefits of peer review and feedback are twofold. First, students are able to incorporate the different perspectives of their peers as they work to polish and refine assignments. Other students will often offer insights that the instructor would not have. Second, the use of peer review is another way to build a learning community. As students contribute their input to fellow classmates, the connections between the students is strengthened.

In online discussions, the instructor must act as the facilitator without controlling the discussion. Balanced instructor presence is essential to this instructional process. Instructors with minimal or no course presence do not generate high levels of student participation. Those who contribute to discussions as participants more than as authoritative instructors generate greater peer dialogue. Another issue for facilitators is when to redirect conversation. Since discussions are largely student led, topics and issues will vary from group to group. Personal and professional experiences can be addressed where problem solving may be needed. The goal is to help students learn to solve their own problems, so as to build their own learning experience, and also to promote the sense of community that results from helping one another accomplish a task. The instructor needs to pass up being the guide each time someone makes a comment. More often, the instructor should allow for response time instead of feeding information to the group.

One of the issues for educators has been recognizing the value of spending time to explore a topic in depth (i.e., stay with the process and what exactly are this group's concerns, including identifying and confronting the issues) rather than breadth (i.e., more and more content—the old teaching expert paradigm). In fact, when time is taken for this type of exploration, students may take the discussion of a topic into an unexpected realm or to an even deeper level than the instructor had planned. Instructors need to allow discussions to flow in whatever direction will produce the deepest level of learning.

In dynamic online discussions, breakdowns can occur due to incomplete understanding of the underlying problem, conflicts among perspectives, or the absence of shared understanding. By supporting the process of reflection within these discussions, opportunities arise for building upon these breakdowns in ways that integrate the various perspectives and expertise while enhancing shared understanding.

Online tools also provide a unique opportunity to interact with experts. Experts are much more accessible when they can interact online with your students from the comfort of their own offices or homes. A guest expert could be an author of one of the books the students are reading, a political candidate or public official, or a person who is an expert in their field. Students need to be prepared for the encounter by reading articles by the expert and by considering prepared questions. If the interaction is synchronous, it often works better to collect questions from students ahead of time to minimize confusion and

Table 1. Sample list of roles for discussion generation

Roles	Task	Procedure	Group Value
Organizer	Provides an ordered way of examining information	Presents outlines, overviews, or summary of all information	Lead thinker
Facilitator	Moderates, keeps on task	Assures all work is done and/or all participants have opportunity	Inclusive
Strategist	Decides the best way to proceed on a task	Organization	Detail
Analyst	Looks for meaning within the content	Realizes potential of content to practical application	Analytical
Supporter	Provides overall support for an individual or group	Looks for ways to help members or groups	Helpful
Summarizer	Highlights significant points; restates conclusion	Reviews material looking for important concepts	Gives the overall big picture
Narrator	Generally relates information in order	Provides group with a reminder of order	
Elaborator	Relates discussion with prior learned concepts or knowledge	Presents previous information as a comparative measure	Application or expansion
Researcher	Supplies outside resources to comparative information	Goes looking for other information with which to compare discussion	Inclusiveness
Antagonist	Supplies contrasting ideas	Looks for opposing viewpoints and presents in a relative way	Opposing viewpoint

to allow the expert time to prepare. Students often report that the topics they are studying come alive as they interact with these types of guests.

Instructors can also use the 'roles' approach to an assigned reading, allowing students to examine a discussion from a particular perspective. Keeping the role titles at a minimum is also an important practice. Using roles for discussion generation will only be effective if the student is able to connect their own reflections and observations to the role. Students should be involved in selecting their own roles before the discussion, allowing them to read material or examine concepts from their assigned perspective. Table 1 is a sample list of roles that could be used to allow members to review material with an assumed perspective in mind.

Relate Learning to Practice

By integrating working and learning, people learn within the context of their work on real-world problems. (Sachs, 1995)

Interaction is an important component of online learning, and when it is related to the learner's current practice, it becomes even more effective. Challenging students to apply new theory to their practice makes for the best learning activities. Adult students typically have challenges in their places of work. Helping them to solve those challenges with new theory and peer support improves their practice and allows the student to internalize the learning in a much more meaningful and lasting way.

Students are highly motivated to discuss content, solve problems together, and apply new concepts to their own professional practice. Students have described this benefit as invaluable, similar to having a team of colleagues and experts available continuously to help them apply new learning to practice. Often solutions and insights come from other students. As students see how concepts can be applied in a variety of settings, their understanding of those concepts is deepened.

Tools for Building an Online Learning Community

New online tools can support and enable collaboration in Web-based environments and can act as a catalyst for building robust digital environments for learning. Each online technology creates a virtual space with distinctive characteristics. These tools can be divided into two categories, synchronous and asynchronous (see Table 2). Synchronous tools require that both people are available to communicate at the same time. Asynchronous tools allow one person to leave a message for another to be read at a later time. These tools enable the social context for community learning and offer huge benefits for learners who master them.

Synchronous tools such as instant message, chat, and online conferences allow for real-time interaction. They allow individuals or groups to interact simultaneously. These tools are ideal for discussions and meetings.

Ideas for Real-Time or Synchronous Interactions

- Discuss a previously assigned reading
- Provide project counseling
- Maintain course housekeeping: assignments, scheduling
- Encourage group investigations and problem solving
- Introduce a new concept
- Schedule student peer teaching
- Plan student presentations
- Continue friendly discussions and community building

Asynchronous tools such as e-mail and newsgroups work best for longer, more in-depth discussions. In the asynchronous discussion area, instructors can post instructions and guidelines, as well as questions that have no simple answers and are open to interpretation. Ideally, the students should post more than the instructor.

Table 2. Online collaboration tools[1]

Online Collaboration Tools				
Tool	Mode	Popular Choice	Summary and Benefits	Definition
E-mail	Asynchronous	Outlook Express; Netscape; AOL.; Earthlink; ATT; Hotmail; Yahoo Mail; MSN mail; MAC mail	Digital communication; recorded; provides responsive feedback	IP based; accessed via software; Outlook Express, Eudora or Netscape; Webmail accessed via Internet Browser software; not stored on local computer
Listservs	Asynchronous	Yahoo Groups; Netware; Topica, Geocities, (there are literally thousands, any user group)	Mass e-mailed information or data sheet; concerns overall subject matter relevance; provides generated information updates; utilizes e-mail	Similar to a group mailing list, but where people can log on to a central location to read updated information
News-groups	Asynchronous	School servers; organization or club Web sites	Digital, recorded location where discussions are 'posted' and read on demand. Allows for continual conversation over extended period of time without the presence of discussants. Discussions are grouped according to topics.	Online discussion group. To be able to read or post to a newsgroup one must "subscribe" to it, i.e., become a member of its list. Typically subject related. Accessed via Usenet utilizing e-mail based software.
Threaded Discussions (BBS)	Asynchronous	School servers; organization or club Web sites; user groups; many independent Webs	Web-based forum; asynchronous conversation on a specified topic with comments visible to all readers. Membership typically not required to post comments.	Same as newsgroup except visible to anyone. Web page-based; non-membership or subscription related.
CHAT (MOO's & MUD's)	Synchronous	Typically server based or school based. EX. TecfaMOO (Univ. of Geneva, Switzerland), Café MOOlano (UC Berkeley) Tapped In	Group discussion 'rooms' designated for specific topics; allows for multiple users to interact simultaneously.	Live "chat" areas. Realtime electronic discussion areas; typically text based. Internet accessible, text mediated virtual environments; good for group or class meetings. Public.
Instant Message (IM)	Synchronous	Yahoo Messenger, AIM, Yahoo Messenger, ICQ, MSN Messenger	Usually a one-on-one discussion software, without an element of recording discussion. Allows for on-the-fly discussion or comments. Can utilize a multi-user element but does not provide a permanent CHAT room for later use.	Live "chat." Typically one-on-one. Good for instantaneous feedback and discussion. Can have the element for opening up a larger "room" for multiple users by invitation. Non-public.
Conferencing	Synchronous	AIM, Yahoo Messenger, ICQ, MSN Messenger; Net Conference;	Similar to CHAT: allows for ability to utilize visual and/or voice elements in order to assist communications	Live "meetings" with the element of visual and/or voice. Can be one-on-one, or multiple.
Application/ Screen sharing	Synchronous	Procomm; Laplink; Timbuktu, PC Anywhere; DirectLink	Allows for remote users to log directly into a colleague's computer in order to access files, explain software use or share files or software.	Remote control of one computer screen by another. Used for problem solving and file sharing.
Learning Suites	either	Placeware, WebCT, Blackboard, Classbuilder, iPlanet	Typically only provides the interface in a Graphic User design, multimedia design or Interactive Web design. The educator, not the suite, provides content.	Software/Groupware that utilizes two or more of the above elements in order to offer an interface for learning.

Ideas for Asynchronous Discussions

- Post assignments, due dates, and updated information
- Initiate discussions by posting in-depth questions
- Continue a discussion begun in a synchronous setting
- Encourage the community the help each other to solve problems
- Poll a class for feedback and opinions
- Allow students to host their own discussion on a topic of interest

The variety of collaboration tools available has increased from simple e-mail to a rich variety including chat sessions, discussion groups, and more recently, screen sharing applications, conferencing tools, and real-time streaming data. Each tool has unique characteristics that can be utilized for learning. As the Web matures, these tools have been integrated into suites providing a common interface and one-stop access to tool sets tailored for specific use. And new applications promoting online collaboration are still being envisioned and designed such as more intuitive social interfaces and software.

Available in both the synchronous and the asynchronous setting is the opportunity for rich, unscripted interaction that allows students the opportunity to ask and respond to questions and explore solutions together. Continued investigation of the tools available and the pedagogical strategies that promote dialogue and collective intellect in a community model will also benefit future design of online learning environments.

Conclusion and Challenges

Once mastered, Web environments are every bit as dynamic as the classroom environment, and instructors can make the most of learning interactions if they are prepared and willing to improvise. The nature of online learning is inherently less controlled than the traditional classroom and demands a more flexible approach. Success requires understanding the dynamic nature of online learning communities, seeing new opportunities for learning, and then letting go and trusting the social constructivist process.

Table 3. Traditional vs. cooperative learning groups

Traditional Learning Groups	Cooperative Learning Groups
No interdependence	Complete interdependence
One appointed leader	Shared leadership
Homogeneous	Heterogeneous
Responsibility only for self	Shared responsibility
Only task emphasized	Task & maintenance emphasized
Social skills assumed and ignored	Social skills directly taught
Teacher ignores group functions	Teacher observes and intervenes
No group processing	Groups process their effectiveness
No individual accountability	Individual accountability

Resourceful new online instructors are gaining insight and proficiency by examining artifacts of successful online classes such as transcripts of real-time sessions, newsgroup postings, and student projects. Online learning environments provide much richer environments for sharing, not just for students but for instructors as well. Imagine the benefit of reviewing the online discussions of several classes from admired online instructors. Leveraging success is the best way to improve the practice as a whole and enables greater opportunities in the future. As Schrage (1995) states, "It takes shared space to create shared understanding."

Table 3 compares the differences between traditional and cooperative learning groups. Cooperative learning activities facilitate intellectual engagement and deep learning. Learning becomes collective, supportive and shared, as well as individual.

Web-based learning environments do pose certain challenges to the learner and instructor. However, these challenges may be overcome by being careful and sensitive with communications, attending to technology issues, and providing learners with sufficient training and support. Students need to master the tools and manage their expectations, and be open to the dynamic nature of Web-based learning environments. Instructors need to build online skills and an environment that encourages collaborative learning.

A constant challenge for instructors lies in keeping online courses "alive" (Krathwohl, Bloom, & Masia, 1964). The major hurdle is how to design learning communities that encourage participation, thus differentiating online courses from being solely correspondence courses by creating a sense of community greater than what is seen in traditional face-to-face environments. The 'Net Generation' (Tapscott, 1998) expects more active ways of seeking entertainment, knowledge, and social interaction. In other words, learners today thrive in a social and educational space with resources that reflect real-life learning activities, which are practical, highly motivating, and challenging.

An unexpected challenge for the instructor is the increased workload that teaching in a Web-based environment brings. Online tools make it possible to continue a never-ending dialogue that can extend to 24 hours a day and seven days a week. Most online instructors report a significant increase in hours spent per online class (Bonk, 2002). This can be seen as a benefit to the student, but poses a challenge to the instructor who must find new ways to manage available time.

A final challenge for online learning designers is the continued development of new collaboration tools and how to incorporate them appropriately into a learning environment. Those designing online learning environments must understand that the technologies are changing rapidly. Focus needs to be on course content to insure the quality of learning. Delivery methods may change, but philosophy and concepts will remain.

Despite the challenges, online learning holds much promise. Online collaborative instruction completely changes the nature of knowledge and the approaches to learning for the future. Clearly, designing Web-based learning environments is an emerging field with room for improving existing models and experimenting with new ones. As new learning theories are developed and design of online learning environments improves, a wealth of online learning opportunities for Web-based collaborative learning will appear. As communication tools continue to evolve, the learning environments designed around them will also change and improve.

References

Abbott, J. (1996). *7 principles of learning: Challenging fundamental assumptions.* Washington, DC: New Horizons Learning, 21st Century Learning Initiative.

Arias, E. G. (1999, December). Beyond access: Informed participation and empowerment. In C. Hoadley & J. Roschelle (Eds.), *Proceedings of the Computer Support for Collaborative Learning (CSCL) 1999 Conference.* Mahwah, NJ: Lawrence Erlbaum.

Bills, C. G. (1997). Effects of structure and interactivity on Internet-based instruction. In *Proceedings of the Interservice/Industry Training, Simulation, and Education Conference,* Orlando, FL.

Bonk, C. J. (2002). *Online training in an online world.* Retrieved July 2002, from http://www.Courseshare.com

Bourdeau, J., & Bates, A. (1997). Instructional design for distance learning. In S. Dijkstra, M. N. See, F. Scott, & R. A. Tennyson (Eds.), *Instructional design: international perspectives, Vol. 2. Solving instructional design problems.* Mahwah, NJ: Lawrence Erlbaum.

Draves, W. (2002). *LERN information that works.* Retrieved November 11, 2002, from http://www.lern.org

Fisher, M. (2003). *Designing courses and teaching on the Web.* Lanham, MD: Scarecrow Education.

Haavind, S. (2001). *Facilitating online learning: Effective strategies for moderators.* Madison, WI: Atwood Publishing.

Institute for Research on Learning. (2001). *IRL perspectives & principles of learning: Challenging fundamental assumptions* (pamphlet). Menlo Park, CA.

Krathwohl, D. R., Bloom, B. S., & Masia, B. B. (1964). *Taxonomy of educational objectives: Handbook II. Affective domain.* New York: David McKay Co.

Matthews, R. (1997). Guidelines for good practice: Technology mediated instruction. *Proceedings of the Academic Senate for California Community Colleges,* Sacramento, CA.

Pepperdine University. (2002, July 17). *OMET online masters in educational technology graduation report.* Data source Eztrieve (SIS).

Sachs, P. (1995). Transforming work: Collaboration, learning, and design. *Communications of the ACM* (Special Issue on Representations of Work), *38*(9), 36-44.

Schrage, M. (1995). *No more teams—mastering the dynamics of creative collaboration.* New York: Doubleday.

Song, J.K.K. (1998, January). Using the World Wide Web in education and training. In *Proceedings of the IT in Education & Training Conference,* Ho Chi Minh City, Vietnam.

Tapscott, D. (1998) *Growing up digital: The rise of the Net generation.* New York: McGraw-Hill.

Wenger, E. (1998). *Communities of practice: Learning, meaning, and identity.* Cambridge, UK: Cambridge University Press.

Endnote

[1]   Mention of these particular companies does not denote recommendation; it merely supplies the reader with a list of popular examples for the type of tool being referenced.

Chapter V

Intercultural Collaborative Project-Based Learning in Online Environments

Karen L. Murphy, Western New Mexico University, USA

Yakut Gazi, Texas A&M University, USA

Lauren Cifuentes, Texas A&M University, USA

Introduction

The growth of online coursework has introduced challenges for learners, instructors, and course designers involved in culturally and linguistically diverse environments. Online learners face the challenges of a lack of visual cues and increased expectations for interaction and collaboration in ways that learners in conventional settings may not encounter. In online environments that include elements of globalization such as international learners, multicultural course content, and twinning projects between universities (Mason, 1998), intercultural communication issues introduce further complexities. This chapter addresses the question, "How can we overcome potential cultural discontinuities in online collaborative project-based learning environments?" We first identify differing worldviews, communication practices, and technological issues that can present barriers that frequently arise in intercultural online courses. We then identify constructivist project-based teaching strategies that reduce these intercultural barriers. Differing worldviews can be reconciled by fostering collaboration, grouping, relevance, and metacognition. Communication barriers can be minimized by attention to language and community building. Technological problems can be reduced by using asynchronous communication, simplifying online communication systems, and providing technical training and ongoing technical support. The chapter concludes with a model for a third, or polycentric culture that minimizes differences among individuals in terms of their worldviews, communication practices, and technological issues.

Online Intercultural Learning

Problems related to online intercultural learning in higher education focus primarily on two interrelated issues: (a) online learning, which frequently requires new ways of interacting and collaborating with others; and (b) intercultural learning, which may include learners and instructors with differing worldviews, communication practices, and technological issues. Online learning raises challenges for learners who may not know how to learn online, and for designers and instructors who may not know how to teach online. As numbers of international students and international twinning projects increase, online instructors and course designers are still expected to provide problem-free intercultural online learning environments.

Online learning characteristics themselves can act as impediments to learning effectively in a largely text-based environment. In the editorial introducing a journal issue about cultural issues of online learning, Mason and Gunawardena (2001) identified three aspects of online courses that contribute to difficulties of teaching and learning: lack of face-to-face meetings, technical and bandwidth difficulties, and challenges presented to nonnative speakers of English. These online learning problems are compounded further by complexities of intercultural learning contexts.

Intercultural Online Learning Contexts

Intercultural communication is described as the "study of distinct cultural or other groups in interaction with each other" (Scollon & Scollon, 2001, p. 539). The requirement for learners in culturally and linguistically diverse environments to communicate effectively with the instructor and with each other involves intercultural communication. Wilson (2001) charges that contact between persons who describe themselves differently can lead to cultural discontinuities.

Cultural discontinuities are obstacles in cross-cultural educational interfaces, brought about by "a lack of contextual match between the conditions of learning and a learner's sociocultural experiences" (Wilson, 2001, p. 52). We have classified the following intercultural factors that impact online learning: (a) worldviews as reflected by cultural dimensions (Hofstede, 1997); (b) communication practices reflected in high and low context communication (Hall, 1976) and in cognition patterns (Tharp, 1989); and (c) technological issues.

Worldviews

Contrasting worldviews related to cross-cultural differences such as individualism-collectivism, masculinity-femininity, uncertainty avoidance, and power distance (Hofstede, 1997) often contribute to cultural discontinuities. These discontinuities are due to differences in social positions of teachers and students, varied relevance of curriculum and of cognitive abilities, and differing socially expected patterns of teacher/student and student/student interaction (Hofstede, 1986). Hofstede (1997) describes individualistic cultures as emphasizing individuals and individual goals, whereas collectivist cultures stress collaboration, group identity and goals, and avoidance of conflict. The masculinity-femininity dimension refers to the rigidity and definition of gender roles: masculinity is characterized by achievement, strength, assertiveness, competitiveness, and excellence; femininity is a preference for relationships, compassion, modesty, and compromise. International learners participating in online classes may face challenges due to unfamiliarity with interactive and collaborative learning strategies (Goodfellow, Lea, Gonzalez, & Mason, 2001).

Hofstede (1986, 1997) describes uncertainty avoidance as the extent to which members of a society can tolerate ambiguity. In weak uncertainty avoidance countries, students are comfortable with ambiguous situations, and teachers are not expected to know everything. In strong uncertainty avoidance cultures, however, students are intolerant of ambiguity and believe in teachers' authoritative expertise. Finally, Hofstede's power distance dimension refers to the different societal approaches to deal with the basic problem of human inequality and explain how concepts such as authority are accepted. Power distance can help explain how students in intercultural courses assume or follow leadership in groups or how they interact with their instructors. Learners may misunderstand each other or the content because of their differing points of view and ways of thinking and making decisions.

Communication Practices

Diverse communication practices that often lead to cultural discontinuities result from high and low context communication (Hall, 1976) and opposing cognition patterns (Tharp, 1989).

High and low context communication. Differing communication practices among cultures result from dependence on the context of communication. According to Hall (1976), people derive different meaning and often key information from contextual aspects of communication. Communication in high-context cultures depends on clues residing in physical context or the individualized person, whereas very little is coded in the actual explicit message. For instance, the Chinese language is flexible and less structured due to expressions with the same meaning that can be understood only within the context. On the other hand, communication in low-context cultures contains most of the message in the actual explicit code without depending on the context. English is concise and rational, and writing in English tends to be concrete in terms of topic paragraphs and topic sentences (Kaplan, 1976). People from high-context cultures can become impatient when communicating with people from low-context cultures; and people from low-context cultures can become frustrated and uncomfortable when the details they need are not present.

Cognitive processing systems. Different cognitive processing systems can also influence how communication takes place. Tharp (1989) presents two types of cognitive processing systems: verbal/analytic and visual/holistic processing. Verbal/analytic learners are verbal oriented and construct a meaningful whole by identifying appropriate elements of a text. Visual/holistic learners prefer learning by observation and doing rather than learning through verbal instructions. Nisbett, Peng, Choi, and Norenzayan (2001) characterized Westerners as analytic, focusing primarily on the object, and favoring abstract analysis, and East Asians as holistic, attending to the entire field and building causality to it, and favoring experience-based knowledge.

Technological Issues

Differences in technological aspects of communication in an intercultural context can contribute to cultural discontinuities in online project-based learning environments due to time-zone differences, access problems, and typing skills. For example, differences in time zones can create technical and bandwidth difficulties that make real-time events challenging for instructors and students (Mason & Gunawardena, 2001). Becoming accustomed to the user-interface interaction, particularly with high-technology communication devices integral to online learning (Hillman, Willis, & Gunawardena, 1994), may be even more critical for international learners, who face particular challenges due to their inability to think and type quickly in English (Murphy, Drabier, & Epps, 1997).

Social Constructivist Teaching Strategies in Intercultural Learning Environments

Social constructivist teaching strategies not only help avoid cultural discontinuities due to differences in worldviews, communication practices, and technological issues; they also lead to positive interaction and collaboration. Social constructivism is the worldview in which individuals create or construct knowledge to bring meaning to new information and to integrate this knowledge with their prior experience in their communication with others (Vygotsky, 1978). Learning constructively, particularly in the social constructivist paradigm, requires an environment situated in "coherent, meaningful, and purposeful activities" (Brown, Collins, & Duguid, 1989, p. 34) designed to support collaboration, personal autonomy, and active learning. Constructivist pedagogical strategies used online include laboratories, field studies, simulations, problem-solving activities, case studies with group discussion, and project-based learning (Jonassen, 1999; Romiszowski, 1997).

Gunawardena, Wilson, and Nolla (2003) examined the impact of culture on communication and the teaching and learning processes in online courses. In contrast, our chapter examines the impact of culture on collaborative project-based learning in online environments. Project-based learning is described as learners working collaboratively over an extended period of time to solve an authentic and challenging problem that results in an end product (Blumenfeld et al., 1991). Project-based learning has the potential for flexibility, capacity for authenticity, and provision for active learning and collaborative problem solving in a social constructivist paradigm (Laffey, Tupper, Musser, & Wedman, 1998).

Online project-based activities provide learners with opportunities for collaborative learning, defined as small groups of people working together to accomplish shared goals to create meaning, explore a topic, or improve skills online (Harasim, Hiltz, Teles, & Turoff, 1995). However, challenges of learning collaboratively in online project-based activities can be overwhelming in intercultural settings.

How can we overcome potential cultural discontinuities in online collaborative project-based learning environments? The next sections address social constructivist teaching strategies that have reduced cultural discontinuities according to the often overlapping and contrasting worldviews, communication practices, and technology-related issues. Examples are drawn from several of our online collaborative project-based learning activities, all of which involved international students. Students used FirstClass computer conferencing software as the primary communication and collaboration tool to accomplish a variety of tasks, including co-facilitating discussions and activities, publishing instructional Web sites, and conducting a needs analysis and instructional design for clients.

Teaching Strategies Addressing Differing Worldviews

Worldviews are based primarily on cultural context, which includes Hofstede's (1997) cultural dimensions. We have identified four design strategies based on differing worldviews that foster intercultural online project-based learning: collaboration, grouping, relevance, and metacognition:

- **Collaboration:** Collaboration in project-based learning can help reduce power distance and uncertainty avoidance. Cifuentes and Shih (2001) report on collaborative problem-solving activities via online tutorials that took place between university partners in traditional and distance classes in Texas and Taiwan. The power distance between teachers and students was clarified during a semester of cultural and instructional exchange such that Taiwanese students gained comfort with Texan teachers' expectations for them to ask questions and interact less formally than is expected in Taiwan. Uncertainty avoidance was reduced during the exchange as participants gained consensus that "college students in Taiwan are not unlike American students and that the two cultures have much in common" (p. 468). In another case, Murphy and Cifuentes (2001) discovered that students writing chapters in online groups used and recommended the following strategies for learning to collaborate online: get to know each other, structure communication, establish leadership roles, respect individual differences, learn from others, and self-regulate.

- **Grouping:** Grouping, which is based on the size, location of the members, and composition of the groups (Cifuentes, Murphy, Segur, & Kodali, 1997), helps reduce cultural discontinuities related to Hofstede's (1997) individualism-collectivism dichotomy. Decisions about how student groups should be formed are best made prior to beginning partnership activities. Murphy and Cifuentes (1999) describe a university partnership between Texas and France in which the instructors established six groups of eight students each for threaded discussions about educational technology. The instructors took into account students' differing levels of expertise in computer conferencing and command of written English.

- **Relevance:** Relevance involves providing meaningful and purposeful activities (Brown et al., 1989) and is associated with Hofstede's (1997) masculinity-femininity, uncertainty avoidance, and power distance dimensions. Relevant learning activities minimize cultural distance resulting from learners' differing personal and professional interests and goals. Activities such as class orientations and bios or "self-portraits" allow students "to understand the learning styles, personalities, and context of each other" (Murphy & Cifuentes, 2001, p. 293). Relevance is established when student teams work with real clients to conduct a needs analysis (Murphy & Chen, 2002) or carry out the phases of instructional design (Murphy, Cifuentes, & Shih, 2004). By working together, team members can reduce the rigidity and definition of gender roles and power distance, while taking pride in ownership of their final products.

- **Metacognition:** Metacognition is knowledge about one's own cognitive processes and the ability to monitor and regulate those processes accordingly (Flavelle, 1976). High degrees of metacognitive awareness are equated with academic performance (Biggs, 1988) and can minimize problems associated with Hofstede's (1986) power distance dimension. Metacognitive strategies used in online project-based learning environments include contributing to collaborative documents, reflective journals, anonymous formative evaluations, and group-learning contracts. Online learners who wrote papers about their reflective journals described their personal growth through new information about themselves and their ability to transition to a new environment (Murphy & Mahoney, 2001). Group-learning contracts foster regulation of learning and group interaction and cohesion by subtly forcing group members to look at the various personalities, skills, and workloads of their team (Murphy, Mahoney, & Harvell, 2000).

Teaching Strategies Addressing Varied Communication Practices

As addressed earlier, variation in communication practices among cultures results from dependence on the context of communication. This context is evident in Hall's (1976) high- and low-context communication systems, and in language with Tharp's (1989) two types of cognitive processing systems. Two communication design strategies that foster intercultural online project-based learning are language and community:

- **Language:** Language is believed to shape our thinking, beliefs, and attitudes, according to the Sapir-Whorf hypothesis (Whorf, 1956). The English language, which is the predominant online language, is a linear thought process, whereas other languages are more cyclical or full of digressions (Kaplan, 1976). Several teaching strategies focusing on language help reduce cultural discontinuities related to Hall's (1976) high- and low-context communication systems and Tharp's (1989) cognitive processing systems. These strategies include specific language use, peer reviews in public conferences, and varied examples.

  Using language that is appropriate to online learning, such as avoiding culture-specific vocabulary and references, slang, in-jokes, and acronyms, will minimize misunderstandings (Pincas, 2001). Murphy and Gazi (2001) report that students in project-based learning activities made conscious efforts to use a conversational writing style to speak directly to fellow participants without regressing into slang and colloquialism. To help adaptation to the text-based environment, instructors can inform students of netiquette and of systematic ways of promoting discussion, including assumptions about modes of interaction such as openers, closers, and polite expressions for disagreement (Pincas, 2001).

  Having students conduct peer reviews of each others' writing assignments at key stages—for example, the first draft of the outline and the first draft of the paper—enhances writing skills. In such cases, international students are paired with native speakers of English who volunteer to be editors rather than reviewers (Murphy & Chen, 2002). Furthermore, students are encouraged to read the drafts and reviews of other students, and often add their comments and suggestions to discussion threads in public conferences.

  Providing varied examples (Chyung, 2001) and models helps all students, particularly international students, in reducing cultural distance. Murphy and Chen (2002) found that Asian students benefit from having an outline to follow and a description of expectations for the final product. They need to know the assignment parameters, and following a suggested outline is particularly advantageous for those verbal/holistic learners who may be unaware of how to outline or use topic sentences and paragraphs correctly.

- **Community:** A community exists when members of a group experience a sense of belonging or personal relatedness (Osterman, 2000). Communities of learners and practice are social organizations in which knowledge, values, identities, and goals are shared (Jonassen, 1999). Lave and Wenger (1991) propose that when learners participate fully in the socially situated practices of a community, learning is a process of becoming part of a community of practice.

  "Without interdependence, there can be no collaboration, and ultimately no community" (Palloff & Pratt, 1999, p. 125). Interdependence is related to learner control, which is characterized by learners making choices in the pacing, sequence, and selection of instructional materials. Giving learners control over their learning environment was empowering to pre-service teachers who were allowed to select their discussion topics and co-moderate their own conferences, and was a chief factor "leading to evolving, relevant discussions that captivated almost all of the participants" (Cifuentes et al., 1997, p. 198). Providing maximum structure and support at the beginning of the course and gradually allowing for more learner control by the end of the course (Murphy, Cifuentes, & Bonham, 1998) may help students in "crossing a threshold from feeling like outsiders to feeling like insiders" (Wegerif, 1998).

For a group to develop into a community that is stronger than the individuals who comprise it, members must hold a "shared objective of continually advancing the collective knowledge and skills" and have "mechanisms for sharing what is learned" (Bielaczyc & Collins, 1999, p. 272). In one online course, the shared objective was for students to collaborate in small groups to conduct a needs analysis and ultimately produce a telecommunications report for a client (Murphy & Chen, 2002). Our online classes incorporate mechanisms for students to share what they learn through group-learning contracts, public workspaces, and formative evaluation of projects. Group-learning contracts guide team members in establishing common behavior guidelines and communication protocols, identifying member roles, and developing contingency plans (Murphy et al., 2000). Encouraging students to peruse other groups' workspaces allows them to review diverse approaches and incorporate best practices into their own work (Murphy & Chen, 2002).

Teaching Strategies Addressing Technological Issues

Technology-related activities are critical for success in online learning. Varied design strategies may reduce technology-related cultural discontinuities in an intercultural context that include time-zone differences, access problems, and varied technical skills. We have identified three technology-related design strategies that foster intercultural online project-based learning: using asynchronous communication, relying on simple online communication systems, and providing technical training and ongoing technical support:

• **Asynchronous communication:** Asynchronous communication is critical to overcome the barrier of time-zone differences and provide for equitable skill development in online project-based activities in intercultural settings. Asynchronous communication, which allows reflection time for participants with wide-ranging skill levels, does not require students to be present at the same time. Collis and Remmers (1997) caution against using real-time interaction in cross-cultural sites because of time-zone differences and "tone-and-style discrepancies in communication norms" (p. 88). Murphy and Cifuentes (1999) speculate that international students with limited typing skills in English may prefer to work with their group members by sending messages asynchronously and working together in collaborative documents instead of participating in real-time chats. As an international student explained, "When we had a chat to discuss our project, my language skill prevented me from exactly expressing my thinking" (Murphy & Gazi-Demirci, 2001).

- **Simple online communication systems:** Using a simple, integrated online communication system can reduce online learners' anxiety, disorientation, and information overload. Chyung (2001) charges that eliminating or reducing "the complexity of the online communication system" (p. 41) helps new online learners. Low system knowledge, or prior knowledge of and experience with a particular information system, in conjunction with weak metacognitive knowledge, have been linked to disorientation and use of ineffective learning strategies (Hill & Hannafin, 1997). Several of our students experienced learner disorientation, due to the requirements for collaboration and the plethora of new Web tools used for communication. For the first time they had to construct conceptual models of various Web tools in order to navigate and communicate (Murphy & Cifuentes, 2001).

- **Technical training and ongoing technical support:** Learners come to the online environment with varied capabilities and prior experiences with technology. The "all-encompassing requirement for successful computer conferencing is adequate technological preparation" (Cifuentes et al., 1997, p. 196). Online students benefit from an orientation session that includes technical training (Chen, 2003; Murphy & Cifuentes, 2001). Technical training should center on helping students learn to function and feel comfortable in the online environment (Winograd, 2001). A method of fostering comfort with a new technology is to have the users play games like "Pictionary" before using the tools to deal with content (Hillman et al., 1994). Students get technological help from peers, classmates in other classes, and library personnel, although they sometimes learn "by plunging in and doing it" (Murphy & Cifuentes, p. 292).

While attempting to learn and use new software features, online learners need continual support (Harasim, 1989). Ongoing training can occur by reducing technological difficulties through pairing students with keyboard partners of unequal ability (Chyung, 2001; Murphy et al., 1998) and maintaining a discussion topic devoted to technical questions and answers (Murphy & Cifuentes, 2001).

Developing a Third Culture

Instructors need to design and teach online courses to accommodate communication and teaching strategies that are effective in both collaborative project-based learning settings and intercultural learning environments. The local or host culture, which generally is the culture where the course is offered, presents challenges for students from different cultural backgrounds. One goal of effective online communication in an intercultural learning environment may be to create a third, polycentric culture (Goodfellow et al., 2001; Mason, 1998). The term "third culture" was first coined by science historian C.P. Snow (1969), who imagined a culture where literary intellectuals conversed directly with scientists. Mason cites Lundin's (1996) depiction of a third culture being con-

Figure 1. Third culture

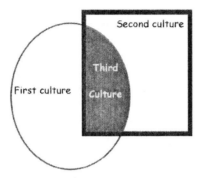

structed when materials from one culture are studied by people in a different culture: "Material from both the interacting cultures is used to fill locally and temporally defined functions outside both cultures but intelligible to participants from both who are involved in the particular interaction" (Mason, 1998, p. 156).

A third culture combines elements of the dominant cultural dimensions and helps move individuals and groups from ethnocentrism to polycentrism, which is "the recognition that different kinds of people should be measured by different standards and the ability to understand the foreigner according to the foreigner's standards" (Hofstede, 1997, p. 211). Forming a polycentric culture would help move learners beyond "non-participation and marginalization in online communities and globally delivered courses" (Goodfellow et al., p. 80). Such a polycentric culture would accommodate differing cultural and linguistic practices that individual learners bring to the learning context.

We propose the model in Figure 1 to describe a third culture in an intercultural learning environment. In this model, the two shapes representing the first and second cultures are equivalent in size, implying that no culture is superior to the other. The two cultures are of different shapes, indicating that they are different from each other. The intersection of the two cultures, or of people's experiences when the two cultures are meshed, creates a third culture, the polycentric culture. The third culture is neither an oblong nor a square but includes attributes of each, indicating its difference from the original cultures and contributions from each. An increase in the size of the intersection represents shared experiences between the first two cultures, with the two cultures moving together on a different dimension—unlike their own or the other culture, but a common third one. The polycentric culture can happen at the individual as well as at the group level.

It should be noted that not all encounters of two cultures end up in a third culture, as course design and activities can either hinder or facilitate this development. Course design that helps reduce cultural distance and foster creation of a polycentric culture includes collaborative project-based learning activities, explicit scaffolding with guidelines for time- and task-management, and assigning control to student activity facilitators to encourage collaboration rather than competition. The course design makes the difference by facilitating an interface for a polycentric culture to develop. As online learners continue to interact through language, they will reshape and define their online space: the polycentric culture. For some students the polycentric culture is small, and for others it is large.

The importance of intercultural online communication increases with the advent of global education. The success of such learning environments will depend on how these distinct identities and cultures are identified as important aspects of online learning, and as Mason (1998) affirms, how successfully these cultural differences are addressed in the globalization movement in education. The interaction of learners with each other, often encouraged by the designers of online environments and instructors, places cultures in constant interaction with each other. Mason's depiction of global education is a positive yet cautionary note:

At its most visionary, the ideal of global education is one of a movement away from the bounded classroom, seen as a haven from the world, self-contained and static, to a dynamic synergy of teachers, computer-mediated instructional devices, and students collaborating to create a window on the world. (p. 6)

References

Bielaczyc, K., & Collins, A. (1999). Learning communities in classrooms: A reconceptualization of educational practice. In C. M. Reigeluth (Ed.), *Instructional-design theories and models: A new paradigm of instructional theory* (pp. 269-292). Mahwah, NJ: Lawrence Erlbaum.

Biggs, J. (1988). The role of metacognition in enhancing learning. *Australian Journal of Education, 32*, 127-138.

Blumenfeld, P., Soloway, E., Marx, R., Krajcik, J., Guzdial, M., & Palincsar, A. (1991). Motivating project-based learning: Sustaining the doing, supporting the learning. *Educational Psychologist, 26*, 369-398.

Brown, J. S., Collins, A., & Duguid, P. (1989). *Situated cognition and the culture of learning. Educational Research, 18*(1), 32-42.

Chen, C.-Y. (2003). *Managing perceptions of information overload in computer-mediated communication.* Unpublished doctoral dissertation, Texas A&M University, College Station, USA.

Chyung, S. Y. (2001). Systematic and systemic approaches to reducing attrition rates in online higher education. *The American Journal of Distance Education, 15*(3), 36-49.

Cifuentes, L., Murphy, K. L., Segur, R., & Kodali, S. (1997). Design considerations for computer conferences. *Journal of Research on Computing in Education, 30*(2), 172-195.

Cifuentes, L., & Shih, Y.-C. D. (2001). Teaching and learning online: A collaboration between U.S. and Taiwanese students. *Journal of Research on Technology in Education, 33*(4), 456-474.

Collis, B., & Remmers, E. (1997). The World Wide Web in education: Issues related to cross-cultural communication and interaction. In B. H. Khan (Ed.), *Web-based instruction* (pp. 85-92). Englewood Cliffs, NJ: Educational Technology.

Flavelle, J. H. (1976). Metacognitive aspects of problem solving. In L. B. Resnick (Ed.), The nature of intelligence (pp. 231-236). Hillsdale, NJ: Lawrence Erlbaum.

Goodfellow, R., Lea, M., Gonzalez, F., & Mason, R. (2001). Opportunity and e-quality: Intercultural and linguistic issues in global online learning. *Distance Education, 22*(1), 65-84.

Gunawardena, C. N., Wilson, P. L., & Nolla, A. C. (2003). Culture and online education. In M. Moore & B. Anderson (Eds.), *Handbook of distance learning* (pp. 743-765). Mahwah, NJ: Lawrence Erlbaum.

Hall, E. T. (1976). *Beyond culture*. Garden City, NY: Doubleday.

Harasim, L. (1989) Online education: A new domain. In R. Mason & T. Kaye (Eds.), *Mindweave: Communication, computers and distance education* (pp. 50-62). Oxford: Pergamon.

Harasim L., Hiltz, S. R., Teles, L., & Turoff, M. (1995). *Learning networks: A field guide to teaching and learning online.* Cambridge: MIT Press.

Hill, J. R., & Hannafin, M. J. (1997). Cognitive strategies and learning from the World Wide Web. *Educational Technology Research and Development, 45*(4), 37-64.

Hillman, D. C., Willis, D. J., & Gunawardena, C. N. (1994). Learner-interface interaction in distance education: An extension of contemporary models and strategies for practitioners. *The American Journal of Distance Education, 8*(2), 30-42.

Hofstede, G. (1986). Cultural differences in teaching and learning. *International Journal of Intercultural Relations, 10*, 301-320.

Hofstede, G. (1997). *Culture and organizations: Software of the mind: New intercultural cooperation and its importance for survival.* New York: McGraw-Hill.

Jonassen, D. (1999). Designing constructivist learning environments. In C. M. Reigeluth (Ed.), *Instructional design theories and models: A new paradigm of instructional theory* (vol. II, pp. 215-239). Mahwah, NJ: Lawrence Erlbaum.

Kaplan, R. B. (1976). Cultural thought patterns in inter-cultural education. *Language Learning, 16*(1), 25.

Laffey, J., Tupper, T., Musser, D., & Wedman, J. (1998). A computer-mediated support system for project-based learning. *Educational Technology Research and Development, 46*(1), 73-86.

Lave, J., & Wenger, E. (1991). *Situated learning: Legitimate peripheral participation.* Cambridge, UK: Cambridge University.

Lundin, R. (1996, November). International education 3: Opening access or educational invasion? In *Proceedings of the Internationalizing Communities Conference,* University of Southern Queensland, Australia.

Mason, R. (1998). *Globalizing education: Trends and applications.* London: Routledge.

Mason, R., & Gunawardena, C. N. (2001). Editorial. *Distance Education, 22*(1), 4-6.

Murphy, K. L., & Chen, C.-Y. (2002, November). An Asian e-learner's experience of cultural differences: Implications for course design. In *Proceedings of the Annual Convention of the Association for Educational Communications and Technology*, Dallas, TX.

Murphy, K. L., & Cifuentes, L. (1999). Exploring conceptions of educational technology between France and Texas. In B. Collis & R. Oliver (Eds.), In *Proceedings of ED-MEDIA 99: World Conference on Educational Multimedia/Hypermedia and Telecommunications 1999* (Vol. 1, pp. 616-621). Charlottesville, VA: Association for the Advancement of Computers in Education.

Murphy, K. L., & Cifuentes, L. (2001). Using Web tools, collaborating, and learning online. *Distance Education, 22*(2), 285-305.

Murphy, K. L., Cifuentes, L., & Bonham, L. A. (1998). Balancing teacher-learner control in computer conferencing. In Z. L. Berge & M. P. Collins (Eds.), *Wired together: The online classroom in K-12, Vol. III: Teacher education and professional development* (pp. 61-69). Cresskill, NJ: Hampton.

Murphy, K. L., Cifuentes, L., & Shih, Y.-C. (2004). Online collaborative documents for research and coursework. *TechTrends, 48*(3), 40-44, 74.

Murphy, K. L., Drabier, R., & Epps, M. L. (1998). A constructivist look at interaction and collaboration via computer conferencing. *International Journal of Educational Telecommunications, 4*(2-3), 237-261.

Murphy, K. L., & Gazi, Y. (2001). Role plays, panel discussions, and simulations: Project-based learning in a Web-based course. *Educational Media International, 38*(4), 261-270.

Murphy, K. L., & Gazi-Demirci, Y. (2001, April). *Role plays, panel discussions, and case studies: Project-based learning in a Web-based course.* Paper presented at the Annual Convention of the American Educational Research Association, Seattle.

Murphy, K. L., & Mahoney, S. E. (2001). Buy-in to online courses: Reflections from e-learners' journal papers. In *Proceedings of the WebNet 2001 World Conference on the WWW and Internet* (CD-ROM), Orlando, FL.

Murphy, K. L., Mahoney, S. E., & Harvell, T. J. (2000). Role of contracts in enhancing community building in Web courses. *Educational Technology & Society, 3*(3), 409-421. Retrieved September 22, 2000, from http://ifets.ieee.org/periodical/vol_3_2000/e03.html

Nisbett, R. E., Peng, K., Choi, I., & Norenzayan, A. (2001). Culture and systems of thought: Holistic vs. analytic cognition. *Psychological Review, 108*(2), 291-310.

Osterman, K. F. (2000). Students' need for belonging in the school community. *Review of Educational Research, 70*(3), 323-367.

Palloff, R. M., & Pratt, K. (1999). *Building learning communities in cyberspace: Effective strategies for the online classroom.* San Francisco: Jossey-Bass.

Pincas, A. (2001). Culture, cognition and communication in global education. *Distance Education, 22*(1), 30-51.

Romiszowski, A. J. (1997). Web-based distance learning and teaching: Revolutionary invention or reaction to necessity? In B. H. Khan (Ed.), *Web-based instruction* (pp. 25-37). Englewood Cliffs, NJ: Educational Technology.

Scollon, R., & Scollon, S. W. (2001). Discourse and intercultural communication. In D. Schiffrin, D. Tannen, & H. E. Hamilton (Eds.), *The handbook of discourse analysis* (pp. 538-547). Oxford: Blackwell.

Snow, C.P. (1969). *The two cultures; and a second look: An expanded version of 'the two cultures and the scientific revolution'* (2nd ed.). New York: Cambridge University.

Tharp, R. (1989). Psychocultural variables and constants: Effects on teaching and learning in schools. *American Psychologist, 44*(2), 349-359.

Vygotsky, L. S. (1978). *Mind in society: The development of higher psychological processes.* Cambridge, MA: Harvard University.

Wegerif, R. (1998). The social dimension of asynchronous learning networks. *Journal of Asynchronous Learning Networks, 2*(1). Retrieved July 1, 1999, from http://www.aln.org/alnweb/journal/vol2_issue1/wegerif.htm

Whorf, B. L. (1956). *Language, thought and reality.* Cambridge, MA: MIT Press.

Wilson, M. S. (2001). Cultural considerations in online instruction and learning. *Distance Education, 22*(1), 52-64.

Winograd, D. (2001). *Guidelines for moderating online educational computer conferences.* Retrieved January 22, 2003, from http://www.emoderators.com/moderators/winograd.html

Chapter VI

We'll Leave the Light on for You:
Keeping Learners Motivated in Online Courses

Vanessa Paz Dennen, Florida State University, USA

Curtis J. Bonk, Indiana University, USA

Introduction

Motivating online learners is a key challenge facing instructors in both higher education and corporate settings. Attrition rates and low participation levels in course activities are frequent instructor complaints about online learning environments. Part of the problem is a lack of sophistication in online tools and courseware (Bonk & Dennen, 1999). Added to this problem is that, even when tools exist for engaging and motivating students, instructors lack training in how to effectively use them. Instructors not only need to know the types of online and collaborative tools for engaging students, but also how to embed effective pedagogy when the technologies are weak.

Consider for a moment a traditional classroom. Why do students attend their classes? Perhaps their presence is being recorded by the instructor, or perhaps they are particularly interested in the topic. Regardless, upon enrolling in a face-to-face course, learners are aware that they are expected to devote significant blocks of time each week to that course. But why do students participate in face-to-face course activities? To start, they already are seated in the classroom, so they may as well participate. Additionally, the effects of instructor modeling of desired activities and peer participation can motivate the reluctant learner to become more active.

In the online class, attendance is distinctly different. Unless explicitly told how their attendance will be noted, such as through a minimum number of messages posted per week, online learners do not know how or if their course participation will be determined. Consequently, online students turn to required assignments outlined in the course syllabus (Dennen, 2001). The end result is that students complete the basic graded components of the course, but little more.

Learner participation in an online class has sometimes been called an "act of faith" (Salmon, 2000). Key problems learners encounter include not knowing participation expectations, not feeling comfortable engaging in activities with people they have never met, and not having enough time to participate in activities. Whereas these first two reasons are clearly linked to motivation, the time factor is also related since highly motivated students will typically budget adequate time to participate.

In reviews of the research on motivation, certain key strategies are consistently found to be effective in conventional classrooms. For instance, effective instructors create a supportive but challenging environment, project enthusiasm and intensity, provide choice, create short-term goals, and offer immediate feedback on performance settings (Pintrich & Schunk, 1996; Reeve, 1996; Stipek, 1998). As these researchers have shown, instructors might also attempt to stimulate student curiosity, control, and fantasy. Naturally, they should make content personal and concrete by using relevant and authentic learning tasks and by allowing learners to create and display finished products. Finally, instructors should foster interaction with peers, create fun and game-like activities, embed structure as well as flexibility in assignments, and include activities with divergence or conflict.

Many of these principles relate to the highly regarded learner-centered psychological principles from the American Psychological Association (1993) and can be incorporated in Web-based instruction (Bonk & Cummings, 1998). In a recent Delphi study of top distance learning experts in the United States, many of these same principles (i.e., relevancy, authenticity, control, choice, interactivity, project-based, collaborative, etc.) were identified as key indicators of effective online learning environments (Partlow, 2001).

If so much is known, why are online courses often suffering from a lack of motivational elements? Problems exist in part because instructors are unsure of how to manipulate this instructional medium, and in part because adequate instructor support is not yet available. According to recent surveys of college instructors and corporate trainers (Bonk, 2001, 2002), the proliferation of Web courseware and training programs has yet to match the pedagogical needs of higher education and industry. When corporate respondents were asked about various intrinsic motivational techniques, activities such as job reflections, team projects, and guest mentoring were considered highly engaging and useful online. When asked about tools and activities that were more motivational for adult learners in the workplace, respondents favored Web-based learning that contained

Table 1. Motivational elements addressed by different online activities

Motivational Element	1. Ice Breakers	2. Self-Assessments	3. Surveys and Polling	4. Cases	5. Conference Tracks	6. Brainstorming	7. Electronic Guest Lectures	8. Debates and Role Play	9. Critical Friends and Peer Feedback Buddies	10. Gallery Tours
1. Tone/Climate	**X**					X				X
2. Feedback		**X**	X	X					X	X
3. Engagement	X		**X**	X		X		X		
4. Meaningfulness			X	**X**	X		X	X		X
5. Choice			X	X	**X**	X				
6. Variety					X	**X**	X			
7. Curiosity			X			X		**X**	X	X
8. Tension				X				**X**		
9. Peer Interaction	X			X	X			X	**X**	
10. Goal Driven		X		X	X	X		X	X	**X**

relevant materials, responsive feedback, goal-driven activities, personal growth, choice or flexibility, and interactivity and collaboration. Unfortunately, such techniques were rarely used online.

According to the findings of these surveys, the motivational climate of online instruction is currently deficient. Therefore, in addition to the evaluation of student learning and completion rates, organizations should step back and evaluate the motivational characteristics embedded within their courses. Of course, there also is a need for further research here since the key motivational principles for online training are only starting to emerge.

As Bonk and Dennen (2003) contend, online instruction is not a simple task; most instructors still do not understand how to adapt different technology tools to engage their students. At the same time, few designers of e-learning tools have thoroughly considered the motivational or pedagogical principles behind adult learning (Firdyiwek, 1999; Oliver, Omari, & Herrington, 1998). How can such tools motivate adult learner participation while fostering student thinking and collaboration? And what can be done to motivate learners in online environments? These questions must be addressed in order for online education to thrive and be a positive learning experience for students.

This chapter focuses on 10 key elements for motivating online learners. Each element is discussed separately, along with corresponding course activities that can be used to address that element. Indeed, it is possible to address multiple motivational principles with one well-designed activity (see Table 1). At the same time, not every instructional situation calls for the use of each motivational element. Context-based instructional design and pedagogical decisions should always be made by the individual instructor.

Tone/Climate

The tone or climate of an online class is set at the beginning. These opening moments have the potential to engage and interest learners so that they want to be active participants for the semester, or alternatively to isolate them and provide little motivation to participate (Salmon, 2000). Much like in the physical world, if one visits an online location and finds little reason to go back, feels uncomfortable in that place, or is uncertain of its purpose, one is not likely to participant actively in that space.

Social ice-breaking activities can be used to set the tone of an online class as well as to help learners become acquainted with one another. They also serve the purpose of familiarizing learners with the course tools without the stress of dealing with course-related subject matter. Some activities that might be employed include:

- **Two Truths and One Lie:** Everyone must post two truths and one lie about themselves. Fellow classmates then try to determine which one is the lie. This activity generates a series of messages and responses, and is a quick way to bring out learner personalities (Kulp, 1999).

- **8 Nouns:** In this activity, everyone is required to post eight nouns that describe him or herself. Near the end of this task, it becomes difficult to come up with nouns, thereby forcing participants to share a good deal of information about themselves that their peers as well as the instructor might refer to later in the course. In effect, it creates some initial shared understandings and common knowledge (Schrage, 1990).

- **Coffee House Expectations:** In this activity, students share their expectations for the class—why they enrolled and what they hope to get out of it. Not only does this activity help the instructor shape the class, it is vital for the goal-oriented behavior of adult learners. In effect, posting expectations gives adults with chaotic schedules something definitive to work toward. As an extension, students also can be asked to share what they have to offer to the class community.

These activities are often fun ways of sharing personal information. While learners may not share this much personal information at the beginning of a traditional course, in an online course it is a way of discovering student commonalities and differences. From our experience, both instructors and learners tend to refer back to the messages generated by these activities to get a better sense of who their classmates are. Using the eight nouns activity, for instance, we have had males describe themselves as "knitters," "tea kettles," and "dishwashers." Such comments have made for interesting, and often humorous, social interactions in each of these courses.

Research by Dennen (2001) indicates that the instructor should model the expected responses to such activities. An instructor, for instance, might post eight nouns about himself so that learners can know him better. Just as the learners need to know who their peers are, they need to know that their instructor is more than a name.

Feedback

Feedback motivates online learners by letting them know how well their performance meets course expectations. Monitoring one's progress toward a goal is motivational to many students (Anderson, 2001). Whereas feedback points are typically built into all courses in the form of graded assignments, in an online class, students often feel the need for feedback at other, more formative points in time. This feedback helps them gauge their own performance and motivates them to either maintain or improve the quality of their work. Feedback may come in many forms:

- **Self-assessments:** Self-assessments can easily be built with most courseware tools, thereby allowing the technology to control the feedback.

- **Reading reactions:** Discussion activities in which learners post their reactions to course readings are useful because they allow the learners to know if they are on-track, and let the instructor know if the learners understand the material. Additionally, learners are more motivated to do the required readings if they know they must discuss them. Peer feedback opportunities can be built into such activities, making sure all learners get a response in a manner that is pedagogically beneficial, yet not labor intensive for the instructor.

- **Instructor feedback:** Feedback to instructors is also critical to online course success. Instructors, for instance, might have anonymous suggestion boxes on the Web. Watson (2000) recommends that the instructor post the suggestions as well as the corresponding decisions for learners to read. Similarly, Brown (2002) indicates that one-minute reflection and muddiest point papers using e-mail or threaded discussion forums also are highly effective in providing formative course feedback.

Engagement

Motivated learners are engaged learners. While all of the motivational methods mentioned in this chapter are in some way engaging, electronic voting and polling is one technique that can be used to engage learners at the beginning of a new unit of instruction. An instructor might survey class attitudes on an upcoming topic using a free survey tool such as Zoomerang, SurveyShare, or SurveyMonkey, and keep the results sealed until an appropriate point during the instruction. The instructor might then use the results to engage learners in a discussion of the minority point-of-view and then have learners revote or self-assess whether their attitudes have changed as a result of the discussion or additional course instruction.

Meaningfulness

Extensive research points to the importance of task meaningfulness and problem-based learning (Singer, Marx, & Krajcik, 2000; Williams, 1992). Simply put, people want to participate in activities that they deem meaningful, authentic, and relevant (Blumenfeld et al., 1991; Savery & Duffy, 1996). In the traditional classroom, meaningfulness is important, but an instructor still can corral students to participate just because they are physically present. In contrast, in the online class, meaningfulness might make the difference between participation and non-participation.

Online activities that are meaningful to students often involve real-world scenarios and allow learners to discuss or present their own opinions and experiences relative to these scenarios. For example, students might be asked to post reflection statements that relate their job or field experiences to the concepts being learned. They also might be asked to develop written cases that exemplify a concept, and then respond to the case of a peer with a possible solution or alternative perspective (Bonk, Daytner, Daytner, Dennen, & Malikowski, 2001; Bonk, Hara, Dennen, Malikowski, & Supplee, 2000). Such meaningful and motivating activities give learners an opportunity to practice and apply what they know with peers around the globe.

Choice

Helping students make a personal investment in a course is one way of providing motivational support (Maehr, 1984). Giving learners choices allows them to be active participants and feel in control of some aspect of their learning environment (Bonk, Fischler, & Graham, 2001). It also demonstrates that the instructor is aware that the learners have entered the learning situation with their own personal goals.

Online classes can be highly designed experiences wherein learners feel they have no choice and must follow the course outline in a lockstep order. Fortunately, there are many ways in which choice may be built into an online experience. Using a motivational perspective, learners may be given the opportunity to select which discussion topics they wish to participate in. In some cases, they may even be asked to help develop the discussion topics as appropriate. Learners might also sign up for leadership roles in the weekly discussion according to personal interests and expertise (Hara, Bonk, & Angeli, 2000). Similarly, the selection of roles or personalities for online role play gives the learners a sense of control over their learning environment as well as an opportunity to be creative and spontaneous. Some classes might use a conference track approach, in which parallel sets of course requirements are proposed, each addressing a slightly different focus. Learners can then choose to fulfill the requirements that most closely match their goals or interests.

Variety

Repeating the same set of online tasks for each course activity or module will be boring for learners. Our experience indicates that learners enjoy variety in online courses—knowing that there is something new for them to master keeps them alert and attentive as well as interested. Thus, instructors should select a range of different online activities rather than redundantly relying on the same ones.

Brainstorming is one simple activity that can interject new life and variety into a course. Learners can be asked to generate as many ideas as possible on a particular topic, without worrying about backing them up, demonstrating the applicability or practicality of the ideas, or ranking them in any way. The results of a brainstorming session might be topics or activities to be addressed or completed later in the course. Collecting multiple class responses, instead of allowing some students to dominate discussion or team projects, is another way to vary the course activities. To really make the course spontaneous, an instructor might utilize "just-in-time teaching" or a "just-in-time syllabus" (Novak, 2000). In this technique, the course skeleton is completed at the start of the semester, but can be modified in response to student interests and course performances as well as current events.

Curiosity

Learner curiosity should be cultivated in an online course, including allowing them to explore ideas beyond those expressed by the instructor. If all learners look to the instructor for answers, their curiosity can only be addressed through limited perspectives. To spark learner curiosity and bring in additional viewpoints, electronic guests may be invited into the online class for short, synchronous chat sessions, some with follow-up asynchronous discussions with those who seek further information. Along these same lines, learners may be mentored electronically by peers or practitioners to help bring in diverse perspectives.

Tension

Points of tension are points of discussion; if we all agree then we probably have little to discuss. The term "tension" frequently has negative connotations, but it can be used to generate fruitful learning discussions. Students, however, may not elect to engage in tension on their own, so debates and assignments that involve role play dialogues can be particularly useful to generate tension in a manner that feels safe to students. Frequently, when students are assigned roles that promote unpopular points of view, they will preface their remarks with statements like "I was told to be the protagonist, so

..." or "As the devil's advocate here ..." Such declarations allow them to engage in the activity while distancing themselves from the viewpoints they uphold in the activity.

Peer Interaction

Peer interaction helps engage students with each other. In traditional courses, even when the instructor does not explicitly facilitate peer interaction, students tend to discuss course-related topics before or after class. In an online class, that informal peer interaction is absent since it is often self-paced or the instructor does not grasp how to facilitate it. As a result, the students may feel extremely isolated and drop the course.

Many of the techniques referenced in this chapter involve peer interaction on various levels. Discussion-based activities tend to require peer interaction in order to be successful; one-person conversations generally are not motivating. Moving beyond generic discussion, goal-oriented interactions such as collaborative problem solving activities are particularly motivating to learners because of both the peer interdependence and the ability to judge their own knowledge and skills against that of their peers (Hacker & Niederhauser, 2000). Student interaction can also be promoted through activities such as online symposia, press conferences, and expert panels. Our research indicates that these techniques are effective, since students in online classes are motivated by measures of how they are performing not only as compared to the instructor's expectations, but also as compared to classmates (Dennen, 2001).

Peer interaction may be considered a key course goal or activity. One technique found effective is the use of the critical friend activity (Bonk, Ehman, Hixon, & Yamagata-Lynch, 2002). In this activity, learners are matched or partnered to provide each other with constructive feedback on assignments. Alternatively, they might be required to send each other reminder messages of upcoming assignments and due dates. These activities may take place publicly via courseware or privately via e-mail. Peer interaction activities help ensure that students are receiving valuable feedback with a minimum of burden on the instructor.

Goal Driven

Student motivation to participate in online class activities tends to be goal driven. If the goals as presented and valued within the course structure and assessments focus on test performance, students are motivated to study for the test. Group problem-solving activities are a great way of avoiding such isolated, low-motivation scenarios. Students who have group goals or final projects to work toward will be motivated to interact with each other. Group problem-solving activities can be semester-long projects or small group-sharing activities akin to a 15-minute group brainstorm in a traditional class. And final projects might be posted online in an online gallery of student work.

Group Based vs. Self-Paced

One of the dimensions of online courses that influences an instructor's motivational options is whether or not it is possible to facilitate group interactions. Many people choose distributed learning to meet their educational needs because they desire the flexibility of working at their own pace. Working in isolation, however, can provide some motivational challenges. In part, motivation must come from within, and in part, it is affected by the design of the learning environment and activities. In group-based activities, learners often are motivated by the knowledge that peers will be reading and commenting on their contributions. However, fostering motivation for the independent learner who operates in the absence of social motivators can pose some extra challenges. Allowing for choice, variety, and independent learning styles can help in this regard, as can using active terminology such as "seek" and "explore" when describing learner tasks (Canada, 2000). Self-assessments also serve to motivate the independent learner who might be hungry for feedback.

Synchronous vs. Asynchronous Communications

Most of the activities presented here may be adapted to accommodate either synchronous or asynchronous communication technologies and may be used across disciplines. Certainly some activities seem better-suited to live interaction, whereas others might be more fruitful when learners take advantage of a lengthy time span for participation or reflection as afforded by asynchronous technologies. In addition, each activity might be varied to further motivate online learners. Table 2 presents some of the adaptations that might be made based on the differences in the communication tools.

Regardless of whether one's communication tools are synchronous or asynchronous, careful consideration should be given to the archiving of learner interactions and work. Such archives prove useful both in promoting learner reflection, as well as in enabling learners who have fallen behind to catch up. For example, a learner who has missed a guest lecture that occurred via a synchronous chat might feel disenfranchised if there were no event archive tools to replay what transpired.

Conclusion

The 10 motivational elements presented here are essential to the success of online learning environments. Online, as well as live, instructors should look for pivotal points where they can comfortably address these principles within their course design. The important point here is to focus on motivational elements and principles, not just on the

Table 2. Synchronous and asynchronous learning issues and elements within different online activities

Type of Activity	General Structure and Elements	Synchronous Issues	Asynchronous Issues
Ice Breakers	Everyone gets an opportunity to share or participate. There are a wide variety of potential activity frameworks, including Two Truths and One Lie, Coffee House Expectations, and Favorite Web Site Postings.	Turn taking is necessary since it is difficult to hear from everyone. Of course, certain activity frameworks will work better than others.	Learners may only selectively participate and read messages. Effort must be taken to encourage them to "meet" all classmates or read all messages in a new topic ice breaker.
Role Play	Learners are assigned a role or personality to play such as optimist, pessimist, journalist, coach, sage, etc. Alternatively, they might be assigned a particular person or author to assume such as Kant, Nietzsche, Mother Teresa, Sir Edmund Hillary, etc.	Learners must fully understand their roles in order to be able to play them out in real time. Some form of turn-taking must be in place to ensure that all participants are active.	Learners must have participation guidelines and deadlines to ensure that dialogue takes place. Summarization of discussion is important to bring closure, though effort must be taken to encourage learners to read the summaries.
Guest Lectures	Guests from outside of the class, such as experts in the field or authors/scholars that the students have read, are invited to join students for a discussion during a particular period of time. Typically, the guest answers learner questions, although the guest may be asked to comment on work the class has already completed.	Turn-taking must be carefully facilitated or the chat should be moderated to ensure the guest is not bombarded with too many questions at once. Preparation of questions in advance is useful.	Expectations of guest participation (how many times the guest will contribute and when) need to be clear for all participants. Early questions should be posted in advance of the guest's first interactions.
Debates	Learners may be assigned a topic and a side, either as an individual or group, and given time to research and generally prepare for the topic.	Turn-taking must be carefully facilitated to ensure equality for both sides and all members of a group.	Timing must be carefully structured to allow for dialogic interchange between sides. Rebuttals should be deeper and more reflective than in a synchronous debate and appropriate resources and references should be cited.
Peer Feedback	Learners are asked to review and comment on each other's ideas and work. Rubrics may be provided to help students focus on the appropriate criteria.	Students providing feedback must review material in advance and be prepared. Students receiving feedback benefit from the ability to seek clarification of muddy points in real time. It is important to have a way of saving feedback for later use.	Asynchronous peer feedback encourages more highly reflective feedback than synchronous feedback sessions. As a result, the timing of making the work available for critique and providing feedback is critical. The instructor may wish to allow learners who receive feedback time to ask their respondents for clarification.

range of possible tasks, since activities are simply vehicles through which effective motivation and learning can take place. In addition, the activities presented in this chapter are not intended to be exhaustive in terms of their exemplification of how to motivate online students. Instead, our intention was to provide a few useful examples and ideas that can be adopted and adapted by online instructors in higher education as well as business learning environments (for additional ideas, see Bonk & Dennen, 2003). And as online motivational ideas are modified and expanded, they can now be instantaneously shared with other instructors around the globe. When that occurs, there will hopefully be fewer bored online learners and frustrated online instructors.

Acknowledgments

Portions of this chapter were presented at the 2001 and 2002 annual meetings of the Wisconsin Distance Teaching and Learning Conference, Madison, Wisconsin.

References

American Psychological Association. (1993). *Learner-centered psychological principles: Guidelines for school reform and restructuring.* Washington, DC: American Psychological Association and the Mid-Continent Regional Educational Laboratory.

Anderson, M. D. (2001). Individual characteristics and Web-based courses. In C. R. Wolfe (Ed.), *Learning and teaching on the World Wide Web* (pp. 45-72). San Diego: Academic Press.

Blumenfeld, P. C., Soloway, E., Marx, R. W., Krajcik, J. S., Guzdial, M., & Palincsar, A. (1991). Motivating project-based learning: Sustaining the doing, supporting the learning. *Educational Psychologist, 26*(3&4), 369-398.

Bonk, C. J. (2001). *Online teaching in an online world.* Bloomington, IN: CourseShare.com. Retrieved January 1, 2003, from http://PublicationShare.com

Bonk, C. J. (2002). *Online training in an online world.* Bloomington, IN: CourseShare.com. Retrieved January 1, 2003, from http://PublicationShare.com

Bonk, C. J., & Cummings, J. A. (1998). A dozen recommendations for placing the student at the center of Web-based learning. *Educational Media International, 35*(2), 82-89.

Bonk, C. J., Daytner, K., Daytner, G., Dennen, V., & Malikowski, S. (2001). Using Web-based cases to enhance, extend, and transform pre-service teacher training: Two years in review. *Computers in the Schools, 18*(1), 189-211.

Bonk, C. J., & Dennen, N. (2003). Frameworks for research, design, benchmarks, training, and pedagogy in Web-based distance education. In M. G. Moore & B. Anderson (Eds.), *Handbook of distance education* (pp. 331-348). Mahwah, NJ: Lawrence Erlbaum.

Bonk, C. J., & Dennen, V. P. (1999). Teaching on the Web: With a little help from my pedagogical friends. *Journal of Computing in Higher Education, 11*(1), 3-28.

Bonk, C. J., Ehman, L., Hixon, E., & Yamagata-Lynch, E. (2002). The pedagogical TICKIT: Teacher Institute for Curriculum Knowledge about the Integration of Technology. *Journal of Technology and Teacher Education, 10*(2), 205-233.

Bonk, C. J., Fischler, R. B., & Graham, C. R. (2000). Getting smarter on the Smartweb. In D. G. Brown, (Ed.), *Teaching with technology: Seventy-five professors from eight universities tell their stories* (pp. 200-205). Boston: Anker Publishing.

Bonk, C. J., Hara, H., Dennen, V., Malikowski, S., & Supplee, L. (2000). We're in TITLE to dream: Envisioning a community of practice, "The intraplanetary teacher learning exchange." *CyberPsychology and Behavior, 3*(1), 25-39.

Brown, D. (2002, January). Interactive teaching. *Syllabus, 15*(6), 23.

Canada, M. (2000). Students as seekers in online classes. *New Directions for Teaching and Learning, 84*, 35-40.

Dennen, V. P. (2001). *The design and facilitation of asynchronous discussion activities in Web-based courses.* Unpublished doctoral dissertation, University of Indiana, USA.

Firdyiwek, Y. (1999). Web-based courseware tools: Where is the pedagogy? *Educational Technology, 39*(1), 29-34.

Hacker, D. J., & Niederhauser, D. S. (2000). Promoting deep and durable learning in the online classroom. *New Directions for Teaching and Learning, 84*, 53-63.

Hara, N., Bonk, C. J., & Angeli, C. (2000). Content analyses of online discussion in an applied educational psychology course. *Instructional Science, 28*(2), 115-152.

Kulp, R. (1999). *Effective collaboration in corporate distributed learning: Ten best practices for curriculum owners, developers and instructors.* Chicago, IL: IBM Learning Services.

Maehr, M. L. (1984). Meaning and motivation: Toward a theory of personal involvement. In R. Ames & C. Ames (Eds.), *Research on motivation in education: Student motivation* (pp. 115-143). Orlando: Academic Press.

Novak, G. M. (2000). Just-in-time teaching: Blending active learning with Web technology. In D. G. Brown (Ed.), *Teaching with technology: Seventy-five professors from eight universities tell their stories* (pp. 59-62). Boston: Anker Publishing.

Oliver, R., Omari, A., & Herrington, J. (1998). Exploring student interactions in collaborative World Wide Web computer-based learning environments. *Journal of Educational Multimedia and Hypermedia, 7*(2-3). 263-287.

Partlow, K. M. (2001). *Indicators of constructivist principles in Internet-based courses.* Unpublished master's thesis, Eastern Illinois University, USA.

Pintrich, P. R., & Schunk, D. H. (1996). *Motivation in education: Theory, research, and applications.* Englewood Cliffs, NJ: Merrill.

Reeve, J. M. (1996). *Motivating others: Nurturing inner motivational resources.* Needham Heights, MA; Allyn & Bacon.

Salmon, G. (2000). *E-moderating: The key to teaching and learning online.* London: Kogan Page.

Savery, J. R., & Duffy, T. M. (1996). Problem-based learning: An instructional model and its constructivist framework. In B. G. Wilson (Ed.), *Constructivist learning environments: Case studies in instructional design* (pp. 135-148). Englewood Cliffs, NJ: Educational Technology Publications.

Schrage, M. (1990). *Shared minds: The new technologies of collaboration.* New York: Random House.

Singer, J., Marx, R. W., Krajcik, J., & Chambers, J. C. (2000). Constructing extended inquiry projects: Curriculum materials for science education reform. *Educational Psychologist, 35*(3), 165-178.

Stipek, D. J. (1998) *Motivation to learn: From theory to practice* (3rd ed.). Boston: Allyn & Bacon.

Watson, G. (2000). PHYS345 electricity and electronics for engineers. In D. G. Brown (Ed.), *Teaching with technology: Seventy-five professors from eight universities tell their stories* (pp. 63-66). Boston: Anker Publishing.

Williams, S. B. (1992). Putting case-based instruction into context: Examples from legal and medical education. *The Journal of the Learning Sciences, 2*(4), 367-427.

Chapter VII

Humanizing Learning-at-Distance:
Best Practice Guidelines for Synchronous Instructors

Kathleen Barclay, University of Phoenix School of Advanced Studies, USA

Introduction

Online learning is taking part in one of the greatest instructional transformations since mass public education was introduced in America in the 1880s. Traditional classroom settings now contend with the implementation of asynchronous (online, self-directed) and, even more recently, synchronous (online, real-time) environments. These uses of technology challenge our historical instructional models, raising many questions about how to appropriately integrate such processes into business and educational instruction.

Distance education research has generally focused on the technological aspects of instruction—does a specific medium help or hinder learning? However, recent research indicates that *quality* of learning depends upon the design of instruction rather than on delivery media, and that information transfer and retention is most strongly impacted by the frequency and quality of learner-centered practice activities (Clarke, 1994; Jones, Valdez, Nowakowski, & Rasmussen, 1994). Researchers strongly agree on the importance of engaged, collaborative learning in schools and business classroom settings. How instructional content is prepared to support engagement, how person-to-person interactions are arranged, and how the complete learning environment matches learner needs are now considered key issues in the creation of successful online instructional design.

Instructor interest in interactivity and engagement as practiced in the live online setting is rapidly increasing as more and more organizations consider this medium for education and communication. Real-time, instructor-led e-learning design and delivery leverages the Internet to improve training efficiency and effectiveness, combining the best of in-person interaction with the dynamics of the Web. Instructors actively request information and techniques to help them adapt to this new live online environment. Comfortable with face-to-face techniques, they now want to facilitate shared engagement between the student and technology, the student and instructor, and the student with other students.

Based on interviews conducted with an international set of experienced synchronous (online, live) instructors, eight best-practice guidelines—considered essential for fostering successful live e-learning instruction—were identified (Barclay, 2001). Assembled from summaries of knowledge, skills, attitudinal aspects, and practices, the following guidelines provide motivated trainers with a theoretical foundation and yet practical set of techniques to support collaborative synchronous e-learning instruction.

Master the Technology

Technology issues are a primary barrier to the implementation of a successful live e-learning environment. The challenges of teaching have always included understanding instructional processes and specific content, but now an instructor must concurrently understand and operate a technologically complex online software application. To become a successful synchronous instructor, technology should be positively and energetically embraced. This translates into mastering the hardware and software use through extensive practice. The goal of the instructor is to move participants in a synchronous session past being fascinated by the technology and tools toward attentive participation in the learning experience.

Techniques instructors may use to overcome the technology barrier include:

- Knowing the features and functions of different tools, and how to use them appropriately

- Selecting only a few of the application's tools to start with and then adding in others as experience with that interface grows

- Accessing instructor and student coaching or training options to learn how to effectively design for and instruct in the media

- Accessing technical support before, during, and after a session to ensure a positive rather than negative online experience for all

- Holding a short test session to help the learner overcome possible technophobia

- Paying attention to technology factors, such as having fast keyboarding skills or a *feel* for bandwidth speed, that help provide a comfortable environment for the learner

- Knowing how to overcome any technical problems that arise
- Knowing when and how to blend online training with face-to-face and self-directed study to provide an optimum learning experience

Acquiring a base foundation in understanding the technology and extensively practicing with technological components will yield higher levels of trainer comfort and confidence when instructing in the synchronous environment. The key message is to become as familiar with hardware and software tools as when operating a slide or overhead projector. Moving past the technology to develop the human connection is paramount for learning success.

Experience the Online Environment

Closely associated with mastering the technology is the provision that a successful instructor must have personal experience with the online environment. Instructors realize they are no longer physically standing in front of a class full of people with whom they have eye contact and can read body language. Software tools should be seen from the student perspective and with an awareness of the student experience.

Critical success factors include the instructor:

- Being a student in one or more synchronous sessions prior to beginning online instruction
- Recognizing effective interactive processes
- Being able to easily enable and disable application tools to provide a smooth flow to a session
- Learning to convey content in acceptable chunks for the online attention span
- Managing questions and answers that are submitted through the various tools
- Staying on time to meet synchronous class time boundaries
- Managing the overall flow of the session to provide a successful learning experience

Synchronous instructors need to develop an outstanding awareness of this innovative model that learners, and trainers, are now facing. An instructor who has experienced the online live environment is in a much better position to effectively train with understanding and thoughtfulness.

Practice Adult Learning
Theory and Application

A fundamental responsibility of the facilitator is to create an experience that causes or enables someone else to learn. A primary factor needed for instructors to thrive in successful synchronous training environments includes the mindset of valuing learning and truly putting adult learning principles into practice. When migrating from the traditional classroom into an online experience, trainers can benefit from practically applying adult learning theory to foster social interaction in a potentially lonely at-distance environment.

The successful synchronous instructor:

- Applies adult learning theory, with a strong learner-centered focus
- Has subject matter knowledge credibility for the appropriate level of instruction
- Practices constructivism (Vygotsky, 1978), a model that assumes students construct their own meaning and the trainer's job is to help facilitate that process
- Integrates stories to make content real
- Sets goals and performance objectives from both trainer *and* learner points-of-view
- Varies the instructional strategies to meet learner needs
- Develops a sense of everyone being part of a group (community), rather than just following the model of presenting information as the expert lecturer

An e-learning instructor should principally consider the student's perception of *what am I getting out of this experience.* Separation of trainer and learner by time and distance in the online environment can significantly alter the roles of trainer-as-expert and student-as-passive-attendee to become roles that foster learning together, a serious challenge and yet great opportunity to provide more effective learning for all.

Figure 1.

Adult Learning Principles by Malcolm Knowles   As a person matures, the self-concept moves from dependency toward self-direction.   Adults have accumulated life experiences that become rich resources for learning.   Readiness of an adult to learn is oriented toward social roles.   Adults are more problem-centered than subject-centered in learning.   Adults are motivated to learn more by internal factors than external ones.

Design Appropriately for
Synchronous Online Learning

Online design surfaces as a major focus of instructor attention for the synchronous environment. Instructional design and engagement techniques specific to the e-learning environment are key. Instructors usually find that designing training for an online course is more complex and requires more up front attention and preparation than design intended for the traditional classroom.

Trainers designing for synchronous classes:

- Use *mini lectures*
- Use alternatives to the lecture method to creatively facilitate interaction
- Present online content simply and clearly in easy-to-read formats and fonts, graphically interesting yet fast-to-load across the Internet
- Modularize content into bites of material that, with instructor facilitation, challenges thinking and enables learners to actively participate
- Present guidelines up front to set learner expectations
- Offer personal acknowledgements throughout a session
- Adapt Accelerated Learning and Active Learning techniques to create innovative class environments
- Provide a learner option to *opt out* or *skip ahead* as needed
- Post before and after session materials;
- Value and promote the *shared learning* of materials
- Give significant attention to pre-, during, and post-session design for interaction rather than emphasizing content development
- Script the class plan into 3-8 minute modules (see Figure 2)
- Practice, practice, practice, and then practice some more to refine the design and delivery

Innovation, combined with well-grounded design, keeps everyone in the class interactive and interested. Instructors who emphasize the authentic design and application of learner-centered instructional processes will provide successful online learning experiences.

Figure 2.

Time	Slide/Content/Materials	Instructor	Attendees
8:05-8:08am 3 min	#4 "INTERACTIVE TOOL BAR"	Explain toolbar	Watch the demo
			Practice tools
Script: We're using XYZ 4.0 today to help demonstrate how live online training works…			

Engage All Participants Frequently

Engagement or interaction of learners with each other and with the instructor is considered a primary aspect for success. This key factor is supported by the findings of the study titled "Quality On the Line" by the Institute for Higher Education Policy (2000). Key success factors for interaction include:

- Adjusting for the lack of visual cues
- Knowing about and implementing group processes
- Implementing exceptional listening, questioning, and facilitation skills
- Emphasizing group or cooperative efforts among instructors and learners
- Integrating content with questions with live demonstration
- Using application tools in a variety of ways to foster attention and participation
- Being able to work with a co-presenter or assistant facilitator to better manage multiple requests

The importance of paying attention to the human aspects of instructor and learner interaction in an online environment is critical. This includes having access to professional development for help with how to best utilize interactive exercises. Engagement is integral to helping learners go beyond what they, and the instructor, already know.

Place Considerable
Attention on Delivery Skills

Instructor delivery skills are significant to producing live e-learning course instruction. The e-learning instructor does not have physical cues such as hand gestures or facial expressions to guide the learning experience and must be very aware of the nature of vocal presentation.

To keep learners interested and engaged, the synchronous instructor:

- Takes cues from broadcast radio skills to develop voice and personality that project comfortably to the students
- Has clear diction and knows how to use a pause appropriately
- Modulates voice tone and pitch
- Is verbally engaging, energetic, and enthusiastic
- Works together with another instructor when possible, introducing a change of voices into the session to help maintain interest (Barclay, Gordon, Hollahan, & Lai, 2003)

- Uses appropriate humor to establish rapport
- Practices, practices, practices

For synchronous instruction, sound becomes the primary way to help make personal connections. Although the visual aspect is accommodated by presenting content slides or other materials on computer monitors, the voice becomes the primary method to foster human relationships and interaction.

Be Flexible and Adaptive

The need to be flexible and adaptable when teaching synchronously cannot be overemphasized. Problems with technology always seem to be present. Visual instructional control normally established in a classroom situation is not present in the online environment. The successful trainer learns not to emphasize a problem, but to just deal with it efficiently and effectively—and have technical support available behind the scenes.

The successful instructor needs to:

- Demonstrate quick and flexible thinking
- Be able to keep track of and balance many tasks at once
- Tightly prepare for a session so that when technical or attendee issues arise, the situation can be handled without losing facilitator control
- Be willing to take risks and try new techniques
- Be open to new ideas and take advantage of them during a session

The ability to creatively *think on your feet* is an important skill to develop for effective synchronous training. This can be perceived as an easy task to accomplish, but it is not. Successful online live instructors must manage the learning environment, the content, and the technology, all at the same time.

Foster a *Fun* and Exciting Learning Environment

Instructional attention to developing engaging, fun, and comfortable live e-learning is considered essential to providing an effective learning experience. An instructional goal should be to generate excitement in students to continue with this form of learning, to sense the *aha*. Instructors must expand their skills in design and delivery to produce a fun and rewarding experience for all involved.

A fun and exciting learning environment includes:

- Using various interactive activities
- Teaching to attendee learning styles
- Using real-world outcome models as best practices
- Facilitating probing questions and *no-holds-barred* discussions to generate deeper critical thinking
- Creating a safe space to reflect on values, challenge ideas, and take risks with behaviors
- Using music and audio files interspersed during a session
- Using interesting and animated graphic presentation practices
- Managing the whole-body environment with exercises like asking participants to stand up to stretch at a midpoint
- Considering the technology as just another tool in the instructional basket
- Using faces, pictures, or video to make the encounter more human
- Embedding relevant puzzles, quizzes, or games
- Showing learners how to use emoticons to show expression ;-) during chat projects
- Giving a lot of feedback with positive comments
- Having a goal and purpose for interaction
- Finding out what is important to the student, not just what is important for the content
- Most importantly, integrating real-world application

The final goals are in the real world, not in the virtual world. When in the distance education arena, synchronous training helps connect content to each individual participant's reason to learn. The synchronous instructor has a wealth of knowledge, skills, viewpoints, and techniques to choose from to create effective—and fun—e-learning sessions to foster the connection of content to learning.

Conclusion

This set of eight guidelines raises awareness of best-practices that novice and seasoned synchronous instructors may use to foster successful live online learning environments. These major themes should encourage those moving into the field of synchronous instruction to carefully attend to the human and social aspects of e-learning. Successful learning experiences are dependent upon instructors receiving appropriate training and continued assistance as they begin to work online, upon the appropriate use and implementation of technology that leads to authentic learning, and upon an application of content and process design that emphasizes interaction and engagement. These critical success factors help support instructors in the search and practice of knowledge, skills, attitudes, and techniques that help foster successful e-learning experiences for all.

References

Barclay, K. (2001). *Humanizing learning-at-distance.* Doctoral dissertation, Saybrook Graduate School, USA.

Barclay, K., Gordon, A., Hollahan, J., & Lai, Y. (2003). *The live e-learning cookbook: Recipes for success.* New York: iUniverse.

Clark, R. E. (1994). Media will never influence learning. *Educational Technology Research & Development, 42*(2), 21-29.

Jones, B., Valdez, G., Nowakowski, J., & Rasmussen, C. (1994). *Designing learning and technology for educational reform.* Oak Book, IL: North Central Regional Educational Laboratory.

Knowles, M. (1989). *Making of an adult educator.* San Francisco: Jossey-Bass.

Institute for Higher Education Policy. (2000). *Quality on the line.* Retrieved from http://www.ihep.com/Pubs/PDF/Quality.pdf

Vygotsky, L. (1978). *Mind in society: The development of higher psychological processes.* Cambridge, MA: MIT Press.

Chapter VIII

Storytelling as a Web-Based Workplace Learning Pedagogy

Nick Nissley, The Banff Centre, Canada

Introduction

This chapter describes the evolution of storytelling in the workplace—from a face-to-face learning pedagogy to the use of storytelling as a Web-based learning pedagogy. The chapter is organized around an improvised version of Koppett's (2001, p. 71) "story spine." The story spine is a tool that Koppett offers to aid people in building stories. Simply, the structure is: (1) "once upon a time," (2) "then one day," (3) "and so," and (4) "and in the end." In this chapter, the story spine structure will help explain or describe the story of storytelling as a Web-based learning pedagogy, as well as aid in the description of its evolution. In addition, this chapter will ask "and so?"—or, what is the significance of this emergent phenomenon of storytelling as a Web-based learning pedagogy?

Once Upon a Time...

Human beings have been captivated by the power of stories for thousands of years. Stories have the power to stir our emotions, stimulate our imagination, make us reflect on our own lives, and motivate us into action. Storytelling has served as a fabric of culture, and stories have been linked to individual health (e.g., Simpkinson & Simpkinson, 1983; Freedman & Combs, 1995; Taylor, 1996; DeSalvo, 2000). For example, Bettelheim (1991) described how in traditional Hindu medicine, the prescription of a fairy tale was not uncommon in the treatment of an emotionally disturbed patient.

It was expected that through contemplating the story the disturbed person would be led to visualize both the nature and the impasse in living from which he suffered, and the possibility of its resolution. From what a particular tale implied about man's despair, hopes and methods of overcoming tribulations, the patient could discover not only a way out of his distress but also a way to find himself, as the hero of the story did.

Today, the practice of narrative therapy (e.g., Freedman & Combs, 1995) similarly understands this healing and restorative nature of story. Coles (1989) has linked the power of story, well-being, and learning, and today many others are beginning to recognize the contribution of storytelling to organizational well-being, primarily due to its educative power.

A key purpose of stories, throughout history, has been to educate—from the handing down of cultural values to the shaping of job-specific behaviors. Egan (1989) asserts, "Of all the techniques invented or discovered for making the lore of a social group securely memorable, by far the most important was the story." But, one may ask, why are stories so helpful in preserving the memorable. Neuhauser (1993) asserts:

Stories allow a person to feel and see the information as well as factually understand it...because you 'hear' the information factually, visually, and emotionally, it is more likely to be imprinted on your brain in a way that it sticks with you longer.

In learning from stories, that which is important is made memorable and retained, so we may better adapt to future events. That is why it makes sense to use stories as a learning pedagogy. A well-told story may have more of an impact on learners than an abstract set of facts that may be forgotten shortly after they are asserted. Stories are more memorable and compelling than alternative ways of conveying information in the classroom.

Stories and Work

Within the workplace, storytelling has become integrated into work processes. Today, stories have become recognized as a means of facilitating strategic planning (e.g., Shaw, Brown, & Bromiley, 1998; Barry & Elmes, 1997), organizational culture development (e.g., Ransdell, 2000; Jones, 1991; Wilkins, 1984), investor relations (e.g., Gurley, 1999), customer research (e.g., Lieber, 1997), marketing (Locke, Levine, Searls, & Weinberger, 2001), managerial communication (e.g., Armstrong, 1992), problem solving (e.g., Mitroff & Kilmann, 1975), organizational design (Browning, 1991), organization development (e.g., Boje, Fedor, & Rowland, 1982; Boje, 1991a; Vance, 1991; Dunford & Jones, 2000), influence (Simmons, 2001), knowledge management (Denning, 2001), organization reflection (e.g., Kleiner & Roth, 2000; Roth & Kleiner, 1999; Learning Histories, 2002), and simply becoming a better leader (Gargiulo, 2001).

Stories and Workplace Learning

More specifically, storytelling has become recognized as an effective pedagogy or means of facilitating learning in the workplace (e.g., ASTD, 2000; Kaye & Jacobson, 1999; Parkin, 1998; Durrance, 1997). Today, one can find specific assistance in how to use stories in the workplace—in coaching (e.g., Parkin, 2001), in leadership development (e.g., Cohen & Tichy, 1997), in facilitating reflective learning, through project retrospective such as learning histories (e.g., Kleiner & Roth, 2000; Roth & Kleiner, 1999; Learning Histories, 2002), and even in assisting organizations to make sense of their future through imaginative storytelling, in Future Search (e.g., Weisbord, 1992; Weisbord & Janoff, 1995) for example. One can even find assistance with specific approaches to storytelling (e.g., improvisational storytelling) that can be used in workplace learning (e.g., Koppett, 2001). Simply, stories are commonly used today as a face-to-face workplace learning pedagogy. In fact, even the mainstream training literature (e.g., King, King, & Rothwell, 2000) identifies and recognizes storytelling as an accepted and proven learning pedagogy.

Stories and Web-Based Workplace Learning

Workplace learning scholars and practitioners have recognized organizations as occurring in and through stories—or as Boje (1991b) asserts, organizations are a big conversation, an ongoing storytelling event. Thus, we may expect storytelling to remain 'center stage' as a valued learning pedagogy. However, within the area of workplace learning, relatively little attention has been paid to storytelling as a *Web-based learning pedagogy* (e.g., Neal, 2002). We generally view the Web as an information resource, rather than a place for engaging in storytelling. Now, as e-learning's sophistication advances, facilitators of e-learning are exploring Web-based storytelling as a comparatively unexploited strategy for embodying and delivering content. In addition to the content-driven interest of some, others (e.g., Weller, 2000) are recognizing the context value of storytelling in the learning environment. In other words, given the first-person nature of story, the learner can identify with an agent—thus, closing a substantial distance between the learner and the material. Or as Weller (2000) says, "The familiarity of the narrative [story] form acts as something of a comforter when a new student is faced with the double impact of being new to study and new to the technology [Web-based learning]."

Storytelling occurring on the Web often is facilitated by the well-known Web-based technologies: asynchronous text communication (e.g., bulletin boards), synchronous text communication (e.g., chat rooms), and Web-based conferencing (e.g., groupware). In addition, Web-based storytelling is also occurring in the following 'places:' Web logs—blogging (e.g., Nichani & Rajmanichan, 2001), cyber salons, virtual theater, multi-user dungeons (MUDs), personal story Web sites, Digital Clubhouses (storytelling centers that provide computer access to seniors, disabled people, and youth groups), and digital storytelling (e.g., Pink, 1999) performances. These are examples of how storytelling is moving from the traditional classroom to the digital world, and these may also function as Web-based learning pedagogies.

Khan (2002) has asserted storytelling as a Web-based learning pedagogy. However, other references to Web-based learning methods (e.g., Loughner, Harvey, & Milheim, 2001; Khan 2001) have not yet recognized storytelling as a Web-based learning pedagogy. This chapter elaborates on Khan's (2002) assertion by: (1) describing the evolution of storytelling in the workplace—from a face-to-face learning pedagogy to storytelling as a Web-based learning pedagogy, (2) asking "and so?"—or, what is the significance of this emergent phenomenon of storytelling as a Web-based learning pedagogy, and (3) positing the future of Web-based storytelling and storytelling as a Web-based learning pedagogy. Examples of Web-based storytelling appear throughout this chapter.

Then One Day...

It is obvious that storytelling has served as a useful workplace learning pedagogy in the traditional face-to-face classroom. However, the focus of this chapter is on the following question: Can storytelling serve as an effective *Web-based* learning pedagogy? So, let us turn from the historical perspective (once upon a time) to the evolving present-day environment. This chapter seeks to provide an overview of the emergence of 'storytelling@work'—as a Web-based learning pedagogy. This next section specifically seeks to explain the movement from "digital page turning" and "e-reading" to digital storytelling@work in e-learning.

From "Digital Page Turning" and "E-Reading"...

First, consider the broader landscape of e-learning. Critics of e-learning are quick to point out that many e-learning course offerings are nothing but "digital page turning" (Masie, 2001), and some refer to the act of taking an e-learning course as "e-reading" (Nichani, 2002). Masie (2001) asserts that about 98% of the e-learning content that is now offered to adult, corporate learners is modeled after a textbook or classroom metaphor.

Masie (2001) reminds us that when television began, our instinct was to make it "radio, but with pictures." For the first years, the development process was to take radio shows, even the same talent, and put them at a microphone, in front of a camera. It appears that Web-based learning has repeated this history—where the textbook 'form factor' has led to extensive collections of text-based information.

Second, more specific to the use of storytelling in a Web-based learning environment, this chapter may hopefully serve as a harbinger—to warn e-learning educators to not merely try copying the face-to-face storytelling form into the Web-based learning environment. For example, like the initial efforts to "make television like radio, but with pictures"; e-learning educators must guard against the overly simplified prospect of 'cut and pasting' story text on to the Web.

Davenport, Agamanolis, Barry, Bradley, and Brooks (2000) also assert that there is much more to story content than just text. For example, photographs, video, illustration, audio, and animation can play a vital role in communicating a story. They also assert that as bandwidth constraints begin to ease for many Web users, and as we become more sophisticated regarding the Web's potential for storytelling, non-text content will become more prominent. Sometimes text is the best solution; often however, Davenport et al. (2000, p. 456) assert: "Seeing the faces or hearing the voices from the story being told conveys a depth and subtlety of experience that text can not rival."

Neal (2002), in a research paper for *E-Learn Magazine,* examines "storytelling at a distance" and is one of the first to alert us to what she refers to as "storytelling's appropriation of the e-learning medium." Despite the interest in using stories in the face-to-face classroom *and* the emerging pedagogical appeal of stories in the Web-based learning environment, we must respect the unique way that e-learners tell and listen to technologically mediated stories. The remainder of this chapter seeks to contribute to our understanding of storytelling as a Web-based learning pedagogy, by beginning to describe the ways that the storytelling phenomenon is emerging and evolving in the Web-based learning environment.

...To Digital Storytelling

As mentioned earlier, storytelling occurring on the Web is often facilitated by the well-known Web-based technologies: asynchronous text communication (e.g., bulletin boards), synchronous text communication (e.g., chat rooms), and Web-based conferencing (e.g., groupware). In addition, Web-based storytelling is also occurring in the following 'places': Web logs—blogging (e.g., Nichani & Rajmanichan, 2001), cyber salons, virtual theater, multi-user dungeons (MUDs), personal story Web sites, Digital Clubhouses (storytelling centers that provide computer access to seniors, disabled people, and youth groups), and digital storytelling (e.g., Pink, 1999) performances. In this section, examples are described, including: "digital storytelling," "blogging," and "story-centered curriculum."

These examples mark the evolution from the early storytelling approaches on the Web—such as the Motley Fool's (The Fool, 2002) "fribble," or simple storied approach to financial education on the Web—to more sophisticated approaches, such as Schank's story-centered curriculum (Socratic Arts, 2002), and the Children's Hospital of Iowa's (2002) experiment in digital storytelling in medical education: "The Virtual Pediatric Patient: A Digital Storytelling System for Teaching Common Pediatric Problems." Yet, these emergent forms of digital storytelling have roots in the simplicity of the storytelling method. For example, for years print-based comics have been recognized as a learning technology (e.g., McCloud, 1994; Eisner, 1996). Today, comics are still recognized as a valuable learning technology; however, we are witnessing the emergence of Web cartoonists and online comics (e.g., McCloud, 2000; Modern Tales, 2002).

First, "digital storytelling" was made popular by Dana Atchley (Pink, 1999; Stepanek, 2000). Digital storytelling uses computers to create media-rich stories and the Web to share those stories. Atchley has made a living helping businesses engage in digital storytelling, particularly with the form of digital storytelling where the digital stories are presented to customers and enable them to tell the company their stories about their relationship with the company and its products. An example of this approach is the *Digital Storytelling Theater* that Atchley created for the World of Coca-Cola in Las Vegas. Other Atchley ventures with digital storytelling include his interactive theatrical performance, *Next Exit* (2002). In this performance, Atchley sits on a log next to a digital campfire, and drawing from a virtual suitcase of 70 stories, creates a unique selection for each audience. *Next Exit* is an excellent example of the positive impact of new technology on the ancient art of storytelling. Companies like NCR and its Global Learning Group have incorporated digital storytelling into the organization's training function. In addition to Atchley's work, the Center for Digital Storytelling (2002) was founded by Joe Lambert and Nina Mullen, and is located at the University of California at Berkley, where they collaborate with the College Writing Program, co-teaching a course—a survey and production course in narrative and new media. Their mission at the Center for Digital Storytelling is to "assist people in using digital media to tell meaningful stories from their lives." While Atchley has popularized the idea of digital storytelling, Lambert and Mullen's Center for Digital Storytelling is ensuring that the training of digital storytellers may continue to evolve the storytelling form and its practice.

Second, bloggers (from the words 'Web log') write online diaries and commentaries. Blogging (Blogger, 2002), similar to digital storytelling, is about using computers to create media-rich stories and using the Web to share those stories. Nichani and Rajmanickam (2001) recognize blogging as a form of storytelling, unique to the Web. Because they are digital and use the Web for publishing and distribution, they have some advantages over traditional means of storytelling. According to Nichani and Rajmanickam (2001): (1) they are much more accessible than face-to-face storytelling mode; (2) they scale very easily across a large network, thus reaching a wider audience; (3) they are easily archived and can be retrieved any number of times; (4) providing context is much easier with hyperlinks and cross references; and (5) they are low on the signal-to-noise ratio on information. Nichani and Rajmanickam (2001) also explicitly speak to the potential use of blogs for knowledge management purposes within large organizations, moving beyond the face-to-face storytelling and knowledge management expressions presently being practiced in the workplace (e.g., Denning, 2001).

Third, story-centered curriculum is an example of how digital forms of storytelling are evolving away from single methods (e.g., blogging and digital storytelling) to holistic approaches to curriculum. Dr. Roger Schank (1995; Schank & Morson, 1995) founded Socratic Arts (http://www.socraticarts.com) to build e-learning programs based on a new approach called the "Story-Centered Curriculum." The Story-Centered Curriculum represents a dramatic departure from traditional curricula and many current e-learning offerings. Socratic Arts is currently working with a number of leading universities to develop new degree offerings based on the Story-Centered Curriculum approach. Some of Socratic Arts' university clients are offering to develop customized story-centered master's degree programs for corporate partners. In Story-Centered Curriculum, rather than creating a curriculum composed of a series of courses, each covering a subject area in depth, learners are immersed in a scenario, or story, that will require them to learn the facts and concepts needed to complete the subject work. Thus, students learn by working together on projects that are part of a larger story in which they are playing a role. Schank's first project is the new Carnegie Mellon West, a virtual university in Silicon Valley, which is founded upon this idea (Warshawsky, 2002).

And So...

While it was asserted that digital forms of storytelling (e.g., digital storytelling and blogs) have begun finding their way into the e-learning medium, one must still ask: So what? What is the significance of such an evolution in the practice of storytelling in workplace learning? Davenport et al. (2000) suggest the following, in terms of the "so what" question.

Throughout the ages storytellers have exploited available technologies to craft compelling stories that entertain and educate their audience. In the 19th and 20th centuries, "radio, television, and motion pictures created forms of media that made the ordinary story seem extraordinary ... however, these forms maintained a single, limited, ordered narrative perspective ... digital narratives of the future are capable of expanding the social engagement of audiences to engage in the collaborative co-construction of meaning and experience." (p. 456)

This speaks to an important issue. The emergence of digital narratives moves us beyond the limited single perspective practiced in face-to-face storytelling. More specifically, Davenport et al. speak to the emergence of a more collaborative telling of stories and the co-construction of meaning—the movement from monologic to more dialogic and multi-vocal storytelling (e.g., Boje, 1995, 2002). Due to the limitations of traditional media, most traditional storytelling has been monologic in nature—a stream that flowed in one direction. Consider for example: television, radio, magazine, or newspaper—you told your story, but seldom was someone able to tell one in response. But now the digital storytelling era is upon us, and the idea of audience begins to be transformed. No longer will the audience of a storyteller be reduced to the role of a passive or detached viewer. Audience members will now be invited to participate in the dialogue and provide their own stories. This evolution in the role of audience in storytelling is similar to the evolution described by Boal (1985), who refers to the theater and the "liberation of the spectator."

Massie (2001) explicitly describes the significance of this evolution to multiple perspectives, in terms of learning pedagogy, stating:

While the classroom is usually focused on a single voice of expertise—the instructor— learners in online programs want to access a wider variety and range of perspectives that often differ. Imagine adding an icon to a program that would give 'the other viewpoint' at any stage of content delivery.

In many ways this is what the potential of digital forms of storytelling will allow to happen in the learning environment.

Massie also reminds us of how storytelling in the workplace connects with knowledge management, asking us to consider the possibilities that emerge from the grassroots ability to share personal stories. Specifically, he reminds us of the possibility for stories in Web-based learning to break down the physical and class barriers to conversation. Weinberger's (1999) commonsensical approach to knowledge management echoes this, as he speaks about knowledge workers and stories:

A knowledge worker is someone whose job entails having really interesting conversations at work. The characteristics of conversations map to the conditions for genuine knowledge generation and sharing: They're unpredictable interactions among people speaking in their own voice about something they're interested in. The conversants implicitly acknowledge that they don't have all the answers (or else the conversation is really a lecture) and risk being wrong in front of someone else. And conversations overcome the class structure of business, suspending the org chart at least for a little while.

In addition to the democratization of storytelling (the movement towards more dialogic and multi-vocal forms of storytelling), the emergence of digital storytelling as a learning pedagogy also announces a movement towards more sensory ways of knowing. Davenport et al. (2000) assert this need to evolve digital storytelling forms that emotionally engage the audience.

We can no longer be doomed to point, click, and type our way through the digital universe, regardless of the task at hand. Complex story environments of the future must actively challenge our ability to act and transform our emotional state. (p. 467)

Digital storytelling allows storytellers to create compelling stories that engage the head *and* the heart—using the full sensory spectrum of video, photography, art, and music. Thus, a storyteller may inspire an emotional response from the viewer that is usually outside the reach of text-based print media. This sort of multisensory stimulation captures the attention and pulls the viewer into the story, and it aids in the memorability of the content. Recall Neuhauser's (1993) assertion:

Stories allow a person to feel and see the information as well as factually understand it...because you 'hear' the information factually, visually, and emotionally, it is more likely to be imprinted on your brain in a way that it sticks with you longer.

Organizations have become aware of this unique aspect and benefit of digital storytelling forms. For example, Dana Atchley, founder of digital storytelling, has applied digital storytelling to the workplace, developing what he refers to as "emotional branding." Also, organizations such as the American Lung Association (2002) have found ways to allow storytelling to work synergistically for their organization. On the association's Web site is a section called "Wall of Remembrance." The wall is a message board where family members or friends post tributes to those special persons who have died from lung-related illnesses. These stories say more in favor of the mission of the American Lung Association than any amount of research data and statistics about lung disease could. Other examples of Web sites that serve as health education vehicles and engage in similar sort of storytelling include: (1) Time Slips (2002), an interactive storytelling project with people with Alzheimer's Disease; (2) Family Caregiver Alliance (2002), a site that is a collection of poignant stories and photos portraying many aspects of care giving—from joy to grief, and from humor to tears; and (3) Time2BreakFree (2002), a site for those seeking to find a way out of domestic abuse—and these personal stories offer hope that the victims may be able to re-story their lives.

While these examples are not the rich media of the future wave of digital storytelling, this Web page technology still captures stories that are written by a real person, about a real person—and they inspire an emotional response.

And in the End...

So, where will this evolution of Web-based storytelling in workplace learning move next? Murray's (1997) *The Future of Narrative in Cyberspace* offers speculations about how cyber bards will engage with new technologies—offering an overview of the prospects digital media offer new forms of storytelling. While she speculates, no one knows for sure. However, Masie (2001) asserts that as we begin to think outside the realm of traditional face-to-face storytelling, every aspect of storytelling has the potential to be morphed by digital contact. So, let us look to the bleeding edge of digital storytelling—to places like the Interactive Cinema Group at MIT's Media Laboratory. But, let us also look to the grassroots forms of story sharing that are emerging in places like *www.netslaves.com* (Net Slaves, 2002), which has been referred to as the "electronic union hall for 21st century info-plumbers." This is an exciting time, as we generally observe the evolution of storytelling in our culture, and more specifically we observe the re-storying of storytelling as a Web-based workplace learning pedagogy.

References

American Lung Association. (2002). *American Lung Association Web page.* Retrieved June 1, 2002, from http://www.lungusa.org/bin/wall/wallview.pl

Armstrong, D. (1992). *Managing by storying around: A new method of leadership.* New York: Doubleday.

ASTD. (2000). *Storytelling* (Info-line). Alexandria, VA: ASTD.

Barry, D., & Elmes, M. (1997). Strategy retold: Toward a narrative view of strategic discourse. *Academy of Management Review, 22*(2), 429-452.

Bettelheim, B. (1991). *The uses of enchantment: The meaning and importance of fairy tales.* New York: Knopf.

Blogger. (2002). *Blogger Web page.* Retrieved June 1, 2002, from http://www.blogger.com

Boal, A. (1985). *Theatre of the oppressed.* New York: Theatre Communications Group.

Boje, D. (1991a). Consulting and change in the storytelling organization. *Journal of Organizational Change Management, 4*(3), 7-17.

Boje, D. (1991b). The storytelling organization: A study of story performance in an office-supply firm. *Administrative Science Quarterly, 36*(1), 106-126.

Boje, D. (1995). Stories of the storytelling organization: A postmodern analysis of Disney as Tamara-land. *Academy of Management Journal, 38*(4), 997 1035.

Boje, D. (2002). *Applications of theater of the oppressed to transorganizational development work Web page.* Retrieved March 4, 2002, from http://web.nmsu.edu/~dboje/Tdpostmodtheatrics.htm

Boje, D., Fedor, D., & Rowland, K. (1982). Myth making: A qualitative step in OD interventions. *Journal of Applied Behavioral Science, 18*(1), 17-28.

Brooke, P. (1995). *Communicating through story characters: Radio social drama.* Lanham, MD: University Press of America.

Browning, L. (1991). Organizational narratives and organizational structure. *Journal of Organizational Change Management, 4*(3), 59-67.

Center for Digital Storytelling. (2002). *Center for Digital Storytelling Web site.* Retrieved June 1, 2002, from http://www.storycenter.org

Children's Hospital of Iowa. (2002). *The virtual pediatric patient: A digital storytelling system for teaching common pediatric problems Web page.* Retrieved June 1, 2002, from http://www.vh.org/Providers/Simulations/VirtualPedsPatients/PedsVPHome.html

Cohen, E., & Tichy, N. (1997). How leaders develop leaders. *Training & Development, 51*(5), 58-73.

Coles, R. (1989). *The call of stories: Teaching and the moral imagination.* Boston: Houghton Mifflin.

Davenport, G., Agamanolis, S., Barry, B., Bradley, B., & Brooks, K. (2000). Synergistic storyscapes and constructionist cinematic sharing. *IBM Systems Journal, 39*(3-4), 456-469.

Denning, S. (2001). *The springboard: How storytelling ignites action in knowledge-era organizations.* Boston: Butterworth-Heinemann.

DeSalvo, L. (2000). *Writing as a way of healing: How telling our stories transforms our lives.* Boston: Beacon Press.

Dunford, R., & Jones, D. (2000). Narrative in strategic change. *Human Relations, 53*(9), 1207-1226.

Durrance, B. (1997). Stories at work. *Training & Development, 51*(2), 25-29.

Egan, K. (1989). Memory, imagination and learning: Connected by the story. *Phi-Delta-Kappan, 70,* 455-459.

Eisner, W. (1996). *Graphic storytelling.* New York: Poorhouse Press.

Family Caregiver Alliance. (2002). *The Family Caregiver Alliance Web page.* Retrieved June 1, 2002, from http://www.caregiver.org/cg.html

The Fool. (2002). *The Fool Web page.* Retrieved June 1, 2002, from http://www.fool.com

Freedman, J., & Combs, G. (1995). *Narrative therapy: The social construction of preferred realities.* New York: W.W. Norton Company.

Friedman, B., Grudin, J., Nass, C., Nissenbaum, H., Schlager, M., Shneiderman, B., & Thomas, J.C. (1999). Trust me, I'm accountable—trust and accountability online. In M. W. Alton & M.G. Williams (Eds.), *Proceedings of the CHI 99 Conference on Human Factors in Computing Systems*, Pittsburgh, PA. New York: ACM.

Gargiulo, T. (2001). *Making stories: A practical guide for organizational leaders and human resource leaders.* Westport, CT: Quorum.

Gurley, J. (1999). The great art of storytelling. *Fortune, 140*(9), 300-304.

Jones, M. (1991). What if stories don't tally with the culture. *Journal of Organizational Change Management, 4*(3), 27-34.

Kaye, B., & Jacobson, B. (1999). True tales and tall tales: The power of organizational storytelling. *Training and Development, 53*(3), 45-50.

Khan, B. (2001). A framework for Web-based learning. In B. Khan (Ed.), *Web-based training.* Englewood Cliffs, NJ: Educational Technology Publications.

Khan, B. (2002). *Web-based learning.* Englewood Cliffs, NJ: Educational Technology Publications.

King, S., King, M., & Rothwell, W. (2000). *The complete guide to training delivery: A competency-based approach.* New York: AMACOM.

Kleiner, A., & Roth, G. (2000). *Oil change: Perspectives on corporate transformation.* Los Angeles: Getty Center for Education in the Arts.

Koppett, K. (2001). *Training to imagine: Practical improvisational techniques to inspire creativity, enhance communication and develop leadership.* San Francisco: Stylus.

Learning Histories. (2002). *Learning Histories Web page.* Retrieved June 1, 2002, from http://www.learninghistories.com

Lieber, R. (1997, February 3). Storytelling: A new way to get close to your customer. *Fortune,* 102-108.

Locke, C., Levine, R., Searls, D., & Weinberger, D. (2001). *The Cluetrain Manifesto: The end of business as usual.* New York: Perseus.

Loughner, P., Harvey, D., & Milheim, W. (2001). Web-based instructional methods for corporate training curricula. In B. Khan (Ed.), *Web-based training* (pp. 185-190). Englewood Cliffs, NJ: Englewood Technology Publications.

Masie, E. (2001). No more digital page-turning. *E-Learning Magazine.* Retrieved May 31, 2002, from http://www.elearningmag.com/elearning/article/articleDetail.jsp?id=5054

McCloud, S. (1994). *Understanding comics.* New York: Kitchen Sink Press.

McCloud, S. (2000). *Reinventing comics.* New York: Harper Perennial.

Mitroff, I., & Kilmann, R. (1975, July). Stories managers tell: A new tool for organizational problem solving. *Management Review,* 18-28.

Modern Tales. (2002). *Modern Tales Web page.* Retrieved June 1, 2002, from http://www.moderntales.com

Murray, J. (1997). *Hamlet on the holodeck: The future of narrative cyberspace.* New York: The Free Press.

Neal, L. (2002). Storytelling at a distance. *E-Learn Magazine.* Retrieved May 31, 2002, from http://www.elearnmag.org/subpage/sub_page.cfm?section=7&list_item=1&page=1

Net Slaves. (2002). *Net Slaves Web page.* Retrieved June 1, 2002, from http://www.netslaves.com

Neuhauser, P. (1993). *Corporate legends and lore.* New York: McGraw-Hill.

Next Exit. (2002). *Next Exit Web page.* Retrieved June 1, 2002, from http://www.nextexit.com/nextexit/nextframeset.html

Nichani, M. (2002). Empathic instructional design. *E-Learning Post.* Retrieved May 31, 2002, from http://www.elearningpost.com/elthemes/empathicid.asp

Nichani, M., & Rajamanickam, V. (2002). Grassroots KM through blogging. *E-Learning Post.* Retrieved May 14, 2001, from http://www.elearningpost.com/elthemes/blog.asp

Parkin, M. (1998). *Tales for trainers: Using stories and metaphors to facilitate learning.* London: Kogan Page.

Parkin, M. (2001). *Tales for coaching: Using stories and metaphors with individuals and groups.* London: Kogan Page.

Pink, D. (1999). What's your story? *Fast Company, 21,* 32.

Ransdell, E. (2000, January/February). The Nike story? Just tell it! *Fast Company,* 44, 46.

Roth, G., & Kleiner, A. (1999). *Car launch: The human side of managing change.* Los Angeles: Getty Center for Education in the Arts.

Schank, R. (2001). *Designing world-class e-learning: How IBM, GE, Harvard Business School, and Columbia University are succeeding at e-learning.* New York: McGraw-Hill.

Schank, R., & Morson, G. (1995). *Tell me a story: Narrative and intelligence.* Chicago: Northwestern University Press.

Shaw, G., Brown, R., & Bromiley, P. (1998, May/June). Strategic stories: How 3M is rewriting business planning. *Harvard Business Review*, 1-8.

Simmons, A. (2001). *The story factor: Inspiration, influence, and persuasion through the art of storytelling.* Cambridge, MA: Perseus Books.

Simpkinson, C., & Simpkinson, A. (1983). *Sacred stories: A celebration of the power of story to transform and heal.* San Francisco: Harper.

Socratic Arts. (2002). *Socratic Arts Web page.* Retrieved June 1, 2002, from http://www.socraticarts.com

Stepanek, M. (2000). Tell me a (digital story). *Business Week Online.* Retrieved May 15, 2000, from http://www.businessweek.com/2000/00_20/b3681103.htm?scriptFramed

Taylor, D. (1996). *The healing power of stories: Creating yourself through the stories of your life.* New York: Doubleday.

Time Slips. (2002). *Time Slips Web page.* Retrieved June 1, 2002, from http://www.timeslips.org/go.html

Time2BreakFree. (2002). *Time2BreakFree Web page.* Retrieved June 1, 2002, from http://www.time2breakfree.com/

Vance, C. (1991). Formalizing storytelling in organizations: A key agenda for the design of training. *Journal of Organizational Change Management, 4*(3), 52-58.

Warshawsky, J. (2002). Tell me a story: A different approach to learning. *Cappuccino: The E-Newsletter for Change, Learning, and Performance.* Retrieved May 31, 2002, from http://www.dc.com/obx/pages.php?Name=cappuccino_elearning

Weinberger, S. (1999). The knowledge conversation. *Journal of the Hyperlinked Organization.* Retrieved September 30, 1999, from http://www.hyperorg.com/backissues/joho-sept30-99.html#knowledge

Weisbord, M. (1992). *Discovering common ground: How future search conferences bring people together to achieve breakthrough innovation, empowerment, shared vision, and collaborative action.* San Francisco: Berrett-Koehler.

Weisbord, M., & Janoff, S. (1995). *Future search: Finding common ground for action in organizations and communities.* San Francisco: Berrett-Koehler.

Weller, M. (2000). The use of narrative to provide a cohesive structure for a Web-based computing course. *Journal of Interactive Media in Education, 1,* 1-18.

Wilkins, A. (1984). The creation of company cultures: The role of stories and human resource systems. *Human Resource Management, 23*(1), 41-60.

Chapter IX

Use of Virtual Exhibits for Promoting Science Learning on The Webs of Science Centers

Leo Tan Wee-Hin, Nanyang Technological University, Singapore

R. Subramaniam, Nanyang Technological University, Singapore

Introduction

Science centers are institutions for the promotion of informal science learning to students and the public (Oppenheimer, 1972; Danilov, 1982; Tan & Subramaniam, 1998; Delacote, 1998). They have come to be regarded as part of a nation's scientific, technological, and educational infrastructure.

Science centers promote their mission objectives in a number of ways: exhibitions on a range of themes, science enrichment programs that complement science lessons taught in schools, mass-based promotional activities such as science festivals and competitions, and so on. However, exhibitions remain the core and distinctive feature of the attractions in science centers.

Exhibits in science centers are incubators of scientific knowledge. By interacting with the exhibits—for example, pushing a button to elicit a response or cranking a wheel to produce an effect the scope for exploratory learning and fostering of functional understanding is enhanced for visitors. A range of scientific concepts can be explored via interactive exhibitry. It is well established that interacting with exhibits in science centers contributes to gains in the affective and cognitive outcomes of the learning process (Sneider, Eason, & Friedman, 1979; Koran, Morrison, Lehman, Koran, & Gandara, 1984).

The World Wide Web presents a unique distribution medium for science centers to reach out beyond the confines of their traditional infrastructures. Many science centers have been compelled to colonize the new media in an effort to stay relevant and tap new avenues for promoting informal science learning. Their Web sites feature a range of resources (Tan & Subramaniam, 2003). Creating compelling online experiences of an interactive nature by hybridizing the traditional fare of science centers with the potential of the Internet presents opportunities for creating new educational experiences in science. Indeed, the Web has spawned a taxonomy of distinctive genres of learning for science centers to capitalize on in the pursuit of their mission objectives.

Virtual exhibits in the portals of science centers are new tools for providing instructional support in the acquisition of scientific concepts. Their utility have, however, not been explored adequately, save for some publications that focus generally on the virtual science center movement (for example, Jackson, 1996; Honeyman, 1998; Orfinger, 1998). In the framework for e-learning advanced by Khan (2001), it is of interest to note that online exhibits find mention as one of the categories.

The principal objectives of this chapter are fourfold:

1.   To show that virtual exhibits in the portals of science centers are effective resources for promotion of informal science learning

2.   To look at the technological tools available for the fabrication of virtual science exhibits

3.   To show examples of some Web sites of science centers where virtual exhibits are used, and to study their interesting features

4.   To comment on some of the issues involved in the popularization of science through virtual exhibits

Virtual Exhibits as Resources for Informal Science Learning

The use of instructional tools contributes greatly to achieving the desired outcomes of the learning process. Some examples of these tools include teacher-centric pedagogy, cooperative learning, simulation, and field trips. Such tools provide scaffolding contexts for anchoring conceptual frameworks related to the subject matter to varying extents, in the process promoting cognitive and affective gains for the learner. Such gains can be gauged through various assessment instruments.

The Internet provides a new media for judiciously transplanting physical exhibits into cyberspace in order for visitors to continue their learning experience in an authentic setting. Features of the new media which augment the utility of the educational experience include the range of technologies now available for creating compelling online experiences, the scope for enhancing interactivity in a manner that is different or not possible with physical exhibits, the opportunities for overcoming constraints imposed by the floor space of science centers, the potential for exploring new ideas not possible in the galleries of science centers, and the flexibility to reach out simultaneously to a large audience.

Virtual exhibits can be defined as cyberspace-based content that aims to illustrate scientific concepts through interaction by the visitor. It is similar to gallery exhibits but differs from the latter in that the curation is done in the digital realm.

A major drawback of the teacher-centered pedagogy in science is that students often do not see the content, as disbursed in textbooks and lecture notes, as being sufficiently engaging or meaningful, and they are not motivated to explore the subtleties and nuances inherent in the scientific concepts, save for the purpose of learning and regurgitating these during examinations. In contrast, virtual exhibits use technological mediation to make the scientific concepts more meaningful and also capitalize on the natural curiosity of students in wanting to explore more about the natural world. Such engagement presents opportunities for incorporating problem-solving skills and reflective thought in the learning process. The locus of control gravitates more towards the student through migration of emphasis from intrinsic content to process, thus providing motivational contexts for him to continue his learning experience.

As will be shown shortly by a few examples, virtual exhibits provide sound instructional contexts for mediating the learning experience in science. The following are some of the reasons:

- It fosters functional understanding via interaction by the visitor.
- It offers a multiplicity of modes for exploring a concept.
- It permits contextual perspectives in the subject matter to be interlaced in the design.
- It permits technological mediation in the learning process.
- It fosters an interplay between learning and leisure through the embedding of game elements in the design.
- It uses visually rich media to position the exhibit to visitors.
- It provides support for the acquisition of learning skills through creative thinking, problem solving, and inquiry.
- Hybridized contexts are provided for the conceptual and practical aspects of the cognitive variables that need to be appreciated for an understanding of the scientific content embedded in the exhibit
- It promotes active learning, in contradistinction to passive learning.

Technological Tools for the Fabrication of Virtual Science Exhibits

The use of new technologies has greatly facilitated the induction of creative and innovative elements in the process of interpretation of various concepts in science through cyberspace exhibitry. Curatorial considerations and the emphasis that science centers wish to foster dictate the kind of exhibit that can be showcased. It can develop along two axes, static and interactive, with the latter being more bandwidth-intensive and expensive to set up.

In the design stage, creative inputs are required from a team comprising curators, designers, educationists, and software specialists. The team has to have an understanding of the traditional elements of conventional exhibitry as well as of how to configure an exhibit idea for the digital realm.

A discussion on some of the important tools used for art museum exhibits in cyberspace has been presented by Duchastel (1996), Tinkler and Friedman (1998), and Spadaccini (2001), and these are generally valid for virtual science exhibits. A brief review of some of these key tools is presented here.

Java

This is a versatile programming language that allows the dreams of the cybercurator to be turned into reality on the Web. It is only limited by the creativity and experience of the programming team.

Java Script

This is the most important tool available for the curator of virtual exhibits. It integrates the various components of a Web page in a harmonious manner, and also allows other tools to be combined in creative and innovative ways.

Shockwave Flash

This software allows for the creation of realistic 'flash' pieces in a virtual exhibit, in a way that does not guzzle up expensive bandwidth. It thus allows for quicker downloads. It is possible to integrate streaming audio with Shockwave Flash and, with the use of Java Script, trigger a flash in any part of the Web page.

Shockwave for Director

These are larger files compared to Shockwave Flash, and are thus ideal for incorporating game elements in the virtual exhibit. Being static files, a disadvantage of both Shockwave Flash and Shockwave for Director is that once they are integrated into a virtual exhibit, it is difficult to upgrade the exhibit further without extensive reprogramming.

Real Media, Windows Media, and Quick Time

These allow for the transmission of streaming video on a narrowband platform, thus obviating the necessity to download entire files. On a broadband platform, the quality of the user experience will, of course, be distinctly superior on account of the greater transmission rates achieved for data and picture frames.

Embedded Audio, MIDI, and Beatnik

For the creation of the appropriate mood setting, sound effects are frequently triggered in the background of a virtual exhibit in the form of sample loops, MIDI, or Beatnik files. While Real Audio is good for narration, WAV files are the choice for interaction-triggered sound.

Dynamic HTML

This tool facilitates manipulation of any aspect of an HTML document in real time. Other functionalities include creation of layers that move upon user interaction or those which appear or disappear.

Quick Cam

This is the tool of choice for providing a streaming video feed, and thus allows the visitor to relish live telepresence in an institution.

Live Picture Viewer

With this Web-interfaced tool, a virtual visitor is exposed to a live show of the exhibition galleries of a science center.

The foregoing tools allow for the authoring of virtual productions that foster innovative learning experiences, as well as create learning interfaces that are not possible in the physical exhibit. It is essential that they be judiciously embedded in context, for otherwise they may appear invasive or detract the user from the learning experience.

It is important to note that there is a difference between real-world manipulation of exhibits and cyberspace manipulation of exhibits. While the former promotes experiential learning via a range of senses, in the latter there would be some degree of impoverishment of the experience; for example, currently cyberspace has limitations in the savoring of tactile and aural feedback.

Even trivial issues such as information layout need to be properly addressed in the design brief so as to lessen cognitive overload and visual fatigue. Economic use of graphics and eschewing of flamboyant design elements are also essential, for otherwise access can be sluggish, and this detracts the user from the learning experience. Multimedia files for downloading must be placed in the lowest hierarchy on the Web page so as to minimize delay in downloading. As a rough guide, images of about 2 Mb or more would generally cause slow downloads on a narrowband platform (Bowen, Bennet, & Johnson, 1998).

With the appropriate design elements, virtual exhibits can confer a new dimension in the learning of science through the creation of compelling experiences. This is important in ensuring that they do not degenerate into surrogate versions of gallery exhibits.

Examples of Virtual Exhibits for Informal Science Learning

Many science centers now have a Web presence, and virtual science exhibits are available for interaction here. We focus in this section on three virtual exhibits from different science centers. In our opinion, these are good examples of how virtual exhibits should be positioned.

Tower of Hanoi

This is a classic exhibit found in most mathematics exhibitions in science centers. Essentially, it challenges the visitor to transfer a fixed number of discs from one peg to another peg in the minimum number of ways, subject to certain constraints—only one disc can be moved at a time, a larger diameter disc cannot be placed on a smaller diameter disc, and the same initial arrangement of discs must be replicated on the other peg. The physical exhibit is fairly easy to interact with if there are three discs. Where it exceeds three discs, the number of moves required becomes progressively more. This puts a stress on the labor, time, and patience of visitors! The online version (see Figure 1), in contrast, mimics the physical exhibit but allows the number of moves to be completed faster and, also, in an interesting manner.

In the version employed at the portal of the Singapore Science Centre (http://www.science.edu.sg), the instructional strategy used is conducive for adding value to the learning experience. Interesting features include:

Figure 1. Virtual exhibit on Tower of Hanoi in the portal of the Singapore Science Center

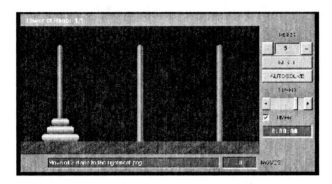

- Flexibility to vary number of discs
- Timer to monitor the duration taken to complete the task (the ticking timer aids in promoting fast thinking!)
- An autosolve option to permit illustration of how the requisite number of discs are moved, while a speed scroll is available to hasten or slow down this process
- A reset button to bring all discs to the starting position for playing the game again or for increasing the level of difficulty by incrementing the number of discs
- Convenient interaction by just clicking on a disc and dragging it to the peg/s

By presenting the mathematical concept of permutation/combination as a game, interest is fostered in the acquisition of concepts through active learning strategies.

Mix-n-Match

This is a virtual exhibit (see Figure 2) found in the portal of the Exploratorium in San Francisco (http://www.exploratorium.edu).

The gallery version of the exhibit can be found in the physical sciences gallery of most science centers. Essentially, it allows the visitor to see how the three primary colors of light—red, green, and blue—can be mixed together in various proportions to produce light of any color. The scope for creative mixing is, however, limited, as light from three monochromatic lamps—representing the three primary colors of light—does not allow for fine control of the light intensity in order to be able to see more than a handful of colors. Also, the ambient light frequently interferes with the color mixing so that the nuances of the color mixing are not readily apparent.

Figure 2. Virtual exhibit on Mix-n-Match in the portal of the Exploratorium

In contrast, the virtual version elevates the gallery exhibit to a higher level of learning through interactive features possible only on the Web. Tremendous scope is afforded to vary the intensity of the three primary colors of light to varying extents to create, in principle, over 16 million colors!

The key features that make the Mix-n-Match exhibit a good example of a virtual exhibit are:

- A good choice of design to showcase the concept—the background color can be changed and the mixture of light at the center can be judiciously manipulated to achieve balance/color parity through click buttons on each of the colors

- At any moment, it is possible to check the color levels used in the game with respect to the theoretical equivalents

- Use of novel context for exploration

- Insightful curation, which has turned a simple concept in physics into an interesting game

Slide Through a Lifetime

This is the online version of the Amazing Aging Machine exhibit found in the gallery of the Ontario Science Centre (http://www.ontariosciencecentre.ca) in Canada. Essentially, it adds decades to the face of a young visitor so that he could see how he would look as he ages.

In the online version (see Figure 3), the screen contains the image of a young boy and girl. By clicking on the bar with the mouse and dragging it slowly along, years are progressively added to their faces. For each age milestone, appropriate textual material comes on screen to convey salient points of biological interest. This is useful in encouraging the visitor to try to understand the science behind aging.

Figure 3. Virtual exhibit on "Slide Through a Lifetime" in the portal of the Ontario Science Centre

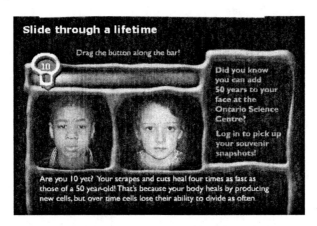

The key features of this exhibit which marks it out as an example of a good online exhibit are:

- Simplicity in design of exhibit
- Ease of navigation, which is achieved by simply dragging the mouse along the bar
- Simple vignettes of scientific information embedded at various age milestones to aid learning
- Seamless morphing of images as they age

The above are just a few examples of virtual exhibits. More examples are available in the portals of other science and technology centers. A listing of all such centers can be found on the Web site of the Association of Science-Technology Centers (http://www.astc.org).

Some Issues Related to the Popularization of Virtual Exhibits

In recent times, online exhibits in the portals of science centers have attracted considerable attention from the public, seeking cyberspace experiences that mimic those available in the galleries of science centers. This has engendered a number of issues of interest, the more important of which are discussed here.

The effectiveness of knowledge transfer though the use of virtual exhibits is very much influenced by the educational elements embedded in the exhibits, though the richness of the experiential environment is also an important factor. They need to be pitched at a level that the public can identify with, rather than at a level for those immersed in the catechism of a science subject! Good instructional contexts and proactive learning scenarios contribute further towards sound pedagogical practice. A learning experience hinging on constructivism is possible with innovative curation. A delicate balance between leisure and learning has also to be struck in the design brief.

The prime determinant in ensuring the quality of the learning experience is the user-friendliness of the virtual exhibit. Instructional contexts that permit guided exploration are important. Site navigability needs to be smooth in order to ensure usability; the requisite tools must be made available to the user for extracting the desired information and to ensure that the learning experience is not distracted by extraneous considerations. A common strategy is menu options, which allow for directedness of the learning experience. A judicious combination of curatorial choice, design elements, pedagogical contexts, and user interfaces can ensure that virtual exhibits, while not engendering the experience of gallery exhibits, do mimic the salient aspects of the gallery experience to a significant extent.

The quality of the user experience is dictated by the choice of network connection, whether narrowband, or broadband via cable modem or digital subscriber lines. On a narrowband platform, pages generally take a longer time to load, while plug-ins—to complement browser capabilities—take an even longer time to download.

Currently, digital exhibits are rather expensive to fabricate since they involve the expertise and efforts of curators, designers, educationists, and software specialists. A gallery exhibit, in contrast, can be developed at modest cost by using in-house expertise and resources in the workshop. On the Web site of any science center, the number of virtual exhibits compared to other resources is thus necessarily low, even though such exhibits are considered to be the choice offerings in the portal.

Though assessment tools for the evaluation of exhibits in the galleries of science centers are available in the literature (Sneider et al., 1979), this is not the case for virtual exhibits. Hit counts are often used to tout the popularity of a virtual exhibit. However, these give only general feedback. Questions such as the effectiveness of the virtual exhibits in promoting learning, the quality of the user experience, and the dwell time are not apparent from hit counts. Also, it makes no distinction between new and repeat visitors. Analysis of server log data would be better.

Conclusion

Virtual exhibits provide useful instructional support for exploring scientific concepts through inquiry. The creation of dynamic learning environments for experimentation through technological mediation, as well as the fostering of endogenous play elements in the learning process, are effective strategies for engaging visitors. This motivates visitors to strive towards acquisition of new skills and knowledge, thus opening up enhanced possibilities for knowledge transfer in cyberspace.

References

Bowen, J. P., Bennet, J., & Johnson, J. (1998, April 22-25). Virtual visits to virtual museums. In *Proceedings of the Museums and the Web Conference*, Toronto, Canada.

Carrie, B. (1998). Museums in cyberspace: Serving a virtual public on the technocratic frontier. Retrieved from http://www.du.edu/-cheaucha/cybermuseums.html

Danilov, V. J. (1982). *Science and technology centers.* Boston: MIT Press.

Delacote, G. (1998). Putting science in the hands of the public. *Science, 280,* 252-253.

Duchastel, P., & Spahn, S. (1996). *Design for Web-based learning.* Paper presented at WebNet '96 Conference, San Francisco.

Honeyman, B. (1998, April). Real vs virtual visits: Issues for science centers. *Australasian Science & Technology Exhibitors Network News.* Retrieved from http://www.astenetwork.net/issues/virtual_visits.html

Jackson, R. (1996). The virtual visit: Towards a new concept for the electronic science center. In *Proceedings of the Conference on Here and How: Improving the Presentation of Contemporary Science and Technology in Museums and Science Centers,* London.

Khan, B. H. (2001). A framework for Web-based learning. In B. H. Khan (Ed.), *Web-based training.* Englewood Cliffs, NJ: Educational Technology Publications.

Koran, J. J., Morrison, L., Lehman, J. R., Koran, M. L., & Gandara, L. (1984). Attention and curiosity in museums. *Journal of Research in Science Teaching, 21*(4), 357-363.

Oppenheimer, F. (1972). The Exploratorium: A playful museum combines perception and art in science education. *American Journal of Physics, 40,* 978-984.

Orfinger, B. (1998). Virtual science museums as learning environments: Interactions for education. *The Informal Learning Review,* 1-10.

Sneider, C., Eason, L., & Friedman, A. (1979). Summative evaluation of a participatory science exhibit. *Science Education, 63,* 25-36.

Spadaccini, J. (2001). Streaming audio and video: New challenges and opportunities for museums. In *Proceedings of the Museums and the Web Conference.*

Tan, W. H. L, & Subramaniam, R. (2003). Virtual science centers: Web-based environments for promotion of non-formal science education. In A. K. Aggarwal (Ed.), *Web-based education: Learning from experience* (pp. 308-329). Hershey, PA: Idea Group Inc.

Tan, W. H. L., & Subramaniam, R. (1998). Developing nations need to popularize science. *New Scientist, 2139,* 52.

Tinkler, M., & Freedman, M. (1998, April 22-25). Online exhibitions: A philosophy of design and technological implementation. In *Proceedings of the Museums and the Web Conference,* Toronto, Canada.

Chapter X

Flexible Learning:
Onsite!

Claus Witfelt, IT University of Copenhagen, Denmark

Introduction

Flexible learning is a term usually connected with IT and the dimensions time and space, for instance when using CSCL-systems (e.g., Blackboard, Sitescape, or FirstClass) to combine onsite learning with online learning in further education, typically with few, intensive onsite seminars separated by online periods where the students work, communicate, and learn via the Internet.

This chapter takes a different approach to flexible learning and how technologies from distributed, flexible learning can be used in everyday university teaching and learning—onsite learning. Onsite learning is characterized not by virtual and distributed processes, but actual presence of the students.

In the current study, we have identified a number of scenarios for these learning contexts and tried a number of systems. In the chapter we will discuss the problems, the pros and cons of the various scenarios, and in short describe some of the technologies we have worked with.

The Course

We have for three years taught the master-level courses *Learning and IT* (LOT) and *Learning and IT Innovation* at the IT-University of Copenhagen. The theme of the course is e-learning—and more: learning, IT, and pedagogy in a broader context, making the students aware of these dimensions in design, communication, and media. The students have very different educational backgrounds and bachelor-level education: medicine, architecture, graphical design, teachers, and many other subjects.

In the courses the students work with both theories, analysis of products and learning contexts, and special needs of various groups. From this point of departure, they define their own projects and implement solutions, for example, design prototypes of CBT, e-learning, or CSCL-solutions. This makes the course both theoretical and practical.

The course lasts for 12 weeks, with 12 full days of lectures, exercises, teamwork, supervision, and other forms—where the students are actually working on campus. Besides the work on campus, the students also study the literature, analyze solutions, and work on projects, usually in a combination of online and onsite work. After the course, many students choose to continue the work in project groups, master projects, and so forth.

The backbone of the course is an educational science textbook (Illeris, 2002), introducing general theories of learning, a compendium, and a lot of digital, supplementary materials, examples, and so forth. The compendium and the digital resource contain various texts about key issues among the themes the students choose to work with, popular issues, current debates, and so on. The general textbooks are the fixed parts of the course; the other texts form the dynamic part which denotes a space in which the course can be flexible.

Students who participate in these courses are usually quite pleased with the flexibility, for instance, that it is possible to add current links and new texts from one lecture to another, for instance if a discussion needs some following up, more materials, and so on. In the last part of the course, the students can actually make requests for lectures about specific themes related to the student projects or current debates. This makes the course dynamic, actual, and plastic, and our students appreciate this plasticity in their evaluations. It is a turn from the sage-on-the-stage, the lonely professor given the same lecture year in, year out, and it calls for a special, very dynamic digital infrastructure. In other studies though, the students have not been interested in this flexibility (e.g., Dehn, Hansen, & Witfelt, 2003).

The Scenarios

In order to meet these needs, we have identified a number of learning scenarios in the course design. We want to support each of these scenarios with digital structure to (1) support learning and (2) teach the students how to use various systems for teaching and learning.

Many of our students after graduation find jobs in the e-learning industry, publishing houses, or other similar teaching and learning context, so we find it very important to use an active learning approach, giving the students concrete experiences with the technology. The use of learning scenarios is described several places, for instance by Bent

Andresen in the European *Pedactice* project (see Andresen, 2002). In a learning scenario we can focus on *who* does *what, when,* and *with* what purpose.

- **Scenario 1. Distributing Dynamic Course Information—Course teachers distribute information to the students, for instance to follow up on discussions in a recent lecture:** One way to make the course flexible is to distribute information, which texts to read, links, examples, and so forth from one week to another. In this way, we as teachers and course designers can use a lot of online materials, giving the course a dynamic nature. This collection of links, text, and examples can be modified and reused next semester.

- **Scenario 2. Distributing Dynamic Content—The teacher distributes actual contents to the students in order to provide new materials and supplementary texts to a forthcoming lecture:** This scenario is not about information and instruction, but about texts (i.e., actual content). Some—few—texts are printed in a compendium with course materials, but then everything has to be prepared a long time before the course starts.

- **Scenario 3. Team Supervision—The supervisor communicates with the students in order to scaffold their project work:** This scenario has to do with supervision of teams, and how supervisors and teams can communicate about projects, texts, and so forth.

- **Scenario 4. Team Collaboration—Students communicate with each other in order to finish their projects:** This scenario has to do with the communication between the members of the teams, but also communication between teams—for example, how the students can communicate about their projects, texts and so on.

- **Scenario 5. Examples and Demonstrations—This includes the use of learning objects and online e-learning solutions:** Teachers present links, texts, cases, and so forth to each other in order to inspire, see how the professionals do things, and so forth.

The Technologies

Information and Content Distribution

The first year we intended to use LUVIT (for all scenarios), a Swedish e-learning system (see http://www.luvit.com). The students preferred to use other systems (such as the Danish system Groupcare [http://www.groupcare.dk], e-mail, and the German BSCW [http://www.orbiteam.de]) for Scenarios 3-4. The only feature which was actually used was the bulletin function (Scenario 1).

Next course, we used e-mail (for Scenario 1) and Usenet newsgroups (Scenarios 2-5). The solution worked quite well on other courses, but here, the students again preferred to use e-mail for Scenarios 3-4. Very few used the opportunity to combine newsgroups with mail.

As a consequence of the fact that the only feature used in the very extensive Luvit-system was the bulletin-function, we chose to use a Weblog/blogger for the third course, also to demonstrate the use of this Web-service in a learning context for the students (for more information on the use of Weblogs in learning and project management, see Schrage, 2004). This system worked quite well and most of the students appreciated it, even though the system only served as solution to Scenario 1 and, to a minor extent, Scenario 5).

The last, but maybe not final chapter of the story about the use of e-learning-systems in the learning and IT courses is about the professional e-learning-system, ABC Academy, produced by Danish Probe (http://www.probe.dk). This content management system is used by Microsoft Business Solutions, Canon, and Kuwait Petrol, among many others.

Communication and IT—Nomadicity (Scenarios 3 and 4)

Introducing e-learning systems in this context can be quite difficult, since a lot of the work and studies are done onsite. We often lack the very good arguments for using conference systems like the arguments used on the Voksplan education (Witfelt 2004), where approximately 75% of the work on the course is done online. In this context, e-mail is, when it comes to digital communication, 'the king'. The system that we had most success with in the first period was actually to e-mail course information to all the students. Still, this system is not without problems: students do not like to receive documents that are too large by e-mail; course teachers must also be IT administrators when students change e-mail addresses, which they do quite often; if someone does not receive the weekly e-mail, a redistribution will have to be made, which can be quite tedious; and to repeat the course is rather tedious.

Another positive problem is that we are dealing with IT professionals and IT nomadic students (the term used in Andresen, 2003). If the students do not like a system, they just find another, like the nomads in the dessert: If there is not enough water and food in an area, they just go to another region.

Collaborative Learning

E-mail and free community services work, but we are lacking one aspect of learning: collaborative learning in the class, not only in the teams. In the Voksplan project (Witfelt, 2001), we used a totally open conference system structure. This made the communication very open, making learning visual and communicatable. Students could benefit not only from their own project work and supervision, but also from others. So it would be very nice to have a very powerful system that integrates students' online communication and collaboration with the material distribution.

ABC Academy can deliver both information and content (Scenarios 1 and 2), and also has some students build communication in a newsgroup style, though our students—the IT-nomads—find other solutions more powerful. Through this system, we can give a course a dynamic nature, inserting new materials, texts, cases, links, or pictures from one week to another.

Senario 5

ABC Academy also facilitates learning objects. We are actually able to see exactly which objects (e.g., texts, etc.) the students have browsed and printed, and how much time they have spent doing it. In a larger perspective it may also be interesting to present modular interactive materials in the shape of learning objects, but at present this is not a very important point. If the themes of the course were more technical/scientific, learning objects would probably be a lot more interesting. Learning object technology is a part of the curriculum, so it is interesting to present a system and some objects to the students. Learning objects is the subject of intense interest from the Danish Ministry of Education (2004).

From Flexible Distributed Learning to Flexible Learning—Onsite

In this chapter, we have presented and discussed some experiences from our course, where we use many of the strategies learned from flexible distributed learning and applied them to onsite courses—hopefully turning this into flexible learning.

In order to describe what technological artifacts we need to make the onsite learning flexible, we have described our course in a scenario-based manner and identified a number of scenarios. Of course there are many more aspects to this (see for instance the multiple dimensions in Badrul Khan's framework for e-learning in Chapter 1 of this book) which need to be taken into consideration and deal with the flexibility: methods, teacher and student roles, classroom interactions, organization, materials, learning environments, learning styles, forms of assessment, time, and space. Other studies will have to cover these important aspects of flexible learning in presence.

We believe that using e-learning systems like the ones mentioned in this chapter can actually be a way to take some of the advantages from distance learning and make education more flexible. Learning objects, SCORM, and IMS compatibility may be very important, but not quite yet.

The bulletin function and functions for the distribution of information are by far the most important (Scenarios 1 and 2). Features for communication between students and supervisors are very important as well, but since our students are 'IT nomads', we have not found the ultimate system yet.

It is still important to the course to be able to demonstrate professional as well as experimental technologies in action (Scenario 5). This scenario has several aspects—we can provide a lot of dynamics by adding links, but right now mostly about how we can demonstrate Scorm-compatible learning objects. Wikipedia or TWiki (Thoney, 2004) could be a fun technology to work with.

E-learning systems like ABC Academy and the others mentioned in this chapter help us reuse materials and create a dynamic course—the first step to having flexible learning in presence. A very powerful technology, which included the communication as well and integrated this communication and project work in the information distribution, would be appreciated.

Acknowledgments

The author wishes to thank the students of the course, Steffen Löfvall from Netstrategen (http://www.netstrategen.dk) and Jesper Hundebøll from Linqx (http://www.linqx.dk).

References

Andresen, B. B. (2001). *WP6—The art of seeing the wood and the trees. Teachers' new competencies in terms of multimedia literacy and ICT genre didactical competences.* Retrieved January 6, 2004, from http://www.vordingbsem.dk/pedactice

Andresen, B. B. (2003). *Nomadiske elevers kommunikative kompetencer—Muligheder og udfordringer.* Retrieved January 6, 2004, from http://www.dpu.dk/site.asp?p=2796

Danish Ministry of Education. (2004). *RUMLO report.* Retrieved January 6, 2004, from http://udviklings.eksperimentrum.dk/doc/logbaseintrorumlo-30.pdf

Danish Probe. (n.d.). Retrieved from http://www.probe.dk

Dehn, S., Hansen, R. E., & Witfelt, C. (2003). *A Sisyphos quest and a IT quantum leap.* Educational Multimedia International. London: Taylor Francis Group.

Friesen, N. (2003, April 13). *Three objections to learning objects.* Retrieved from http://phenom.educ.ualberta.ca/~nfriesen/

Illeris, K. (2002). *Learning between Freud, Piaget and Marx.* Samfundslitteratur.

IT University of Copenhagen. (2004). Retrieved January 6, 2004, from http://www.itu.dk

Schrage, M. (2004). *The virtues of chitchat.* Retrieved January 6, 2004, from http://www.cio.com/archive/051504/work.html

Thoney, P. (2003). *TWiki™—A Web-based collaboration platform.* Retrieved January 6, 2004, http://twiki.sourceforge.net/

Witfelt, C. (2001). *Voksplan, en antologi om en fleksibelt tilrettelagt uddannelse.* Retrieved from http://claus.witfelt.person.emu.dk/antologi.pdf

Chapter XI

Asynchronous Content Design for Flexible Learning:
The Macro and Micro Level of Frameworks to Share Knowledge Online Between Professionals and Community

Gülsün Kurubacak, Anadolu University, Turkey

T. Volkan Yuzer, Anadolu University, Turkey

Introduction

Gradually, more institutions around the globe are becoming involved in dynamic change over a long period to provide time- and location-independent asynchronous e-learning opportunities. With the potential of network-based technologies, asynchronous e-learning has become a powerful, global, interactive, economic, and dynamic as well as democratic tool of virtual learning (Khan, 1997). Asynchronous e-learning provides an opportunity to build flexible online programs for sharing knowledge with virtual educational contents. To generate cogent asynchronous e-learning opportunities, however, it is important to analyze the principles, ethics, and pitfalls of sharing knowledge online between professionals and community. Therefore, asynchronous content must be designed carefully based on macro- and micro-level frameworks, which provide us with elaborating *open, flexible*, and *distributed* virtual learning milieus.

Asynchronous content must be designed based on democratic and multicultural curriculum understandings and approaches for diverse racial, ethnic, economical, political, educational, and cultural groups. It also must investigate the principles, ethics, and pitfalls that professionals (all online workers, such as online designers, policy makers, virtual workers, online learners, etc.) and community members (all stakeholders, such as parents, siblings, administrative personnel from outside organizations, knowledge workers in other organizations, etc.) can combine—the learning philosophy, concepts, and resources for multicultural theory and praxis—to share knowledge online.

The main purpose of this chapter is to discuss the design principles, ethics, and pitfalls of asynchronous contents in e-learning systems, and also to introduce macro- and micro-level frameworks on how to share knowledge online between professionals and community members. The developed frameworks will acquire learning roles for educators who integrate distance online activities in their traditional courses, and online workers who design, deliver, implement, and evaluate asynchronous course content. Moreover, these frameworks can provide useful assessment methods and techniques for e-learning providers and producers to improve their understanding of the cutting-edge technology applications into asynchronous milieus. Finally, these frameworks can encourage professionals and communities to plan and manage their learning activities with a high degree of personal control and autonomy, to reflect on their personal learning experiences and incorporate new information on how to share knowledge and work together online.

Theoretical Background of the Study

There is a need to investigate clearly how asynchronous e-learning content actually features collaboration between professional and community (Lessing, 2001). Also, focusing on how virtual learners can negotiate the meaning and usability of e-content by themselves is very important to assess their understanding, founded on culturally shared procedures for constructing meaning in online contexts. Online knowledge sharing to construct new schemas and revised existing ones in individuals' minds must offer virtual participants a wide range of viewpoints to reverence individual cultural differences and give more attention to diversity issues in the new millennium.

These frameworks help online workers and learners understand how they manage their tasks, how they keep a diverse attention, and how technology features in their activity in asynchronous online content. Finally, in this chapter conducted within these frameworks, the researchers largely focus on categorizing collaboration, interaction, and communication according to degrees of shared knowledge with the principles, ethics, and pitfalls of asynchronous content design.

The Macro-Level Framework
for Asynchronous Contents

The most essential elements of the macro-level framework to design, implement, and evaluate asynchronous e-learning content are the social, political, economical, institutional, technological, and educational backgrounds of the country, which uses asynchronous content for educational purposes in virtual learning programs. This macro-level framework for any developed, developing, and underdeveloped countries must be discussed based on the existing circumstances and potential of their educational systems. Regardless of the developments and improvements in the digital world over the decade, there are still many challenges and risks to establish, deliver, and implement online content via asynchronous programs.

Figure 1. The macro framework to design asynchronous contents

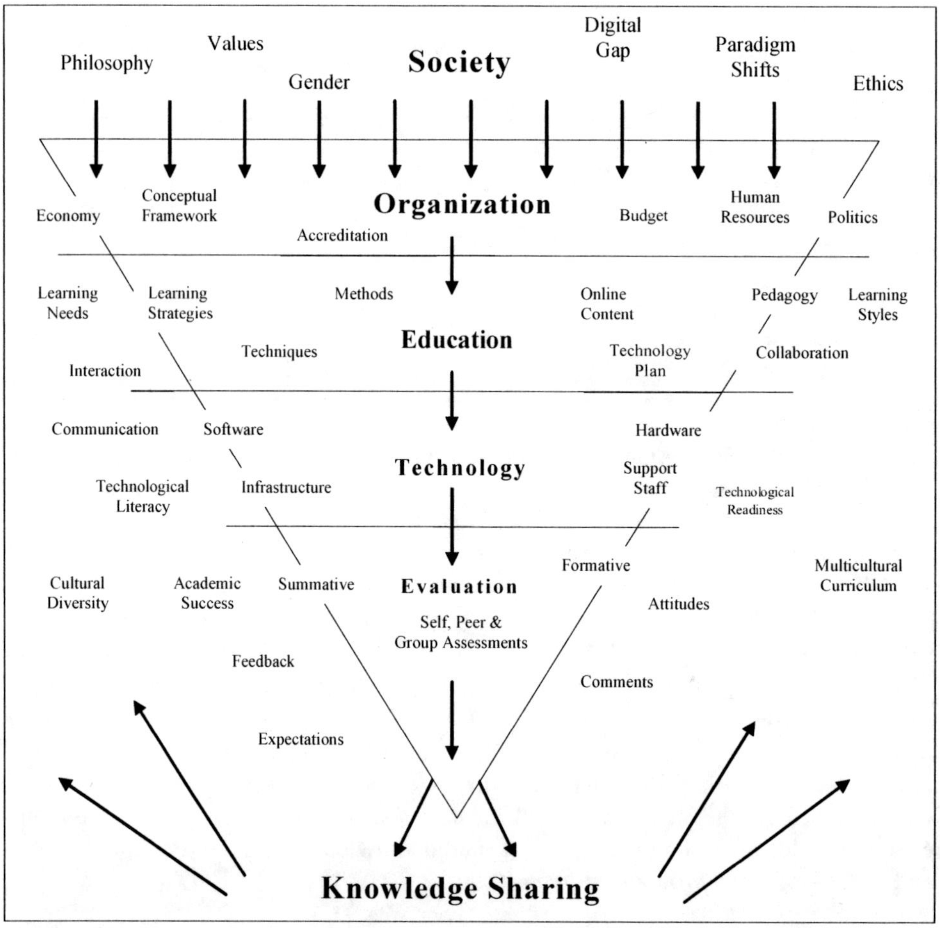

Launching and maintaining e-learning content needs not only money and other funds, but also well-educated human resources for online support services (Bonk & King, 1998). For that reason, each country cannot use and integrate the same frameworks into their asynchronous online content. Online workers can largely focus on the complex learning problems with their unique answers of their societies based on the presented ideas of these developed frameworks in this chapter. Moreover, online workers can help their colleagues and stakeholders in communities build not only progressive, but also integrated asynchronous virtual content together to share and exchange knowledge with these flexible frameworks. These workers also focus attention on the principles, ethics, and pitfalls of sharing and exchanging knowledge in virtual milieus to create asynchronous online course content with learning objects and work on e-learning policies within the assessment of asynchronous design processes based on the opportunities of their society.

Yuzer and Kurubacak (2003) discuss a SITE (Society, Intuitions, Technology, and Education) framework to integrate the cutting-edge technologies in enhanced-TV applications in distance education. Based on this framework, to share knowledge via any asynchronous content designs in any developed, developing, and underdeveloped countries, first we have to define and analyze the five indispensable components that help us clearly realize the *open, flexible,* and *distributed* nature of asynchronous e-learning content, to share knowledge online between professionals and community (see Figure 1): (1) society, (2) organization, (3) education, (4) technology, and (5) evaluation. The perspectives of social values and ethics, organizational structure and management, educational policies and strategies, technological improvements and innovations, and evolutional methods and techniques help learners, workers, and stakeholders in e-learning communities accept this framework broadly.

Society and Asynchronous Content Design

Society, one of crucial elements of the macro-level framework for designing asynchronous e-learning content, has different dimensions. There is no doubt that the emerging technologies create digital gaps between younger age groups and older people. The generation growing up with the digital world can accept network-based communication without problems (Burniske & Monke, 2001) whereas the older, not living in the digital world, can refuse to share knowledge with others online. In the developing countries, more elder people have a greater chance to interact with others via cutting-edge technologies. The society can upgrade its lifestyle with digital technologies gradually, and help its citizens get ready for these innovations. On the contrary, because of the lack of money sources and budgeting problems to buy or produce and invest new technologies, it can be too early for the elders in developing and underdeveloping countries to communicate with this asynchronous content to create a knowledge network among participants in the society.

Therefore, the economical conditions of society are the second important element to improve learning through asynchronous content. To share knowledge online, learners must have some devices, such as a computer with a high-speed Internet connection, printer, scanner, and so forth, to interact with other learners from the globe. There is no difficulty if online learners already have these gadgets; the problems arise when they must buy all the essential digital tools, which are very expensive, or borrow these devices for long-term or short-term use from their institutions or other foundations. This depends on the financial conditions and budgeting politics of online learning providers and communities.

Online workers must focus on the ethics and values of their society to design asynchronous contents for diverse learner groups, especially those from underserved communities. They also must design asynchronous e-learning content with a democratic and multicultural curriculum to transform the related concepts of diverse racial, ethnic, economic, and cultural groups in their community and also from the world. Asynchronous content design must help virtual learners improve their higher-order skills (Jonassen, 2000) to better understand what cultural, ethnic, economical, and political diversity is. Moreover, it does make professionals and community members demystify the design, and deliver and implement strategies for effective online learning based on existing philosophical and political arrangements in society.

Organization and Asynchronous Content Design

Organization is concerned with the administrative and academic affairs, and online learner support services based on its conceptual framework. These issues associated with network-based asynchronous education systems are related with the needs assessment, organizational change, budgeting and return on investment, and partnerships with other organizations. The most crucial element of organization issue is that online learning providers must give attention to accreditation, technology support services for learners with and without disabilities, and marketing and recruitment information.

For professionals and communities to share knowledge successfully, administrative, technological, and educational support staff are vital in the design of efficient asynchronous content, as communicating via online learning applications can be quite complex for end users. Traditional educational organizations may not use and integrate these new ways in learning successfully. The major reason is that they do not have adequate financial investments and budgeting strategies for developing asynchronous learning materials, and hiring and training support staff regularly (Palloff & Pratt, 1999). Accordingly, without well-educated staff support, conventional organizations can deliver educational methods and strategies with weak quality via asynchronous content.

Needless to say, any high-quality asynchronous content design requires well-budgeted strategies and opportunities. For that reason, the operating budget for online education must provide extensive support services with regular upgrading activities to professionals and participants of communities. Therefore, the number of enrollments can be increased whereas the dropout rate can be reduced.

Education and Asynchronous Content Design

Virtual education with the emerging technologies strongly addresses at least two-way interaction, collaboration and facilitation for sharing knowledge online. This issue is related with knowledge distribution and inside collaboration as well as external interaction via asynchronous contents, which provide new rich learning experiences for global learners (Thomas & Carswell, 2000). Asynchronous content design, also, has an enormous impact on creating well-design communication activities between professionals and community; because it can provide totally new ways and experiences to share knowledge and resources from the world.

Asynchronous content design must address variety of learning styles and types (Collier & Yoder, 2002). Therefore, there can be some challenges for online learners that these issues affect not only their attitudes, but also success when they do interact with each other via asynchronous contents: (1) the degree of communication, collaboration, and interaction between professionals and community; (2) the amount of difficulty and barriers in sharing knowledge via asynchronous contents; (3) equal access opportunities to asynchronous content; (4) the difficulty level of delivered asynchronous content; (5) the communication abilities of virtual learners; and (6) the amount of valuable knowledge to share online. When sharing knowledge online, professionals and community members can face the educational issues of culturally, ethnically, and racially mixed heritage. Therefore, if their perceptions are based on any stereotypes and misconceptions on race, ethnicity, gender, social class, sexual orientation, religion, disability, and so forth, they must review their insights about others from around the globe.

Technology and Asynchronous Content Design

Based on their technological experiences and knowledge, as well as their savings accounts, professionals and community members influence asynchronous content providers to select the best technological solutions for knowledge sharing online (Picciano, 2001). Especially in the developed societies, most virtual learners can have at

Figure 2. The micro framework to design asynchronous contents

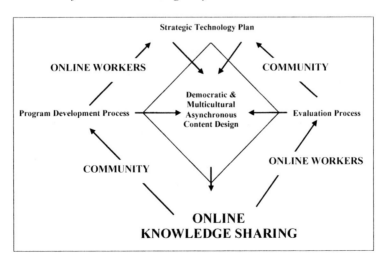

least one computer with a high-speed connection at their homes. These users in the knowledge share network can also have a computer with an Internet connection in their offices. Therefore, technically, these people can access asynchronous content easily and communicate with each other by using high-level interaction methods and techniques. Asynchronous content design to share knowledge online can be one of the best choices for these people, because of the lack of efficient time for interaction with others and the limitations of hectic lifestyles in this century.

Designing and delivering asynchronous content also can be the best way for the developing and underdeveloping countries, because of inadequate technological investments at their homes and offices. Although poor-design, low-budget asynchronous content provides limited interaction between professionals and community members, organizations have a chance to deliver these contents several times. Moreover, the contents can be edited later by online designers to provide maximum performance for virtual communication.

Evaluation and Asynchronous E-Learning Content

Evaluation in education is a general term used for measuring learners' performance in a course against the objectives (Resta, 2002). Like any educational setting, it is fundamental for asynchronous content designs to improve the quality and quantity of knowledge sharing between professionals and communities. There are many forms of evaluation in virtual learning, including learner self-assessment, group and peer assessment, and formative and summative assessment.

There is a paradigm shift simulated by several diverse characteristics to assess asynchronous content design: (1) providing equal access to knowledge and resources; (2) delineating the needs and expectations of virtual professionals and community; (3) expanding learning opportunities lifelong; (4) reducing staff numbers and expenses, but increasing participant enrollment to asynchronous learning-based actions; (5) maximizing communication activities between online participants; and (6) creating multicultural curriculum for sharing knowledge via asynchronous content. Therefore, the macro-level framework supports self-, group, and peer assessments to revise asynchronous content to respect much more multicultural learning.

In the next section, the micro-level framework for asynchronous content design to establish pluralistic online education derives effective learning strategies that reflect ethnic (race, religion, etc.) and cultural (language, exceptionality, poverty, socioeconomic status, gender, etc.) diversity.

The Micro-Level Framework to Asynchronous Content Design

The micro-level framework to design asynchronous content helps professionals and community members in developed, developing, or underdeveloped countries share knowledge online based on respecting their diverse needs and expectations from around the globe. This framework can also show new ways of thinking skills, sharing knowledge, and actively learning online. Finally, this framework is a very useful resource providing strategies, principles, and suggestions for working with professionals and community members of culturally diverse backgrounds in a variety of forceful online learning opportunities via synchronous content design. With this micro-level framework, therefore, online workers can help community members envision why it is vital to know about the cultural backgrounds of individuals in particular and in general.

There are three important elements in the micro-level framework to design asynchronous content for any developed, developing, or underdeveloped country. These elements help online participants understand undoubtedly the *open, flexible,* and *distributed* nature of asynchronous content: (1) developing a strategic technology plan to share knowledge online; (2) implementing an online program development process (type, purpose, strategies, and components) to create multicultural understandings; and (3) evaluating implementation processes to support best practices between professionals and community members. This theoretical framework has multi-dimensions to design asynchronous content for professionals and communities. It also is practicable, inexpensive, and convenient to deliver asynchronous content to construct knowledge networks in societies (see Figure 2). Moreover, the framework encourages sharing and exchanging knowledge between professionals and communities so to provide knowledge and a deeper understanding of asynchronous online learning.

Developing a strategic technology plan provides unique answers to accomplish successful asynchronous content designs (Wiburg, 2001). The first step is to find a creative solution to create well-quality online content based on the needs and expectations of individuals from around the world. This plan to share knowledge virtually has seven important stages to construct multicultural online societies: (1) defining clearly the current needs and expectations of professionals and communities; (2) planning technology requirements based on the budgeting strategies and the existing technical opportunities of an organization; (3) examining personal knowledge, resources, and skills in society; (4) communicating with stakeholders to construct a knowledge network with prospective community, business, school, universities, colleges, and so forth; (5) creating standards based on the conceptual framework of organizations to cope with future challenges; (6) developing goals and objectives to define outcomes based on the ethic and value codes of society; and (7) creating learning statements for multicultural asynchronous content designs. This plan, moreover, must provide a specific description of the assessment of asynchronous content design to share knowledge online.

The second step is implementing an online program development process, which has these two main steps: (1) working on project timelines to define online project tasks to work effectively and efficiently, and (2) budgeting to estimate all costs to identify fund sources in advance. The timeline and financial plan have extremely vital roles to design and deliver asynchronous contents without any delay. The program development process also has four sub-steps based on the project timeline and the budgeting strategies: (1) type—deciding the design and delivery methods and techniques of asynchronous content; (2) purpose—clarifying goals and objectives for knowledge sharing online; (3) strategies—highlighting which critical thinking skills will be used and improved; and (4) components—defining which cutting-edge technologies that are needed.

Evaluating the implementation process, the last step of the micro-level framework, has two critical stages: (1) receiving feedback from professionals and community members to clarify whether asynchronous content design meets their needs and expectations successfully, and (2) managing change process to provide helpful guidance for online providers to create more open and flexible asynchronous milieus. In the evaluation process, data must be collected from different sources and then analyzed to discuss findings. Finally, findings must be summarized and reported to revise asynchronous content designs to share knowledge online.

Therefore, this process must allow professionals and community members to make the right decisions on the ethics and values of online learning. It also must produce specifics answers about the ill-structured steps and e-learning circumstances of asynchronous content designs, and provide guidelines for professionals and communities sharing knowledge.

The micro-level framework provides necessary principles and strategies to improve asynchronous content design to knowledge sharing. Moreover, this framework helps online participants examine their ability to share and exchange knowledge rather than to memorize and reproduce it. Also, given learning activities in asynchronous content, encourage learners to access and share knowledge, and motivate others to learn. Moreover, in virtual learning settings, each participant can observe others' works and contribute reflective comments on postings. Sophisticated knowledge construction and development activities can build group activities for professionals and communities to work together as a group, and to achieve the goals of the online program. Finally, this framework also describes, explains, and predicts the cognitive processes and experiences of online participants, because it helps them actively engage in complex learning activities, which provide a link between conceptual and experiential learning.

Conclusion

The e-learning communities in the 21st century are in conversions due to social, economical, and political pressures from decreasing costs and time boundaries for culturally diverse learners (Bonk & King, 1998). The critical question is to how educational organizations in developed, developing, and underdeveloping countries respond to these changes and demands efficiently. There is no universally applicable guideline for designing asynchronous content. The planned strategies for necessary changes in educational systems to integrate these programs need to be developed within the macro and micro frameworks. Therefore, most professionals in communities can reap knowledge from diverse learning resources in their paces, places, and times. They also can plan and manage their learning, have a high degree of personal control and autonomy, reflect on their learning experiences and incorporate new knowledge into preexisting knowledge, and engage in sharing knowledge and working together.

Asynchronous content designed by the micro- and macro-level frameworks helps participants actively engage in learning progress and critically reflect upon what they share with each other. These also help them to effectively transfer their knowledge to new contexts. Therefore, online participants improve their complex critical thinking and higher-order skills to create, produce, or demonstrate their knowledge in asynchronous content. Finally, these frameworks also provide rubrics for assessment criteria to promote collaborations and interactions among professionals and community members. They involve innovation in assessment to meet their changing needs and to realize new opportunities for sharing knowledge online.

References

Bonk, C. J., & King, K. S. (Eds.). (1998). *Electronic collaborators: Learner-centered technologies for literacy, apprenticeship, and discourse.* Mahwah, NJ: Lawrence Erlbaum.

Burniske, R. W., & Monke, L. (2001). *Breaking down the digital walls: Learning to teach in a post-modem world.* Albany, NY: State University of New York Press.

Collier, C., & Yoder, M. (2002). Successful online discussion and collaboration: Techniques for design and facilitation. *Proceedings of the Society for Information Technology and Teacher Education International Conference 2002,* (1), 2351-2355. Retrieved from http://dl.aace.org/11448

Jonassen, D. H. (2000). *Computers as mindtools for schools: Engaging critical thinking.* Englewood Cliffs, NJ: Prentice-Hall.

Khan, B. (1997). *Web-based instruction.* Englewood Cliffs, NJ: Educational Technology Publications.

Lessing, L. (2001). *The future of ideas: The role of the commons in a connected world.* New York: Random House.

Palloff, R. M., & Pratt, K. (1999). *Building learning communities in cyberspace: Effective strategies for the online classroom.* San Francisco: Jossey-Bass.

Picciano, A. G. (2001). *Distance learning: Making connections across virtual space and time.* Columbus, OH: Merrill Prentice.

Resta, P. (Ed.). (2002). *Information and communication technologies in teacher education: A planning guide.* Paris: UNESCO.

Thomas, P., & Carswell, L. (2000). Learning through collaboration in a distributed education environment. *Educational Technology and Society, 3*(3), 1-15.

Wiburg, K. M. (2001). Effective technology planning. In G. Ivory (Ed.), *What works in computing for school administrators.* Maryland: Scarecrow Education.

Yuzer, V., & Kurubacak, G. (2003). A framework for integrating Enhanced TV (ETV) into distance education. *Information Technology and Teacher Education Annual,* (1), 817-825. Albuquerque, NM: Association for the Advancement of Computing in Education (AACE). Retrieved from http://home.anadolu.edu.tr/~gkurubac/SITE2003VolkanGulsun.pdf

Chapter XII

Online Faculty Proficiency and Peer Coaching

Jason D. Baker, Regent University, USA

Shauna Tonkin, Regent University, USA

Introduction

By the time someone becomes a teacher, regardless of whether he or she enters the K-12 school system, higher education arena, or corporate training environment, he or she has literally had decades of experience with face-to-face instruction. While new teachers vary in their pedagogical training and student teaching experience, they still benefit from a lifetime of experience as students themselves. Accordingly, most of today's teachers have a fairly common set of experiences and expectations to draw from when planning and evaluating traditional instruction. This is not so when the educational environment is shifted from the four-walled classroom to the online Internet environment. According to Bork (2002), the results of a survey of university instructors revealed that experienced online instructors had taught between four and seven online courses either partially or fully online. While not an insignificant number, it pales in comparison to the teaching experience of the same respondents (e.g., 36% having more than 20 years of experience and 34% with 10-20 years of experience), as well as the nonteaching history that such instructors invariably had.

Moving into the comparably new territory of online teaching and learning thus requires a renewed emphasis on training and continual improvement. The central question is not whether this new approach to education is effective—the plethora of "no significant difference" studies largely render that question moot (see Russell, 1999, 2002 for hundreds of examples). Rather, greater attention should be given to ensuring that individual courses are pedagogically effective, and traditional faculty are trained to become quality online instructors.

In their 2000 report, *Quality on the Line: Benchmarks for Success in Internet-Based Distance Education*, the researchers at the Institute for Higher Education Policy (IHEP) identified 24 benchmarks for ensuring effective online education. Among the faculty support benchmarks were the following:

- "Faculty members are assisted in the transition from classroom teaching to online instruction and are assessed during the process" (p. 37).

- "Instructor training and assistance, including peer mentoring, continues through the progression of the online course" (p. 3).

Reliance upon student and faculty self-reporting instruments as the sole forms of evaluation are particularly problematic since the online learning environment is significantly less familiar to participants than the classroom. Such unfamiliarity is likely to result in feedback which by itself is ill-suited to meeting these quality benchmarks. Incorporating peer mentoring or coaching into the instructors' training and support plan may enhance initial experiences with the online environment, which may contribute to improved teaching effectiveness. Furthermore, the use of peer coaching as a means of regular professional development will encourage faculty toward continual improvement of their online pedagogical strategies in light of increasing student and technological sophistication.

Changing Faculty Roles

Current Faculty Perspectives

In order to understand the current state of online teaching and the environment in which such a peer coaching model would be implemented, surveys addressing technological proficiency and online pedagogy were administered to the faculty at a private university in the American Southeast. This university offers multiple degree programs, primarily graduate degrees, through asynchronous online learning. The majority of online classes are taught by the same full-time faculty who teach on campus. Over 90% of the full-time faculty responded to surveys about technological proficiency and the pedagogical uses of technology.

There were three technologies with which the majority of faculty respondents indicated that they were comfortable: finding information on the World Wide Web, using Blackboard, and creating and using PowerPoint presentations. Faculty identified a number of technologies which they indicated they would like to use in their online and on-campus courses, if they could learn how. In ranked order, these included multimedia, streaming media, videoconferencing, Acrobat/PDF files, Web page creation, and digital photography. When asked what resources or services faculty would like to have in order to more effectively use technology in their teaching, the responses were mixed. Almost half of the responses revolved around a request for more/better equipment, a quarter expressed a desire for more training, and a handful identified more or better trained support personnel. When asked about technical training, the most common requests were for an increase in the number of technical support staff to assist faculty with their online course development and for additional instructor training sessions to be offered on campus and online.

In general, faculty indicated that various technologies either added to or significantly added to teaching effectiveness in campus-based and online courses. For example, almost two-thirds indicated that e-mail communication with students added significantly to teaching effectiveness, while approximately one-third said that it added to teaching effectiveness. Similar results were found for class-related Internet assignments (44% said that they added significantly to teaching effectiveness, 30% said that they added to teaching effectiveness), the Blackboard CourseInfo system (51%, 25%), posting material online (53%, 33%), online threaded discussions (43%, 25%), audio/video resources (52%, 34%), online library databases (66%, 27%), and PowerPoint presentations (41%, 44%). The only technologies that significantly deviated from this pattern were chat rooms (51% indicated that they had no effect on teaching effectiveness) and online tests/quizzes (48% indicated that they had no effect).

Sixty-nine percent of faculty respondents indicated that their annual teaching load included online courses, with 36% of the total respondents indicating that over half of their annual teaching load consisted of online courses. Of those faculty that taught online, regardless of load percentage, the plurality of faculty (36%) had been teaching online courses for three or four years. Twenty-four percent of faculty teaching online courses stated that they logged into their courses daily, with another 38% logging in four to six times per week. Sixty-five percent agreed or strongly agreed that they were effective online teachers, although 52% indicated that they still were more effective teaching campus-based courses.

New Faculty Pedagogy

Despite the integration of information technologies throughout higher education, many professors still cling to traditional perspectives of instruction that view faculty as arbiters of knowledge. Students who do not successfully conform to institutional expectations are seen as lacking in ability or effort; rarely are student deficiencies attributed to shortcomings in program design or instruction. This was evident in the aforementioned faculty survey, since when asked about their online pedagogical approaches, the majority of faculty indicated that the content of their online and off-line courses was basically the same (57%) as were the assessment tasks (53%), but 66% stated that their teaching techniques differed between online and off-line courses. Sixty-six percent indicated that their online students were either as active or more active in class discussion than their on-campus students. Faculty indicated that they were able to develop collegial relationships with online students, with 32% indicating the same level as with on-campus students and 24% indicating that they were stronger relationships than with on-campus students. Despite these seemingly positive factors, 41% of faculty teaching online courses stated that their campus students learn more than their online students.

An alternative view of a professor's role shifts the focus from providing information to facilitating learning (Van Dusen, 1997). Schulman (1999) argued that the use of new technologies at colleges and universities makes it "increasingly difficult to ask about teaching…without asking about evidence for learning" (p. 4). In an era where information is available from a host of reputable sources, students may not regard faculty members as the final authority for content issues. Instead, professors must guide the students in making sense of the knowledge. The "guide on the side" as opposed to the "sage on the stage" is a commonly used metaphor for the professor's role in e-learning, indicating that collaborative and supportive strategies are more effective than telling and directing (Collison, Elbaum, Haavind, & Tinker, 2000). For some instructors, this change requires a rethinking of course purpose and procedures, and the development of new teaching skills. To facilitate student participation and foster learning in the online classroom, Stevens-Long and Crowell (2002) stated that effective teachers:

1. Define conceptual and administrative structures for their course and clearly communicate expectations related to assignments and process

2. Provide regular and meaningful feedback on student work, both through evaluating assignments and overseeing course activities

3. Demonstrate patience with students who approach online learning with anxiety

4. Accept unforeseen technical problems as part of the experience, and create strategies to continue the teaching and learning process in spite of these problems

In the open-ended questions, a number of faculty teaching online indicated that they were anxious for a more media-rich learning experience. The current mode of online learning, which is largely text based, was often criticized for taking too much time and hindering the relational connection between teacher and student. The desire to see more audio and videoconferencing in online courses was the single most commonly cited feature when asked in an open-ended question how they imagined their courses looking in five years. Clearly there is a desire among existing online faculty to make the online learning experience richer and more personal, and the authors believe that peer coaching can provide a valuable nonthreatening means of improving online instruction.

Peer Coaching Cycle

The role of continuous instructional improvement becomes particularly important when one considers how quickly teaching patterns (good or bad) can become ingrained. Like many institutions, the university under consideration adopted the Blackboard CourseInfo platform as the primary content delivery framework because of its ease of use for both faculty and students. However, in the years since developing the first Blackboard-based courses, it has been evident that the initial course design and delivery efforts quickly became the model for all subsequent course development. While this is not inherently bad—the asynchronous discussion model has been particularly rich for seminar-style graduate courses—it also has tended to blind some instructors to alternate instructional approaches. It appears that the instructors have either consciously or subtly adjusted their pedagogical approach to conform to the limitations of the software.

Peer observation and coaching activities are an accepted means of generating data for assessing teaching effectiveness, and adopting this practice reinforces the concept that faculty are the best judges of institutional quality (DeZure, 1999). However, in the absence of established procedures and adequate training, peer coaching is benign at best and in many cases wastes valuable faculty resources. The university has employed a method of peer coaching for face-to-face courses throughout the past six years, and in the past two years has adapted this model for the online instructor. This method is taught in a yearlong teaching improvement seminar. Participants engage in a coaching cycle with another colleague, sharing their findings with the larger group when the process has been completed.

The peer coaching cycle used consists of three stages: a planning conference, instructional observation, and a reflecting conference. The planning conference is a structured meeting in which the instructor and his/her peer coach discuss their collaborative effort with a particular focus on the goals of the instructor. Unlike other observation and feedback models, this peer coaching model does not promote open-ended feedback. Rather, during the planning conference the instructor briefs the peer coach on the specifics of the upcoming class session, including such factors as the topic under consideration, the objectives for the session, the planned teaching and learning activities, the sequence and pacing of the session, and formal or informal assessments included in the session. With this background established, the instructor requests specific aspects that he/she would like the peer coach to observe. For example, the instructor may have difficultly sustaining a robust class discussion, and would like the peer coach to observe the discussion dynamics and offer recommendations for improvement. It is important that the instructor have a clear purpose for engaging in peer coaching and can communicate such requests to the peer coach during the planning conference, especially since feedback on topics other than these prearranged ones is generally off limits. Such focused requests help to build trust between the instructor and coach, ensure that the observation and feedback will support the instructor's goals, and promote genuineness and vulnerability (rather than an instructional "performance") during the lesson.

The second phase in the peer coaching cycle is the actual instructional observation. For online courses, we expect that the peer coach will commit to at least one week of observation, logging into the course site multiple times throughout the week as well as examining the prior weeks' efforts. Since the majority of our online classes follow a traditional semester schedule but break the lessons into week-long intervals (highlighted by asynchronous threaded discussions), one week in Blackboard is equivalent to a week's worth of face-to-face class time. The peer coach takes notes based on his/her observations of the class, using the planning conference requests as a framework. In addition, there are many observations that we encourage the peer coach to make, even if he/she does not directly communicate the findings to the instructor. We encourage the online peer coach to take particular notice of the virtual classroom environment and interpersonal communication dynamics. Such facets include the design and layout of the Blackboard Web pages, the tone of the announcements and course materials, the level of learner-instructor and learner-learner engagement in class discussions, the types of media used for presenting materials, the ease of navigation, the clarity of course instructions, and the instructor's mastery of the course content and effectiveness at presenting it to the class. In addition, the level of instructor participation, student reactions, questions posed to the class (e.g., type, frequency counts, and even time between question and answer), communication style, content knowledge, use of rich media, and balance between online and off-line assignments are all facets that the peer coach could use to assist in the evaluation of the instructor's requests. Following the observation exercise, the peer coach is encouraged to review and organize his/her notes in preparation for the follow-up conference.

The final phase is the reflecting or post-observation conference in which the instructor and peer coach meet to debrief the observed class session. During this meeting, the peer coach begins by providing the instructor with feedback based on his/her observations of the class. The feedback presentation typically includes describing the relevant observations, analyzing and interpreting the observations in light of the questions posed during the pre-observation meeting, and offering additional data which support the focus questions. After presenting such feedback to the instructor in an informational (vs. judgmental) manner, the peer coach elicits the instructor's inferences, opinions, and feelings. This provides an opportunity for the pair to dialogue about the observations and their consequences rather than having the peer coach simply debrief the instructor. The peer coach is discouraged from giving direct advice, but instead is encouraged to listen intently, ask clarifying questions, focus on the specific observations rather than offer personal commentary, and seek to agree on the meaning of the observations. The peer coach then closes the conference on a positive and productive note by helping the instructor develop an action plan to improve in the focus areas.

As a postscript to the peer coaching process, we have encouraged peer coaches to document their relevant observations in an essay or letter to the instructor as a means of helping the instructor use the experience for significant professional development. Furthermore, subsequent to the reflecting conference, the instructor is asked to comment on the collaborative coaching process (preferably in writing). This provides a final opportunity for reflection by the instructor and also helps to provide feedback which can be used to improve the peer coaching process.

Peer Coaching Checklist

The collaborative coaching model can be presented in a checklist format as follows:

Pre-Observation Meeting

1. Identify the instructor's concern about instruction
2. Translate the concerns into observable behavior
3. Identify procedures for improving the instructor's teaching and students' learning
4. Set goals and content, arrange time for observation, and choose appropriate instruments

Online Classroom Observation

1. Class online atmosphere
2. Learner-instructor interaction
3. Learner-learner interaction
4. Mastery of content
5. Manner of presentation
6. Media for presentation
7. Use of Blackboard and the Internet
8. Design usability

Post-Observation Meeting

1. Provide the instructor with feedback
2. Elicit instructor's inferences, opinions, and feelings
3. Close conference on a positive and productive note
4. Evaluate the process

Peer Coaching Benefits

Often the first reaction of faculty committed to online teaching is to devise ways to recreate the face-to-face classroom experience via computer. When one faculty member first learned of a proposed new online program, he wanted to put a camera in front of himself and lecture to the online students. Other colleagues also envisioned themselves as seated in front of their computer screen with small square images of each of their students dutifully looking back at them. We are reminded of McLuhan and Fiore's (1967) rearview mirror syndrome. They noted that we tend to live one medium behind and offered the example of filming plays as the first mainstream use of film cameras. Such cameras were usually set up in the center aisle of a theatre house and just filmed what appeared on the stage—how far removed that is from the film experience of today.

As major stakeholders in online learning, faculty require assistance in discovering new teaching methods that would be more suitable to effective Web-based instruction. In traditional higher education models, instructors do all aspects of course design and development by themselves. After all, they are the content experts and are best equipped to design a quality learning experience for their students. Now that the instructor-learner dynamic is mediated through online communication, the medium itself affects the learning experience. Furthermore, the typical faculty member is trained in his or her particular field, not in instructional design. It is simply unrealistic, and a poor use of resources, to expect a faculty member to be content expert, Web developer, multimedia designer, and systems administrator all rolled into one. While there are numerous books, conferences, and consultants available to assist faculty and students make the transition to online instruction—and we highly recommend such texts to our faculty—we have found that the peer coaching approach has been more personal and beneficial. One benefit of such peer coaching is that faculty can encourage one another in developing quality instruction without feeling that they are being forced into one style or model that is being dictated by the administrators or technologies. The authors have observed this in multiple university settings where skeptical professors were much more likely to respond to an enthusiastic colleague than someone from outside the faculty. Further-more, the peer coaching model provides faculty increased exposure to the online education environment (rather than limiting themselves to only their assigned courses). We have also found that such exposure has been particularly effective for new online instructors.

Just as businesses have learned the value of work teams, so too should online instructors team up with faculty colleagues using peer coaching and perhaps even bring in others who could provide specialized expertise to the table. Willing faculty should consider partnerships with instructional designers, multimedia developers, or student assistants. Instructional designers bring insight into how to design the contents to maximize student learning. They will have the most insight on the media selection, layout of Web pages, and overall instructional approach, and can help the faculty member translate his/her content into a quality course to be delivered at-a-distance. Multimedia developers not only can convert much of the content into an online format (e.g., creating a streaming audio or video segment based on a classroom lecture), but they can offer a sense of style to the course design. Finally, to accommodate laborious work involved in developing and improving online courses, there should be student or staff assistants who can assist the development team in accomplishing such tasks.

This is no small undertaking, as it requires a commitment not only from the instructor to collaborate on the course redesign, but also from the institution, which needs to commit the resources necessary for instructional design support. Despite the potential limita-tions of the current online educational efforts (e.g., text only, lack of real-time sponta-neity, etc.), they have shifted the tenor of adult learning from lecture to interactive discussion. Once high-bandwidth access is the norm, we may have the opportunity to see a richer multimedia educational experience. Unfortunately, it may also tempt faculty to simply broadcast their lectures online and abandon the constructivist interaction that current online courses benefit from. The determining factors will likely be instructional design and providing the resources necessary to support quality instructional design. We believe that the effective use of peer coaching has the potential to help not only improve instructional efforts in the present, but also serve as the catalyst for a significant rethinking of effective online instruction for the future.

References

Bork, C. J. (2002). Online teaching in an online world. *USDLA Journal, 16*(1). Retrieved July 4, 2004, from http://www.usdla.org/html/journal/JAN02_Issue/article02.html

Collison, G., Elbaum, B., Haavind, S., & Tinker, R. (2000). *Facilitating online learning: Effective strategies for moderators.* Madison, WI: Atwood Publishing.

DeZure, D. (1999). Evaluating teaching through peer classroom observation. In P. Seldin (Ed.), *Changing practices in evaluating teaching: A practical guide to improved faculty performance and promotion/tenure decisions.* Bolton, MA: Anker Publishing.

Institute for Higher Education Policy. (2000). *Quality on the line: Benchmarks for success in Internet-based distance education.* Retrieved July 7, 2004, from http://www.ihep.com/Pubs/PDF/Quality.pdf

McLuhan, M., & Fiore, Q. (1967). *The medium is the massage: An inventory of effects.* San Francisco: Hardwired.

Russell, T. L. (1999). *The no significant difference phenomenon.* Raleigh: North Carolina State University.

Russell, T. L. (2002). *The "no significant difference phenomenon" Web site.* Retrieved October 7, 2004, from http://www.nosignificantdifference.org/nosignificantdifference/

Schulman, L. (1999). *Visions of the possible: Models for campus support of the scholarship of teaching and learning.* Retrieved February 19, 2002, from http://www.carnegiefoundation.org/eLibrary/docs/Visions.htm

Stevens-Long, J., & Crowell, C. (2002). The design and delivery of interactive online graduate education. In K. Rudestam & J. Schoenholtz-Read (Eds.), *Handbook of online learning* (pp. 151-170). Thousand Oaks, CA: Sage Publications.

Van Dusen, G. C. (1997). The virtual campus: Technology and reform in higher education. *ASHE-ERIC Higher Education Report, 25*(5). Washington, DC: The George Washington University Graduate School of Education and Human Development.

Chapter XIII

What Do They Learn?

Carla R. Payne, Vermont College of Union Institute and University, USA

Introduction

Significant learning is marked by transformation in ways of thinking and in the making of meaning. As Winn (1997) put it: "Information is not knowledge and knowledge is not wisdom." He goes on to point out that "the acquisition of knowledge from information requires effort and involves perceptual and cognitive processes that decode symbols, deploy literacy skills to interpret them, and apply inferencing [*sic*] abilities to connect them to existing knowledge." I have argued elsewhere that the instructor must make cognitive development an overall course goal (Payne, 2004). The possibility that there can be developmental change must be an underlying assumption of effective course design. But even given a strong commitment to our students' cognitive growth, how can we know that the most careful course design and the most thoughtful discussion facilitation are having a positive impact on their thinking abilities? We need some evidence about the impact of our strategies to guide us in improving them. In this chapter, I suggest that the transcripts generated by asynchronous discussion can be more than the objects of quantitative analysis, and that our practice as teachers in any discipline can also benefit by attention to these highly accessible records of our students' work.

Dewey and his heirs, the educational constructivists, set forth certain conditions for significant learning: that students are active, interactive, and reflective, within any particular learning environment (Payne, 2004). In this chapter, one emphasis is on interaction, the social aspect of the construction of knowledge, as it may occur and be fostered in a specific context, asynchronous discussion. The other is on the identification of indicators of development in transcripts of those discussions. In this case, the indicators selected are for interactivity and for inference, one of those higher-order thinking skills considered to be an aspect of reflective thinking.

Most courses in any format require students to submit written work, and these, of course, are subject to ongoing assessment. Online discussions yield additional records or transcripts not available in the traditional classroom setting which can be useful in evaluating the effectiveness of course design. As a demonstration of how these records can assist us in improving our teaching practices, I review some models for the content analysis of online transcripts and select criteria for identification of growth in critical thinking skills. Indicators for the selected skills are identified in the transcripts generated in the early and later stage discussions in an undergraduate ethics course. The course structure is described and the results of the trial analysis are presented, with their implications for design and for effective discussion facilitation.

The Developmental Perspective

Adopting a developmental perspective is key to assessing the effectiveness of course design. Unless improvement in students' knowledge, skills, and understanding is the objective of any course, it has no value as an educational experience. Here we focus on improvement in critical thinking or higher-order thinking abilities, a desirable outcome in any disciplinary context.

A conventional research design that seeks evidence for development would include the establishment of a baseline measure of these abilities prior to the start of the course to be evaluated. However, given the logistics of populating a college course, the opportunity to identify such a baseline is usually not available to the instructor planning a course. The next best strategy might be to evaluate target abilities (e.g., skills in manipulating information, critical analysis) just after the start of the course, in this case, using the transcript of online discussions from the first weeks. Without the developmental perspective—that is, the focus on positive change—the value of any analysis of student performance is questionable. Thus, a comparison of the performance of students participating in threaded discussions with those who do not, undifferentiated as to whether the participation took place early in a course or later (as in examples reported by Weasenforth, Biesenbach-Lucas, & Meloni, 2002), serves at best to provide support for the weak conclusion that "higher-order thinking can and does occur in online discussions" (Meyer, 2003). This may be a counter to those who still doubt that written conversation can have the same qualities as spoken conversation, but it does little to advance the project of using the online environment to help student development.

The developmental perspective implies a belief in the possibility and the probability that students will exhibit positive change in an appropriate environment; with this commitment, the task of the teacher is clearly to design and realize that environment. Without this commitment, the analysis and assessment of transcripts—or of any other aspect or record of a course—is essentially sterile, because it cannot have any purpose beyond the analytical exercise itself. Weasenforth et al.'s (2002) exclusion of the constructivist principle of "developmental influences on learning" from the framework of his study "because it is not particularly relevant for adult students" implies in part that we cannot expect these students to benefit from particular course design features.

Interactivity or Interaction?

Terminology can lead us astray in our search for recognizable signs that course design is encouraging desired changes. *Interactivity,* for instance, frequently describes certain features of computer software, as in "self-paced" learning systems; they require individual learners to interact with computer applications or programs, rather than with peers or mentors. "Interactivity" and "interaction" are sometimes used interchangeably (e.g., the Web site of the Stanford University Interactivity Lab at http://interactivity.stan ford.edu/), but in this context both interaction and interactivity will be used to denote a social function, conversation between human beings.

Content Analysis

The value of the transcripts of online discussions for understanding the learning process has been recognized by many researchers. A variety of systems of analysis have been developed, resting on different assumptions and having different purposes in regard to which aspects of learning are being investigated. For example, Aviv, Erlich, Ravid, and Geva (2003) consider "three aspects of ALNs: the design; the quality of the resulting knowledge construction process; and cohesion, role and power network structures." ("Asynchronous Learning Network" or "ALN" is used to refer to online discussions conducted in asynchronous mode.) They apply an interaction analysis model which assumes a five-stage process of knowledge construction, but caution that "In general, in assessing the success or failure of an ALN, one should consider the aims of the ALN and its design." Essentially, transcript analysis consists of "reading each message and classifying it…" (Aviv et al., 2003).

The classification system adopted in any particular analysis stem assumes criteria for distinguishing certain qualities of individual messages and a method for coding them. The qualities most valued in higher education settings are commonly given the collective label "critical thinking," but unpacking this bundle yields a variety of specific lists. Each individual list itself implies presuppositions about the nature of cognition and the learning process. Newman, Webb, and Cochrane (1995) note that "Critical thinking is not just limited to the one-off assessment of a statement for its correctness, but a dynamic activity, in which critical perspectives on a problem develop through both individual analysis and social interaction."

138 Payne

One technically sophisticated example of transcript analysis is that developed by Jeong (2003), who distinguishes his methodology from *content analysis* by its focus on interactions and "examining how specific event sequences affect subsequent discussion and cognitive outcomes." Jeong's Discussion Analysis Tool (DAT) "was used to identify patterns in interactions and determine which interactions promoted critical thinking," and is a computational instrument, yielding graphical illustrations of the probabilities of certain types of responses to specific types of interactions. With respect to critical thinking skills, Jeong adopts a complex model proposed by Gunawardena, Lowe, and Anderson in 1997, but he does not approach the analysis from a developmental point of view. That is to say, he does not seek to identify change over the duration of the graduate course which generated the transcript. This seriously limits the usefulness of the analysis for evaluating the course design. Further, since "the instructor abstained from intervening and participating (in the recorded debates)," this particular analysis provides no guidance as to the effectiveness of facilitation style. Jeong's Forum Manager (at http://bbproject.tripod.com/ForumManager/index.htm) is another tool that enables multidimensional analysis of discussion forums in BlackBoard, but its use for identifying the cognitive relevance or function of individual messages requires their labeling by category at the time of posting by participants, compromising the exchange as *conversation,* or the genuine exchange and testing of ideas.

Henri's work has been seminal in influencing the development of transcript analysis methodologies which focus on cognitive growth. Henri's analytical model for assessing cognitive skills (as cited in Lally, 2001) could be applied to the evaluation of student progress. Henri also presented a set of criteria for distinguishing *surface processing* in discussion postings from *in-depth processing.*

Bullen (1998) noted Henri's distinction between independent and interactive messages, having previously (1997) elaborated it as *intermessage reference.* According to Henri's scheme, *independent messages* deal with the topic of discussion, but make no implicit or explicit reference to any other message. *Interactive messages* deal with the topic, but also refer to other messages by responding to them, elaborating on them, or building on them in some fashion. Interactive messages in this sense define *conversation,* and we may take an increase in their occurrence as a positive indicator with regard to the conditions of knowledge construction.

Henri's 1992 categories for distinguishing specific cognitive skills were *elementary clarification, in-depth clarification, inference, judgment,* and *strategies* (Lally, 2001). This classification has been refined and further distinctions drawn by various theorists including Garrison, Anderson, and Archer (2001). Newman et al.(1995) drew on a 1991 list of criteria developed by Henri, as well as on her 1992 list of paired indicators for surface and in-depth processing (as cited in Lally, 2001), to develop a much longer list of indicators: relevance; importance; novelty ("new info, ideas, solutions"); bringing outside knowledge/experience to bear on problems; ambiguities ("clarified or confused"); linking ideas, interpretations; justification; critical assessment; practical utility; and width of understanding. Any of these could be applied in an assessment of discussion transcripts for a course, or even to track the progress of individual students. In the demonstration presented here, the selected transcripts were coded for *intermessage reference* (as an indicator of interaction) and for evidence of *inference.* Several commentators, including Garrison et al. (2001), concede the technical difficulties—for example, interrater reliability—involved in complex content analyses of discussion transcripts.

Nevertheless, the case can be made for a practice-level analysis which can be carried out as part of ongoing evaluation of course design.

Online Discussion as an Integral Part of Overall Course Design

It is now widely recognized that effective course design means integrating online discussion into the course fabric, rather than treating it as an ancillary feature (Weasenforth et al., 2002). "Integration" would mean, at a minimum, matching the topics of the readings, the written and other assignments, and the topics of threaded discussions. Beyond that, the presence of the facilitator/teacher in the conversations supports their status as the venue for important learning, as does a defined rating system for individual participation. The absence of such integrative elements casts doubt on the value of any conclusions from transcript content analysis for improvement of overall course design.

Application: Interaction

Key steps in performing a practical transcript analysis to assess learning are:

- Select course objective(s) to be tracked
- Identify indicator(s) for desired change
- Select course segments to be tested

The course selected for this test analysis was a 15-week introduction to ethics, offered entirely online, using BlackBoard 6. Ten students were enrolled. The coursework consisted of readings from an ethics textbook, supplementary readings, two short written assignments per week, midterm and final essays, and mandatory participation in a weekly discussion, which was rated *Strong, OK,* or *Poor.* (The college required at least one posting per week as an indicator of attendance.) Most important for present purposes, a new discussion question was set each week, keyed to the readings and written assignments. The previous weeks' discussions were then accessible on a read-only basis.

The discussion transcripts for weeks 2, 3, 13, and 14 of the ethics course were selected for analysis.

- **Week 2 Forum Question:** Read Case #22 on Hinman's Web site. (Click on the Web site's button at the left, then on "Cases for Discussion" under "Resources" on Hinman's page.) If the judge in this case is an ethical relativist, how might he rule? If the judge is an ethical absolutist, what might her decision be?

- **Week 3 Forum Question**: Read case #54 on the Hinman Web site. What light does it shed on the "divine command" theory of "right" and "wrong?"

- **Week 13 Forum Question:** Do animals have rights in and of themselves? Or should our behavior toward them be governed by one of the ethical systems we have studied?

- **Week 14 Forum Question:** Read the article on the banning of head scarves in French schools at http://www.nytimes.com/2003/12/11/international/europe/11CND-FRAN.html?ex=1082260800&en=c250cc14b7580f62&ei=5070. What light does this case shed on how diversity can be accommodated within a system of moral and legal principles?

The first message coding was for intermessage reference. The two possible categories were "student responses to instructor," which included all postings responding to the week's initial question, as well as responses to further postings by the instructor and "student-to-student messages."

Coding for Intermessage Reference

Student 1: Coded as "Student Responses to Instructor"

I think that animals should have the same rights that people do. I think that sometimes people think of animals as…plants or as dirt or something of the like. Animals have feelings just like the rest of the world, just as people do.

Student 2: Coded as "Student-to-Student" Message

"I think that animals should have the same rights that people do." This is a very bold statement. An animal should have the right to sit in a public restaurant? Enter a public restroom? Swim in the public pool? Maybe what you meant was that animals deserve the same emotional considerations that we would give to a fellow human being. This issue is really one in which you have to be on one side or the other. Referring again to your quote above, have you had any of the following food items lately; a burger, steak, piece of chicken, turkey sandwich, etc.? Does your car have leather seats? You see the point I'm getting at. If you aren't a vegetarian, if you own a pet, or enjoy going to the zoo than [sic] the statement that you made has no ramifications. If you believe that animals should have the same rights that people do, you would never consume or use any animal products or confine an animal in any way.

The results of this coding and subsequent tabulation are shown in Figure 1.

Figure 1. Change in intermessage reference, response to instructor or student-to-student postings

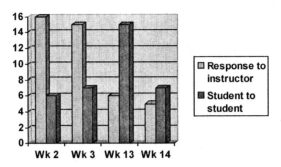

The change in the type of interactivity—from messages directed to the instructor to messages directed to those of other students—paralleled a decrease in instructor postings during the portion of the course tested, from 15% of the weekly totals during weeks 2 and 3, to 5% in week 13 and 8% in week 14. Further research would be required to determine whether this is a causal relationship, and how the level of instructor presence affects the type and quality of student postings.

Discussion of Interaction

Given the discussion format, in which students were required to respond to a weekly question, it was not surprising that there were no independent (isolated or unrelated) messages in any of the transcripts; the distinction was drawn in the analysis between postings directed to the week's original question or to the instructor's subsequent postings, and those directed to other students. Determining whether or not this is a useful distinction implies an answer to whether the facilitator or instructor can be an authentic conversation participant. The danger that student-to-student interaction will be stifled or overwhelmed by instructor/facilitator postings is real; on the other hand, the instructor's presence or "immediacy" has been found to be a crucial element in community building (Wegerif, 1998; Rourke, Anderson, Garrison, & Archer, 1999), as well as in integration of the discussions. If the instructor's principal role is to coach, guide, and model, rather than to transmit information, then skillful participation in the discussions appears to be a necessary condition of collaboration and interaction toward knowledge construction. The limited samples examined in this case show that decreased instructor participation after the posting of the opening question paralleled increased student-to-student interaction.

Application: Inference

The second dimension for coding messages was *inference,* using Henri's definition: "induction and deduction, admitting or proposing an idea on the basis of its link with propositions already admitted as true." Henri's indicators for the presence of inferential thought were: "Drawing conclusions. Making generalizations. Formulating a proposition which proceeds from previous statements" (cited by Lally, 2001). Skill at constructing and recognizing sound arguments, which is central to a philosophy course and a significant element in higher-order thinking across disciplines, rests on the ability to perform this linking. In this test of discussions from the ethics course, the focus was on the inferential process, rather than on the content of the reasoning; messages which contained any of Henri's indicators for inference were coded "I+," regardless of whether they were strictly relevant to the topic of discussion. Other messages were coded "I-." ("Relevance" is another element of critical thinking or cognitive processing which could be separately tracked.)

Coding for Inference: Sample Messages

Week 2. Coded Inferential: Drawing Conclusions

I think I would argue for Miriam Wilngal. It seems to me that if it was moral for that culture to force their women to do what they want, then that would also mean it would have been moral for Americans to have slaves. I don't think we have a right to suppress human life.

Week 3. Coded Inferential: Formulating A Proposition Which Proceeds from Previous Statements

I am conflicted on this very tough case. If I put myself in the parents' shoes I would probably come to the same conclusion they did. However, if I was the judge I would have ordered that the hospital should go through with the surgery. While the parents seemed to arrive at their decision through faith and passion, the judge arrived at his or her decision through reason and compassion. Although, one could argue that there is not much compassion in going against a parent's decision and letting the hospital go through with an operation that they have never performed successfully. And when it is all said and done, and the surviving child (if she survives) will be presumably be cared for and brought up by the parents, not the judge or hospital. (sic)

Week 13. Coded Inferential: Generalization

I do think that animals do have emotional rights. Unfortunately I myself do use animals as instruments. I believe that we should not harm animals, but not because of how it will

Figure 2. Occurrence of postings indicating inferential thought

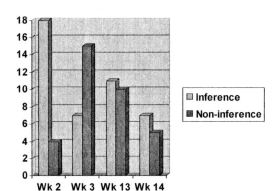

affect us, but how it will affect them. I think that most animals are smarter than we give them credit for.

Week 3. Coded Non-Inferential

This is a real tough case. I am not sure what I would do if I was in this position. I found it interesting that the judge ruled for the hospital even though they didn't have one successful....

Week 14. Coded Non-Inferential

I loved your answer. You have a lot of really great ideas!! I just wish they could work!

The results of this coding and subsequent tabulation are shown in Figure 2 for the four weeks analyzed.

Discussion of Inference

The lack of any general pattern or trend in respect to inferential thought in this case over the duration of 14 weeks may indicate that the type of questions posed by the instructor affects the nature of the responses more than the passage of time or increasing familiarity with the material. This suggests that special attention might be given to the framing of discussion questions to encourage specific kinds of thinking.

Selecting any one factor out of a complex concept such as "critical thinking" tends to skew our perspective, if only temporarily. In this illustration, it is important to remember that messages coded as non-inferential (**I-**) may or may not exhibit other salient characteristics, such as relevance and judgment; this is true also of messages coded positively for inference (**I+**), since any single posting can itself be a complex communication.

Conclusion

Do the results of the sample analyses presented here support the assumption that examination of discussion transcripts is a useful exercise? Even repeated analyses of this kind could not tell us conclusively whether it is course design as a whole (including readings, written assignments, and individual e-mail exchanges with the instructor) that is influencing apparent changes, or the particular level and kind of instructor participation in the discussions which support increased interaction between students. The fact, however, that this type of analysis is not entirely definitive does not diminish its utility for the improvement of teaching practice. An individual instructor examining the discussion records of a specific course, for example, might be guided in future facilitation to alter the content, tone, or frequency of her postings so as to foster student-to-student interaction, and to elicit more cognitive in-depth processing. Combined with the rating of written assignments, the results of transcript analysis can be the recognition of the impact of the various "inputs" on learning outcomes, with regard to particular objectives. Assuming flexibility on the part of the instructor in designing and redesigning courses, such analyses can be a useful tool for achieving greater teaching effectiveness.

References

Aviv, R., Erlich, Z., Ravid, G., & Geva, A. (2003). Network analysis of knowledge construction in asynchronous learning. *Journal of the Asynchronous Learning Network, 7*(3). Retrieved June 25, 2004, from http://www.aln.org/publications/jaln/v7n3/v7n3_aviv.asp

Bullen, M. (1997). *A case study of participation and critical thinking in a university level course delivered by computer conferencing.* Unpublished doctoral dissertation, University Of British Columbia. Retrieved October 23, 2003, from http://www2.cstudies.ubc.ca/~bullen/diss/thesis.doc

Bullen, M. (1998). Participation and critical thinking in online university distance education. *Journal of Distance Education/Revue de L'Enseignement à Distance.* Retrieved October 23, 2003, from http://cade.athabascau.ca/vol13.2/bullen.html

Garrison, D. R., Anderson, T., & Archer, W. (2001). Critical thinking, cognitive presence and computer conferencing in distance education. *American Journal of Distance Education, 15*(1), 7-23.

Jeong, A. C. (n.d.). *Forum manager.* Retrieved May 26, 2004, from http://bbproject.tripod.com/ForumManager/index.htm

Jeong, A. C. (2003). The sequential analysis of group interaction and critical thinking in online threaded discussions. *American Journal of Distance Education, 17*(1). Retrieved May 26, 2004, from http://dev22448-01.sp01.fsu.edu/Research/Publications/SequentialAnalysis_Jeong2003.pdf

Lally, V. (2001). *Analyzing teaching and learning in networked collaborative learning environments: Issues and work in progress.* Retrieved October 23, 2003, from http://www.mmi.unimaas.nl/euro-cscl/Papers/97/doc

Meyer, K. A. (2003). Face-to-face versus threaded discussions: The role of time and higher-order thinking. *Journal of the Asynchronous Learning Network, 7*(3). Retrieved June 25, 2003, from http://www.aln.org/publications/jaln/v7n3/v7n3_meyer.asp

Newman, D. R., Webb, B., & Cochrane, C. (1995). *A content analysis method to measure critical thinking in face-to-face and computer supported group learning.* Retrieved August 21, 2004, from http://www.qub.ac.uk/mgt/papers/methods/contpap.html

Payne, C. R. (2004). Design for success: Applying progressive educational principles online. In C. Vrasidas & G. V. Glass (Eds.), *Current perspectives on applied information technologies: Preparing teachers to teach* (pp. 231-237). Greenwich, CT: Information Age Publishing.

Rourke, L., Anderson, T., Garrison, D. R., & Archer, W. (1999). Assessing social presence in asynchronous text-based computer conferencing. *Journal of Distance Education/Revue de L'Enseignement à Distance, 14*(2). Retrieved November 13, 2002, from http://cade.athabascau.ca/vol14.2/rourke_et_al.html

Stanford University Interactivity Lab. (n.d.). Retrieved August 21, 2004, from http://interactivity.stanford.edu/

Weasenforth, D., Biesenbach-Lucas, S., & Meloni, C. (2002). Realizing constructivist objectives through collaborative technologies: Threaded discussions. *Language, Learning & Technology, 6*(3), 58-86. Retrieved June 25, 2004, from http://llt.msu.edu/vol6num3/weasenforth/default.html

Wegerif, R. (1998). The social dimension of asynchronous learning networks. *Journal of the Asynchronous Learning Network, 2*(1). Retrieved August 24, 2004, from http://www.aln.org/publications/jaln/v2n1/v2n1_wegerif.asp

Winn, W. (1997). *Learning in Hyperspace.* Retrieved October 23, 2003, from http://www.umuc.edu/ide/potentialweb97/winn.html

Chapter XIV

Mobile Learning Technologies

Diane M. Gayeski, Ithaca College, USA

Introduction

While educational and corporate training environments have made large investments in getting wired to high-speed Internet connections, our work and social environments are rapidly becoming more mobile and flexible. The Internet and organizationally based intranets are powerful learning and performance tools, as long as users have a high-speed connection and up-to-date computing equipment. Online learning and information is not nearly as convenient or reliable when learners need to access sites from their homes, hotel rooms, client locations, or while on the road. In corporate settings, large numbers of critical employees such as factory engineers, health care professionals, builders, and maintenance workers often do not even have offices in which to use a computer.

Beyond the need for fast and flexible access to interactive learning, the field of online learning is being reshaped by several important economic and professional trends:

1.   **Many corporate training departments are moving towards a more holistic professional model of "performance consulting" in which they provide solutions beyond instructional interventions; the trend is to provide short performance support tools and job aids that are meant to be used in the process of actually performing work.** Thus, the need for small and wireless media devices is even more pressing.

Even the smallest laptop is a clumsy reference device when one is trying to troubleshoot a telephone system in a cramped equipment closet or when attempting to develop specs for a new manufacturing facility while walking around a construction site. Moreover, constantly updated information is often needed in tasks such as order-taking or quality control; therefore, some type of wireless connectivity, sometimes called "persistent computing," is needed.

2.   **On the education front, many colleges and universities are attempting to broaden their student base and income by offering courses and noncredit educational experiences to adult learners who are already in the workplace.** Because of this, distance technologies often need to be able to be accessed in nontraditional locations, such as during commuting time. INSEAD, a large international business school based in France and Singapore, is already using applications that run on cell phones to allow their students to collaborate and check on course updates and grades. This is especially useful because many of their students are busy executives who can use their very limited time (such as while commuting or waiting to be served in a restaurant) to engage in coursework. These applications run in coordination with traditional classroom learning as well as WBT-based course materials.

3.   **While interactive learning and Web browsing have become second nature even to very young children, it is expensive and cumbersome to equip elementary and high-school classrooms with traditional computers.** Thus, some other more mobile and less expensive devices that still offer the immediacy and interactivity of the Web are desirable. Many schools have purchased or received grants to equip every student with a small personal digital assistant.

4.   **As education and business are becoming more global, there is a need to provide information and instruction to regions that are not well served by high-speed Internet connections or even good phone service.** In many developing countries, it is much easier and cheaper to use wireless connectivity than to attempt to install conventional wired access. The prevalence of cellular technologies in areas such as Japan, Singapore, and Scandinavia make it attractive to employ wireless systems because of the large installed base of users.

5.   **Finally, millions of personal digital assistants and other handheld technologies such as MP3 audio players are now in the hands of users worldwide.** Many businesspeople already use palm-type computers as date books, and they would like to leverage their investments to use these devices for more applications. Digital audio players and other multifunction devices, including cell phones that connect to the Internet and share pictures, are becoming popular among young people; again, this rapidly growing installed base makes it inexpensive to offer instructional programs on them.

The Rapid Move
Toward Wireless Computing

The communications landscape is becoming wireless even more quickly than it became wired. For example:

- By 2009, there will be more than 61 mobile workers in the United States alone.
- Almost 2 billion people now have cell phones worldwide.
- Of the 9 million handheld computer units purchased in the last few years, 80% are synchronized to some corporate user's computer at work.
- Laptops and personal digital assistants now outnumber conventional desktop computers.
- Over two-thirds of the telephone numbers issued worldwide are for cellular phones.

Today, it is common for office workers to have both cell phones and some type of mobile computing device. For less than the price of lunch for a corporate project team, one can buy wristwatch audio players, a credit card-sized organizer that will store thousands of phone contacts and appointments, or a digital camera that can directly send its pictures via wireless e-mail and browse the Web. New software systems can now turn a home or office PC into a mini-server which you can access from anywhere by using a variety of devices, so you can be sitting in a traffic jam and download an MP3 audio file from your home PC and listen to it on your cell phone, or use your personal digital assistant to retrieve a user's manual from your office server while you are at a client site. College campuses are quickly adopting wireless networks to make instruction, collaboration, and scheduling available at a lower cost per delivery medium and networking than conventional desktop computers and wired campuses (Loh, 2001). Finally, there are literally thousands of "hot spots," which are wireless Internet connections in public locations such as hotels, libraries, airports, and parks (Wi-Fi Freespot Directory, 2004).

New Philosophies of Learning

Being tethered to an Internet line or being saddled with a laptop is not always effective or even possible, but this is not the biggest limitation of typical Web-based training. Beyond the technical constraints, there is a philosophical mismatch between what typically passes as good online training and what modern organizations need to improve performance. Most Web-based training is conceptualized and managed as courses which are designed, produced, and deployed by trainers, and which are in turn taken and passed by learners. These courses mimic college curricula more than workplace performance improvement efforts. This idea of both the course and the learner ever being "done" is a fundamental mismatch with the kind of continuous improvement systems in

Table 1.

PDAs	Personal digital assistants are handheld computers whose built-in software includes an address book, calendar, to-do list, and which also may include miniature versions of word processors, spreadsheets, and email clients. There are two major operating system platforms, Palm OS and Windows Mobile for Pocket PCs. Short training courses, documentation, and expert systems can easily be deployed on these.
MP3 players	These are the next generation Walkmans, but instead of playing cassettes or CDs, they play back digital audio files. The files are typically downloaded from the Web or "ripped" from your own CDs, using a conventional computer. Then they are downloaded into the MP3 player via a simple cable. You listen to files through a headset or adapter that lets you play it through your car radio. Beyond listening to music, trainers can record auditory instructional materials, and major website services provide audio versions of popular management books and magazines.
Digital text, audio, still picture, and video capture devices	A plethora of devices let you capture text, pictures, audio, and motion video. Besides the familiar digital cameras, small hand scanners, the size and shape of pens, are now available. Some of these are stand-alone devices while some (including audio capture devices and small digital still cameras) are built into PDAs. These allow you to create materials for training or documentation, and they also allow end-users to capture pictures or sounds on the job so that they can consult with colleagues or experts.
Tablet computers	These are basically laptops without the keyboard (or with a detachable keyboard) and they are very useful for performance support and data entry on the job. The user draws on the screen itself, or uses a stylus to tap on menu items. They can be strapped onto vehicles such as a truck dashboard or forklift truck, or carried around a construction site or storeroom.
Smart cell phones and pagers	"Smart" cell phones, widespread in Europe, are becoming more popular in other parts of the world; they allow you to wirelessly browse miniature versions of web sites, type short messages to other users, or receive automatic notifications of information such as flight delays or stock prices. Some universities are already employing these in graduate and continuing education courses.
GPS	Global positioning devices use a system of satellites to pinpoint your location—down to a couple of feet—using a small device that periodically sends out signals. These are used, naturally, for locating yourself on a map and creating routes to a destination. Companies with a mobile workforce use these to track performance and as security devices to locate employees who may need help.
Wearable devices	Remember Dick Tracy? Futurists say we'll soon be wearing wrist watches that are cell phones and web browsers, earrings that play music, and necklaces that carry our ID and medical information. They are being employed as performance aids especially within factory and equipment maintenance applications.

place in most organizations. For example, is a course on leadership or negotiation ever really complete and up-to-date—and is a learner ever completely through adding to his or her knowledge in this area?

Instead of courses, many training experts feel that we need "learning bytes": little packages of content and job aids that people can access at the peak moment of "teachability" and performance enhancement. Ideally, learning would occur when and where people need it most, and where it can most readily impact the success of their work. The information would be completely up-to-date, and would be interactive in its style and content.

In order for communication, documentation, and training professionals to align their efforts more closely with the emerging landscape of the modern workplace, they need to move:

- from producing courses to developing learning and performance systems that "grow themselves";
- from managing certification to encouraging continuous learning and collaboration;
- from developing curricula to building structures to capture and store knowledge bytes;
- from teaching and telling to aiding performance; and
- from creating schedules and managing facilities to adapting to the schedules and locations of the workers.

Types of Mobile Devices

Many types of mobile devices are potential platforms for information and collaboration that support learning and performance improvement in the workplace.

So, envision this: instructional designers now have a mobile delivery system for instruction, communication, collaboration, and performance aids that combines the following:

- Phone calls
- Music or audio playback
- Video and still-frame picture capture
- The ability to browse Web sites online
- E-mail send and receive
- Text and voice paging
- Global positioning and interactive map directions
- Multimedia, hypertext training, and documentation
- Expert systems and smart job aids
- Programs that monitor performance or take measurements or perform calculations for workers

Applications

Many corporations are already creating innovative and highly effective applications for mobile computing devices. For example, Cisco has created a small documentation and job aid program on one of its routers that can be downloaded from its Web site onto a PDA. Intel uses video clips on a Pocket PC to disseminate best practices to technicians in their chip factories. Maines Paper and Food service uses GPS systems and Palm computers to aid in the accuracy and efficiency of its delivery system to restaurants. Location scouts in the film industry use wirelessly connected video cameras to shoot and e-mail pictures of potential shooting sites to producers, saving days in their schedules. Cypress Semiconductor's Vice President of Marketing creates MP3 audio news programs that his staff can download on their computers or on portable MP3 players to listen to as they jog or commute. Telecommunications repair fleets for SBC Corporation are using ruggedized laptops that combine computer-based training, expert systems, and actual testing devices. And BOC Gases deploys wearable computers with interactive documentation that allows technicians in factories to quickly inspect and repair refrigeration systems.

In educational applications, Drexel University now uses a Web-based infrastructure that allows students to access their e-mail, pay bills, check on grades, and work with course materials either using conventional computers or wireless devices such as cell phones and personal digital assistants. One math teacher in Irvine, California has a class set of 40 (numbered) PDAs that she uses to give quizzes; the devices have become very popular with the students. The students are given the quiz ID of the assessment for that day, and they enter their student ID and quiz ID into the Classroom Wizard program. After answering the questions on the PDA, a student beams his or her answers to the teacher's computer, which scores it right away, and the student's score appears on his or her PDA. Medical residents in anesthesia in Great Britain use a program developed by their professors to access information about prescribing the right form and dosage of medications. And even elementary school students are using quizzes and games that run on handheld computers, thanks to simple and inexpensive authoring programs that any teacher can learn.

The challenge will not be in learning how to use and create programming for these devices: this is actually quite simple and versions of popular authoring tools are being introduced. Rather, this next revolution in technology will bring about discontinuities that will require a change in the fundamental approach to training, communication, collaboration, and performance support in the workplace. These devices are already being used widely in elementary schools, high schools, and colleges; the new workforce will not only accept this technology, but will demand it.

Acknowledgment

This chapter is derived from the author's latest book, *Learning Unplugged*.

References

Gayeski, D. (2002). *Learning unplugged: Using mobile devices for organizational learning and performance improvement.* New York: AMACOM.

Loh, C. S. (2001, November-December). Learning tools for knowledge nomads: Using personal digital assistants (PDAs) in Web-based learning environments. *Educational Technology,* 5-14.

Wi-Fi Freespot Directory. (n.d.). Retrieved July 29, 2004, from http://www.wififree spot.com/

Chapter XV

Strategies for Sharing the ReMoTe:
Changing the Nature of Online Collaboration

Richard Caladine, University of Wollongong, Australia

Brian Yecies, University of Wollongong, Australia

Introduction

Online learning or e-learning has had an impact on the way many institutions around the world provide opportunities for learning. For the past five years, the University of Wollongong, like many others, has taken a blended approach to online learning. Blended learning combines face-to-face and online learning. In the online component, learners interact with Web pages and online resources under the umbrella of a course management system (CMS). While the CMS has been highly successful, there are some online teaching and learning functions that could not be easily undertaken. These involve group work, and it was believed that an online system that fostered cooperation, collaboration, social and active learning would provide opportunities for deep learning (Ramsden, 1992). For some time many researchers have sought a solution for online collaboration or group work that moved beyond text-based discussions. The work by others in the area of Computer-Supported Collaborative Learning (CSCL) has provided insightful theoretical contributions (Crawley, 2003; Jefferies, 2002; Paavola, Lipponen, & Hakkarainen, 2002). To explore CSCL, the University of Wollongong funded an initiative that proved the concept of online collaboration through the use of database-driven Web pages. The initiative was called CUPID.

A Description of CUPID

A CUPID—or Collaborative, User-Produced Internet Document—is a new way of using the World Wide Web. Functionally, CUPIDs enable users to add content to Web pages or edit existing content on CUPID pages. The technology that makes this possible is centred around a database that is a repository for the information to be displayed on the Web page. To add new content or edit existing content, users add or change information using Web forms. When the new information is submitted, the database is updated and a rebuilding of the Web page is triggered. This technology is functionally similar to that used in Wiki Wiki Web (http://c2.com/cgi/wiki?WikiWikiWeb) and in the Xerox PARC-developed Sparrow (http://www2.parc.com/istl/projects/sparrow/).

A significant benefit of CUPID is that no programming skills are required of users since they input information via pre-designed Web forms. Once the information has been submitted to the database, it then rebuilds the Web page. In this way the database constructs or "drives" the Web site. Once material has been added to the page, it may be edited by users with the appropriate permission by selecting a link to an edit function from the page. Reloading then adds the new and changed material to the displayed page, thus generating the latest iteration of a collaboratively produced Web page. An administration page, generally controlled by the course coordinator, allows for control of the content and layout to ensure the suitability of content developed by the group (see Figure 1).

Figure 1. Collaborative User-Produced Internet Document (CUPID)—schematic

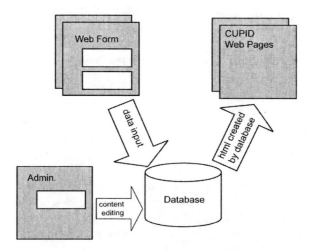

Figure 2. Learning activities model (adapted from Caladine, 2003)

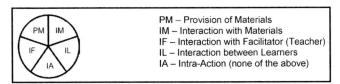

PM – Provision of Materials
IM – Interaction with Materials
IF – Interaction with Facilitator (Teacher)
IL – Interaction between Learners
IA – Intra-Action (none of the above)

Why CUPIDs Were Developed

Online learning has developed quickly in many institutions, with sophisticated course management systems being *de rigueur*. The tools available in most CMSs can be classified as one-way or two-way tools that are used in learning and in administration. Examples of administration tools include lists of marks and indicators of students' progress through courses. Examples of learning tools include materials, such as the Web pages they interact with, and communication tools like e-mail, discussions, and chat.

The learning activities model (Caladine, 2003) provides a classification system for these tools (see Figure 2) in which they can be categorised as tools for interaction with materials or tools for interaction with people. Unfortunately, to date the technology has caused a separation of these two groups of tools which contrasts to the learning experience in many classrooms, particularly where group work is concerned. In many instances it is the norm that communications between learners and the teacher happen coincidently to and with interaction with materials. It is suggested that the imposition of the separation of communications from the interaction with materials can impact on the effectiveness of learning. CUPID technology removes this separation. CUPID technology also creates opportunities that foster the social and collaborative aspects of learning that lead to deeper learning. One example is to facilitate online teamwork in which groups of learners produce materials.

Developing skills of group work or teamwork is considered an important part of education by many institutions. The University of Wollongong has developed a number of attributes of university graduates. One of these is: "a capacity for, and understanding of, teamwork" (University of Wollongong, 2004a), and the university's code of practice states:

Many members of staff believe that group work develops capacity for teamwork and prepares graduates to be effective in employment where they will be expected to work as part of a team. (University of Wollongong, 2004b)

As the university has a number of campuses and approximately 60% of learners undertake the online component of their learning from home, there is a need to provide opportunities for teamwork to learners who are geographically dispersed. One of the common teamwork tasks is the creation of group reports. In the past, some attempts at online group reporting have been less than satisfactory. This was due to the time and lack of synergy inherent in the serial process of successive group members adding their contribution to the report being circulated between members of the group. CUPIDs allow students who are at a distance to collaborate on group projects in a parallel fashion.

Technologically, database-driven Web pages, or CUPIDs, refer to a functionality rather than an application. A clearer understanding of how CUPIDs work and their scope can be achieved through the ways in which CUPID technology has been applied to learning.

CUPID technology was developed in two stages, which were referred to as CUPID 1 and CUPID 2. With CUPID 1 applications, users' input is restricted to ASCII characters. In CUPID 2 applications, files can be uploaded to the database. Clearly there are many issues in the use of CUPID 2 technology, not the least of which concern securing of the database from unwanted input. In addition, users need to be provided with guidelines for file type and size limitation. Although the use of CUPID 2 is complicated by placing constraints on what may be uploaded, the advantages are usually worth the extra work.

To date two types of CUPID applications have been developed. Firstly, some standard templates for CUPID technology have been built to provide the following applications:

- Collaborative Online Glossary (COG)
- Collaborative Online Reporting (COR)
- Online Student Collected and Annotated Resources (OSCAR)

Secondly, a small number of highly specific and customised applications have been developed. One of these is ReMoTe.

Figure 3. ReMoTe homepage

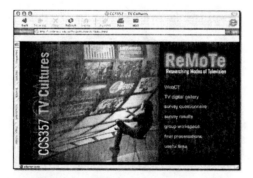

A Description of ReMoTe

Researching Modes of Television (ReMoTe) is a Web-based tool and environment that allows participants to add their own contributions to a Collaborative, User-Produced Internet Document. It is a virtual group workspace that facilitates learning activities between learners based in Wollongong, and in four other satellite campuses located throughout the South Coast and Southern Highlands of New South Wales (NSW), Australia. ReMoTe enables students to upload survey research results and digital images of multiple respondents' televisions. A digital gallery links these images and their corresponding survey findings. A series of pre- and post-production spaces permits each student to contribute an individual critical analysis, which is then expanded into a group report and finally published on the site.

ReMoTe was the major assessment task for students enrolled in the 2003 offering of the Television Cultures (CCS357) course in the School of Social Sciences, Media, and Communication at the University of Wollongong. The project began as a challenge to create opportunities for high levels of interactivity between small groups of students across five different campuses. The general aim of the project was to enable students to work more effectively in groups as well as negotiate roles and task responsibilities. It was designed to:

- Help students develop a capacity for, and understanding of, teamwork
- Give them a basic understanding of information literacy and specific skills in acquiring, organising, and presenting information, particularly through computer-based activity

The specific aim of the project was to investigate and analyse the television cultures of a sample of residents living in the Illawarra, South Coast, and Southern Highlands—regional areas of NSW, Australia. The project addressed the following questions:

Figure 4. Digital gallery
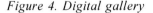

Figure 5. Group workspace

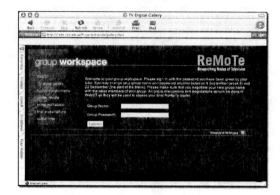

- What makes television cultures of these regions distinct?
- What do our TVs look like?
- What do we place around them?
- What are our favourite kinds of TV shows?
- What types of functions do our TVs serve in our lives?
- In what ways has TV influenced our lives?
- How can we share these findings and other thoughts with our classmates and the larger community?

These were some of the core research questions that drove the project, made it relevant to the CCS357 course, and tied it to the overall aims of the Communication and Cultural Studies program at the University of Wollongong.

How ReMoTe Worked

Students used the following steps in their interactions with the ReMoTe project.

1. Students from eight tutorial discussion groups across five different campuses were randomly assigned to small groups of five. Each group was allocated their own production workspace, which was protected by a password.

2. Each group member introduced themselves to one another via asynchronous postings in their group space and selected specific tasks to perform such as writing the abstract, introduction, or conclusion; overall editing (spelling, style, grammar); creating subheadings and transitions between paragraphs; scanning; uploading; and so forth.

3. All members of each group conducted a research survey of local people living in the surrounding communities. A photo of the interviewee's TV was taken as part of the data-collection process.

4. Students scanned and uploaded the image into the digital gallery space.

5. Each group member—working in their group's pre-production project space—selected one TV image to analyse from the digital gallery and wrote an individual 500-word analysis.

6. The group joined together all of the individual analyses in a post-production area and expanded their analysis by adding the abstract, introduction, and so on, and at least one Excel chart/graph, reflecting the collected aggregate data displayed in the digital gallery. The length of all final ReMoTe group reports was intended to be between 4,000 and 5,000 words (approximately 1,000 words per each group member).

7. Students sent the instructor their peer-evaluations regarding the contributions their fellow ReMoTe group members had made.

8. Finally, all of the group projects were published in the site's final project space and were available for viewing.

Feedback from Learners

For many students, the online collaborative report writing assignment provided a new type of learning experience. ReMoTe was different. It was more dynamic than most of the individual and small-group assignments they had completed for other courses at the University of Wollongong. ReMoTe moved away from a learning model involving a high level of interaction with the teacher (IF category in Figure 2) and concentrated more on facilitating interaction between learners (IL category in Figure 2). ReMoTe taught them how to communicate with classmates over the Internet and created opportunities to make new friends. They seemed to enjoy working with their randomly selected group members. Overall, the positive feedback from each group indicated that the site offered a level of peer support that an individual assignment may not have facilitated. The project provided students with a better understanding of how people could work together in an online environment. Enabling a flexible working schedule also had great appeal for students. The online aspect of the project allowed them to complete their group work from home with ease and interact with others in their own time. In addition, the constant communication between group members that the online environment offered and the project required was seen as a positive attraction to the assignment. Another helpful dimension was how all the assignment tasks were divided, self-nominated, and negotiated among group members in asynchronous discussion postings. This better ensured the burden of all the work did not fall on one person, as often happens with more traditional face-to-face group projects. Regarding basic layout and aesthetics, the site was easy to navigate, as there were simple links to follow and all of the different workspaces within the site were clearly labelled. Learners considered the layout to be simple but attractive. Thus, the concluding findings from the learner's feedback was that the project succeeded in its goal of bringing a small, geographically diverse group of students together in a user-friendly online environment.

While a majority of learners enjoyed their online, collaborative, group experience, those who were less computer savvy had a frustrating time with the site. For this smaller group, the site did not seem to work as it was supposed to. However, this seemed to be due to technological issues concerning browser incompatibilities and/or slow dial-up speeds. Part of the frustration also originated from less dependable group members who either fell behind with deadlines or showed little interest in maintaining frequent communication (discussion postings) with their group. The unreliability of a small number of group members was seen as downright rudeness. Other learners lost work they thought had been saved in the site and experienced minor problems with file and image size uploading limitations. Finally, those with less online experience were daunted by the "computer" aspect of the overall project and at times felt as if they were enrolled in a computer course. These are all real-world concerns that come with participating in a collaborative group exercise like ReMoTe, and the comments have been taken on-board for future revisions.

Lessons Learned

The 10 key lessons learned from ReMoTe were:

1. Assignments with collaborative online environments can help learners develop negotiation skills and encourage them to work as team members.

2. Participants are more likely to avoid their task responsibilities in a group report writing assignment if they fail to communicate frequently with their group members.

3. Successful groups—that is, groups that worked well together and met all of their deadlines—consisted of individuals who were friendly and willing to take the initiative by encouraging others to keep up with the tasks.

4. The more a group communicated with one another via asynchronous discussion postings, the less stress the group seemed to experience.

5. Online environments like ReMoTe—used in conjunction with face-to-face meetings—offer a blended learning experience that students seem to prefer. Blended learning can be an opportunity to combine the richness of human interaction with the flexibility of online learning.

6. Protecting the security of login names, passwords, and written materials in a group's pre- and post-production workspace is an important concern of most participants.

7. Enforcing strict deadlines and requiring periodic progress reports from each group helps learners keep up with the different production stages of the project.

8.   Providing an opportunity for distance learners to work in real time—or at least offering synchronous chat in the group workspace—would solve problems of losing data in the group workspace and/or wasting time by unknowingly working on older versions of group work.

9.   Setting deadlines for 1:00 p.m. on weekdays when IT support is available (and networks are less likely to be down for servicing), rather than at midnight on Sunday evenings, provides better continuity of service.

10. Nearly all students indicated that participating in the ReMoTe online collaborative site was worthwhile despite any initial learning curves and minor technological problems experienced.

Developer's Reflections

In retrospect, the most difficult task of the project was creating a relevant research project that was congruent with the larger aims of the Television Cultures course, while offering small groups of students from geographically dispersed locations a meaningful opportunity to collaborate in an online environment. The questions that were addressed included:

•   How could this be done?
•   What would a collaborative online space look like?

The answers lay in creating a project that: (1) enabled learners to work more effectively in groups and negotiate roles and task responsibilities, (2) gave learners field research experience, and (3) created a database of survey findings concerning how television has influenced the lives of people living in regional New South Wales.

There are significant issues for designers of such projects to consider. Developing and maintaining the ReMoTe site has been more time consuming than originally imagined. An initial internal e-learning grant assisted with the project's start-up development. However, securing additional funding for making revisions and addressing ongoing maintenance issues has been more challenging. In addition, the current workloads model at the University of Wollongong, and possibly other universities like it, could benefit from an appropriate way to account for and encourage teaching innovations such as ReMoTe and other CUPIDs like it.

Nevertheless, would I do it again? Was it worth it? Yes and yes. The ability to facilitate interactions between learners at five different campuses has made it all worthwhile. Clearly, to undertake a project of this nature requires a significant amount of time. Given the large workload implications of ReMoTe, it has become apparent that future projects will need to coincide as closely as possible with one's research interests.

The Future of CUPID

As CUPID technology is embraced by teachers and learners, it is expected that patterns of demand and usage will emerge that will indicate some common applications. For example, Collaborative Online Glossary (COG) and Collaborative Online Reporting (COR) have proved popular to the degree that automation of establishment is being tested. A possible future scenario could be that when a teacher is organising the online material for a course, he or she could elect to include a CUPID. Through a Web interface, he or she would submit the required information. This would stimulate a database to create a CUPID of the requested type and URLs for the CUPID, and the administration page would be e-mailed by the database to the teacher. Another proposed development is the convergence of CUPIDs with other communications applications. For example, an online audio chat in parallel with a CUPID could enhance the interactions between users. Of course, this would reduce the flexibility of when learners interact with CUPID.

The functionality afforded by CUPIDs to online collaboration can provide opportunities for a host of new activities and hence they occupy a vital place in online learning of the future. CUPIDs can support deeper learning through the provision of opportunities for learning in a social context where individuals have clear responsibilities for the work of the group, engage with concepts through their own learning, connect them to concepts presented by peers—and do all this with the convenience of flexibility of time and place.

References

Caladine, R. (2003). *New theoretical frameworks of learning activities, learning technologies and a new method of technology selection.* Unpublished doctoral dissertation, University of Wollongong, Australia.

Crawley, R. (2003). *What is CSCL? Computer-Supported Collaborative Learning or just another name for groupware?* Joint Information Systems Committee, University of Brighton. Retrieved July 26, 2004, from http://www.bton.ac.uk/cscl/jtap/what_is.htm

Jefferies, P. (2003). ICT in supporting collaborative learning: Pedagogy and practice. *Journal of Educational Media, 28*(1), 35-48.

Paavola, S., Lipponen, L., & Hakkarainen, K. (2002). Epistemological foundations for CSCL: A comparison of three models of innovative knowledge communities. *Proceedings of Computer Support for Collaborative Learning* (CSCL 2002), Boulder, Colorado. Retrieved July 26, 2004, from http://newmedia.colorado.edu/cscl/228.html

Ramsden, P. (1992). *Learning to teach in higher education.* London: Routledge.

University of Wollongong. (2004a). *Attributes of a Wollongong graduate.* Retrieved March 19, 2004, from http://www.uow.edu.au/about/teaching/attributes/

University of Wollongong. (2004b). *Code of practice—teaching and assessment.* Retrieved March 19, 2004, from http://www.uow.edu.au/handbook/codesofprac/teaching_code.html

Chapter XVI

Integrating Multimedia Cues in E-Learning Documents for Enhanced Learning

Ankush Mittal, Indian Institute of Technology, India

Krishnan V. Pagalthivarthi, Indian Institute of Technology, India

Edward Altman, Institute for Infocomm Research, Singapore

Introduction

The digitization of educational content is radically transforming the learning environment of the student. A single lecture, as well as supporting reference material, textbook chapters, simulations, and threaded chat system archives, may be captured on one hour of video, a set of 20 or more slides, and ancillary text resources. A single course may contain 25 such lectures and a single department may have 30 distinct courses that have been digitized in a single year. If, while taking one course, a student wants to find a relevant definition, example, discussion, or illustration of a concept, then the student would potentially need to search as much as 750 hours of video, 15,000 slides, and a huge volume of text in order to find the desired information. Thus the online student is overwhelmed by a flood of multimedia data which inhibits the development of insight.

Insight is a key ingredient of education and is most often achieved by the manipulation of information through the discovery of new relationships, identification of hidden structures, or the construction of domain models. The methodology of instructional design may be used to anticipate the needs of the student in the controlled environment of a classroom with novice learners, but it is inadequate for the needs of a heterogeneous population of online learners. Intelligent tutoring systems provide an additional degree of flexibility for the independent learner, but are difficult to produce and maintain. The advanced learner needs powerful search and organizational tools to support self-guided learning. In all three cases there is a need for content-based retrieval of multimedia resources ranging from simple indexing and navigation of lectures to ontology-based mining of information nuggets from large repositories of heterogeneous content.

The needs of the independent learner are particularly demanding due to the requirements for real-time, context-dependant, and precise retrieval of unstructured and incomplete information distributed across multiple media sources. Due to the large size of the corpus and the highly focused nature of the target information, the systematic labeling (either manually or automatically) of the media is not feasible. Instead, we propose a system for *media hot spotting.*

Media hot spotting is the process of finding *hot spots* within the text, audio, video, and other media content. A hot spot may be a distribution of key terms in a text document; a matching distribution of terms in the speech track of a lecture video; or a sequence of writing, emphasis, and gesture events in the video stream of a lecture, where an event is a spatial or temporal set of interrelated features. Individually, each piece of information does not convey sufficient semantic information to identify the informational content of the media. In combination, they provide significant evidence, for instance, that a Definition event has occurred in the media and that a particular term has most likely been defined within the context of this event. Thus, given a model for how information co-occurs across different media objects, hot spotting enables the rapid retrieval of candidate media content for further analysis and reference.

Content-based solutions are available for domains like sports and news, but have not yet been systematically explored for educational videos (Idris & Panchanathan, 1997; Mittal & Cheong, 2003; Woudstra et al., 1998). This chapter describes a new method of content-based retrieval for e-learning videos using camera motion cues, audio features, slide layout, and associated decision rules. Using this technique, we are able to separate the lecture videos into several component states and personalize the video from these states. For our experiments, we used 26 lecture videos from the Singapore-MIT Alliance, along with the associated PowerPoint slides.

This chapter is organized as follows. The next section presents a discussion of an existing distance learning program (SMA) and other related work. Then an overview of our approach is presented, followed by the section titled "Multimedia Indexing Features," where we show the framework for modeling multimedia information and present a list of the most useful features used in the video segmentation task. The section titled "Indexing of Lectures" elaborates upon the mapping of low-level features to lecture semantics. Finally, we discuss the experimental results and significance of this approach.

Distance Learning Paradigm

Singapore: MIT Alliance Educational Setup

The work presented here relates to the materials used in the Singapore-MIT Alliance (SMA)[1] development program. SMA is an innovative engineering education and research collaboration among the National University of Singapore (NUS), Nanyang Technological University (NTU), and the Massachusetts Institute of Technology (MIT). SMA classes are held in specially equipped classrooms at the Singaporean institutes and at MIT using live video transmission over the Internet. The synchronous transmission allows participants at both locations to see each other and speak normally. However, because of the 12-hour time zone difference, SMA has made a great effort to find and develop tools to enhance asynchronous learning.

SMA lectures are given daily, and it is expensive to process, index, and label them through manual methods. Immediate availability of the lectures is also important because the courses are fast paced and build sequentially upon earlier lectures. Techniques for the efficient indexing and retrieval of lecture videos are required in order to cope with the volume of lecture video data produced by the SMA program and other media-intensive programs.

SMA is just one example of how the application of information technology to digital media is rapidly enhancing the field of distance education. The effective use of information technology enables institutions to go beyond the classroom to create personalized, lifelong learning for the student. This results in a repository of potential learning experiences that is available not only for the student, but also available for incremental refinement and elaboration by the lecturer.

Related Work

Using video for educational purposes is a topic that has been addressed at least since the 1970s (Chambers & Specher, 1980; Michalopoulos, 1976). Recently the focus of the research has been on the maximum utilization of educational video data which has accumulated over a period of time. Ip and Chan (1998) use the lecture notes along with Optical Character Recognition (OCR) techniques to synchronize the video with the text. A hierarchical index is formed by analyzing the original lecture text to extract different levels of headings. An underlying assumption is made that the slides are organized as a hierarchy of topics, which is not always the case. Many slides may have titles which are in no way related to the previous slide.

Bibiloni and Galli (1996) proposed a system using a human intermediary (the teacher) as an interpreter to manually index the video. Although this system indexes the video, it is highly dependent upon the vocabulary used by the teacher, which may differ from person to person. Moreover, even the same person may have a different interpretation of the same image or video at different times, as pointed out by Ip and Chan (1998).

Hwang, Youn, Deshpande, and Sun (1997) propose a hypervideo editor tool to allow the instructor to mark various portions of the class video and create the corresponding hyperlinks and multimedia features to facilitate the students' access to these prerecorded sequences through a Web browser. This scheme also requires a human intermediary and thus is not generalized.

The recently developed COVA system (Cha & Chung, 2001) offers browsing and querying in a lecture database; however, it constructs the lecture index using a digital textbook and neglects other sources of information such as audio or PowerPoint slides. A similar work (Mittal, Dixit, Maheshwari, & Sung, 2003) concentrated on deriving semantic relationships between concepts and answering queries solely based on PowerPoint slides. Thus, it can be concluded that the integration of the information present in various e-learning materials has not been systematically explored.

State Model for Lectures and Overview of Our Approach

The integration of information contained in e-learning materials depends upon the creation of a unifying index that can be applied across information sources. In content-based retrieval systems, it is often convenient to create a *state model* in which nodes represent semantically meaningful states and the links between nodes represent the transition probabilities between states. Thus, the methodology for constructing an educational video information system begins with the creation of a state model for the lecture, where the states are based on the pedagogical style of teaching. For the purpose of illustrating the concept, let us consider computer science courses, especially theoretical ones like Introduction to Algorithms. In this case, each lecture can be said to contain one or more topics. Each topic contains zero or more of the following:

- **Introduction:** general overview of the topic
- **Definitions and Theorems:** formal statement of core elements of the topic
- **Theory:** derivations with equations and diagrams
- **Discussions:** examples with equations and diagrams
- **Review:** repetition of key ideas
- **Question and Answer:** dialogue session with the students
- **Sub-Topic:** branch to a related topic

A simple state model for a video-based lecture can be represented as shown in Figure 1. This model for indexing e-learning videos is a state model consisting of 10 different states linked by maximal probability edges. Each state follows the probabilistic edges to go to another state. For example, from state Topic, one potential next state is Definition with a probability of 0.91 and another potential next state is Discussion with a probability

Figure 1. State diagram model of a lecture

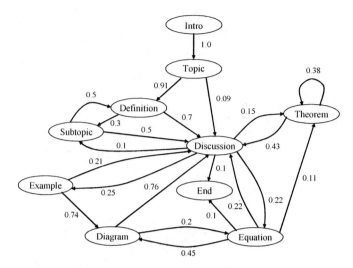

Each state follows the probabilistic edges to go to another state. For instance, an Example in a lecture is preceded by a Discussion, and can be followed by Discussion again or a Diagram. Only the most likely edges from a state are depicted. Thus, in this model the state Example will most likely go to either Discussion (0.21) or Diagram (0.74).

of 0.09. Figure 1 shows the corresponding probabilities of transitions from one state to another based on our analysis of the SMA lecture corpus.

The state model implicitly encodes information about the temporal relationships between events. For instance, it is clear from Figure 1 that the introduction of a topic is never followed by a theorem without giving a definition. The state model, supplemented with our indexing techniques (discussed in later sections), provides useful information regarding the possible progression of topics in the lecture. For example, if a lecture is in the Discussion state and has some special attribute such as a camera zoom on the blackboard, we can say with a high level of confidence that it will go next to the Example state. Thus, the state diagram provides a framework for making inferences about lectures which can be used to determine the probable flow of pedagogical transitions that occur in the lecture.

Overview of Our Approach

Various camera motion techniques such as zooming in, zooming out, and panning can be extracted from educational videos. We match sequences of such camera motions to various states in the lectures, such as Theorem, Equation, and so forth (see Figure 1). In addition, we use the information available through the nonvisual media, including text from PowerPoint slides and audio from the lecture, to correctly correlate the heterogeneous media sources. Lastly, we are able to perform contextual searches for media content with minimal use of manual annotations.

The semantic analysis of raw video consists of four steps:

1. **Extract low- and mid-level features:** Examples of low-level features are color, motion, and italicized text. Some mid-level features are zoom-in and increased hand movement of the lecturer. Numerical representations of these features for a particular video segment are then assembled into a vector for subsequent processing.

2. **Classify the feature vectors into a finite set of states within the lecture:** States may correspond to Definitions, Emphasis, Topic Change, Q&A, Review, and so on. These are the objects and events identified in the lecture which are likely to be associated with semantically meaningful events.

3. **Apply contextual information to the sequence of states to determine higher-level semantic events:** such as defining a new term, reviewing a topic, or engaging in off-topic discussion.

4. **Apply a set of high-level constraints to the sequences of semantic events:** to improve the consistency of the final labeling.

Multimedia Feature Extraction and Analysis

Feature extraction is a widely accepted initial step towards video indexing. Features are interpretation-independent characteristics that are computationally derived from the media. Examples are pitch and noise for audio, and color histogram and shape for images. Experience across a wide range of multimedia applications has resulted in the identification of a large number of features that are useful for indexing (Gonzalez & Woods, 1992). The next step is to add semantics to the collection of features (e.g., high pitch in audio, pointing gestures, hand velocity, etc.) so one can use relationships among the features to infer the occurrence of higher level events (Gudivada & Raghavan, 1995).

Multimedia Indexing Features

The key influencing factor for the success of any video indexing algorithm is the type of features employed for the analysis. Many features have been proposed for this purpose (Idris & Panchanathan, 1997). Some are task specific, while others are more general and can be useful for a variety of applications.

Audio Features

There are many features that can be used to characterize audio signals. The three features of volume, spoken word rate, and spectral components have proven to be useful for lecture analysis. Volume is a reliable indicator for detecting silence, which may help to segment an audio sequence and determine event boundaries. The temporal variation in volume can reflect the scene content. For example, a sudden increase in volume may indicate a transition to a new topic. Spoken word rate and recurrence of a particular word are indicators for the scope of a topic or cluster of words within a discussion (Witbrock & Hauptmann, 1997). Finally, spectral component features refer to the Fourier Transform of the samples of the audio signal. Analysis of the frequency components of audio signals using signal processing methods provides support for speaker change detection and other advanced tasks.

Video Features

A great amount of research has gone into summarizing and reviewing various features useful for video segmentation (Wang, Liu, & Huang, 2000). The color histogram, which represents the color distribution in an image, is one of the most widely used color features. The simplest histogram method computes the gray level or color histogram of two frames. If the difference between the two histograms is above the threshold, a boundary shot is assumed.

Motion is also an important attribute of video. Motion information can be generated by block matching or optical flow techniques (Akutsu, Tonomura, Ohba, & Hashimoto, 1992). Motion features such as motion field, motion histogram, or global motion parameters can be extracted from motion vectors. Other video features include texture, compression, and shape, which have been addressed in many papers. The features presented above have been used in different image retrieval systems to effectively perform a video segmentation.

Text Features

In the distance learning paradigm, text is one of the most important features that still has not been researched and utilized extensively. Ip and Chan (1998) propose text-assisted video content extraction, but only to synchronize the video with the text. Text extracted from PowerPoint slides, which are generally provided with educational videos, inherently stores a great deal of information, as we shall see with the SMA lectures.

Indexing of Lectures

The most important and basic steps in a video indexing engine are to extract salient features and then combine these to get the most efficient indexes. A potentially rich source of pedagogical information is the blackboard activity during the presentation of the lecture, which in turn is highly correlated with the content of the lecture notes. Thus, a proper analysis of the lecture notes, which occur as PowerPoint slides, along with the properties discussed below provide an effective means for identifying pedagogical structures in the lecture video.

The PowerPoint slides that are distributed as lecture notes inherently store important information regarding the lecture, which is still largely untapped. Information in the form of the size, shape, color, and boldness of fonts reveals important aspects of the lecture. The state model for the educational videos discussed before enables us to divide the full lecture into four basic categories, namely: Definitions & Theorems, Examples, Proofs, and Formulae. In the analysis of the SMA lectures, we found that there exist stylistic conventions in the PowerPoint slides such as: all the important words (keywords with definitions) are in red and italicized; the special names are always in quotes; the slides having an example always have the word "example" in it; the questions and FAQs have a question mark in the particular slide; and the common names are always in square brackets. Some video features such as camera *zoom in* or *zoom out* to the blackboard or to the audience also specify a transition in the lecture from one state to another state, say from Diagram to Discussion state. The rules for indexing the slides in the above-mentioned four categories can be summarized as follows.

Category 1: Definitions and Theorems

The keywords or defined terms are always red and in italics, so if there is a definition in the slide, it should have a red italicized word. The word *definition* or *theorem* may be present, but the string queried (the string is the set of words that one is searching for) must be found in the slide.

Category 2: Examples

The course material under consideration for Introduction to Algorithms has an associated image file for all the examples to represent special graphics or equations. The presence of the text pattern *'examples'* or *'examples:'* along with the string queried, is mandatory for a slide to qualify as one containing examples.

When analyzing the text, the context of the current slide is related to the previous slides. Figure 2 illustrates a case where a single example is presented in a sequence of slides. The sequence of processing steps for the well-known sorting algorithm called merge sort is illustrated in these slides. Progressive changes between consecutive slides provide evidence for labeling the associated video as the Example state. In the case of Figure 3, there is an example embedded in a definition as indicated by the word *example* found towards the bottom of the slide. Thus, the context of the particular example is linked to the contents above it and the topic currently being discussed.

Category 3: Proof

The word *proof* along with the string queried is assumed to be present in the slides having relevant information associated with the query. This assumption is a generalized one and can be used for all distance courseware.

Figure 2. Slides illustrating the determination of context on the basis of text

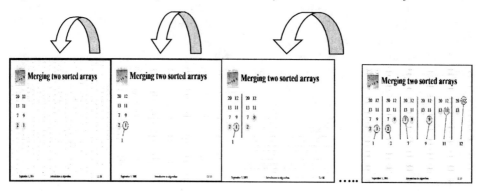

A definition is followed by the solved example. As shown in the above slides, there is no mention of the word "example," though clearly this is an illustration of how a sorting technique works (Merge Sort). Notice the minor differences between consecutive slides that help in detecting the Example state.

Figure 3. This slide shows the definition of a concept with an embedded example

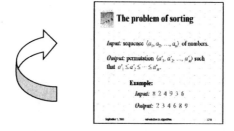

Note that there are no words in the slide explicitly referring to a "definition."

Category 4: Formulae

Slides containing embedded formulae can be easily identified through the identification of special symbols used to represent the mathematical expressions. Queries for mathematical expressions can be resolved by converting the query expression into a string of characters and then performing pattern matching. Special attention must be given to matching expressions that may assume alternate forms, such as fractions and summations.

This set of rules for indexing the slides is supplemented by video features to improve the overall quality of the video indexing. It is well known that video features taken in isolation are highly ambiguous. The video feature for *zoom out* may indicate either discussion in the class, the presentation of a definition, or simply a technique to reduce the tedium of the video (see Figure 4). Similarly, we find that the video feature *zoom in* may indicate the occurrence of the Topic, Example, Diagram, Theorem, or Equation states. Although

Figure 4. (a) Zoom in to the lecturer; (b) Zoom out to the room

(a)   (b)

Table 1. Summary of the video and text features

State	Video Features		Text Features	
Topic	1.)	Zoom In	1.)	Slide Title.
	2.)	Stay Zoomed In		
	3.)	Underline on board		
Definition	1.)	Zoom Out	1.)	Defined Word is Red Italicized.
	2.)	Input and Output on board	2.)	Presence of word Definition or Theorem along with defined word.
Example	1.)	Zoom In	1.)	Presence of word Example: or Examples along with topic.
	2.)	Ex: on blackboard	2.)	An associated *.gif file.
Discussion	1.)	Zoom out for entire class	1.)	No or much less blackboard activity.
	2.)	Change in voice		
	OR			
	1.)	Zoom In on lecturer		
	2.)	Increased hand movement of lecturer		
Theorem	1.)	Zoom In	1.)	Defined Word is Red Italicized.
	2.)	Theorem or Proof or Corollary in PPT	2.)	Presence of word Definition or Theorem.
	3.)	Same as (2.) but on blackboard		
Formulae & Equation	1.)	Zoom In on blackboard	1.)	Associated *.gif file.
			2.)	Associated *.wmf file.

Notice that there is overlap of some features in two states, but by using other features, some distinction can be achieved.

there is a large overlap between pairs of features, the combination of multiple features given in Table 1 dramatically improves the accuracy of the state classification.

After the entire lecture has been classified, the labeled metadata can be used to perform multiple functions. The first one is searching in context. Several automatic frameworks exist for searching in context (e.g., Mittal and Altman, 2003). Here we employ a simple contextual searching algorithm. To enable searching in context, we need to manually enter the topic names for each video clip associated with a significant pedagogical event identified by the application of the classification rule set. Once the topic names have been keyed into the topic lists, we can then perform a contextual search just by searching for all occurrences of the queried subject and returning the results. This method is accurate because under our definition of the Topic state, all subject matter that is important enough to be explained separately is classified as a Topic or a Subtopic. For example, when *quicksort* is mentioned under the divide-and-conquer method (divide-and-conquer is a generic technique and quicksort is its specific application), our system classifies *quicksort* as a subtopic. Again, when *insertion sort* is compared with *quicksort,* it classifies *insertion sort* as another subtopic. As a result, the topic list is comprehensive in covering all material that is of importance. Hence, we are able to retrieve all instances of a particular query by searching through the topic list.

Experimental Results and Applications

The key idea is to create a system that automatically segments the educational videos so students can then use it to view the desired sections of the lectures without going through a linear search, thereby saving them time and effort. We tested our method on 26 lecture videos from the Singapore-MIT Alliance course SMA5503. The semiautomatic classification results are tabulated in Table 2.

Overall, our method has an accuracy of 85.1% in detecting the correct state. The personalization rules dependent on the first algorithm also have an accuracy of 85.1%. The contextual search algorithm is solely dependent on the correct classification of the topic state and has an accuracy of 90%.

Further, we are able to efficiently and accurately search in context throughout the video database. For example, by searching for the string *merge sort,* we return not only the video clip that teaches *merge sort,* but also other clips from other lectures where some aspect of *merge sort* is further explained (see Figure 5). In this particular case, *merge sort* is mentioned in video lecture 1 under the topic Sorting. It is also mentioned again in lecture 3 under Time Analysis, and in lecture 7 where it is compared to *quicksort.* Hence, when

Table 2. Experimental results for the detection of the lecture states

TOPIC	DETECTION ACCURACY (%)
Introduction	100
Topic	90
Definition	80
Discussion	86
Theorem	87.5
Example	83
Equation	62
Diagram	92.3

Figure 5. Search for Merge Sort

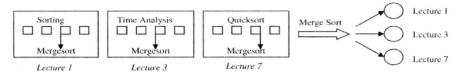

The occurrence of merge sort in three different lectures is determined. Appropriate context would then be used to find out whether it is one of the following: (a) discussion on sorting, (b) time analysis, or (c) comparison with quicksort.

Figure 6. Graphical user interface (GUI) for the presentation of lecture content in response to a query

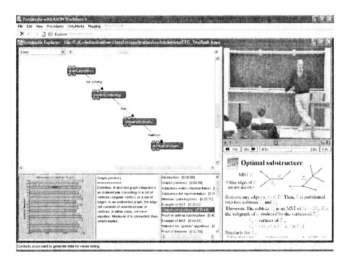

The display contains the following frames (clockwise from top-left corner): graphical display of terms related to the query, lecture video player, synchronized slide presentation, index of all slides, display of text from lecture notes, and a multiple timeline display of search results, with hot spots highlighted along the bar chart for each lecture in the course.

a student uses this system to search for *merge sort,* he has immediate access to all three related video clips even though they are taught in completely different lectures and different parts of the course. As a result, a student searching for *merge sort* will get a much clearer idea of how it actually works and all its different aspects. The combination of semiautomatic analysis of lecture videos to identify pedagogical events and key topics along with techniques for discovering emergent semantics from the media metadata provides the student valuable insights into the finer concepts of the queried subject. By using a simple user interface, users can enter keywords, view topic associations, and search for related materials as shown in Figure 6 (Altman & Wyse, 2005).

Conclusion

This chapter presents a system for indexing videos using audio, video, and PowerPoint slides and then segmenting the video content into various lecture components. The use of multiple media sources ensures accuracy in the classification of lecture content. This is of critical importance for the effective support of e-learning tasks and maintenance tasks performed by students and instructors. By dynamically manipulating these lecture components, we are able to personalize the lecture videos to suit individual needs. This helps to make the videos more suitable for absorption of the subject matter by students. While full-text indexed retrieval systems have been proposed earlier, our method is more efficient as it uses all forms of media to segment and index the video. It also allows us to perform efficient contextual search with a minimum of human supervision. Future integration work will focus on increasing the automation of media analysis for the courseware and the automatic construction of media models. Additional work on an enhanced learning environment involves the creation of query mediation tools that bridge the gap between the semantically labeled media and a domain ontology. The combination of media models and query mediation will enhance insight generation and provide support for the personalized construction of knowledge by the individual student.

References

Akutsu, A., Tonomura, Y., Ohba, Y., & Hashimoto, H. (1992). Video indexing using motion vectors. In *Proceedings of SPIE Visual Communications and Image Processing* (pp. 343-350), Boston.

Altman, E., & Wyse, L., (2005). Emergent semantics from media blending. In U. Srinivasan & S. Nepal (Eds.), *Managing multimedia semantics* (pp. 363-390). Hershey, PA: Idea Group Inc.

Bibiloni, A., & Galli, R. (1996). Content-based retrieval video system for educational purposes. In *Proceedings of the Eurographics Workshop on Multimedia, "Multimedia on the Net" (EGMM '96)*. Retrieved May 20, 2003, from http://citeseer.nj.nec.com/53258.html

Cha, G. H., & Chung, C. W. (2001). Content-based lecture access for distance learning. In *Proceedings of the IEEE International Conference on Multimedia and Expo (ICME 2001)* (pp. 160-163).

Chambers, J. A., & Specher, J. W. (1980). Computer-assisted instruction: Current trends and critical issues. *Communications of the ACM, 23,* 332-342.

Gonzalez, R. C., & Woods, R. E. (1992). Digital image processing. Reading, MA: Addison-Wesley.

Gudivada, V. N., & Raghavan, V. V. (1995). Content-based image retrieval systems. *IEEE Computer, 28*(9), 18-22.

Hwang, J.-N., Youn, J., Deshpande, S., & Sun, M. T. (1997, October). Video browsing for course-on-demand in distance learning. In *Proceedings of the IEEE Computer Society International Conference on Image Processing (ICIP)* (pp. 530-533).

Idris, F., & Panchanathan, S. (1997). Review of image and video indexing techniques. *Journal of Visual Communication and Image Representation, 8*(2), 146-166.

Ip, H. H. S., & Chan, S. L. (1998). Automatic segmentation and index construction for lecture video. *Journal of Educational Multimedia and Hypermedia, 7*(1), 91-104.

Michalopoulos, D. A. (1976, February). A video disc-oriented educational system. In *Proceedings of the ACM SIGCSE/SIGCUE Technical Symposium on Computer Science and Education* (pp. 389-392).

Mittal, A., & Cheong, L.-F. (2003). Framework for synthesizing semantic-level indices. *Journal of Multimedia Tools Applications, 20*(2), 135-158.

Mittal, A., Dixit, S., Maheshwari, L. K., & Sung, W. K. (2003, July). Enhanced understanding and retrieval of e-learning documents through relational and conceptual graphs. In *Proceedings of the AIED'03 Workshop on Technologies for Electronic Documents for Supporting Learning*, Sydney, Australia (p. 9).

Mittal, A., & Altman, E. (2003, January). Contextual information extraction for video data. In *Proceedings of the 9th International Conference on Multimedia Modeling*, Taipei, Taiwan (pp. 209-223).

Wang, Y., Liu, Z., & Huang, J. C. (2000, November). Multimedia content analysis using both audio and visual cues. *IEEE Signal Processing Magazine, 17*(6), 12-36.

Witbrock, M. J., & Hauptmann, A. G. (1997, July). Using words and phonetic strings for efficient information retrieval from imperfectly transcribed spoken documents. In *Proceedings of the 2nd ACM International Conference on Digital Libraries*, Philadelphia (pp. 23-26).

Woudstra, A., Velthausz, D. D., de Poot, H. G. J., Hadidy, F., Jonker, W., Houtsma, M. A. W. et al. (1998). Modeling and retrieving audiovisual information: A soccer video retrieval system. In *Proceedings of the Advances in Multimedia Information Systems 4th International Workshop (MIS'98)*, Istanbul, Turkey (pp. 161-173).

Endnote

[1]   Retrieved from http://web.mit.edu/sma/ (last accessed September 4, 2004).

Chapter XVII

Interface Design for Web Learning

Lorna Uden, Staffordshire University, UK

Introduction

"Usability rules the Web!" (Nielsen, 2000). It is very easy to recommend that a Web-learning application should be usable, but it is often a difficult design objective to achieve. We believe that usability can be achieved by bringing the interface closer to the user's way of thinking and working. It is important to design applications that are based on the mental models of users in order to achieve high usability. Designing high usability can be achieved by adopting user interface design models and an object-oriented approach. We have developed a methodology—the Web user object modelling (WUOM) method—to guide designers to develop Web learning applications that have high usability. This chapter describes the WUOM method to develop a Web application for learning circuits based on WUOM. Evaluation of the Web application shows that it has high usability.

Models are Useful

The design of a product's user interface is critical to its user acceptance and success. Without a well-designed user interface, even a system with outstanding features will not be successful. The best way to give a user a better product interface is to design with the user's beliefs, wants, needs, experiences, and expectations in mind. The way we interact with things around us is determined by our past experiences with those objects (and other objects like them) and our expectation of how things should work when we use them. We believe that models are useful for designing and analysing the user interface of a Web application. Models can be used to describe an interface in terms of objects, properties, beliefs, and relationships between objects. Models can provide a framework for communication, understanding, and decision making. Three models are relevant to the design and implementation of a user interface. Each model provides a different perspective on the interface, beginning with the user's perspective and including the designer's perspective and the implementing programmer's perspective. The user's conceptual or mental model, the designer's model, and the programmer's model, as well as their importance, are well documented in the IBM Common User Access (CUA) guidelines (IBM, 1992).

Designer's Role

The user interface designer's role is to create a designer's model or blueprint of the user interface, just as the architect creates a blueprint of a house. To do this, the designer must understand the user's conceptual model. Just as an architect would understand a client's needs and expectations, the user interface designer must understand users, their tasks, and their expectations. An architect must use basic principles that apply to housing design. Similarly a user interface designer needs to have a knowledge of accepted and proven principles in interface design. In addition, just as an architect knows the strengths and weaknesses of building materials and the skills of the tradespeople who will build the house, the user interface designer must understand the capabilities and restrictions of operating systems, the skills of the programmer, file systems, programming toolkits, and so forth. It is essential that we create a designer's model (blueprint) that reflects the architect's understanding of these requirements.

User Interface Design Models

The user's conceptual models or mental models of a system are mental images that each user subconsciously forms as he or she interacts with the system. Research by Norman and others indicates that users' conceptual or mental models play an important role in the design of high usability user interfaces (Redman-Pyle & Moore, 1995). A mental model (or conceptual model) is an internal representation of how users understand and interact with a system (Mandel, 1997). It helps people to predict what will happen next in a given situation and serves as a framework for analysis, understanding, and decision making. Having an appropriate mental model enables users to use a system effectively, because they can work out what to do in order to achieve their task goals and can interpret information displayed on the screen correctly.

The designer's model represents the designer's intent in terms of objects users will see and how they will use the objects to accomplish their tasks. It identifies objects, and how these objects are represented to users (views), and how users interact with those objects using the views. Traditionally, the user interface of a product has been considered to be the "look-and-feel" aspect of the product. The emphasis, recently, has been shifted to the objects needed by users to accomplish their tasks. This is the basis of our Web User Object Modelling approach. According to Roberts, Berry, Isensee, and Mullaly (1988), a computer system can be thought of as being like an iceberg. Only a fraction of it is visible at the surface. The look and feel is what is immediately visible, but the most important aspects are encapsulated in the object. The object model is the main component of the designer's model in WUOM.

The programmer's model describes the system internals used to implement the designer's model. It includes details relevant only to the programmer. The programmer's model is the easiest to visualise because it is explicit and can be more formally defined.

Benefits of Using User Object Modelling

The WUOM approach is based on user interface design models and an object-oriented approach. There are many advantages to adopting such an approach to Web learning applications. Users of an object-oriented computer user interface need not be aware of computer programs and underlying computer technology in order to be able to use the Web. An object-oriented user interface enables a user to focus on objects and work with them directly, which more closely reflects the user's real-world way of doing work.

This is in contrast to the traditional application-oriented interface, in which the user must find a program appropriate for both the task they want to perform and the type of information they want to see. Applying an object-oriented approach to design promotes the usability of Web applications by ensuring that serious thought is given to how the user will conceptualise and comprehend the objects in the system. It provides a design for the end user's mental model. It also provides a useful basis for the initial definition of windows and promotes an object-action style of user interface.

The general principle of WUOM is to model the real world as the user normally interacts with it and to map the environment onto the Web. Another advantage is that it brings rigour to the interface design process and produces output that feeds directly into code design, thus reducing the risk of introducing interface errors later in the development.

Applying WUOM

This section describes the use of WUOM to develop a Web learning application for learning circuits for 8- to 9-year-olds in one of the schools in the UK. An important part of the design of effective learning user interfaces is to assist the user in forming a suitable mental or conceptual model of the learning environment to be used. Users always have mental models and will always develop and modify them, regardless of the particular design of a system. Users rely on models to guide their interaction with computers in transferring knowledge of the world around them to the Web. The Web learning environment must be designed to fit in with the way users view the computer system they are working with. It is difficult to capture users' mental models. We believe that it is possible to assist designers in developing an interface that achieves an effective mental model by the use of user object modelling. The user object model is the agreed design for the user's mental model—it is specification of the way we want the users to think of the objects in the application. User object modelling also contributes to the usability of our application in other ways. Shneiderman (1992) proposes that to make an interface usable, it should represent task domain objects and actions, while minimising the computer concepts and command syntax that the user needs to learn and remember.

WUOM adopts an object-oriented approach to designing Web interfaces. An object-oriented user interface focuses the users on objects—the "things" people use to accomplish their work. Users see and manipulate object representations of their information. Each different kind of object supports actions appropriate for the information it represents. Object-oriented design is built on the belief that users know their way around an office—the desktop metaphor: they are familiar with the office environment, know how to use objects in that environment (folders, cabinets, telephone, notepads, etc.), and understand the idea of an office desktop as a working space.

In order to develop the user's object model, we use the Dollhouse as a metaphor to learn about the appliances in the house. In the Dollhouse, learners can dim the lights, turn on the hairdryer at low speed and high speed, press the door buzzer, and so forth. The program is highly interactive. For example, learners can press the door buzzer of the house and it will open to the various rooms within. Clicking on the light enables the light to come on. This will then take the learners to see the circuit of the light. The whole purpose of the program is to provide an environment that children can explore in order to come to a coherent understanding of how circuits work. To help them in managing their tasks, children were provided with notebooks containing templates for recording their findings. These templates helped the children manage their work and the process of interpreting the circuits. The children had to construct their own answers and explanations, based on the interaction they had available. They were also required to discuss, write, and represent the work to the teacher. The simulated Dollhouse allowed children to engage in authentic activities without overwhelming them with the complexity of formal circuit instruction. The learning environment mediated the children's learning-about-circuits-working using household appliances familiar to their conceptual models.

From the scenario of the learning environments, we identified the user's learning objects to form the user's object model. The user object model provides a useful basis for the initial definition of windows and promotes an object-action style of user interface. Inputs to the object user modelling include task and learner analysis. A user object model is a model of the learning objects which learners believe they will interact with in the learning environment. The model includes:

- What type of objects these are (learner objects)
- What information the learner can know about an object of a particular type (learner object attributes)
- What actions the learner can perform on (or with) an object of a particular type (learner object actions)
- How objects may be relate to other objects (relations)
- Object types having 'subtypes' which have additional specialised action or attributes

The learner object model identified contains:

- **Learning objects:** electricity, circuit, light bulb
- **Container:** a folder, list, or directory containing other objects

A user learning object can also have relationships with other user learning objects, be specialised to user learning object subtypes, and have attributes and user learning object actions. It is often convenient to group the attributes of objects together in a container rather than having to deal with each item of a collection separately. Container objects can have their own attributes and actions.

User learning objects are identified from task analysis and scenarios. The most effective approach is to discuss each subtask and determine what objects are used or referred to in performing the task. Review these task objects to decide which are required as user learning objects. For each object, consider a number of questions. Does the learner need to see and interact with the object to perform their tasks? Does the object exist in the instruction and will it continue to exist within the learning environment? Does the object group together related information in a way that helps the learner to perform a specific task? The user learning objects should reflect the educational world and the requirements of learner tasks. Besides identifying the learner objects, it is necessary to define the attributes of each object. For example, a light bulb might have state and colour. The state may be on or off. Objects also have actions that learners can perform on or use—such as turning on the light, turning off the light, connecting the battery, testing the circuit, connecting the light bulb, and so on.

Another aspect of the design of WUOM is dynamic modelling. Dynamic modelling is used where there is significant state-dependent behaviour—that is, where the behaviour

Figure 1. Screen shot from Dollhouse program

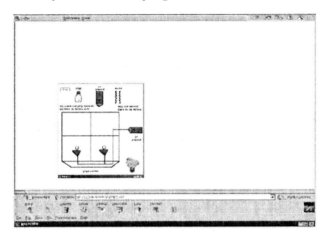

of an object changes through time, depending on the state that object is in. The dynamic modelling can be used to analyse and design the behaviour of windows (i.e., the window states in which the learner is allowed to perform particular window actions). A dynamic model is a useful practical input to Web learning systems, particularly to the design of error handling. It shows when an action will be invalid and steps the designer can take to cope with the learner's inappropriate attempts to perform them. This may be either by some preventive actions in the user interface such as menu-dimming, or by some recover action, such as informing the learner via a warning that the action he or she tried to perform was not allowed. Dynamic modelling encourages designers to ask questions about preconditions for actions and the effects (post-conditions) of those actions on object states. It can also be used to validate task scenarios by checking that each scenario consists of a valid sequence of user object actions. It can check that task scenarios do not specify actions in an invalid sequence or where action preconditions are not satisfied.

A statechart is used to describe the behaviour of an object, as a set of states, with transitions between states each labelled with the name of the action (event) which caused the transition. Some user learning objects have dynamic behaviour that involves concurrent states (i.e., an object is in two or more states simultaneously). This normally reflects different aspects of the object's life, and the concurrent states may change independently of each other.

Our Dollhouse learning environment was built using Macromedia Director Version 5. A sample screen shot is shown in Figure 1.

Evaluation

Usability testing is a key part of WUOM. The goal of usability testing should be to measure user behaviour, performance, and satisfaction. We have conducted usability testing at various stages of our development, beginning with early user walkthroughs of initial designs using prototyping. Feedback from our usability testing was incorporated into the development model to improve the user object model of our application. The application developed was used by the children to learn about circuits.

The children enjoyed using the learning environment, and the teacher found that children were more motivated in their learning using the Web application than traditional classroom learning.

Conclusion

Web learning applications should be useable. User interface models play an important role in the design of effective Web learning interfaces. Having an appropriate conceptual or mental model enables users to use a system effectively, because they can work out what to do in order to achieve their goals, and can interpret information correctly. User object modelling can assist a designer in developing a learning interface that achieves an effective mental model. The main benefit of using object models for interface design is that of real-world appreciation. Object models represent the real world as we understand it. The real world can be represented as a collection of interacting entities, each of which exhibits well-defined behaviours. The way we interact with things around us is determined by our past experiences with these objects (and other objects like them), and our expectations of how things should work when we use them.

If users do not know much about the Web, they will attempt to relate to it in a way similar to how they relate to other things in the world. By adopting a WUOM design model to develop Web learning environments, we can help users to use the interface more intuitively. This had been demonstrated in our study.

Acknowledgment

The author wishes to thank D. Meir for the contribution of Figure 1.

References

IBM Corporation. (1992). *Object-oriented interface design: IBM common user access guidelines*. New York: QUE.

Mandel, T. (1997). *The elements of user interface design*. Chichester, Sussex: John Wiley & Sons.

Nielsen, J. (2000). *Designing Web usability*. Indianapolis: New Riders Publishing.

Norman, D. (1988). *The psychology of everyday things*. New York: Basic Books.

Redmond-Pyle, D., & Moore, A. (1995). *Graphical User Interface Design and Evaluation (GUIDE): A practical process*. Englewood Cliffs, NJ: Prentice-Hall.

Roberts, D., Berry, D., Isensee S., & Mullaly J. (1998). *Designing for the user with OVID: Bridging user interface design and software engineering*. Indianapolis, IN: Macmillan Technical Publishing.

Shneiderman, B. (1992). *Designing the user interface: Strategies for effective human-computer interaction*. Reading, MA: Addison-Wesley.

Chapter XVIII

Improving the Usability of Distance Learning Through Template Modification

Linda L. Lohr, University of Northern Colorado, USA

David A. Falvo, University of Northern Colorado, USA

Erin Hunt, University of Northern Colorado, USA

Ben Johnson, University of Northern Colorado, USA

Introduction

Navigating distance-learning environments can be a frustrating experience for users. Many find themselves confused about where they are, how they got there, or where they need to move next, a condition coined as "lost in cyberspace" (Webster, 2001). Even finding what they need is no guarantee that they will avoid similar disorientation at a later date when they need to perform the same or a parallel task. The question "Where was the place that I found that?" takes precedence over "What is important for me to learn?" The focus of this study is to discover if there are methods that an instructor can use to reduce user disorientation in distance learning environments.

Review of the Literature

One solution to information access problems in distance settings is good interface design. Learner-to-interface interaction is considered one of four types of critical online interactions that a learner experiences. The other three interactions are learner-to-content, learner-to-instructor, and learner-to-learner (Shelton, 2000). An interface is considered the instructional cues between a system and a user (Hackos & Redish, 1998; Marchionini, 1995). The interface in a distance learning environment is simply the cues that direct the user towards the learning goal. Those cues include signs or signals in the form of headings, buttons, and screen numbers that imply "go here to find...instructional content, the teacher's e-mail, the unit test..." When the signals are clear, the user knows where they are and where they are going.

Unfortunately, most educators using distance authoring tools (course templates) are not aware of what an interface is, or that when they create their classes, they have the option to modify the interface (or signals) to accommodate the learner. Instructors simply use what is given to them, adding their syllabus to a designated Syllabus space, their grades to a Grade Book space, and lessons to a Course Materials space. Though limited, there are tools in template authoring environments such as eCollege™, Blackboard™, and WebCT™ that allow some degree of modification to the instructional interface. Areas designated for Course Materials, and named as such, can be renamed to more directly address the composition of the topic at hand. For example, Course Materials could be renamed to something more specific, such as *Web site Links* or *Mini Lectures* if these titles are more relevant to the instructional strategies of the course. Buttons or link names can also be rearranged to fit the course content and sequence.

Despite the opportunities, many instructors give little thought to how easy it will be for the learner to find the information and navigate the learning space. It is likely that most instructors use the prescribed spaces, regardless of whether they are easily understood or not. This practice is not unusual. Pedagogy may take the backseat in many distance learning environments (Firdyiwek, 1999).

Lohr (2000) suggests three critical roles of the instructional interface that should be accounted for in its design: (1) to provide learner orientation to instructional content, (2) to provide navigational tools to access instructional content and instructional strategies, and (3) to provide feedback. Mayer's (1993) identification of selection, organization, and integration cognitive processes is a convenient way to emphasize the organization suggested by Lohr.

Selection is the process that takes place when the learner notices the important information and is able to isolate it from less important information. As seen in Table 1, many of the orientation features of the interface address this function. Instructional interface designers should seek to help the learner notice the most salient information when first accessing instruction. For example, a clearly identified topic is an important piece of information that can set the stage for greater understanding.

Organization is the process where the learner is able to chunk or sequence information in a way that is meaningful. In interface design, organization elements include visual cues and features similar to a table of contents that helps a learner mark where they are in the instruction. Navigation panes, menus, page or screen numbers, and links all become important organization features.

Integration is the process where the learner is able to assimilate or accommodate new information into memory. Integration interface elements are those that facilitate access to and understanding of learning spaces. Buttons that link to extra help, pop-up windows that explain new terms, graphic organizers integrated into the interface, and space for practice, feedback, and interaction with the teacher and other students help the learner integrate.

Table 1 shows a list of anticipated learner questions and how these questions relate to cognitive processes involved in accessing information.

Given this information, a highly usable interface for learning could be considered one that would facilitate learner selection, organization, and integration. Usability is a term used by different disciplines to address the science of making things easier for people to use (Krug, 2000; Nielsen, 2000).

This study examines the usability of one of the widely used courseware authoring tools, Blackboard™. The focus of this study is twofold: First, the study tests how easy it is for instructors to perceive opportunities to modify the Blackboard™ interface for learner selection, organization, and integration. Second, the study assesses the effectiveness

Table 1. Cognitive processes associated with anticipated learner questions

Cognitive processes involved	Anticipated learner questions (Lohr, 2000; Lohr, 2003)
Selection (Noticing the critical information)	**Anticipating the Following *Orientation* Questions:** • What is the topic of learning? • How do I begin learning? • What is the learning climate? • What is the breadth of this environment? • What, in general, is expected of me in this learning environment? • Do I feel comfortable welcome in this environment?
Organization (Chunking or sequencing information)	**Anticipating the Following *Navigation* Questions:** • What is the depth ? • Where am I in this process? • Can I mark where I am? • How do I go back? • What do I do now? • What do I do next? • When am I finished? • How do I get out of this?
Integration (Assimilating or accommodating information)	**Anticipating the Following *Instructional Strategies Access* Questions:** • How do I interact with this instructional strategy? • Can I get more/less information? More or less examples? • Can I skip this information?
	Providing Interactive Feedback • Am I doing the right thing? • Am I right/wrong? • How did I end up here? • Can I undo what I just did? • Can I customize this?

of modifications by comparing student use of a standard template interface to student use of a modified interface, essentially asking, Do modifications make any difference? Two specific questions asked include: Do designers see the potential to change the template to accommodate selection, organization, and integration? Do learners using that template demonstrate greater ease with selection, organization, and integration tasks?

Methodology

Small samples were used to test usability based on Nielsen and Landauer's (2000) recommendation that small sample sizes (approximately 5) yield the best results, making it costly and ineffective to test more. This advice stems from the observation that user testing commonly fails to reveal any new information after a fifth user has view a product. The first five users typically find 85% of the usability problems. A second user test, of the modified product, tends to find the remaining 15% of the errors.

Subjects were grouped to answer the two research questions: (1) distance learning instructors (who act as authors/designers in a distance setting); and (2) distance learners, the individuals who used the distance environments created by the instructors.

Distance Learning Instructors

Instructors consisted of three individuals with authoring experience. The lead researcher categorized the instructor's skill level along usability and authoring dimensions. Low-level usability skills were assigned to instructors with little or no training in concepts of user-centered design or hands-on application of usability concepts. Medium-level usability skills were assigned to designers with some training (a minimum of one class or reading that defined usability and required a general understanding of usability as well as application of user-centered design concepts). High-level usability includes training and application of user-centered design concepts over a period of several years.

Low-level authoring skills were assigned to designers with little or no experience creating with the distance learning authoring tool. Medium-level authoring skills were assigned to designers with at least one year of authoring experience. High-level authoring skills were assigned to designers with three or more years of experience authoring in distance

Table 2. Usability and authoring skill levels of instructors

Instructor	Instructor 1	Instructor 2	Instructor 3
Usability level	High	Medium	High
Authoring experience	Low	High	High

learning environments. Table 2 shows the distribution of skill level for the three instructors.

Each instructor was shown the authoring panel of the distance learning environment and was asked to identify the presence or absence of selection, organization, and integration functions. In other words, were there features in the authoring environment that the instructor could use to facilitate student selection (or organization and integration) of content? If present, the designer/instructor would indicate if the feature was obvious (the function was immediately recognizable as something that could be used to modify the learning environment) or indirect (the designer/instructor would need to think about how to adapt the feature, or would use some indirect method to modify the learning environment).

Seven questions were asked that centered on the instructor's perceptions of whether the interface could be altered to produce a more learner-friendly environment. Questions focused on selection (i.e., Can you help the learner find lesson objectives or key points?), organization (i.e., Can you provide the learner with cues to help move them from one task to the next?), and Integration (i.e., Can you provide the learner a space to seek out additional information if they want to explore a topic or interact with an instructional strategy more deeply?). See Table 4 in the Results section for a complete listing of questions.

Distance Learners

Twelve volunteer graduate students in an intact Introduction to Computers in Education course were assigned to two groups: those who had a year or more of experience using the Blackboard™ distance learning tool, and those whose Blackboard™ experience was limited. Random assignment to a treatment group (modified Blackboard™) and a control group (default Blackboard) followed.

Figure 1. Treatment group interface buttons

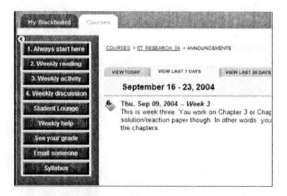

Figure 2. Control group links

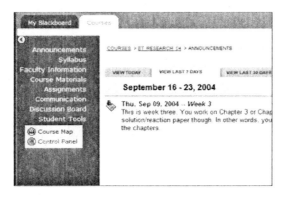

Table 3. Comparison of standard and modified Blackboard™ interface features

Standard Blackboard™ Interface Element	Modified Control Group Interface Element	Type of Content
Announcements	1. Always Start Here	Introduction to the unit, objectives, key topics
Course Materials	2. Weekly Reading	Reading Assignments and Discussion Assignments
Assignments	3. Weekly Activity	Project descriptions and examples
Discussion Board	4. Weekly Discussion	Discussion questions
Communications > Discussion Board	Get Help	Frequently Asked Questions posed during the week and answered by the teacher
Student Tools > View Grades	See Your Grade	Current grades and feedback
Communicatons > Send E-mail	Email Someone	E-mail functions
Syllabus	Syllabus	Overview of semester

Treatment Materials

Both groups received the same instructional content, which included a reading assignment, a learning activity, and discussion question on the topic of contrast, alignment, repetition, and proximity. The treatment group (see Figure 1) used the Blackboard™ interface modified by the lead researcher using Lohr's guidelines (see Table 1). The control group (see Figure 2) used the default interface provided by Blackboard™. The standard and modified Blackboard™ interface features and their relationship to content are compared in Table 3.

Twelve students usability tested the control and treatment interfaces in one-on-one sessions with three researchers. Students spent five minutes exploring the interface while talking aloud with the researchers recording all comments. Following the talk-aloud, students were instructed to locate specific places on the interface. The researchers noted student comments, whether the student could find the correct item, and the time spent, rounded to the nearest second. Following the timed activity, students answered two five-point Likert scale questions and two open-ended questions regarding the learning environment in general.

Table 4. Instructor identification of modification opportunities

		Instructor 1 High Usability Low Authoring		Instructor 2 Med. Usability High Authoring		Instructor 3 High Usability High Authoring	
		No	Yes	No	Yes	No	Yes
Selection Questions	Can you provide the learner with specific instruction on how to get started?		X (I)*	X			X
	Can you help the learner find the lesson objectives, or key points?		X	X			X
	Can you make the environment friendly and welcoming?		X (I)	X			X(I)
Organization Questions	Can you provide the learner with cues to move them from one task to the next task?		X	X			X (I)
	Can you provide the learner with feedback on how they are doing to help them know where to go next?	X			X		X(I)
Integration Questions	Can you provide the learner a variety of feedback sources?		X (I)		X(I)		X
	Can you provide the learner a space to seek out additional information if they want to explore a topic or interact with an instructional strategy more deeply?		X(I)	X			X

Note that (I) indicates indirect opportunity, or something the instructor would need to think through to make happen

Results

Instructor Perceptions

Three instructors assessed the modification potential of the Blackboard™ authoring tool. Instructor 1, rated high on usability skills and low on Blackboard™ authoring skills, indicated that features of the template could be altered to accommodate learner Selection for each of the three questions (see Table 4). Fewer opportunities for modification of the template were noted by this instructor for Organization and Integration intervention. Instructor 2, rated medium on usability skills and high on Blackboard™ authoring skills, saw no opportunities to modify the template to improve learner Selection. This instructor saw mixed potential for improving organization and integration of the interface. Instructor 3, rated high on usability skills and high on Blackboard™ authoring skills, indicated potential to modify the interface to improve learner selection, organization, and integration for each of the questions asked.

Student Actions and Comments

Both the treatment and control group were similar in terms of experience with Blackboard™. Approximately half of each group had taken one or more courses using Blackboard™ or a similar distance learning platform, with the other half of the group new to Blackboard™.

Table 5. Treatment and control group response times, Likert ratings, and open-ended comments

Question	Mean Time Regular Interface	Mean Time Modified Interface
Show me where you would go to learn how well you are doing in this class/lesson.	Mean = 7	Mean = 3.5
Show me where you would find the main topics of this unit.	Mean = 33	Mean = 14
Show me how you would get help from someone else.	Mean = 7	Mean = 3.5
Show me where you would begin the lesson?	Mean = 15	Mean = 8
Show me where to get more information about what you are supposed to complete for this lesson.	Mean = 13	Mean = 9.6
Show me where you would go to ask a question from either the teacher or other class members.	Mean = 15	Mean = 8
Show me how you would get out or start over if you got lost.	Mean = 28	Mean = 4
Likert Scale Questions		
Rate how the environment is or isn't friendly or welcoming on a Likert 5 point scale with 5 very friendly/welcoming, and 1 very unfriendly unwelcoming	Mean = 3.6	Mean = 4
Rate how easy it was for you to know the expectations of the lesson/class.	Mean = 3.3	Mean = 5

Table 6. Open-ended student responses to usability questions

Open-Ended Questions	Control Group	Treatment Group
What would you tell the designer of this class to do differently to make it more understandable/usable?	"[Instruction] for starting over if lost." "More help on where to put new work"	"Not fond of black buttons" (2 comments). Too much stuff/information (2 comments).
Overall, did you like or dislike this environment, why or why not?	Equal mix of likes and dislikes (no comments)	Five of the 6 liked. "Just easier to use than the regular Blackboard", "Easier to navigate" "Weird, different [than the regular Blackboard] "Very clear that you would learn something in this class." "Lots of creative options." "Liked the way lessons were broken down...activities separated from readings, discussions"
Overall, how easy was it for you to find things in this environment?	Easy (5 comments) So-so (1 comment)	Very easy (1 comment) Hmm...easy (1 comment) Easier than regular Blackboard (1 comment) Easy (3 comments)

Most similarities between the two groups ended there. Mean response times for the control group, the regular Blackboard™ interface, were higher than the response rates for the treatment group, the modified Blackboard™ interface, on all items tested. Likert scale means, assessing the usability of the two interfaces, were higher for the treatment group, although the means comparing the friendliness of the setting were similar (3.6 for the regular Blackboard™ interface, and 4 for the modified Blackboard™ interface). Clarity of learning expectations was higher for the modified Blackboard™ interface (a mean of 5 compared to a mean of 3.3).

Students using the modified Blackboard™ interface had more to say about their likes and dislikes as well (see Table 6). The control group, the regular Blackboard™ interface, did not offer any illuminating comments regarding their likes or dislikes.

Discussion

Data collected from both the instructors and student groups suggest differences in how instructors perceive the modification potential of template interfaces as well as differences in how students experience the learning environments. Given the small sample sizes (3 instructors and 12 students), these differences are discussed more as items worthy of exploration, rather than as significant findings to guide future design of learning environments.

Instructor Skills

Perceptions of how easily the interfaces could be modified to accommodate selection, organization, and integration tasks varied among the different instructors (see Table 4). Instructor 3, rated as highly skilled in both usability and authoring, identified the most options (direct and indirect) for modifying the interface. Generally, the instructors with greater knowledge and skill in usability testing as well as authoring, were more likely to see opportunities to modify Blackboard™ to facilitate student selection, organization, and integration (see Table 4).

Of these two skills, experience with usability testing appeared to be related to the ability to see more options for modifying the interface. Low authoring skill paired with high usability skills (Instructor 1) was associated with increased opportunities for interface modification than medium usability skills (Instructor 2). Opportunities noted by Instructor 1, however, were more often categorized Indirect (not immediately obvious) as compared to the opportunities classification by Instructor 3.

Student Behavior and Comments

Students using the modified Blackboard™ interface located information more quickly and made more positive comments about the instructional attributes of the environment that did the regular Blackboard™ interface users for all questions and tested items. Notable differences in response rates for locating feedback on grades (50% faster for the modified interface group) and the ability to relocate oneself after getting lost (70% faster for the modified interface group) were recorded. While no students commented on the instructional or learning aspects of the regular Blackboard™ environment, two students commented on the educational dimension of the modified Blackboard™ environment when they mentioned: "Very clear that you would learn something in this class"; "Lots of creative options"; "Liked the way lessons were broken down…activities separated from readings, [separated from] discussions."

Implications

Based on the findings of this study, exploration of how training in usability and instructional design influence an instructor's ability to see options for modifying templates is suggested. In this research, the two instructors with the most usability and design experience indicated seeing more opportunities to change the interface to facilitate student access to instructional material. A future study might question how usability training as well as hands-on design experience influence an instructor's ability to perceive modification options and in turn adapt an interface. For example, does understanding of design impact one's ability to create more learner-friendly environments? Further, what aspects of design seem to be the most influential in facilitating learner selection, organization, and integration? Are there unique variables that influence an instructor's ability to translate an understanding of design into its application, such as design aptitude, skill, or a combination of both?

In this study, a fairly superficial modification in the Blackboard™ interface seemed to positively influence the student experience. Simply changing link or button names, reorganizing, and re-sequencing interface options had an impact. The modified interface, overall, allowed quicker information access and elicited more positive comments than did the regular interface. Although use of small sample sizes for usability testing is an accepted practice (Nielsen & Laundauer, 2000), the difference in student response rates varied widely when students were asked to locate specific items, suggesting the need to use a larger sample size to more accurately represent the reaction time means.

Likewise, investigation into student comments to determine the presence of a more educational focus would be worthy. In this study, two of the six students in the modified template mentioned the educational attributes of the environment where none of the students in the other group did so. A larger sample size might uncover a greater number of comments, perhaps encouraging template manufacturers such as Blackboard™, eCollege™, and WebCT™ to provide more opportunities for template modification. An investigation into the status and potential to modify these other widely used authoring tools is needed.

Improved insight into learner cognition when using a distance learning environment is needed. In addition to researching a larger audience, inquiry should also be made into thought processes, such as an exploration of short- and long-term memory. Measuring immediate and delayed recall would increase validity of the study, and would additionally provide more accurate information regarding learner perceptions that influence information access.

Regardless of platform, questions regarding both micro and macro levels of instruction are needed. Instructors and students in this study focused on interface issues at a micro level, specifically the lesson level. Equally important are macro- or curriculum-level issues. For example, how quickly does a student become adapted to an interface? In this study, the findings were counter-intuitive. Two students who had used Blackboard™ for several classes reported that the modified interface was "strange," yet they outperformed similarly experienced students in the regular Blackboard™ setting. While it might seem that once an interface becomes familiar, navigation response times decrease, the results of this study do not support that idea.

Summary

This study examined how three instructors and 12 students interacted with a distance learning environment. Instructors were asked to identify options available in the Blackboard™ authoring template to make its learning interface easier to navigate. The two instructors with the highest ranking of design knowledge and skills were able to identify more options to modify the template to improve the learner experience. When a modified Blackboard™ environment was user tested in the treatment group, faster location times were recorded for all tasks requested. Additionally, students using the modified template made more positive comments about the experience, and mentioned phrases relating to the instruction and educational feel of the environment more frequently. While these findings seem favorably positioned for proposing design guidelines, further studies are recommended in order to improve validity.

References

Firdyiwek, Y. (1999). Web-based courseware tools: Where is the pedagogy? *Educational Technology, 39*(1), 29-34.

Hackos, J. T., & Redish, J. C. (1998). *User and task analysis for interface design.* New York: Wiley Computer Publishing.

Krug, S. (2000). *Don't make me think: A common sense approach to Web usability.* Indianapolis, IN: Macmillan USA.

Lohr, L. (2000). Designing the instructional interface. *Computers in Human Behavior, 16*(2), 161-182.

Lohr, L. (2003). *Creating graphics for learning and performance: Lessons in visual literacy.* Columbus, OH: Prentice-Hall.

Marchionini, G. (1995*). Information seeking in electronic environments.* Melbourne, Australia: Cambridge University Press.

Mayer, R. (1993). Illustrations that instruct. In R. Glaser (Ed.), *Advances in instructional psychology* (Vol. 5, pp. 253-284). Hillsdale, NJ: Lawrence Erlbaum.

Nielsen, J. (2000a). *Designing Web usability.* Indianapolis, IN: New Riders Publishing.

Nielsen, J., & Landauer, T. K. (2000, March 19). Why you only need to test with five users. *Jakob Nielsen's Alert Box.* Retrieved from http://www.useit.com/alertbox/20000319.html

Shelton, A. (2000). *Catering to students taking an online course for the first time.* (ERIC Document Reproduction Services No. ED4467755).

Chapter XIX

Management of the Learning Space

Susan M. Powers, Indiana State University, USA

Christine Salmon, North Harris Montgomery Community College District, USA

Introduction

Dr. Villez looks up from her papers and sighs as her e-mail beeps again for what seems the 100th time this morning with yet another incoming mail message. She checks the subject line and sender—yes, it is from another student in one of her online courses. She sighs again. She has barely started reading the last assignment that came in 20 minutes ago, and here is yet another assignment being turned in that needs to be graded and feedback given to the student as soon as possible. Dr. Villez looks at her watch and then back at her pile of e-mail. She might need to rethink her agreement to participate in her institution's online programs. The online courses were taking so much of her time; it was beginning to cut into her time for scholarship.

There are a multitude of reasons why an institution may elect to engage in distance education (Oblinger, Barone, & Hawkins, 2001). One of those reasons might be to generate greater revenues and to expand its access. With projections that an estimated 15% of all students in higher education will be engaged in distance education (International Data Corporation, 1999), the related pressures on faculty can become enormous. While these reasons may have a basis in institutional survival and transformation, the implications may come at a cost to those who must deliver the instruction through greater teaching loads and class sizes.

This scenario presented above may seem extreme, but it is not unusual on college campuses (Moore, 2000; Moore & Kearsley, 2005). Many faculty are reluctant to move into Web-based instruction (WBI) because they have heard from peers about the overwhelming time demands of this form of instruction (Visser, 2000). However, we contend that the time involved in *delivering* and *maintaining* online courses is not greater than well-maintained face-to-face courses. Rather, WBI requires a different *kind* of time. The key to a successful distance education experience for both faculty and students is to effectively manage the learning space. There are three principal issues involved in effective learning space management of an online course: workload management, student management, and time management.

Workload Management

There is no single, universal manner in which faculty workload is handled in all institutions. However, regardless of the university policy regarding workload, it is imperative that distance education become an integral part of the load and not figured as an "add-on" or overload. Parker (2003) found that faculty who participate in distance education are motivated by more intrinsic factors, in particular, self-satisfaction. However, when obstacles or disincentives are examined, issues related to *time* are a common theme (Rockwell, Schauer, Fritz, & Marx, 1999). The function of traditional workload is an important institutional element for faculty.

Guidelines provided by national organizations lend credence to the concept that "a course is a course is a course," meaning from an institutional perspective, translated to faculty workload, all courses should be treated as equal. The North Central Association of Colleges and Schools (NCA) provides guidelines related to curriculum and instruction in distance education (NCA, 2000). Several of these, while not directly indicating workload, require a manageable instructional level. For example:

- Programs provide for timely and appropriate interaction between students and faculty, and among students.
- The institution's faculty assumes responsibility for and exercises oversight of distance education, ensuring both the rigor of programs and the quality of instruction.
- The institution ensures the currency of materials, programs, and courses (NCA, 2000).

The American Association of University Professors (AAUP) also provides guidelines and suggestions regarding faculty workload through its *Statement on Distance Education* document (AAUP, 1999). First, institutions should develop policies that delineate teaching-load credit for both the preparation and delivery of distance education, and these specific arrangements should be carried out within faculty units. Second, the expectation or requirement of a faculty member to carry distance education as part of a teaching load should be clearly contained within the faculty contract. Finally, its strongest statement that affects workload is found in AAUP's *Suggestions and Guidelines on Sample Language for Institutional Policies and Contract Language* (AAUP, n.d.). This document discusses teaching load based on the *Statement on Distance Education,* but also addresses course size. These guidelines emphasize the importance that course size is dictated by pedagogical need and that larger sections should be compensated as additional workload. The American Federation of Teachers (AFT) also strongly supports the notion that it is critical to maintain a workable class size that allows for high levels of interaction (AFT, 2001).

Findings by the National Center for Educational Statistics (NCES) support the concern of the AAUP on workload. Distance faculty (both part time and full time) taught about one class or section more than their non-distance teaching counterparts (NCES, 2002). This additional workload carried through for additional numbers of sections, but also in increased numbers of course preparations. Fortunately, the NCES did not find that distance education faculty were teaching significantly more students in their distance education courses.

Ultimately, effective workload management is not in the personal hands of the faculty member, but relies upon careful administration by the academic units and university administration. Without a successful workload and teaching load policy and subsequent implementation, and if loads for faculty who teach distance education continue to increase, universities will find increasing numbers of faculty who feel that distance education programs are contrary to institutional goals, are frustrated by a lack of institutional support, and ultimately refuse to deliver distance education courses and programs.

Time Management

Time management is usually considered in terms of a series of strategies. Effective time management can be achieved by using these principles. To that end, three time management principles based upon established techniques are offered.

Conceptualize All Relevant Activities Related to Learning Goals

The essential time management principle applied here is that by setting a goal and knowing the desired end result, we will become more focused and better able to achieve that goal (Cvach, 1989; Huffstetter & Smith, 1989). This same principle is the important first step to manage the time related to WBI because there is a desired end goal. The instruction should have a desired student outcome, and all the energy directed toward the course should support this outcome.

Unfortunately, instructors and students often expend a great deal of time and effort in directions that are at best tangential to learning outcomes. For example, faculty may need to spend inordinate amounts of time accessing multiple file formats of e-mail attachments or troubleshooting a computing problem for a student. While all these may be superfluous issues to the instructor, they are of great concern to the student and directly related to his/her ability to achieve the ultimate learning goal(s). It is not dissimilar to the concerns of the young single father who must miss class because of a sick child or the student who struggles to pay attention in class because she must work many hours to earn her tuition. Software incompatibility and network issues are equally real to distance students. Therefore, the instructor who keeps the end learning goal(s) and the byproduct to facilitate student learning in mind will see these seemingly tangential tasks as part of the instructional activity that must also be managed according to other techniques.

Organizing and Planning the Learning Time

Once the goal has been set, or in this instance, conceptualized, the tasks necessary to manage the overall online instructional picture must be organized. Effective time managers organize through listing and prioritization (Cvach, 1989; Norris, 2001; Starr, 1984). Experienced faculty may do this with their traditional classes naturally and must draw upon these same elements for the online classroom.

First, the WBI syllabus, just like a traditional teaching syllabus, has already organized and prioritized the term. The act of posting it to the Web does not automatically send these priorities out into cyberspace. Instructional priorities have been predetermined for the students and in turn for the instructor. The ebb and flow of the course can be plotted and tracked. The time management element is to remember these periods where assignments will come due or questions will arise, and plan ahead. For example, for a face-to-face course, faculty know that prior to an exam or research paper, additional office hours might be needed to accommodate questions and problems. Additionally, once those items have been submitted by the student, additional time is needed to provide feedback and scores. An instructor will often plan ahead and block out calendar times to accomplish this requirement. The online course is no different. As major assignments or learning goals are reached in the online course, e-mail and phone messages will increase that require additional response, and assignments will show up electronically. Ultimately, the skilled instructor can even micromanage the instructional waves to occur at manageable points in the term.

Table 1. Typical work week

	Faculty Time	Student Time
Seat-time in class	3 hrs/week	3 hrs/week
Preparation time for course (reading, organizing notes, etc.)	2 hrs/week	4 hrs/week
Time on assignments (grading, completing, etc.)	3 hours/week	2 hrs/week
Total	**8 hrs/week**	**9 hrs/week**

Planning time for tasks is important not only for the online instructor, but also as a learning tool that the instructor can model to the student. For the most part, faculty and students know how to plan the time necessary for traditional face-to-face instruction. A typical week for an undergraduate seminar may flow as shown in Table 1.

In addition to these faculty hours, the instructor is likely to have dedicated office hours and appointments to deal with student questions or concerns. This workload is not typical of every week, and the ebb and flow of the course would modify the amount of time needed for time on assignments. However, because of the scheduled class meeting time, much of the time is very planned and regimented.

The lessons and habits learned from face-to-face instruction are often not translated to WBI. A course that has synchronous components (real-time conferencing, for example) has some level of schedule. Unfortunately, an online course that generates a great deal of e-mail and correspondence also generates an instructor who feels that he/she is a slave to e-mail. The technology is still novel enough that we may feel a need to instantly read and respond to every message. The telephone may at one time have had the same impact on people. Now it might not be uncommon for people to use voicemail and answering machines to selectively screen calls.

Develop a Tiered Priority System

"With learning materials available 24 hours a day, 7 days a week, time is no longer a limitation to learning" (Oblinger et al., 2001, p. 2). Aligned with the organization and prioritization principles, an instructor can develop tiered response systems. Learning materials may be available at all times, but there is no equivalent expectation that an instructor be available to that same degree; online faculty need to make this clear from the outset of a course. Create a database or templates of replies that can be sent automatically using your e-mail system's filtering function—for example, "I received your assignment and I will be looking it over. When I have completed all assignments for the class, I will return your assignment with comments."

The important first element is to reassure students that an assignment has been received and is not lost in 'cyberworld'. Depending on the type of assignment, two additional levels might be necessary. Using your organizational syllabi developed earlier that lets you know when an assignment is due from everyone, schedule chunks of time to grade that assignment. Students who have turned assignments in early may wait for a period of time for this next stage after being notified of receipt. Assignment scores can often be determined more quickly than full, detailed feedback, so first provide students with the grade from the assignment, with the comment that detailed feedback will follow. Finally, use the technology to help you give feedback. Word processors will allow you to insert comments into a document, highlight text, track changes, and correct text, all of which can be sent to the student. However, learn to do this on the computer instead of first editing by hand and then doing it again on the computer. Alternatively, if it must be done by hand, scan that document and/or fax it back to the student. Look for creative technology solutions that reduce the amount of your effort. Naturally, to help students with their management of the learning space, an instructor must make it clear from the outset of the course that a tiered response system will be used.

Student Management

To best manage the course workspace, an instructor needs to avoid a scenario whereby he/she is conducting multiple independent studies with students enrolled in the same online course. The opening scenario of this chapter illustrates the overwhelming workload that can occur within WBI. Student management depends a great deal upon the ability of the instructor to develop a community of learners whereby students themselves take on much of the responsibility of learning and course management. Applying theories of active and adult learning, faculty can handle student management issues, such as timely submission and grading of assignments, shared expertise, and peer mentoring.

Active Learning and Adult Learning

Design for WBI draws from the field of constructivist theory which emphasizes that learning occurs when students rely upon their prior experiences and knowledge to form or "construct" new concepts and new ideas. Learning does not take place in a vacuum, but rather is a social, collaborative process and activity (Vygotsky, 1978; Bruner, 1990). While constructivist theory is aimed at understanding and exploring the ways in which children learn, many researchers and instructors in higher education have applied constructivism to adult learners (Huang, 2002; Murphy, 2001; Oliver, 1999; Wilson & Lowry, 2000).

Theories of adult learning share certain concepts with constructivism, including the value of previous experience and knowledge, and the focus on learning as shared activity. Conceptions of adult learners also stress self-direction, responsibility, motivation, expectations, and authentic tasks (Courtney, Vasa, Luo, & Muggy, 1999; Knowles, 1990).

The picture of the adult learner is that of a person who brings many of their own ideas and experiences into every learning situation, and whose learning will be shaped by real-life relevance and real-life constraints. The adult learner is at the same time independent and dependent, motivated and distracted by multiple responsibilities, and rich in life experience (Nichols, 2002).

Relying on these theoretical frameworks, the instructor can design an online course where students rely upon each other as content and process experts, and thus share (with the instructor) the responsibility for information management. This strategy for managing students is consistent with both constructivist and andragogical theories, emphasizing that the experience and prior knowledge that students bring to the class are valued. Markel (2001) acknowledges that students should understand that their peers are "holders of knowledge." Duffy and Jonassen (1992) point out that shared dialogue with others is an important factor in the social negotiation of knowledge.

Students as Process Experts

Using a learner analysis at the beginning of the course, the instructor can identify those students who are experienced in online learning. These students possess valuable knowledge that can be shared with beginning or less experienced online students. Armed with this information, an instructor can implement measures to help students share what they already know and mentor each other.

- Create a system of "online buddies" pairing an experienced learner with one new to the online environment. Encourage students to make regular contact with their buddies.

- Create topics or forums on the discussion board that allow students to share previous WBI experience.

- Set up chat sessions for students to share concerns, difficulties, and suggestions with each other. You can set the time but make it known that this is "student time."

- Use the discussion board to take care of specific course-management-related topics such as Questions about the Course, Questions about Specific Assignments, and Technical Questions. Ask students to check the discussion board for questions and answers before contacting you. Encourage other students to answer peers' questions. It is likely that other students in the course can and will answer the question. You should, of course, monitor the discussion board. If, after a time, no student has responded or if several students express confusion and post similar questions, you can step in and answer the question. By waiting and allowing students to post and respond, you save time for yourself by responding to the entire class instead of to separate e-mails. Additionally, passing the responsibility to the students builds community, thereby contributing to the sense of a community of learners. Students become "experts" or "mentors" for each other.

Students as Content Experts

One of the best ways for students to share their expertise and knowledge is on the discussion board. When students lead a discussion, either individually or in a group, they gain what Savery and Duffy (2001) call "ownership" of the learning task or problem.

- **Let students lead the discussions, taking more responsibility for their learning:** The instructor in this context will serve as facilitator or guide. The instructor should, however, provide clear guidelines and step in when needed. To help learners know what is expected of them, provide samples of acceptable posts and responses. The instructor should also not rely on students to lead all discussions. Doing so places an unnatural burden on those who may be new to discussions in either the role as participant or leader.

- **Use groups as the basis for discussion:** Assign tasks or topics to groups. The groups work on their own by e-mail, chat, or discussion board (many course management systems, such as BlackBoard and WebCT, permit private group areas). Group members create a summary of the topic and post it to the Web. The advantage is twofold—the instructor reduces work time by grading group summaries instead of summaries from each student, and students collaborate and become content experts.

- **Implement peer and self-evaluation:** For specific discussion assignments or for a group discussion activity, ask students to evaluate their own performance and that of their peers. Provide clear and consistent guidelines or rubrics for evaluation. Graham, Cagiltay, Craner, Lim, and Duffy (2000) and Moore, Winograd, and Lange (2001) offer detailed suggestions on managing course discussions effectively.

Timely Submission of Assignments

Online students, especially those new to the environment, sometimes have difficulty budgeting their time appropriately, especially in courses that are not strictly structured by the instructor. Faculty report that these students may procrastinate, waiting until near the end of the course to do and to submit their assignments (Graham et al., 2000). At some institutions this is called "dumping." Dumping can cause a burden on the instructor who then must grade a chunk of assignments in a very short time span. Dumping also does not allow the instructor to adequately determine what students have really learned, especially if they did all or most of the assignments in a few days. While online courses can be designed either to follow an instructor-set schedule or to be self-paced study, to effectively manage student assignments, a structured, regulated learning space that delineates due dates contributes best to learning effectiveness and to the instructor's ability to grade and return assignments. Structured courses provide students specific or semi-specific due dates on assignments. Semi-specific due dates allow a range of time for submitting specific assignments. For example, the instructor might specify "Assignment 3 is due the week of February 12, but must be submitted by noon Friday, February 16." This allows online students some flexibility, while at the same time granting the instructor a necessary time expectation for assignment submission. Whatever your specifications or schedule for submitting and grading assignments, be sure to inform students of these specifications.

Receiving Assignments

Acknowledgement feedback confirms or acknowledges receipt of assignments. Online students take advantage of the 24-hour nature of e-mail and electronic drop boxes to submit assignments at any time. Often the students' timeframe for response does not match the instructor's, especially if the instructor has not clearly stated e-mail or assignment turnaround policies. In one case, an instructor began to receive almost hourly messages from a student who had submitted an assignment the night before but had not received an acknowledgement from the professor. While the faculty response to students is a time management issue (see Time Management section), to assist students with their course management skills, an instructor must make it clear to the students what can be expected when assignments are received.

Conclusion

There is no guarantee that by following every tip and practical guide detailed here, an online course can be delivered without any problems. Just like traditional instruction, good WBI takes practice, training, and often patience. Recent research shows that faculty, in fact, can spend less preparation time on WBI as they progress from semester to semester when compared to traditional courses (Pachnowski & Jurczyk, 2003). When time and student interactivity are well managed, and workload is not an issue, online faculty will find that weekly, and even daily, course management is not a time-eating beast but rather a new and different way to consider the learning space.

References

AAUP. (1999). *Statement on distance education.* Retrieved August 15, 2004, from http://www.aaup.org/statements/Redbook/StDistEd.HTM

AAUP. (n.d.). *Suggestions and guidelines on sample language for institutional policies and contract language.* Retrieved August 15, 2004, from http://www.aaup.org/Issues/DistanceEd/Archives/speccmt/deguide.htm

American Federation of Teachers. (2001). *A virtual revolution: Trends in the expansion of distance education.* Retrieved August 15, 2004, from http://www.aft.org/higher_ed/downloadable/VirtualRevolution.pdf

Bruner, J. (1990). *Acts of meaning.* Cambridge, MA: Harvard University Press.

Courtney, S., Vasa, S., Luo, J., & Muggy, V. (1999). *Characteristics of adults as learners and implications for computer-based systems for information and instruction.* Minneapolis, MN: America's Learning Exchange, Minnesota Department of Economic Security. (ERIC Document Reproduction Service No. ED451340.)

Cvach, P. (1989). *Time management: Strategies for achieving success.* McLean, VA: Interstate Research Associates, Inc. (ERIC Document Reproduction Service No. ED329076.)

Duffy, T., & Jonassen, D. (Eds.). (1992). *Constructivism and the technology of instruction: A conversation.* Hillsdale, NJ: Lawrence Erlbaum.

Graham, C., Cagiltay, K., Craner, J., Lim, B., & Duffy, T. (2000). *Teaching in a Web-based distance learning environment: An evaluation summary based on four courses*

(CRLT Tech. Rep. No. 13-00). Center for Research on Learning and Technology, Indiana University, USA.

Huang, H. (2002). Toward constructivism for adult learners in online learning environments. *British Journal of Educational Technology, 33*(1), 27-37.

Huffstetter, S., & Smith, S. C. (1989). *Managing time and stress.* In S. C. Smith & P. K. Piele (Eds.), *School leadership: Handbook for excellence.* Eugene, OR: ERIC Clearinghouse on Educational Management, College of Education, University of Oregon. (ERIC Document Reproduction Service No. ED309518.)

International Data Corporation. (1999, June). Online distance learning in higher education, 1998-2002. *Council for Higher Education Accreditation (CHEA) Update, 2,* 1.

Knowles, M. S. (1990). *The adult learner: A neglected species* (4th ed.). Houston, TX: Gulf Publishing.

Markel, S. (2001). Technology and education online discussion forums: It's in the response. *Online Journal of Distance Learning Administration, 4*(2). Retrieved August 15, 2004, from http://www.westga.edu/~distance/ojdla/summer42/markel42.html

Moore, G. S., Winograd, K., & Lange, D. (2001). *You can teach online: Building a creative learning environment.* Boston: McGraw-Hill.

Moore, M. G. (2000). Is distance teaching more work or less? *American Journal of Distance Education, 14*(3), 1-5.

Moore, M. G., & Kearsley, G. (2005). *Distance education: A systems view* (2nd ed.). Belmont, CA: Thomson Learning.

Murphy, K. L. (2001). Using Web tools, collaborating, and learning online. *Distance Education, 22*(2), 285-305.

National Center for Educational Statistics. (2002). *Distance education instruction by postsecondary faculty and staff: Fall 1998.* Retrieved May 25, 2002, from http://nces.ed.gov/pubs2002/2002155.pdf

NCA. (2000). *NCA distance learning guidelines.* Retrieved August 15, 2004, from http://www.ncahigherlearningcommission.org/resources/guidelines/gdistance.html

Norris, G.A. (2001). We asked our multilane readers to respond to this question: What is your favorite time management strategy? *Advisor Today, 96*(6), 86.

Nichols, M. (2002, April 15). Principles of best practice for 21st century education. In *Proceedings of the International Forum of Educational Technology & Society, Formal Discussion Initiation.* Retrieved May 15, 2002, from http://ifets.ieee.org/discussions/discuss_april2002.html

Oblinger, D. G., Barone, C. A., & Hawkins, B. L. (2001). *Distributed education and its challenges: An overview.* Washington, DC: American Council on Education and EDUCAUSE.

Oliver, R. (1999). Exploring strategies for online teaching and learning. *Distance Education, 20*(2), 240-255.

Panchowski, L. M., & Jurczyk, J. P. (2003). Perceptions of faculty on the effect of distance learning technology on faculty preparation time. *Online Journal of Distance*

Learning Administration, VI(III). Retrieved August 15, 2004, from http://www.westga.edu/~distance/ojdla/fall63/pachnowski64.html

Parker, A. (2003). Motivation and incentives for distance faculty. *Online Journal of Distance Learning Administration, VI*(III). Retrieved September 20, 2004, from http://www.westga.edu/~distance/ojdla/fall63/parker63.htm

Rockwell, S. K., Schauer, J., Fritz, S. M., & Marx, D. B. (1999). Incentives and obstacles influencing higher education faculty and administrators to teach via distance. *Online Journal of Distance Learning Administration, II*(IV). Retrieved September 20, 2004, from http://www.westga.edu/~distance/rockwell24.html

Savery, J. R., & Duffy, T. (2001). *Problem-based learning: An instructional model and its constructivist framework* (CRLT Tech. Rep. No. 16-01). Center for Research on Learning and Technology, Indiana University, USA.

Starr, L. (1984). The productive executive: Top ten time tips. *Performance and Instruction, 23*(5), 5.

Visser, J. (2000). Faculty work in developing and teaching Web-based distance courses: A case study of time and effort. *American Journal of Distance Education, 14*(3), 21-32.

Vygotsky, L. S. (1978). *Mind in society: The development of higher psychological processes.* Cambridge, MA: Harvard University Press.

Wilson, B., & Lowry, M. (2000). Constructivist learning on the Web. *New Directions for Adult and Continuing Education, 88,* 79-88.

Chapter XX

Ethical Issues in
Web-Based Learning

Joan D. McMahon, Towson University, USA

Introduction

If you were to survey course syllabi on your campus, you would probably find the standard syllabi to include:

- Course title and number
- Instructor's name and contact information
- Course objectives
- A list of required and recommended readings/materials
- A detailed outline of the topics for consideration
- Detailed descriptions of assignments and due dates
- Percentage of final grade
- A schedule of topics by date

You would also find a campus curriculum or departmental committee that initially approves such courses. Once the course is approved, it is not usually subject to review or scrutiny by the campus, unless the department requests a course change.

Meanwhile, faculty who teach the course change the syllabus at will based on new material in their discipline, changes in textbooks, and so forth. This is encouraged so that the students get the most up-to-date information in the discipline.

If faculty switch courses, retire, or resign, then their syllabus is passed on to the successor to revise, again at will. There seems to be little or no systematic accounting of the legitimacy of the course originally approved to the course now taught. Department chairs are supposed to do this. Many take their responsibility for quality control seriously; many others delegate this to their capable administrative assistant who may not know enough about the subtleties of the curriculum to have recognized that an inconsistency exists.

What is the Overall Ethical Problem?

The problem is that course information is now being posted to the Web, thus creating problems with values, rights, and professional responsibilities specifically in curricular quality control, advising, intellectual property rights, and succession planning (University of Washington, 1996).

What is the harm in not having quality control in developing and posting courses on the Web? This is best addressed through a series of questions about rights and values, and is illustrated in Figure 1.

1.   Has the delivery mode of the Web changed the approved course's integrity? How does faculty pedagogical style affect course integrity? Has the course changed from the campus's officially approved version? What is the professional responsibility of the faculty and the department in keeping courses current and still protecting curriculum integrity? How does one handle and value course updates without changing the course? This is a *departmental* problem.

Figure 1.Curricular quality control

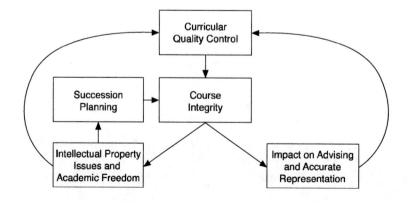

2.   Do students have the right to get what they "pay" for? From an advising perspective, does the course reflect what is "advertised" in the campus catalog so that those seeking credit for the course elsewhere are assured that the course description in the official catalog is the same course taught or desired? This is an *institutional* problem.

3.   How are the intellectual property rights of the faculty valued and protected by posting course material on the Web? This is an *institutional* problem.

4.   How will successive faculty comply with the course integrity whether they put their material on the Web or not? This is a *departmental* problem.

There need to be policies or procedures in place that allow faculty to upgrade their syllabi routinely within the accuracy of an approved course process to address the ethics of advising, course and curriculum integrity, intellectual property, and succession planning. With the advent of courses being developed online and faculty now able to easily state to the world that "I have my syllabus on the Web," this plethora of ethical issues arises.

The Course Integrity Problem

The course integrity problem stems from the overall issue of quality control. Faculty are encouraged to keep up to date in their discipline and pass this on to their students. Currency of intellectual thought is valued. Yet the bureaucratic process of reapplying for course "approval" whenever a course/syllabus is revised, or each time it is taught by a new faculty member, would be untimely. Curricular policies typically do not allow for easy and quick updates within the framework originally approved. The Web and online learning only exacerbate the problem. Faculty can and do change their courses quickly and without bureaucratic approval. Ethically, how are they being professionally responsible? This feeds another problem of altering courses that might not match catalog descriptions. The process of course approval and revision needs to be reexamined at the departmental level; for now, many faculty are caught in the middle.

The Advising Problem

When a campus prints a catalog of approved course descriptions, it is inherent that the course syllabi has been approved by the required committees. If students want to take a course on another campus or want their credits reviewed for transfer, it is the official course description in the catalog that is assessed. If a syllabus has been changed or updated so often by different faculty that it no longer reflects the approved course description, then there is an ethical problem of "misrepresentation." Similarly, students who wish to enroll in a course, using the official course catalog description, fully expect that the course will reflect what is described. Students drop the course when they realize the course description and the actual course syllabus do not match. This was not the course they thought it was going to be. This issue denies students fundamental rights of "buying" what is advertised. Is there an issue of public trust being violated? These are issues that need to be raised institutionally

The Intellectual Property Problem and Academic Freedom

With each new iteration of a course, the syllabus has taken on the personality and pedagogical style of the professor. What worked for one instructor does not work for his/ her successor. Their pedagogical styles and beliefs are reflected in how and what they teach, and how they assess the learning in their assignments. So they revise the course to reflect their own styles and personalities, and are permitted by academic freedom to do so (Hecht, Higgerson, Gmelch, & Tucker, 1999, p. 138).

When a faculty changes the course by changing the emphasis of the content, the type of assignments, and the new pedagogical material that helps student learn, they are developing their own intellectual property in the course. Who owns the intellectual property of the course is the subject of much current ethical debate. On some campuses, if you are an employee of the institution, the institution owns the intellectual property because the faculty member was "hired" to develop and teach it. This is "work for hire" (Kelley & Bonner, 2001). Other campuses feel that the faculty members own the intellectual property of the course. The course itself—that is, the course description— and the originally approved syllabi are the intellectual property of the institution. The faculty member's interpretation of how to teach the course, the emphasis on the content, how the learning is assessed, and so forth is the intellectual property of the faculty member. The ethical problem is who owns what? And for how long? Is it the course or the syllabus that is sacred? What is posted to the Web for public access? And what is "secured" information to be obtained through enrollment fees, if any, that protect the intellectual property of the faculty? These are ethical issues for institutions to address.

The Succession Planning Problem

If a faculty member switches courses, goes on sabbatical, resigns, or retires, what happens to the course integrity? Does the course go with the faculty member who developed it? If given a copy of a previous syllabus, will successor faculty recognize it as the one originally sanctioned by the department, be able to recognize multiple modifications to it, or recognize the customized interpretation and intellectual property of the previous instructor? Do they know they can customize the course to fit their own scholarly interpretation without compromising the course and curriculum integrity? Again, is it the course or the syllabus that is sacred? The face-to-face version may look different from the online version. How will these successor faculty be coached on keeping the original course integrity intact while offering their own customized interpretation online? Who in the department will coach and monitor them?

Table 1. Ethical issues reflecting values, rights and professional responsibilities

Ethical Issue	Value(s)	Rights	Professional Responsibilities
Course Integrity	Information delivered should be current.	What are the rights of faculty and students to provide and learn up-to-date information?	What are the policies and procedures to allow for updates within approved course structures?
Advising	The institution values curricular quality.	What rights do students have for accurate representation of what is printed versus what is delivered?	What is the responsibility of the institution and department in providing accurate information?
Intellectual Property	Faculty have unique teaching styles and pedagogical instructional design preferences	What rights do faculty have to carry their intellectual interpretation of the course to another campus? What rights does the campus have to protect curricular integrity?	What are the policies on "work for hire" and how are intellectual property rights of the faculty and the institution clarified? How long can an institution use the intellectual property of a faculty member who leaves the institution?
Succession Planning	Faculty grow and move on. Successor faculty should be of equal or greater quality.	What rights do faculty have to develop their own intellectual property Academic freedom)? What rights do successors have to customize their interpretation of the approved course and not necessarily copy an old syllabus from someone else?	To what extent should adjunct faculty and other successor faculty comply with approved course syllabi? Who monitors the quality of what these successors teach?

What are Some Solutions?

An ethical problem is one that can be solved with a win-win solution if people think through it long enough to figure out what to do. Can campuses support or justify their actions within the context of their values, rights, and professional responsibilities? (See Table 1.)

Using the Web, campuses can now do several things: (1) protect the intellectual integrity of the curriculum if a faculty member leaves or no longer teaches a course, which in turn affects advising; (2) protect the intellectual property of the faculty so that only those who are "buying" the credits actually get to use it; and (3) hold the departments accountable for the accuracy of the course offerings. To do these, two simple solutions are recommended:

1.   Publish a "generic one-page common course syllabus" on the campus Web site reflecting the approved generic syllabus

2.   Develop a customized "schedule" of the course which changes from semester to semester depending on who teaches it

Publish a Generic Common Course Syllabus that Does Not Change Over Time

This is a one-page document that has been approved by the department and campus curriculum committee or other required approving bodies. It can be posted on a campus Web site and provides enough information to viewers about whether the course meets their needs. This should be placed on top of any instructor's own interpretation of the course. No matter who teaches the course, this is a "guarantee." It only changes with official departmental/campus approval. The campus "owns" this course. It is a building block of a curriculum and is not subject to the changes in staffing. It is a course preview and could include the following elements:

1.   Heading that specifies department, course number, course title, and institution

2.   Approved course rationale

3.   Approved course catalog description

4.   Prerequisites

5.   Approved course objectives or goals

6.   Approved content outline of about 10 topics

7.   Possible learning assessments/assignments

8.   Required departmental standards/readings/materials

9. Required campus policies on cheating/plagiarism, attendance, and so forth (or these can be addendums)

10. An approved statement on disabilities assistance

11. Approved campus plagiarism policy

12. Campus attendance policy

Develop a Customized "Schedule" of the Course Which Changes from Semester to Semester Depending on Who Teaches It

A course schedule reflects whatever is changed in a course from semester to semester. If different faculty teach the course each semester, the course itself will not change, but rather the scholarly interpretation of the course will be dependent on who teaches it (Palloff & Pratt, 1999, p. 88). It reflects their teaching style and education philosophy. It is their intellectual property, the way they interpret and view the course based on the students they serve at the time. They can carry this course with them to another campus and adapt it to the needs of a different student body. It protects the fundamental rights of the faculty while complying with the course requirements of the institution. Several faculty teaching the same course ensures that the course objectives, content, and assessments are covered, while giving academic freedom to the faculty to implement their creativity and scholarship in unique ways in their customized version of the "schedule." It could include the following:

1. Instructor name, credentials, and contact information

2. Office hours

3. Room assignments

4. A statement of their personal assumptions about learning (their educational philosophy about teaching and learning)

5. Their current list of required and recommended readings

6. Their interpretation of the topics (more detail than the general outline)

7. A timetable for implementation of topics and assignments

8. Their interpretation of the learning assessments/assignments and weighting of such

These are two relatively simple solutions to solving the complexity of these ethical problems. Other ethical innovative solutions are possible, given the right processes to generate win-win solutions (Joseph & Conrad, 1995). Regardless, the solutions will suggest departmental faculty collaboration, faculty training, workshops, seminars, policy analysis, and perhaps external peer reviews.

Long Range Implications

Ethically, the long-range issue affects curricular quality control, course integrity, and potentially accreditation. But the implementation of such a simple strategy as recommended above, the adoption of a one-page generic common syllabus and a changeable schedule, affects departmental decision making to the core.

Having a departmental discussion about each course, what the central elements are and how they are a part of the larger curriculum whole, is an insightful exercise in interpersonal group dynamics, organizational development, and change management. These cannot be handled in a single faculty meeting. With the number of online courses being developed within departments, many faculty will simply say that "the delivery method" has changed and there is no need to review the online version of the course. But an in-depth analysis of the course in that delivery method may show the problems mentioned earlier. Palloff and Pratt (1999) pose guiding questions to consider in developing courses online and how they might differ from their face-to-face counterparts (p. 109). Regardless, online course assessment should be considered in light of its impact on the department's curriculum.

Another long-range implication is that of succession planning. If adjunct faculty step in for regular faculty, what assurances are there that the course will remain "intact?" What does "intact" mean now? If a faculty member resigns or retires, what happens to the course and curriculum integrity? By having a generic syllabus available for successor faculty, it provides them with the guidance and structure needed to develop their own materials in the course. The generic common course syllabus theoretically forms the basis for accreditation review.

Conclusion

With the advent of online courses, departments will have to reexamine what it means to offer a course in this new delivery method. They will have to think through the issues of values, rights, and professional responsibilities specifically in curricular quality control, advising, intellectual property rights, and succession planning. The delivery of courses online and visible worldwide brings fundamental ethical problems to the forefront. They need to be grappled with by departments, curriculum committees, and other approval bodies. What an opportunity we have to dialog about these issues!

References

Hecht, I., Higgerson, M., Gmelch, W., & Tucker, A. (1999). *The department chair as academic leader.* Phoenix, AZ: The American Council on Education and The Oryx Press.

Joseph, V., & Conrad, A. P. (1995). *Essential steps for ethical problem-solving.* Retrieved from http://www.socialworkers.org/pubs/code/oepr/steps.htm

Kelley, K., & Bonner, K. (2001). *Courseware ownership in distance education: Issues and policy models.* Unpublished manuscript, University of Maryland University College, USA.

Palloff, R., & Pratt, K. (1999). *Building learning communities in cyberspace.* San Francisco: Jossey-Bass.

University of Washington. (1996). *Recommended core ethical values.* Retrieved from http://www.engr.washington.edu/~uw-epp/Pepl/Ethics/ethics3.html

Chapter XXI

Moving Toward the Implementation of Contextualized Educational Technology

Esko Kähkönen, University of Joensuu, Finland

Erkki Sutinen, University of Joensuu, Finland

Introduction

As a result of the rapid development of information and communication technologies, educational software has become readily available in the global market. Although the international transfer and trade of most technological products seems straightforward, the actors in the field must have cultural sensitivity when it comes to implementing technology-based learning tools and digital materials. This is due to the individual and cultural diversity of the global e-learning community. This diversity should be recognized when designing and implementing modern learning environments or when activating technology-based study zones.

First of all, by *contextualization,* we refer to the various methods and processes related to design issues, pedagogical aspects and approaches, contents, or applied technologies that are needed for a learning environment to be functional and useful in a particular cultural setting. Consequently, we need to discuss contextualization from diverse perspectives. As such we have identified: *cultural differences in producing e-learning materials and tools,* culturally flavored learning paths, technical platform and cultural factors, and taking a multidisciplinary approach to contextualization.

Cultural Differences in Producing E-Learning Materials and Tools

Producers and consumers, when they come from different cultural backgrounds, should collaborate in a way that cultural heterogeneity can enrich the learning process and bring about new, intercultural perspectives (Kähkönen, 2003). Somewhat surprisingly, this applies not only to materials, but also to learning tools that are occasionally called *mind tools* or *instruments of the mind* (Jonassen, 2000; Sutinen, Vesisenaho, & Virnes, 2002). For example, not all people consider certain types of visualization tools beneficial for their learning process because of the different roles imagery takes on in different cultural contexts.

Culturally Flavored Learning Paths

Individualized learning paths are widely recognized as success factors in learning outcomes; however, little attention is paid to the cultural background and conceptualization of cultural factors in the development of student learning paths (Kähkönen, 2003).

Technical Platform and Cultural Factors

From the users' point of view, technologies should make certain tasks easier or provide some kind of added value. Applied to learning technologies, this principle means that an economically sound technical platform helps learners focus on and overcome the main barriers of the learning process. Many of these difficulties and bottlenecks are related to one's cultural situation. In order to help learners avoid unnecessary learning obstacles and save time for the most relevant issues, the technical learning platform should modify the pedagogical content to fit the needs of the particular cultural setting.

Taking a Multidisciplinary Approach to Contextualization

A multidisciplinary research approach is needed to be able to adapt the learning process to the endless varieties of human behaviors and cultural identities. An interdisciplinary approach should cover all the dimensions of the learning process: knowledge, skills, attitudes, and values. We believe that novel approaches in these fields enable identifying the most meaningful factors in the comprehension of concepts—whether they are abstract and computational or concrete and culturally bound—in multiple, culturally diverse learning settings.

Collis and Remmers (1997) write about two kinds of Web sites—local sites and cross-cultural sites. Local sites are those designed for participation in one context and one culture; cross-cultural sites are those designed for cross-cultural participation. Collis and Remmers state that there is a special need for instructional design when sites have to be suitable for a wide, intercultural audience.

One should ask, anyhow, if this local/cross-cultural approach is helpful in the development of truly contextual, culturally sensitive e-learning. This pragmatic division might also create a certain dichotomy where in an imagined monocultural situation, the prevailing pedagogic approach is taken as a given. Instead of focusing on the local/cross-cultural dichotomy, we focus on the prerequisites of learning and the application of adaptive technologies.

Action and Awareness in the Implementation of Contextualized Educational Technology

In instructional design, little attention has been paid to the diversity of the cultural backgrounds of learners. No wonder that in the U.S., institutions of higher education, even the ones that are most active in Web-based learning, omitted *accommodating different learning styles* from their list of crucial factors for quality teaching and course development (Institute for Higher Education Policy, 2000). This is understandable, however, because it is a challenge to transform curricular content in a wider pedagogic and communicative sense. Regarding the design of culturally sensitive learning content, we need to be aware of the fact that "the lack of shared meaning can make communication very difficult for two people from very different cultures" (Duffy & Cunningham, 1996).

Much of the present attraction to the field of information and communication technologies seems to be rooted in technological optimism. Technological optimism implies that a new world culture should be created; however, a strong emphasis in this direction seems to leave no place for cultural diversity. Although *localization* is a word from the software industry, it is unclear how meaningful the software industry's various localization strategies really are.

In the field of higher education, the tradition of distance learning, which gained competence in a variety of contexts even before the advent of Web-based technologies, always has had to deal with issues of contextualization. The tradition of distance learning lives on, both challenged and enriched by ICT-based learning, for instance in the world conferences of the International Council for Open and Distance Education (ICDE). The proceedings of the latest ICDE conferences (ICDE, 2001, 2004) show a wide variety of topics related to the practical issues of education, with a strong emphasis on Asian and African contexts. In the ICDE proceedings, theoretical approaches are quite rare however.

Now that multinational education companies are looking for new global markets, the issue of contextualization gains new relevance. The decision of the Massachusetts Institute of Technology (MIT) to deliver materials through the Internet (Goldberg, 2001) has brought about a variety of reactions, despite the fact the materials are freely distributed. Some are pleased to get world-class learning materials for free, whereas others fear a new kind of imperialism. Surprisingly, for some at least, one of the authors of this chapter has experienced positive comments while doing research in Iran (Kähkönen, 2003), a country in great isolation and which has mutual animosity with the U.S. For example, a university physics teacher, who very much welcomed the initiative, valued it as a source of very helpful learning materials.

From the point of view of cultural contextualization, the global availability of the MIT materials has to be viewed in light of the fact that it is not ready-made courseware that MIT is delivering, since they only deliver materials, animations, lectures, and such. One point, according to MIT itself, is that developing countries can rapidly develop their system of higher education with the help of their materials. Developing courseware based on these materials would become easier, and this again would add to development of new curricula and the exchange of ideas globally.

Theoretical clarification of the cultural context as an issue in educational technology is just beginning. A short review shows that the situation of minorities has largely guided the debate. Henderson (1994) and McLoughlin and Oliver (2000) pay special attention to the Australian context and its aboriginal students in institutions of higher education. In that case, a certain multicultural setting dominates the discussion; hence, the majority of educational policies have come under fire. It has also become common to discuss, in the Australian context, whether constructivist education necessarily works with indigenous groups of students.

McLoughlin and Oliver (2000) recommend that systematic attention be paid to design guidelines for the sake of cultural sensitivity. Of importance are such factors as responsiveness to learner needs, and community and cultural contextualization of learning activities. They regret that despite the fact that many current design models and paradigms are socially and culturally determined, the need for cultural contextualization is not acknowledged. McLoughlin and Oliver also present 10 rules for the design of "flexible, culturally responsive Web design" aimed at indigenous Australian learners. They consider an approach to be *pragmatic* if it promotes constructivist and contextualized learning, especially in situated cognition.

McLoughlin and Oliver strongly support measures and tasks that motivate students to connect the curriculum to the everyday sphere of the student. They also point out the need for multimodal delivery and assessment mechanisms.

McLoughlin (1999) is in favor of binding teaching with high levels of cultural inclusion and with high levels of constructive alignment. Similarly, McLoughlin hypothesizes that low levels of cultural inclusion necessarily correlate with low levels of constructivism. McLoughlin makes it clear that the constructivist approach is appropriate when it comes to considering cultural differences and practicing cultural sensitivity.

Henderson (1994) claims that the consideration of culture sensitivity is imperative in instructional design. She assumes that the dimensions of cultural sensitivity infiltrate every aspect of the learning process. Here she makes remarks on Tom Reeves' model of interactive learning. However, regarding the Australian indigenous perspective, she maintains that a constructivist pedagogy does not necessarily work. She says, for example, that *why* questions are not expected in the sociolinguistic framework of indigenous Australians. Reeves (1997) acknowledges Henderson's remarks, but also questions what, comprehensively, culturally sensitive computer-based education would be like. Boman (2001) addresses the same issue by stating that computer-mediated communication "allows more open platforms from which to situate radically different dynamic, intercultural learning contexts."

Here the core question and the main challenge is drafted at the same time. It is clear that the need for new developments is engrossing. The viewpoints presented above, on one hand, illustrate the preliminary research paradigm and the need for further investigations. On the other hand, the viewpoints also make the case for the use of new approaches.

Multiple Representations for Contextualized Educational Technology

The learning process and its outcomes depend on, at least, the following factors that always reflect the learner's cultural background: learning styles, learning goals, and learning prerequisites.

Although learning styles are primarily individual characteristics, the other two are determined largely from the context of the learner. It needs to be considered that even learning styles might be influenced by the local context. For example, some cultures rely upon visual aids more than others.

The potential of computers in learning environments can be viewed from multiple perspectives. From the perspective of computer science, one needs to analyze, in particular, the role of computing (i.e., the process of transforming given input by an algorithm into the required output). There might be other aspects to add, like user interface design or software engineering, as well.

For the learning process, it is crucial that learners can proceed in a way that is in accordance with their personal learning styles, goals, and prerequisites (Kähkönen & Sutinen, 2002; Kähkönen, 2003). They all relate to the issues of cultural background, values, and ethical issues.

Courses of Action for Implementing Contextualized Educational Technology

The implementation of contextualized educational technology brings forth mutual benefits since the flood of information flows reciprocally between cultural learning settings. This means, for example, that a certain African story, myth, or approach could be beneficial for Western students as much as a Western story, myth, or approach could be beneficial for African students.

An important thread in the contextualization process is the implementation of dialogical learning over the Web. Kähkönen, Silander, and Gerdt (2004) drafted a pedagogical and communicative framework for intercultural encounters over the Internet. They report that some of the key issues involve implementing a narrative approach where stories and memories of mankind serve as common heritage. From the communicative viewpoint, common experiences should be integrated more strongly. A strong communal bond, where the community forms the rules, makes the encounter more realistic, while at the same time reducing the use of deceptive virtual personalities. James F. Fowler (as cited in Kähkönen et al., 2004) states that at the highest level of personal maturation, "a synthetic logic prevails as an attitude of mutuality, strongly bound to the commonwealth of being." Acknowledging Otherness is one of the key concepts in cultural contemporary cultural studies (During, 1999). Thus, the understanding of a dialogical encounter as a part of the contextualization process is important.

Concerning our orientation in computer science, we have introduced the concept of 'ethnocomputing' (Tedre, Sutinen, Kähkönen, & Kommers, in press). By the term ethnocomputing, we refer to the analysis and use of computational concepts within a culture. Ethnocomputing challenges the prevailing way of thinking: in order to keep up with the West, other cultures have to adapt to Western ways of thinking, including Western scientific traditions. The problem of the Eurocentric view of science is manifested in the learning of computer science. Non-Western students not only face a new subject, they also face an entirely new philosophy and new problem-solving methods that may differ greatly from their own. For example, a program or an algorithm makes use of concepts which have obvious cultural bindings, like recursion or divide-and-conquer heuristics. The extent to which students can make use of these concepts or even form new ones depends on the level of assimilation between their cultural backgrounds and the computational technologies available. As proponents of ethnocomputing, we argue that the universal theories of computing take different forms in different cultures. Studying and developing the concept of ethnocomputing may thus lead to new findings for improving computer science education.

References

Boman, M. (2001). *Pedagogic practice: How appropriate is computer-mediated communication (CMC) to culturally inclusive teaching and learning?* Retrieved November, 2004, from http://ispg.csu.edu.au/members/keustace/research/analysis/cultureCMC

Collis, B., & Remmers, E. (1997). The World Wide Web in education: Issues related to cross-cultural communication and action. In B. Khan (Ed.), *Web-based instruction* (pp. 85-92). Eaglewood Cliffs, NJ: Educational Technology Publications.

Duffy, T. M., & Cunningham, D. J. (1996). Constructivism: Implications for the design and delivery of instruction. In D. Jonassen (Ed.), *Handbook of research for educa-*

tional communications and technology (pp. 170-198). New York: Simon & Schuster Macmillan.

During, S. (1999). *The cultural studies reader.* New York: Routledge.

Goldberg, C. (2001, April 5). No net profit: MIT courses are going online (Free!). *New York Times Service, International Herald Tribune.* Retrieved November 4, 2004, from http://www.uni-muenster.de/PeaCon/medkomp/kurs/bt-mit.htm

Henderson, L. (1994). Reeves' pedagogic model of interactive learning systems and cultural contextuality. In C. McBeath & R. Atkinson (Eds.), *Proceedings of the 2nd International Interactive Multimedia Symposium* (pp. 289-298). Perth: Promaco Conventions.

ICDE. (2001). *Proceedings of the 20th World Conference on Open Learning and Distance Education.* Oslo, Norway: International Council for Open and Distance Education.

ICDE. (2004). *Proceedings of the 21st ICDE World Conference on Open Learning and Distance Education.* Oslo, Norway: International Council for Open and Distance Education.

Institute for Higher Education Policy. (2000). *Quality on the line. Benchmarks for success in Internet-based distance education.* Retrieved November 4, 2004, from http://www.e-guana.net/organizations.php3?action=printContentItem&org id=104&typeID=906&itemID=9239

Jonassen, D. H. (2000). *Computers as mindtools for schools: Engaging critical thinking* (2nd ed.). Upper Saddle River, NJ: Prentice-Hall.

Kähkönen, E. (2003). Cultural and pedagogical aspects for a contextual approach in e-learning. In E. Kähkönen & E. Sutinen (Eds.), *Proceedings of the 1st International Conference on Educational Technology in Cultural Context* (International Proceedings Series 3, pp. 9-18). Joensuu, Finland: University of Joensuu Press.

Kähkönen, E., Silander, P., & Gerdt, P. (2004). Towards dialogical learning in the Web. Intercultural encounter as a challenge for technology and pedagogy. *International Journal of Continuing Engineering Education and Lifelong Learning, 14,* 32-45.

Kähkönen, E., & Sutinen, E. (2002). Context and ethics as factors in the design of educational technology. In I. Ebrahimzadeh, A. Farahani, B. Zandi, & S. Abbabandi (Eds.), *Proceedings of the 2nd Conference of Open and Distance Learning* (pp. 1-8). Tehran: Payame Noor University Press.

McLoughlin, C. (1999). *Crossing boundaries: Curriculum and teaching implications of culturally inclusive online learning.* Retrieved November 4, 2004, from http://www.aare.edu.au/01pap/mcl01720.htm

McLoughlin, C., & Oliver, R. (2000). Designing learning environments for cultural inclusivity: A case study of indigenous online learning at tertiary level. *Australian Journal of Educational Technology, 16*(1), 58-72.

Reeves, T. (1997). *Evaluating what really matters in computer-based education.* Retrieved November 4, 2004, from http://www.educationau.edu.au/archives/cp/reeves.htm

Sutinen, E., Vesisenaho, M., & Virnes, M. (2002). E-based and contact-based computing studies for Tanzania: Action research from challenges via changes to chances. *Proceedings of the 7th International Working Conference of the International Federation of Information Processing (IFIP): Information Technology in Developing Countries (WG 9.4)* (pp. 444-452).

Tedre, M., Sutinen, E., Kähkönen, E., & Kommers, P. (in press). Universal is local in computing: ICT in cultural and social context. *Communications of the ACM.*

Chapter XXII

Evaluation Strategies for Open and Distributed Learning Environments

Thomas C. Reeves, The University of Georgia, USA

John G. Hedberg, Macquarie University, Australia

Introduction

Evaluation falls into the category of those often neglected human practices such as exercise and eating right. All of us involved in education or training know that we should engage in systematic evaluation when designing or implementing any type of learning environment, but we rarely get around to it. Perhaps this lapse stems from the fact that most instructional design models such as the ubiquitous ADDIE (Analysis, Design, Development, Implementation, and Evaluation) model (Molenda, 2003) appear to suggest that we can postpone evaluation until the end of the process. Whatever the reason, evaluation often remains in the realm of promises made, but not kept, such as "I'll eat better tomorrow."

Even when we do evaluate interactive instructional products or programs such as open and distributed learning environments, we often do so in an ill-conceived manner, the evaluative equivalent of thinking that if we eat a salad with a burger and fries, we have somehow engaged in healthy eating. For example, quasi-experimental comparisons of open and flexible learning environments with traditional classroom learning environments continue to dominate studies published in refereed research journals or presented at research conferences. Did we really need another large-scale meta-analysis such as the one recently reported by Bernard et al. (2004) to tell us that such comparisons are "of low quality" (p. 416) and that the final outcome is almost always of "no significant difference." Bernard et al. (2004) produced an excellent piece of scholarship, but as with most such meta-analyses of educational technologies (e.g., Dillon & Gabbard, 1998; Fabos & Young, 1999), their analytical synthesis provides precious little to guide designers or practitioners in their efforts.

With these failings in mind, this chapter is focused on recommending a set of practical strategies for evaluating open and distributed learning environments. A much more extensive treatment of this important topic can be found in a book titled *Interactive Learning Systems Evaluation* (Reeves & Hedberg, 2003).

A point of clarification about terminology is necessary. In his innovative *Framework for Web-Based Learning*, Khan (2001) includes "Evaluation" as one of the eight key dimensions. Under Evaluation, Khan lists both "assessment of learners" and "evaluation of the instruction and learning environment" (p. 78). In our work (Reeves & Hedberg, 2003), we have preferred to separate these two factors, reserving the term "assessment" to refer to activities focused on measuring characteristics of human learners (their learning, motivation, attitudes, etc.), a process that we see as a sub-dimension of pedagogy. We use the term "evaluation" solely to refer to activities focused on estimating the outcomes and worth of products, programs, and projects. In short, we assess people and evaluate things. The remainder of this chapter is exclusively focused on evaluation issues.

Why Evaluate?

We recommend a primarily pragmatic philosophy of evaluation that maintains that you should evaluate in order to provide the information that you and other decision makers need to make better decisions about the design and implementation of open and distributed learning environments. We view this as analogous to the conclusion that you should exercise and eat right to provide the necessary ingredients for a long and healthy lifespan. Exercise and evaluation are not ends in themselves in most contexts, but means to longer life on the one hand and better decision making on the other.

As a developer, manager, or implementer of open and distributed learning environments, you must make decisions, similar to those made by other professionals. For example, before rendering a diagnosis, a physician usually questions a patient to ascertain the patient's presenting complaint and medical history, conducts a thorough examination, and runs various tests. In fact, the quality and reputation of a physician is determined largely by how skillful he or she is in conducting "evaluative" acts such as interviewing, examining, and testing. The same is true of an evaluator.

Years of experiences as designers and evaluators of interactive learning environments have convinced us that decisions informed by sound evaluation are better than those based on habit, ignorance, intuition, prejudice, or guesswork. This may seem painfully obvious, and yet, far too often, we have seen people make poor decisions about the design and implementation of open and distributed learning environments simply because they failed to seek pertinent information that would be relatively easy to obtain. The e-learning field is replete with horror stories of bad choices related to factors such as course management systems, pedagogical design, and graphical user interface (Reeves, 2003).

Evaluation Functions

From time to time in the United States, the federal government's Department of Agriculture issues recommendations for healthy eating, usually presented in the format of a food pyramid. Recent versions of these dietary pyramids suggest that the broad base of the pyramid should encourage us to exercise and consume plentiful helpings of whole grains, fruits, and vegetables, whereas the narrow pinnacle of the pyramid should limit us to the relatively infrequent consumption of red meat, sweets, and butter.

We suggest a similar pyramidic metaphor for evaluation as illustrated in Figure 1. There are six types of evaluation functions represented in this evaluation pyramid: (1) Review, (2) Needs Assessment, (3) Formative Evaluation, (4) Effectiveness Evaluation, (5) Impact Evaluation, and (6) Maintenance Evaluation. The pyramid signals that the largest investments in time, money, and resources should go into the first three of these functions, especially formative evaluation. These first three aspects are often omitted from popular models of evaluation which focus more on Effectiveness and Impact and little else. From the pyramid in Figure 1, smaller "servings" of effective, impact, and maintenance evaluation are suggested because, although these are "good" for you, the

Figure 1. Evaluation pyramid

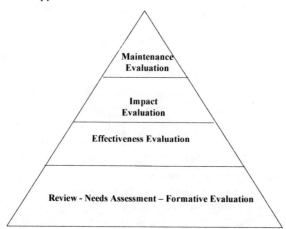

return-on-investment from these types of evaluation is lower than for the baseline functions.

The function of Review as an evaluation strategy is most important during the initial conceptualization of an open and distributed learning environment. Two key activities of the Review function are studying the published literature related to flexible learning and examining similar learning environments. In short, you should carry out Review activities to find out what is already known about the type of interactive learning environment you plan to develop and to understand the state of the art of design of learning environments of that kind. The failure to engage in Review can be seen at almost any large e-learning trade show where products with remarkably similar objectives and designs are marketed by multiple vendors.

The function of Needs Assessment as an evaluation strategy is to identify the critical needs that the proposed learning environment will address. A need is any significant gap between desired levels of performance and current levels of performance. Most needs stem from deficiencies (the lack of required knowledge, skills, and attitudes) or discrepancies (differences between what people can do and what they normally do). For example, there may be a need to expand professional development opportunities for teachers with respect to technology integration, in which case an open and distributed learning environment may be a viable solution. Alternatively, there may be a need to enhance the quality of the outcomes of educational programs concerning responsible alcohol consumption by young adults, and again, the provision of an e-learning environment may be the best way of meeting such a need. The primary activities carried out during Needs Assessment are task analysis, job analysis, and learner analysis (Rossett, 1987).

The function of Formative Evaluation as an evaluation strategy is to provide the information required to guide decisions about creating, debugging, and enhancing an open and distributed learning environment at various stages of its development. Formative evaluation should drive the instructional design and development process regardless of whether a traditional instructional systems design (ISD) or rapid prototyping model is pursued. Two of the primary activities carried out during Formative Evaluation include expert review and usability testing (Flagg, 1990; George & Cowan, 1999; Rubin, 1994).

The function of Effectiveness Evaluation as an evaluation strategy is to determine whether an open and distributed learning environment accomplishes its objectives within the immediate or short-term context of its implementation. It is essential to evaluate the implementation of a program with the same rigor as outcomes are evaluated. Some of the primary Effectiveness Evaluation activities include field tests, observations, interviews with different stakeholders, and performance assessment (Horton, 2001; Reeves & Hedberg, 2003).

The function of Impact Evaluation as an evaluation strategy is to determine whether the knowledge, skills, and attitudes (or more broadly "outcomes") learned in the context of an open and distributed learning environment transfer to the intended context of use, for example, the workplace or into further education. Inevitably, practical impact evaluations, including return-on-investment studies, entail considerable degrees of inference from results to decisions. Some of the primary Impact Evaluation activities include document analysis, interviews, and observations, as well as experimental methods. The

Figure 2. Relationships between development and evaluation functions

DEVELOPMENT FUNCTIONS	Should be informed by	EVALUATION FUNCTIONS
Project Conceptualization	⟵	Review
Design	⟵	Needs Assessment
Development	⟵	Formative Evaluation
Implementation	⟵	Effectiveness Evaluation
Institutionalization	⟵	Impact Evaluation
Project Re-Conceptualization	⟵	Maintenance Evaluation

latter are quite expensive in most cases, impractical in others, and yield results that are inevitably subject to multiple interpretations.

The function of Maintenance Evaluation as an evaluation strategy is to examine the continuing viability of an open and distributed learning environment over time. This is perhaps the most infrequently applied evaluation function, but the importance of it is growing, as the size and scope of e-learning enterprises rapidly expand. Some of the primary activities carried out in the name of Maintenance Evaluation are document analysis, interviews, observations, and automated data collection. In this function, the role of critical incidents is becoming one of the most common indicators of a need to change. For example, most managers of large implementations of learning management systems can tell nightmarish tales about how a database was corrupted or some other catastrophic event occurred which disrupted learners' access to an online learning system at critical times.

Another way of envisioning the interrelationships of these six evaluation functions is to illustrate them in relationship to the major development functions carried out when an open and distributed learning environment is designed, produced, and put into operation. Figure 2 demonstrates how the major development functions (conceptualize, design, develop, implement, institutionalize, and re-conceptualize) should be informed by the major functions of evaluation (review, needs assessment, formative evaluation, effectiveness evaluation, impact evaluation, and maintenance evaluation).

Case Studies

To illustrate how evaluations of open and distributed learning environments can be carried out, two case studies are described below, one related to formative evaluation issues and the other related to impact evaluation issues. The two case studies are hypothetical, although we have actually conducted related evaluations with similar results. The case studies are organized around the following key steps that are required for the planning, implementation, and reporting of any evaluation:

1. Identify the decisions that the evaluation should inform.

2. Specify the questions that must be answered to provide the information needed to inform the identified decisions.

3. Select reliable, valid, and feasible evaluation methods.

4. Implement the evaluation methods in a rigorous and professional manner.

5. Report the findings in an accurate and timely manner so that decisions can be informed as intended.

Formative Example

- **Scenario:** A large pharmaceutical company commissioned the development of e-learning materials related to GMP (Good Manufacturing Practice) by an entrepreneurial e-learning firm.

- **Decisions:** Decisions needed to be made about the graphical user interface (GUI) for the e-learning materials. The final programs provide more than eight hours of interactive training for pharmaceutical workers who range in education levels from two-year associate degrees to doctorates. The GUI had to be designed to provide user-friendly navigation, and allow multiple forms of interactions and clear readability of text.

- **Questions:** Based on graphical design principles, learner analysis, and other instructional design techniques, the e-learning firm developed a prototype GUI for the GMP programs. To inform decisions related to GUI enhancement, the developers require answers to the following questions:

  o What enhancements do e-learning experts recommend for the prototype GUI?

  o What enhancements are required on the basis of user testing of the prototype GUI?

- **Methods:** Heuristic review and usability testing are the two most commonly used evaluation strategies carried out to improve the navigation and user-friendliness of interactive computer programs (Nielsen, 1993). The developers first subjected the GUI to heuristic review (Nielsen, 1994) using a panel of five experts. Heuristic review involves the following procedures:

  a. Each member of the panel of experts reviews the prototype e-learning screens using a set of heuristics such as the ones provided by Nielsen (1994) or ones specifically developed for open and distributed learning environments. A typical heuristic would be: "Minimalist Design: Screen displays should not contain information that is irrelevant, and media features such as animation and sound should not be gratuitously added to the e-learning program."

  b. After identifying violations of the design heuristics, each expert independently exams each violation to rate its severity (How seriously will the

Figure 3. Severity scale for rating violations of e-learning screen design heuristics

Severity Scale for Rating Violations of Screen Design Heuristics
1.   **Cosmetic:** fix if possible.
2.   **Minor:** fixing this should be given low priority.
3.   **Medium:** fixing this should be given medium priority.
4.   **Major:** fixing this should be mandatory before the system is launched. If the problem cannot be fixed before launch, ensure that the documentation clearly shows the user a workaround.
5.   **Catastrophic:** fixing this is mandatory; no workaround possible.

Figure 4. Extensiveness scale for rating violations of e-learning screen design heuristics

Extensiveness Scale for Rating Violations of Screen Design Heuristics
1.   Single case
2.   Several places
3.   Widespread

violation affect the learner's experience?) and extent (How pervasive is the violation within the overall program?). Sample severity and extensiveness scales are illustrated in Figures 3 and 4.

c.   The expert reviews are synthesized and shared at a group meeting conducted face to face or online. Based upon the severity and extensiveness ratings, opportunities for improvements are identified and specific recommendations about how to redesign the GUI are made.

Some of the advantages of heuristic review are: (1) it is relatively quick because you do not need to find or schedule users to review the program, (2) it is relatively easy to review problem areas many times, and (3) it is relatively inexpensive because no fancy usability testing facilities are needed. Some of the disadvantages of heuristic review are: (1) its validity is weaker than usability testing because no actual learners are involved, (2) it generally finds fewer problems than usability testing, (3) recruiting good experts can be challenging, and (4) building consensus among experts can be difficult sometimes. In most cases, heuristic review should be conducted as a precursor to usability testing.

•   **Implementation:** The heuristic review takes place over a period of five days and costs almost $6,000. The costs include consulting fees paid to each of the five experts and the expenses associated with a half-day review meeting, including the time of the two primary instructional designers from the e-learning firm.

- **Reporting:** Significant changes are made to the e-learning screen designs based upon the analysis of the heuristic review. However, the developers know that heuristic review, while valuable, is no substitute for user testing, and they subsequently engage in formal usability testing. Reeves and Carter (2001) provide an introduction to usability testing, and detailed guides to usability testing have been written by Nielsen (1993) and Rubin (1994).

Impact Example

- **Scenario:** An international wireless telecommunications company wishes to increase sales of its products and services when customers call for support of products they already own. The company develops an e-learning program to help its customer service representatives (CSRs) recognize and take advantage of additional sales opportunities when engaged in customer support.

- **Decisions:** The e-learning program is ready for rollout at one of the company's regional customer support centers. Decisions must be made about two key issues: (1) should the e-learning program be disseminated to other regional customer support centers, and (2) should a generic version of the e-learning program be developed as a commercial product for marketing to other companies providing telephone customer support?

- **Questions:** To inform decisions related to internal and external dissemination of the CSR sales e-learning program, the corporate decision makers require answers to the following questions:

  o How does CSR call performance change as a result of completing the e-learning program?

  o How are the sales of related wireless products affected as a result of the rollout of the e-learning program?

- **Methods:** To collect the data needed to answer the aforementioned questions, three types of evaluation methods are planned. First, a random sample of transcripts of CSR call performance before and after completion of the e-learning program are analyzed by an independent specialist in qualitative data analysis to determine the rate at which opportunities for additional sales have been recognized and acted upon by the CSR. The qualitative specialist is unaware of which transcripts were recorded before or after the training.

  Second, Web surveys are distributed to all the CSRs at the call center where the program was originally implemented as well as to their immediate supervisors. The survey for the CSRs seeks to determine the extent to which the CSRs performed each of these sales promotion tasks after the e-learning course in comparison with how they performed these tasks prior to the course (much better, better, same, worse, much worse). The survey for the supervisors seeks to determine whether the supervisors had observed the changes in their CSR staff after the e-learning program related to behaviors such as:

o The CSRs seem to know more about our products and services than they did before the e-learning.

o The CSRs seem to have more confidence dealing with customers.

o The CSRs seem to be able to recognize sales opportunities when speaking to customers.

o The CSRs seem to be able to increase their sales of related products and services.

Third, the sales figures for wireless products generated at this call center are compared with the sales figures of the previous 12 months of the fiscal year, as well as with the sales figures generated at each of the other call centers.

- **Implementation:** The discourse analysis takes two weeks to complete and costs $8,000. The data analyst charges $800 per day for her services. The surveys are designed, distributed, and analyzed in house at a cost of $5,000 over a period of three months. Sales figures are tracked for two quarters after the e-learning program is released at the one regional call center. Analysis of the sales data is done in house at a cost of $3,000.

- **Reporting:** Results are positive on all counts. Although the average length of a customer's call increases by two minutes, this time is totally focused on additional sales of wireless products and services. Survey results indicate that CSRs feel more confident in responding to client calls, recognize sales opportunities, and act upon them. Sales increase by 40% during the two quarters after the initial rollout at the participating call center, whereas sales at the other sales center report no comparable increases. As a result of the evaluation, the e-learning program is immediately rolled out to all other call centers and design of a generic e-learning product commences.

Conclusion

Can we guarantee that you will receive the types of positive results noted above if you invest more of your time, money, and people resources in evaluation? No. Your results may be less than compelling, but what we can promise is that your decision making will be enhanced. You will have the critical information you and others need to make informed decisions about the design, use, and outcomes of e-learning. Returning to exercise and diet with which this chapter began, no one can guarantee that you will not be hit by a car while jogging or that you will not suffer food poisoning from dining at the salad bar rather than the hamburger joint. But, on average, exercise and eating right lead to longer, healthier, and happier lives. Similarly, on average, appropriate evaluation of open and distributed learning environments at key times in their development and use will enhance the decision making required to make these environments the best they can be.

References

Bernard, R. M., Abrami, P. C., Lou, Y., Borokhovski, E., Wade, A., Wozney, L., Wallet, P. A., Fiset, M., & Huang, B. (2004). How does distance education compare to classroom instruction? A meta-analysis of the empirical literature. *Review of Educational Research, 74*(3), 379-439.

Dillon, A., & Gabbard, R. (1998). Hypermedia as an educational technology: A review of the quantitative research literature on learner comprehension, control and style. *Review of Educational Research, 68*(3), 322-349.

Fabos, B., & Young, M. D. (1999). Telecommunications in the classroom: Rhetoric versus reality. *Review of Educational Research, 69*(3), 217-259.

Flagg, B. N. (1990). *Formative evaluation for educational technologies.* Hillsdale, NJ: Lawrence Erlbaum.

George, J., & Cowan, J. (1999). *A handbook of techniques for formative evaluation: Mapping the student's learning experience.* London: Taylor & Francis Group.

Horton, W. (2001). *Evaluating e-learning.* Alexandria, VA: American Society for Training and Development.

Khan, B. H. (2001). A framework for Web-based learning. In B. H. Khan (Ed.), *Web-based training* (pp. 75-98). Englewood Cliffs, NJ: Educational Technology Publications.

Molenda, M. (2003). In search of the elusive ADDIE model. *Performance Improvement, 42*(5), 34-36.

Nielsen, J. (1993). *Usability engineering.* Boston: Academic Press.

Nielsen, J. (1994). Heuristic evaluation. In J. Nielsen & R. L. Mack (Eds.), *Usability inspection methods* (pp. 25-64). New York: John Wiley & Sons.

Reeves, T. C. (2003). Storm clouds on the digital education horizon. *Journal of Computing in Higher Education, 15*(1), 3-26.

Reeves, T. C., & Carter, B. J. (2001). Usability testing and return-on-investment studies: Key evaluation strategies for Web-based training. In B. Khan (Ed.), *Web-based training* (pp. 547-557). Englewood Cliffs, NJ: Educational Technology Publications.

Reeves, T. C., & Hedberg, J. G. (2003). *Interactive learning systems evaluation.* Englewood Cliffs, NJ: Educational Technology Publications.

Rossett, A. (1987). *Training needs assessment.* Englewood Cliffs, NJ: Educational Technology Publications.

Rubin, J. (1994). *Handbook of usability testing.* New York: John Wiley & Sons.

Chapter XXIII

Components of Effective Evaluation in Online Learning Environments

Steven R. Terrell, Nova Southeastern University, USA

The Components of Effective Evaluation in OLEs

Dringus and Terrell (1999) defined evaluation in an OLE as:

...an iterative process for assessing the efficacy and validity of online learning environments (OLEs). Evaluation should take place from the conceptual stage of OLE development through the measurement of learning outcomes of an online course. Accurate and ongoing assessments of learners, teachers, the instructional process, the course content, and the OLE as an entity will include a combination of formative and summative evaluations for each of these components and their effectiveness as a unit. (p. 61)

Other authors (e.g., Bunderson, 2003; Govindasamy, 2001; Hirumi, 2000; Khan, 2000; Williams, 1999) have addressed similar issues on a conceptual and theoretical level, but there is a need for further examination at the application level.

In the traditional face-to-face environment, the instructional process consists of integrating three primary components: curricular material, instructional methods, and the learner. A valid and accurate assessment of a traditional learning environment includes evaluation of these components in the form of program evaluations (e.g., periodic program or course curricula reviews), evaluation of the instructional process (e.g., end of term teacher evaluations), and student evaluations (e.g., examinations, term papers, or presentations).

In an online learning environment, where the environment is an open space of static and dynamic information, where there is discovery and sharing of information and ideas through electronic means, and where the OLE itself is an interface between the stakeholder and the online activity, the same three components are of equal importance. There is, however, an additional component that must be considered.

In the traditional setting, little emphasis is placed on the assessment of the physical environment because, as much as they are a necessity, most people do not conscientiously view buildings and walls as critical learning components. In an online setting, the OLE itself—the interface, the organization of online courses, information, material, activities, and communication modes—serves to create a sense of presence, atmosphere, and a state of being for stakeholders accessing the OLE. Because of this, the online learning environment must be evaluated.

Taking this into consideration, Figure 1 shows the iterative process that includes the formative and summative evaluation of *course content,* the *instructional process, learners,* and the *online learning environment as an entity.* The *content* component includes not only course content in terms of syllabus, course objectives, goals, and curricular material, but also the assessment of information resources that may be available in large scale via information on the World Wide Web. The *instructional process* component involves evaluation of teaching and learning styles, instructional methods, communication and interaction methods, as well as overall instructional processes. *Learner* assessment involves measures of student success (e.g., exams, term papers, case studies, etc.) as well as self-assessment by the learners themselves. Assessing the *OLE as an entity* involves evaluating the OLE as an interface between the instructor, the learner, the instructional material, and the information at large.

With these four components viewed as an entity, it is then possible to produce an effective evaluation process for online courses and the instructional process as a whole. When these components are evaluated as a unit, it is likely that administrators, course developers, and instructors will gain useful information concerning what may be needed to enhance the online experience and achievement of learners. These four components of effective evaluation in online learning environments will be discussed in terms of how they can be approached in both the context of assessing the online experience as well as the overall instructional process.

Figure 1. Components of effective evaluation in OLEs

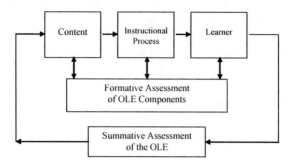

Assessing Course Content

Instructors working in an OLE are faced with two problems. First, as in any learning environment, the goals and the objectives of a given course must be clearly conveyed to and understood by the learner. Second, due to the nature of an OLE being essentially an open space of fluid information and activity, stakeholders must pay strict attention to outside information sources. This must be done in order to ensure the Web sites referenced are pertinent to course objectives and are not erroneous in fact or by omission.

The Evaluation of Goals and Objectives

A thorough evaluation of any learning environment requires the assessment of course goals and objectives. Gagné and Briggs (1979) proposed a framework that, in part, addresses evaluation at this level. In their framework, the authors emphasize the use of a hierarchical approach: the instructor should first develop general goals followed by specific goals (i.e., course objectives) whose completion would lead to attainment of the general goals. Doing so, they believed, helps the instructor focus on ways of organizing the instruction. These same ideas can be used when developing goals and objectives for an OLE. It is important, however, to remember how these goals and objectives are conveyed to learners, and in what presentation form a given learner may interpret goals and objectives differently through electronic means.

Providing a standard syllabus online may not be an efficient method for providing directions regarding general goals, objectives, and assignment requirements. Given that, consideration should be given to the following questions for evaluating the effectiveness of relaying essential directives related to course goals, objectives, expected outcomes, and exit competencies:

- Are the course goals and objectives clearly stated in the OLE?

- Do the exit competencies of the online course demonstrate mastery of the course goals and objectives?

- Can the goals and objectives of the course be achieved through the organization of information in the OLE?

- Are outcomes measurable considering the topic and structure of the online course?

- Are assignments and other requirements clearly stated with satisfactory information or directives given for completing work?

The Assessment of Information Sources

Due to the open nature of OLEs, it is easy to adopt a credo of "more is better" and include an overabundance of material into the presentation schema of the OLE. Due to the wealth of information afforded by the Internet, the amount of information presented to and used by the learner is potentially limitless. In an effort to include only resources that are valid and pertinent to course content, instructors should ask questions such as (partially adapted from Fabos, 2004):

- Who is the author of the information?

- Is contact information provided?

- What was the author's purpose in creating the Web page?

- Are links from the source being evaluated active and appropriate for the subject matter being studied?

- Is the material useful in helping achieve course goals?

- Is the material accurate and valid? When was it last updated?

- Does the author provide references for material presented on the site?

- Is the material appropriate for the population of learners?

- How does the material in the OLE compare with similar material used in a traditional environment?

In addition, presentation techniques such as information sequencing, timing, filtering, and orientation for posting information are also essential factors in assessing the effectiveness of presented material in an OLE. For example, hundreds of information links posted at the start of an online course may not be perceived as useful by students. Problems of this type can be recognized and addressed by first evaluating the presentation techniques in the manner prescribed above, followed by asking questions such as the following:

- Is the material presented online meaningful (i.e., related to a specific assignment) at the time of posting?

- Is there a balance of static and dynamic information that is useful?
- Can the learner discern the potential use of the material found on the site?

To assist in the process of answering these questions, educators can borrow the idea of content validity from psychometric theory (Gay & Airasian, 2000). Content validity deals with whether the material in the data source is correct and relevant to the course objectives, and whether the course objectives are sufficiently addressed by the data sources. If either of these concepts is violated, instructors and students should question whether a given information source should be used.

For example, an instructor in a learning theory class might develop material for an OLE using the same materials used in a traditional classroom setting. The instructor is assured of the validity of these materials if students in a traditional class are able to satisfy course objectives by using them. To engage and expand the horizons of students in the OLE, the instructor might decide to include links to one of the many learning theory resources available on the Web (for example, using a common search engine, inputting the words "learning," "theory," "distance," and "education" recently returned hits on 4,142 possible sites on the Web). An instructor wanting to incorporate any of these sites into his or her online course needs to ensure the validity of the site by asking the aforementioned questions. A negative answer to any of these questions may lead to the learner becoming confused or not adequately using the extent of the resources on the site.

Because of this, educators have to be especially concerned with search engines embedded in or used by students as part of the OLE. Like instructors, students have to question whether any information retrieved via a search is applicable to the course objectives. In order to do this, students should be trained, or have access to, reference material readily available that details effective search strategies. Additionally, students must be aware of the validity of retrieved information. Using our previous example of a learning theory class, students should learn to limit retrieved material to sources more likely to be valid. These would include refereed electronic journals, university and professional Web sites, and material posted by known authorities in the field. Online learners should question materials posted from a secondary source or Web sites where the author is unknown or unidentified. To assist in this process, if learners are able to share resources with peers in an organized manner such as in an asynchronous forum thread, the class as a whole could collectively assist their peers in determining the validity of retrieved information.

Assessing Instructional Processes

Working from a traditional classroom model, it can be easy for an instructor developing an online course to attempt to emulate the historically teacher-led, didactic style of teaching. Selecting this one teaching style alone may limit the instructional process in an online course. It is imperative that OLEs be developed in a manner that supports a wide range of teaching and learning styles. To do this, the effective evaluation of instructional processes must focus on specific instructional methods, communication practices, and the overall instructional process. To achieve this effectively, one must understand the relationship between the learner and the instructor in terms of the processes used to convey information.

Receiving information (Rose, 1985) is the function of the three main processes—vision, hearing, and movement. Although most students use all three forms of sensory input, learners are labeled by the modality they prefer. These labels—auditory learner, visual learner, and kinesthetic learner—are referred to as a person's preferred learning style. Research has shown that if an OLE does not support a given student's preferred learning style, they are at risk for attrition (Terrell & Dringus, 1997). To address this problem, online instructors need to ensure that their instructional methods, communication practices, and the overall instructional process support multiple learning styles. In evaluating this aspect of an OLE, the following questions could be used as guidelines (adapted from Clark, 2000):

- Does the OLE use material that includes graphs, charts, and illustrations whenever appropriate and possible (visual learners)?

- Do developers include organizers and outlines to allow students an overview prior to getting into the detail of the given subject matter (visual and kinesthetic learners)?

- Are resources such as streaming video and audio provided whenever appropriate and possible (visual and auditory learners)?

- Are assignments developed wherein students have to respond to presented material with written responses (visual and kinesthetic learners)?

- Does the OLE allow students to highlight or manipulate text-based information in order to better understand the subject matter (visual and kinesthetic learners)?

- Do developers include the use of synchronous and asynchronous communication tools that afford learners of this type the ability to control the level and flow of communication (visual, auditory, and kinesthetic learners)?

- Does the OLE use audio introductions to inform the student about what they will be covering in a given lesson or segment (auditory learners)?

- Following the presentation of material, does the OLE offer learners a summation in order to help enhance retention (visual, auditory, and kinesthetic learners)?

- Does the OLE provide for synchronous communication (auditory or visual)?

These are only a few examples by which the effectiveness of instructional methods, communication, and instructional processes can be measured. There is a need for ongoing formative and summative evaluation of these processes. Asking the question "Do the techniques and tools used in an OLE support the attainment of goals and objectives at the individual assignment and the course level?" can help identify ways by which the OLE can be designed to better meet the needs of the learner.

Instructors of an online course may also be evaluated in terms of their efforts to maintain a sense of presence and availability during an online course. The issues of course organization, structure, and quality of course presentations need to be addressed in formative and summative evaluations, by administrators and students alike, to determine what areas of instruction learners perceive to be satisfactory and what areas need improvement.

Assessing Learners

Traditionally, assessment has often been equated to having monitored examinations. With respect to learner assessment in an OLE, related concerns involve the process of ensuring accurate and adequate evaluation of student performance, and the extent to which students have mastered the content and have met course objectives. Despite the lack of physical proximity in OLEs, educators can design and administer meaningful assessment methodologies in online courses. In doing so, it is imperative to break the historical mindset of "pencil and paper" tests and work toward a more holistic manner of assessment. Bloom, Englehart, Furst, Hill, and Krathwohl (1956) support this idea by noting that a broader approach allows for the evaluation of skills ranging from discrete, concrete facts to higher-level cognitive skills.

Holistic assessment of student performance should take into consideration the three Ps—participation, performance, and production. There are many techniques available for assessment of this type; these include examinations, online interactive forum contributions, student-led synchronous chat sessions, and project-oriented work (group or individual). The appropriateness of each of these techniques depends on, among other things, the needs of the learner, resources available, technologies used within the OLE, and the subject matter being studied. Educators are encouraged to consider many alternatives and choose those that meet their needs and the needs of learners. The following are examples of questions that can help guide the educator's approach to student assessment:

- Did the student participate in and contribute to bulletin board sessions (participation)?

- Did the student meet stated requirements for student-to-student or student-to-instructor e-mail (participation and performance)?

- Did the student participate in and contribute to chatroom discussions (participation)?

- How did the student perform on both objective and subjective testing (performance)?

- How did the student rate in terms of projects assigned (performance and production)?

- Were students able to assume different roles (e.g., leader, teacher, student, or moderator) in the communication forums used (participation and performance)?

- What was the perceived level of quality of interaction among students as a collective group (participation and production)?

- Was the student able to self-assess his or her progress in the online course (participation, performance, and production)?

Assessing the Online Learning Environment

The OLE itself is essentially an interface to the formal instructional process that connects stakeholders to each other and to online activities. The OLE replaces traditional arrangements of physical proximity and synchronous "time-on-task" activity with spatial latitude and synchronous or asynchronous "learning-on-task activity." In an online course, considerable attention should be given to the tasks related to the learning activity and the degree of interaction needed to achieve the learning objectives, particularly if the course is strictly online without face-to-face communication. It should also be assessed for its efficacy as an interface between instructors and learners, and as an interface to information. The OLE should be assessed in terms of quality as a medium of instruction and interaction.

OLE Organization

An OLE should be assessed for clear organization of course information, clear structure for the presentation of student activities that require interactivity, the extent of efficient mechanisms for information management, and the extent to which the OLE enables learners to organize and manage their own course activities. It cannot be assumed that clear organization, clear structure, efficient mechanisms for information management, and flexible management are things that occur simply by presenting a course on a Web site.

Usability

Current learning management systems such as WebCT™, Blackboard™, and others offer extensive mechanisms for creating online courses. However, the creation of a rich OLE is a challenge and requires concentrated planning for the presentation and functionality of the course interface. Usability of an online course from a human-computer interaction view is not a naturally occurring process; it must be planned for in an OLE. The usability of an OLE must be evaluated in terms of how the OLE as an entity promotes a sense of presence of school or of learning or other important metaphors. Usability attributes such as usefulness, utility, ease of learning, ease of use, and other attributes must be assessed to ensure the quality of the learning experience and the quality of the learning environment that serves as an interface between stakeholders. Usability testing can also be useful in locating problems related to navigation, error recovery, locating information, and the selection of hyperlinks. By developing and following a routine evaluation process, instructors can improve the design of their courses and determine the proper mix of technology and human intervention needed in online activities.

The following questions to be raised in a formative or summative evaluation of an OLE or an online course may be useful in determining the usability of the interface:

- Were students able to readily access and get started in the OLE?

- Were errors discovered while navigating the OLE?

- Were users able to navigate to and from external links with relative ease and convenience?

- Using the communication tools available in the OLE, were learners able to effectively participate in online class discussions?

- Were participants able to gain a sense of presence or a sense of being part of a class in an OLE?

- How can the OLE interface be improved?

- Was the OLE effective in helping learners achieve learning goals and to meet expectations?

Conclusion

In this chapter, a traditional model for assessment and evaluation was expanded to assist in identifying the components of effective evaluation in online learning environments. Each component was discussed to provide a general overview of the unique items and issues that must be assessed in an OLE or an online course relative to the component. The model supports traditional approaches to evaluation, but also expands and includes factors that are unique to online learning environments. Formative and summative evaluation is stressed to form a routine and iterative process for evaluating content, instructional process, the learner, and the OLE as an entity. Evaluative questions were raised in the discussion of each component to spark ideas for effective assessment. While each component was summarized in terms of providing general scope, practical considerations were given as a starting point for addressing these components in an effective manner.

Current learning management systems or other online tools do not yet provide comprehensive assistance for evaluating online learning and instructional processes. Current tools are limited in helping stakeholders formulate an iterative plan to evaluate the effectiveness and quality issues associated with online learning and instruction. New tools and methods for evaluating the instructional and learning processes in an OLE must emerge to tighten the gap between the perceived and actual quality and effectiveness achieved in online learning.

Acknowledgment

The author would like to thank Dr. Laurie Dringus, a professor at Nova Southeastern University, for her assistance in an earlier draft of this chapter. Her insight, perspective, and support helped me focus on the problem at hand and develop an approach that gets to the very core of the evaluation of online learning environments.

References

Bloom, B., Englehart, M., Furst, E., Hill, W., & Krathwohl, D. (1956). *Taxonomy of educational objectives. The classification of educational goals. Handbook I: Cognitive domain.* New York: Longman Green.

Bunderson, C. (2003). Four frameworks for viewing blending learning cases: Comments and critique. *Quarterly Review of Distance Education, 4*(3), 279-288.

Clark, D. (2000). *Instructional system design* (chapter 4). Retrieved October 24, 2001, from http://www.nwlink.com/~donclark/hrd/learning/styles.html

Dringus, L., & Terrell, S. (1999). The framework for DIRECTED online learning environments. *The Internet and Higher Education, 2*(1), 55-67.

Fabos, B. (2004). *Wrong turn on the information superhighway: Education and the commercialization of the Internet.* New York: Teachers College Press.

Gagné, R., & Briggs, L. (1979). *Principles of instructional design.* New York: Holt, Rinehart and Winston.

Gay, L., & Airasian, P. (2000). *Educational research: Competencies for analysis and application.* New York: Merrill.

Govindasamy, T. (2001). Successful implementation of e-learning: Pedagogical considerations. *Internet and Higher Education, 4*(3-4), 287-299.

Hirumi, A. (2000). Chronicling the challenges of Web-basing a degree program: A systems perspective. *Quarterly Review of Distance Education, 1*(2), 89-108.

Khan, B. (2000). A framework for e-learning. *Distance Education Report, 4*(24), 3-8.

Rose, C. (1985). *Accelerated learning.* New York: Dell.

Terrell, S., & Dringus, L. (1997). An investigation of the effect of learning style on student success in an online learning environment. *Journal of Educational Technology Systems, 28*(3), 231-238.

Williams, D. (1999). *A framework for evaluating Web-based instruction.* Retrieved October 18, 2001, from http://mse.byu.edu/ipt/williams/webnet.htm

Chapter XXIV

Flexible Assessment:
Some Tensions
and Solutions

Chris Morgan, Southern Cross University, Australia

Jenny Bird, Southern Cross University, Australia

Introduction

Flexible learning is now well entrenched in the policy, curriculum, and course delivery frameworks of many higher education sectors in the Western world. However, because of the ambiguous nature of the terms, teachers are often faced with ill-defined expectations from their institution to 'be flexible'—to make choices about where, when, and how they will offer the various elements of their curriculum. The negotiable meanings of flexibility cluster around the divergent perspectives of a range of stakeholders, including pedagogists, managers, and technologists. Teachers are often unsure of the motives behind the push towards flexible learning: Are they being asked to save money by putting their courses online and reducing their face to face teaching? Are they being asked to better meet the needs of 21st century students and therefore increase enrolments? Is it about improving student learning by refocusing on student-centred learning and lifelong learning? Is it about harnessing the educational potential of new technologies? Tucked within this confusing area of higher education sits flexible assessment—a relatively neglected theme in the flexible learning story.

Whilst attempts to define and describe flexible learning remain elusive, essentially flexible learning is about increasing student choice over the time, place, pace, content, learning style, assessment, and opportunities to collaborate with others (Ling, Arger, Smallwood, Toomey, Kirkpatrick, & Barnard, 2001). As such, flexible learning is about:

1. **Pedagogy:** Flexible learning is informed by a number of pedagogies, including the more traditional open learning, student-centred learning, and lifelong learning, as well as more recent pedagogies associated with technology and online learning.

2. **Delivery:** Flexible delivery allows teachers and students to choose the media through which units of study are offered: face-to-face teaching, print materials, online materials and/or communications, audio and video, CD-ROM, and so on.

3. **Institutional policies, systems, and structures:** Institutions necessarily support flexible learning and flexible delivery with policy related to issues such as advanced standing, flexible entry, enrolment categories, flexible course structures; and with systems and structures that support multi-modal delivery (Bird, 2004).

However, teachers who attempt to operationalize even some of these grand claims for flexible learning soon learn that very real tensions can appear between the various elements of flexible learning. A choice to increase flexibility in one domain of flexible learning limits flexibility in another. For example offering online learning materials affords students increased flexibility in time, place, and pace of study, but will not accommodate all learning styles and may not offer opportunities to collaborate with others. Choosing to run and assess online debates or other forms of group work offers opportunities to collaborate with others, but limits choice in time, place, and pace of study (Ling et al., 2001). Teachers, when designing units of study, need to be explicit in deciding which types of flexibility they want to build in and which types they do not.

Inside this perplexing array of choice, teachers must also make choices about the flexibility of their assessment tasks, about what type and what degree of flexibility is appropriate. There is little in the literature specifically about flexible assessment to guide teachers. This omission is odd given the accepted view that student assessment drives learning, and that for students studying at a distance from their institution, "assessment has if anything an even sharper focus in the students' experience" (Thorpe, 1998, p. 269). Hyde, Clayton, and Booth (2004) conducted a literature review of assessment in flexible learning in the tertiary sector and found that in a number of studies, assessment practices had not changed to keep pace with other changes in flexible learning. These studies showed teachers falling back on traditional assessment methods such as invigilated exams which offer students no choice in the time, place, pace, or content of their assessment. According to Roberts (2002), "despite the fact that across courses assessment methods are likely to vary considerably, students rarely have a choice of how to be assessed in any particular course."

The following two definitions of flexible assessment offer a starting point for our discussion:

Assessment practices are flexible if they can accommodate the scope of knowledge and skills encompassed by the assessment criteria, the variations in contexts in which assessment may be conducted and the range of needs and personal situations of potential candidates. (Rumsey, 1994, p. 20)

The three tests for flexibility in assessment processes can be exemplified by the following questions:

- *Can students be assessed from remote locations?*
- *Can students be assessed at times of their own choosing?*
- *Can students be assessed by a variety of methods?* (Roberts, 2002, p. 4)

Morgan and O'Reilly (1999) argue that special attention needs to be paid to assessment in distance and open learning contexts. They subsequently developed a set of 10 key qualities for online assessment which apply just as well to flexible assessment:

1. A clear rationale and consistent pedagogical approach
2. Explicit values, aims, criteria, and standards
3. Relevant authentic and holistic tasks
4. Awareness of students' learning contexts and perceptions
5. Sufficient and timely formative feedback
6. A facilitative degree of structure
7. Appropriate volume of assessment
8. Valid and reliable
9. Certifiable as students' own work
10. Subject to continuous improvement via evaluation and quality enhancement (Morgan & O'Reilly, 2006, pp. 86-87)

Hyde et al (2004, p. 23) identify the following strategies for increasing the flexibility of assessment:

- Adopting a range of assessment methods, tasks, and modes of delivery
- Providing users with opportunities for choices among and within assessment methods, tasks, and modes of delivery
- Ensuring assessment methods and tasks are accessible to all potential users
- Using assessment as a basis for the recognition of prior learning, leading to variations in learning arrangements

Tensions in Flexible Assessment

Although there are many reasons to recommend a flexible approach to assessment, in time, place, and choice, the realities of conceptualising and implementing it are entirely another matter. There is a range of tensions operating in both the purposes and processes of flexible assessment that deserve some closer examination. Many of these tensions arise in our efforts to adopt a flexible approach to assessment, yet deal with the competing interests of institutional policies and culture, and ever-increasing workloads. Tensions may also be felt in the form of students themselves, protesting at the flexible arrangements that were supposedly designed for their benefit. We also experience tensions in relation to the separation of teacher and learner, and the technological abilities and capacities of students as we push the limits of conventional assessment practice and explore what can be reasonably managed in the way of flexibility. The following section explores these tensions, and is derived and further developed from an earlier exploration of assessment tensions in the context of open and distance learning (Morgan & O'Reilly, 1999).

The Role of the Assessor—
Formative Guide or Summative Examiner?

When faculty move to flexible teaching and assessment, there are certain philosophical assumptions that are likely to accompany this move. It is likely, for example, that the teacher will be interested in facilitating learning opportunities that are more constructivist in style. Teachers are often interested in reshaping their relationship with learners as more of a joint venture or a collaboration in which we engage in mutually rewarding dialogue. Teachers may conceptualize their role as a learning facilitator or mentor, or even colleague of the learner, in acknowledgement of the considerable bodies of knowledge and experience brought by the learner to the encounter. Yet when it comes to assessment, teachers find themselves making unilateral judgements about student achievement using traditional methods (exams) and traditional grading schemes (competitive ranking, norm referencing). Our role as facilitator of learning is somewhat undermined by inherent power relationships in traditional assessment arrangements. In acknowledging that assessment is a powerful driver and shaper of student learning behaviour, most of the benefits intended through constructivist style encounters are undermined by the traditional assessment.

How can we shape our role primarily as a learning facilitator rather than subject examiner, without abrogating our responsibilities as assessors and certifiers of student achievement? How do we strike a particular balance between the competing demands and tensions that arise from these two roles? One of the most important areas for consideration is the relative emphasis or balance we place between formative and summative assessment. When focussing on formative assessment, we are strengthening our roles as guides and facilitators, and reinforcing the values of flexibility by encouraging students to actively shape and construct their own learning. Considered below are examples of three types of assessment schemes that bring fresh emphasis to our formative role, while still providing for summative judgements to be made for the purposes of certification.

1. **Contract assessment:** Although learning contracts have been around as an educational tool for many years (e.g., Knowles, 1983), they gain fresh currency in the context of flexible, constructivist style encounters. Nowadays, however, we do not necessarily assume that self-directed learning is the natural domain of adults. Indeed we know that many learners may flounder with the high level of autonomy associated with learning contracts, and they may need to be introduced incrementally over a whole program of study. However, substantial components of self-directed activity in any course provide the opportunity for the teacher to really focus on the developmental and formative aspects of assessment. Here the teacher's role is primarily a diagnostic one, helping students to devise their own learning needs, to locate resources, to shape learning activities, to make their own meaning, to devise outcomes and criteria for assessment, and to evaluate and reflect on their learning. Although the teacher may still be involved in summative judgement, the process is shared with students with a high level of built-in flexibility, choice, and autonomy.

2. **Mastery assessment:** Mastery assessment provides the opportunity for students to pace themselves towards preordained or self-selected learning goals in partnership with the teacher. It is accepted that students enter courses with a variety of abilities and prior learning. With mastery assessment, students may, by negotiation, 'set the bar' at whatever height is appropriate to their particular ambitions in the subject. They may also improve low grades by repeated efforts with support of the teacher. Again, the teacher's role is primarily one of a facilitator, with an emphasis on mentoring and developmental feedback. Mastery assessment, of course, is difficult to implement in higher education systems that demand that students be ranked competitively rather than simply acknowledged for their attainments or competencies; however, it is an excellent example of the kinds of assessment appropriate to flexible and constructivist learning environments.

3. **Self- and peer-assessment:** Self- and peer-assessment are also excellent ways in which teachers can reshape their role as learning facilitators and provide emphasis to the formative, developmental aspects of their assessment role. When learners themselves are called upon to make judgements about their own or others' work, they are encouraged to adopt a higher level of responsibility for their learning, and they also become more skilled at making informed judgements and providing constructive feedback to others—vital lifelong learning and workplace skills. The teacher's role in self- and peer-assessment is to ensure that learners are sufficiently supported to make judgements and are competent in the use of marking criteria that have been thoroughly discussed and problematized. It will also be necessary to ensure that good moderation processes are in place to ensure that grades have been fairly and appropriately awarded (e.g., Gibbs, 1995).

Each of these assessment schemes provide an example of the ways in which we can reconceptualize our assessment practices to place particular emphasis on our formative developmental assessment role, and to offer students greater flexibility in terms of learning outcomes. Yet they are not to be entered into lightly. To move away from time-honoured traditional assessments requires considerable planning and preparation of students for a new learning and assessment culture. To dabble in flexible methods without adequate preparation will often see teachers falter and revert the disheartened to more traditional methods.

What to Assess? Getting the Mixture Right

In flexible learning and assessment encounters, we are under additional pressure to meet student learning needs, yet cover the curriculum, develop key graduate skills and attributes, and prepare students for a transition into professional life. Although we may aspire to broad components of self-directed learning in any program of study, failure to meet vocational requirements, or to inadequately instil key workplace skills, may render the program irrelevant to employers and students who are pursuing vocational goals. Yet rigid adherence to vocational requirements may only leave students with a body of knowledge that is rapidly outdated, without the skills or mindset of the lifelong learner, who is able to continually update and upgrade qualifications as required.

The question of competing stakeholders needs—including those of the teacher, the student, the university, the employer, and the accrediting agency—tends to coalesce around assessment, and in particular, what balances we strike in assessment between vocational content, broad academic enquiry, and self-directed learning. The challenge for us in providing flexible assessment is to strike a particular balance between these competing needs which retains a strong student focus.

Getting this mixture right will certainly involve two key flexible assessment strategies: (1) a diversity of assessment methods, and (2) a strong focus on authentic assessment tasks. A diversity of assessment tasks is critical both as a means of developing a broad repertoire of abilities and attributes in learners, and provides learners with the opportunity to shape their learning in new and challenging ways. Diverse assessment schemes take account of broad abilities such as critical thinking, problem solving, information literacy, written and oral communication skills, ethical awareness, creativity, self-direction, and lifelong learning skills. With their heavy reliance on pen-and-paper tasks such as examinations, traditional assessment neglects many of these learning outcomes.

In a similar vein, authentic assessment tasks are those that are drawn from the working world and are usually complex integrated tasks that call upon learners' higher-order thinking skills. They often require students to identify issues or problems, draw upon their developing expertise to carry out solutions, respond to contingencies as they arise, and evaluate their results. As many online learners are already working, there are rich opportunities for authentic, integrated assessments that may be individually tailored, if appropriate, to learners' own working worlds. With a focus on a diverse range of assessment methods, and assessment tasks that pose authentic or 'real-world' problems, we are far more likely to satisfy a range of stakeholder needs while retaining a flexible, student-centred focus and a concentration on higher-order academic thinking skills.

Flexible Assessment and Standards—Is It Rigorous?

New flexible forms of assessment, when contrasted with time-honoured traditional forms, suffer from various types of concerns and misconceptions, particularly relating to fears about standards, rigour, and lack of reliability in marking. Some have noted, for example, a tendency for higher marks in flexible assessment schemes, by comparison to traditional methods. Gibbs (1995) argues, however, that this could be the result of more effective learning on the part of students, who are offered greater challenges and are therefore more highly motivated to achieve. Certainly flexible assessment tends to focus on different values than traditional assessment. Whereas the focus in traditional assessment is on content coverage and knowledge reproduction, flexible assessment seeks to also validate students' own personal meanings and reflections, as well as efforts to apply theory to students' own worlds and workplaces.

Flexible assessment arrangements are often criticized by those who consider them to be lacking in rigour. These perceptions often reside with those who believe academic standards are embodied in traditions such as formal lectures and examinations, where the decisions regarding what is learned, how it is learned, and how it is assessed are tightly controlled by the teacher. Unquestionably there is a necessary cultural shift in the widespread acceptance of flexible learning and assessment, and there will be tensions felt in the way we prepare learners for assessments, such as the pace at which learners opt to progress, the balance of formative and summative assessment, and where we, or indeed learners, may choose to set goalposts at various points in their pathway. Yet flexible assessments are in no way inherently less rigorous than traditional forms—to the contrary they are likely to extend learners in ways that are often unexpected by teachers.

A further concern raised in relation to individualized assessment is reliability. When tasks are individualized, assessors will often find a greater than usual degree of difficulty in comparing student work for the purposes of grading. When there are multiple markers involved, this difficulty could be compounded by the differing values and expectations of individuals. However, even the most open ended of assessments should have broad criteria and standards that communicate the assessor's expectations about the nature and quality of student work, and that enable judgements to be made with an acceptable degree of reliability. There is no easy or definitive measure that will guarantee that standards or rigour in one program are equivalent to those of another. The solution lies more in quality assessment processes. These issues are picked up in further detail in the next section of this chapter on validity and reliability.

Can Flexible Assessment Be Valid and Reliable?

As teaching and learning activities come under greater scrutiny from quality assurance agencies, industry stakeholders, and sometimes external accreditation bodies, the focus on the validity and reliability of student assessment sharpens. Ultimately, summative student assessment is the only activity where students measurably demonstrate to themselves, their peers, their teachers, and their current and potential employers what they have learned and to which standards they have performed. In this climate many teachers are only just beginning to apply the concepts of validity and reliability to their student assessment tasks, and their marking and grading practices.

(a) Challenges with Validity

Ensuring and demonstrating validity of assessment within the context of flexible assessment raises additional challenges compared to more traditional assessment practices. The emphasis on providing students with a diverse range of graduate skills and abilities inevitably requires an equivalent diversity of assessment tasks. Some attributes, such as oral communication skills, are both difficult to assess and expensive to mark in flexible learning contexts where students are geographically distant from their teachers/assessors. The temptation to compromise the validity of assessment in these circumstances is very real, and all too often skills such as oral communication and teamwork are put in the 'too hard basket' or the 'too expensive basket'. However emerging technologies, which provide opportunities for online group work and digital audio and video streaming, are rapidly resolving the problems associated with assessing logistically difficult skills. Many of these technologies are realistically priced, easy to use, and compatible with most computers.

But how do faculty offer students choice in their assessment without compromising validity? What happens to the important element of equivalence between students' work? Put more simply, how do faculty compare apples with pears when they offer students choice in the 'how' and 'what' dimensions of flexible assessment? Student choice in assessment is a continuum—at the 'limited choice' end, for example, the faculty member might offer a few alternative assessment questions from which students can choose. As long as the set questions are aligned with the learning outcomes of the course and are equivalent, then the validity of the task is not compromised. At the 'maximum choice' end of the continuum, students may, for example, negotiate individual learning contracts. Again, as long as students are instructed that their choice of assessment must align with the learning outcomes, and marking and grading criteria are negotiated with faculty, then the validity of the task is not compromised.

Dunn, Morgan, O'Reilly, and Parry (2004, p. 32) describe three benchmarks by which teachers can establish the validity of their assessment:

1.   that the learning objectives for individual units of study align and fit with the outcomes for the overall program;

2.   that the assessment tasks 'hold up' to external benchmarking with similar programs in other educational institutions, accrediting bodies, or other external stakeholders in the same discipline or field of study; and

3.   that the assessment tasks align internally to other elements of the curriculum within the individual course, such as the unit's learning objectives, the teaching and learning activities, the syllabus, and so on.

(b) Challenges with Reliability

Ensuring and demonstrating the reliability of assessment within the context of flexible assessment raises another set of challenges. Whilst questions about validity focus on the types of assessment being offered to students (and their alignment and equivalence), questions of reliability focus on faculty practices which will ensure consistency of marking, both across students and between markers. Flexible learning environments are increasingly characterized by large student enrolments, geographically dispersed student cohorts, and teams of contracted teachers and markers who might work anywhere in the world.

The following strategies will help bolster the reliability of assessment in flexible learning contexts:

1.   Every assessment task has tailored performance criteria which have been developed with all markers (or students in the case of negotiated learning contracts) and are provided to students at the beginning of the teaching period.

2.   Grading standards are developed, either at the program, unit, or assessment level, depending on the institution's assessment policy and/or practice, with all relevant staff involved, and are provided to students at the beginning of the teaching period.

3.   Develop, as a team, model answers for each grade.

4.   In situations with large teams of markers, the teacher with overall responsibility conducts 'spot checks' on other markers to compare standards of marking and rectify inconsistencies.

5.   Randomly select a paper, distribute it to all markers for marking, and then discuss the results as a team.

6.   Double blind mark a selection of papers, discuss results, and resolve inconsistencies.

7.   As an individual marker, be careful of any previous perceptions you may have of particular students which might affect your marking—marking towards the average, and hard or soft marking (TLC, 2003).

With rigorous moderation processes such as these built in to the management and administration of the unit of study, reliability in assessment can be protected, even in circumstances of high degrees of flexibility in assessment.

Costs and Benefits: Can We Afford Flexible Assessment?

With so much of the assessment literature focusing on assessment as an *event,* it is easy to overlook the fact that assessment is also a *process* that occurs within complex institutional *contexts.* All assessment is constrained or supported to varying degrees by institutional and faculty-based policy, budgets, infrastructure, management systems, administrative processes, teaching workload formulae, and so on. Economic and political pressures to offer more courses to more students in more locations with more flexibility can result in compromised teaching, learning, and assessment practices which are in direct contrast to what we assume to be the best conditions for effective student learning. We know, for example, that well-designed assessment tasks, timely and adequate feedback, and proactive student support are critical to both retention rates and successful learning in flexible learning contexts. We also know how quickly these activities can be shaved from a shrinking departmental budget.

Flexible assessment (both the processes which surround it and the events themselves) is particularly vulnerable in environments of financial constraint. Whilst the flexible learning policy rhetoric claims to offer students greater choice over the 'where, when, and how' of assessment, in reality flexible assessment takes time to design, plan, and deliver, particularly when large and/or distributed student cohorts are involved. To achieve best practice in flexible assessment (like that described earlier in this chapter by Morgan & O'Reilly, 2005), teachers require time, resources and institutional support.

(a) At the Institutional Level

Ultimately the development of best practice flexible assessment requires a whole institution approach, with a well-resourced and coordinated plan that aligns with the institution's strategic goals and mission. Best practice flexible assessment requires considerable institutional support. Clearly, adequate IT infrastructure is required to support both students and staff with ready access to online learning environments, and associated IT training and helpdesk support. Administrative systems need to be adequately resourced in order to accommodate the extra administrative loads inevitably associated with offering flexible assessment. Institutions can support, through innovation grants and professional development programs, the considerable developmental work associated with designing flexible assessment.

However, contradictory policies and budgetary constraints often inhibit the design and delivery of best practice flexible student assessment. One such tension surrounds the authentication of student work and other matters related to academic integrity. Phillips and Lowe (2003) claim that these issues dominate policy debate for online assessment. Invigilated exams are the first resort solution to this problem; however, invigilated examinations are the most inflexible of assessment events. Hidden within the 'exam/authentication debate' resides another issue: examinations can be a cheap form of assessment. Multiple choice examinations that can be computer marked offer huge savings in marking costs, as do written examinations which are not returned to students with feedback. Whilst these are seductive options from a budgetary perspective, they are not defensible from a best practice flexible assessment perspective. Alternatives to invigilated exams which diminish opportunities for plagiarism, encourage deep learning, and offer degrees of choice to students include continuous assessment, online collaborative work, and open book examinations (Phillips & Lowe, 2003). With thoughtful design these alternatives need not necessarily be a huge drain on resources. For example teachers might readily trade the exhausting experience of marking large numbers of long assignments with quick turnaround times for the experience of a more distributed spread of marking across a semester associated with continuous assessment. Similarly, online collaborative work can be designed in such a way that only select 'best samples' of work are submitted for marking.

(b) At the Departmental Level

Within a department a whole raft of policies and processes either support or inhibit flexible assessment. Policies which pertain to extensions on the submission of assignments, the resubmitting of assignments, recognition of prior learning through assessment, the incompletion of units of study, and so on all have a significant impact on the flexibility of assessment in relation to 'when'. Very few higher education programs are offered as fully self-paced programs, as the resources required to support, track, and administer large cohorts of students are prohibitive. However, within the constraints of semester or trimester teaching periods, individual departments balance the extra academic and administrative costs associated with these aspects of flexible assessment against their commitment to offering students greater choice.

Another set of decisions are made at the departmental level about the degree to which students will be supported within flexible learning environments. Student support in flexible learning is both administrative and academic, and requires appropriate resourcing. This aspect of providing flexible learning is easily overlooked when departments decide to design their programs for flexible learning. It is here that managers might imagine that savings will occur, when in fact the opposite is true.

(c) At the Individual Level

In a fully online course, with no face-to-face contact between teacher and student, all of the following activities are normally associated with assessment: providing individual and group feedback on assessment items, marking and grading, answering queries about assessment-related matters, designing quality assessment, moderating assessable online discussion forums, establishing online groups for the purposes of assessment, and so on. However, with increasing degrees of student choice, the workload associated with many of these activities increases. Take for example offering students greater choice in the methods by which they are assessed (i.e., the 'how' of flexible assessment). Marking 40 papers that are identical is a much faster and therefore cheaper exercise than marking 40 papers that are different as a result of students being given choices about their assessment tasks. Similarly, setting one assignment question is a much more straightforward exercise than negotiating with students about individual learning contracts.

Therefore the workload implications associated with offering students choice over how they are assessed must be realistically anticipated. Faculty need to make "individual assessment plans that are logistically feasible in the light of available resources" (Hyde et al, 2004, p. 97). Opportunities for timely formative feedback on assessment work, and realistic allocations of time for marking and grading of assessment must be factored into flexible assessment workload models.

Conclusion

Underlying the adoption by teachers of flexible assessment methods has been a concern that traditional teaching and assessment methods have tended to result in students going through the motions of their study in a relatively passive, superficial manner, focussing on reproductive learning strategies for quick returns in traditional assessments. Not only does this call into question the lack of relevance of this kind of education for the future lives and careers of students, but also the return on investment for the price of a university education.

Although flexible teaching and assessment methods offer some alternatives for teachers and students, they clearly require considerable thought and planning. In this brief chapter we have outlined only some of the many tensions that will inevitably arise as teachers devise more diverse and authentic forms of assessment, offer degrees of student choice, defend and advance standards, cater more overtly for student needs, ensure validity and reliability, and generally swim against the tide of institutional policy and funding arrangements. Yet there is much that individual teachers can achieve, both in terms of student learning outcomes and personal satisfaction in the role. At the heart of the move to flexibility is a philosophy of openness and student-centeredness in education, a conscious desire to subvert some very old-fashioned power relationships in education, and the opportunity to create more meaningful opportunities for learning.

References

Australian National Training Authority. (1996). *National Flexible Delivery Taskforce final report.* Brisbane: ANTA.

Bird, J. (2004, July 4-7). Mapping flexibilities. In F. Sheehey & B. Stauble (Eds.), *Transforming Knowledge into Wisdom: Proceedings of the Annual International Higher Education Research and Development Society of Australia (HERDSA) Conference* (Vol. 27), Miri.

Dunn, L., Morgan, C., O'Reilly, M., & Parry, S. (2004). *The student assessment handbook.* London: Routledge Falmer.

Gibbs, G. (1995). *Assessing student centred courses.* Oxford: Oxford Centre for Staff Development.

Hyde, P., Clayton, B., & Booth, R. (2004). *Exploring assessment in flexible delivery of vocational education and training programs.* Adelaide: National Centre for Vocational Education Research.

King, B. (2003). *The future of distance education and the role of ODLAA.* Retrieved July 10, 2004, from http://www.odlaa.org/summit.html

Knowles, M. (1983). *Adult learning and education.* London: Open University Press.

Ling, P., Arger, G., Smallwood, H., Toomey, R., Kirkpatrick, D., & Barnard, I. (2001). *The effectiveness of models of flexible provision of higher education.* Canberra: EIP Higher Education Division DETYA.

Morgan, C., & O'Reilly, M. (1990). *Assessing open and distance learners.* London: Kogan Page.

Morgan, C., & O'Reilly, M. (2006). Ten key qualities of assessment online. In M. Hricko & S. Howell (Eds.), *Online assessment and measurement.* Hershey, PA: Information Science Publishing.

Phillips, R., & Lowe, K. (2003, December 7-10). Issues associated with the equivalence of traditional and online assessment. In G. Crisp, D. Thiele, I. Scholten, S. Barker, & J. Baron (Eds.), *Interact, Integrate, Impact: Proceedings of the 20th Annual Conference of the Australasian Society for Computers in Learning in Tertiary Education,* Adelaide.

Rumsey, D. (1994). *Assessment practical guide.* Canberra: Australian Government Publishing Service.

Roberts, T. (2002, December 8-11). Flexible learning: How can we get there from here? In A. Williamson, C. Gunn, A. Young, & T. Clear (Eds.), *Winds of Change in the Sea of Learning: Proceedings of the 19th Annual Conference of the Australasian Society for Computers in Learning in Tertiary Education (ASCILITE)*, Auckland.

Teaching and Learning Centre. (2003). *Pathways to good practice, a guide to flexible teaching for quality learning.* Lismore: Southern Cross University.

Thorpe, M. (1998). Assessment and "third generation" distance education. *Distance Education, 19*(2).

Chapter XXV

Toward a Comprehensive Model of E-Learning Evaluation:
The Components

Curtis J. Bonk, Indiana University, USA

Robert A. Wisher, U.S. Department of Defense, USA

Matthew V. Champagne, IOTA Solutions, USA

Introduction

Whether one is at conferences, responding to e-mail, or chatting with colleagues, the topic of e-learning is bound to prompt a discussion related to assessment and evaluation. But there are many aspects of e-learning evaluation. Naturally, most are interested in comparisons between online and traditional instruction. Others want to know about the effectiveness of the instructors or the instructional designers in designing interactive and engaging courses. Of course, given the newness of this area, some ask for information about what the training actually provided them. Still others might inquire about what makes some courses and programs highly popular while others are seemingly hidden from view. Those focused on pedagogy might analyze the course tasks and syllabi, while those with technological interests might favor an exploration of the courseware tools and services. Finally, administrators and managers of e-learning might request evaluations of e-learning policies, partnerships, return on investment, and strategic planning. When asked to evaluate e-learning, therefore, the focus of that evaluation must be clearly specified and detailed.

Evaluation is often confused with assessment. According to Susan Millar (2001), director of the Learning through Evaluation, Adaptation, and Dissemination (LEAD) Center at the University of Wisconsin, assessment typically refers to an instructor's efforts to obtain specific information about student learning within a course in order to improve her teaching or to demonstrate student learning and achievement to others. More generally, it is a way of using information obtained through various types of measurement to determine a learner's performance or skill on some task or situation (Rosenkrans, 2000). Hence, it is typically learner focused.

Evaluation is often at a more encompassing level, though it can include the assessment of student learning. Simply put, an evaluation is concerned with judging a program's worth and is essentially conducted to aid the decisions of the stakeholders (Champagne & Wisher, 2000). The level of evaluation will depend on articulating the type or level of the stakeholders. In corporations, the stakeholders may range from high-level executives to training managers to the developers or instructors of that training. In higher education, the stakeholders might be the learners, the directors of distributed learning, the local community, the faculty, the campus administrators, or the state. In the government, stakeholders include human resource development department heads, agency directors, and congressional committee members.

Duin and Bear (2002) point out that evaluation becomes even more complex when there are partnerships between one or more of these entities. For instance, if an e-learning company partnered with a major public university to develop and test a new courseware platform or component, each might be interested in different outcome data. According to Duin and Baer, students should benefit from enhanced course availability, efficient scheduling, increased career opportunities, and the availability of learning resources on demand. In addition, the university may benefit from new capabilities in offering online content, growing enrollments, enhanced learning, and new marketing opportunities. State politicians might be interested in cost efficiencies, increased competitiveness, improved student learning, and higher student completion rates. College faculty members might focus on how the partnership fosters a more relevant curriculum and increased opportunities to facilitate student learning and problem solving. In addition, corporate partners might be interested in how the courseware platform will retain customers, provide a competitive advantage, and of course, increase revenues through retaining customers as well as developing new revenue streams (CIO, 2001; Docent, 2000). Clearly, the focus of e-learning evaluation differs widely and depends on the stakeholder's perspective.

So while some in higher education might target questions such as whether students learned more online than in traditional classes, corporate concerns might focus solely on return on investment (Aldrich, 2002; Reddy, 2002; Worthen, 2001). Given the complexity of e-learning evaluation, the goal of this chapter is to expand on a key section of Khan's (2000) eight-part framework for Web-based learning—namely, the area of evaluation.

Components in E-Learning Evaluation

Evaluation of e-learning is often squarely focused on whether the online course or component is better than a comparable face-to-face version of the course. Unfortunately, most Web-based learning studies are deficient in one or more areas. Moreover, there is little consensus as to what variables to measure and compare (Champagne & Wisher, 2000; Olson & Wisher, 2002). Part of the problem is that few e-learning courses are purely online, but instead, most rely on a blended approach, combining online and live components.

Taking this complexity into account, Figure 1 displays the range of considerations for an e-learning evaluation plan. Each slice of the eight-part evaluation pie involves a number of issues and questions. For example, in terms of the first slice or "student" level of evaluation:

1.   What are student attitudes toward the e-learning course or program?
2.   Do they recommend it to others?
3.   What is the retention rate of students in the program?
4.   Do they display increased comprehension and overall achievement?
5.   Exactly what did they learn?
6.   Are they better prepared for a job or higher-level course?
7.   Do they actually get placed in full-time jobs or internships?

Answers to these questions might be obtained from experimental studies, focus groups, interviews, observations, surveys, or learning outcome measures (e.g., exams, home-

Figure 1. E-learning evaluation considerations

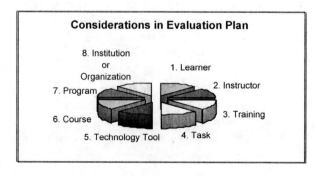

work, projects, etc.). As detailed below, each of these measures might help evaluate e-learning at the learner, instructor, training, task, technology, course, program, and institution or organizational levels.

Learner Measures

Evaluation at the student or learner level can include basic data, as well as more complex and rich measures. Basic data includes student grades, attitudes, achievement test scores, and computer log data (Chen, Liu, Ou, & Liu, 2000; Spooner, Jordan, Algozzine, & Spooner, 1999). Eventually, electronic portfolios will allow one to assess a range of potential learning gains, skills, and competencies from basic terminology to advanced levels of performance (Bonk, 1998). Unfortunately, instead of access to student electronic portfolios, anecdotal and attitudinal data are currently among the most common data reported (Usip & Bee, 1998). In addition to simple questionnaires about course quality and instructor effectiveness, learner perceptions regarding the type and quality of course interactions are also vital (Fulford & Zhang, 1993). Moreover, computer log data might indicate the raw number of posts, participation patterns, peak usage, time on task or in the system, and messages per day. Log data can help determine whether learners participate more often than in traditional settings and whether certain types of courses or activities enhance those contributions.

More complex or high-end learner measures might analyze message complexity, degree of interactivity, depth of posting, level of questioning, or collaboration skill levels. One might be interested in learner ability to find a problem or critically reflect on issues. In addition, the ability to challenge or debate people might be targeted by the course. Many educators, of course, are interested in the degree to which students back up their claims or note their assumptions (Bonk, Angeli, Malikowski, & Supplee, 2001). Problem-based learning activities and authentic performances might help measure student higher-level abilities.

Corporate and military training organizations that are investing significant sums of money in e-learning are concerned whether the online material applies to specific jobs or work responsibilities (Horton, 2001). Basically, they want to know if the online training worked (Wisher, Curnow, & Drenth, 2001). The retention of what was learned over a period of time is another aspect of learner measures (Wisher, Curnow, & Seidel, 2000).

Instructor or Trainer Measures

E-learning evaluation programs might explore factors related to instructor, trainer, or moderator success. Though less of a concern for self-paced courses in corporate training environments, instructors have a vital role in e-learning in most higher education courses. Even if they do not deliver the course, instructors might help in the course design efforts as subject matter experts.

Of course, a common evaluation measure includes the reliance on student reactions and attitudes toward the course, as well as the instructor or trainer. Such reaction data are common in both corporate training (Van Buren & Erskine, 2002) and higher education (Freitas, Myers, & Avtgis, 1998) settings. For instance, learners might be asked whether the trainer or instructor was effective at promoting online interaction, addressing multiple learning styles, and projecting a friendly image (Thach, 1993). They might also assess if the instructor made the course intellectually satisfying and suitable to their needs (Horton, 2001). Actual course transcripts offer clues about the effectiveness of instructor mentoring or online facilitation. Such transcripts can help determine whether the instructor was skilled in varying the forms of online feedback. Other signs of successful online instruction will include learner completion rates, enrollment trends, and the ability to acquire funding for online ideas and projects. As Web courses continue to proliferate, trainers and instructors may be evaluated for their ability as well as willingness to share their pedagogical ideas with others online.

Training Measures

Another evaluation component is the preparation of students, instructors or trainers, and instructional designers for the online environment. Too often this area is ignored or assumed to be adequate. Focusing evaluation at the instructor level illuminates many needs since few trainers or instructors are adequately prepared for the world of online instruction. In response, many universities and consultants now provide train-the-trainer types of services and certificates. Some of these programs offer multiple tracks—one for higher education and one for corporate training settings. But what is the quality of this instruction? Has anyone performed a content analysis of these train-the-trainer courses? And where can one find reviews of the accuracy and value of online newsletters, publications, and related Web resources offered by train-the-trainer portals and online instructor communities?

Internally, an organization or institution should evaluate the quality of student orientation sessions as well as its train-the-trainer programs. Questions raised here include whether tutorials and other support services for registration, administration, and technical advice match student and institutional needs. Are instructors supported with training programs to teach online (Lawrence, 1996-1997). These programs should also assess the impact of innovative instructor training and mentoring initiatives, as well as equipment support such as laptop programs. In addition, they might keep track of the number of instructors attending e-learning technology fairs, workshops, colloquiums, and other professional development opportunities, and assess their overall utility.

Task, Activity, or Pedagogical Measures

In terms of the online tasks or pedagogical measures, there are many measures to determine how engaging and intrinsically motivating the task is. First of all, is it relevant? Do the learners find the tasks authentic and meaningful? Second, is the online experience individualized for the learner(s)? E-learning should offer unique opportunities and challenges for each user. Third, the online experience should offer learners opportunities for in-depth processing of information and, when appropriate, deep discussions. Learning requires extensive interaction with the material and other participants in the learning process. Fourth, the chosen task should be interactive. Learning best takes place when learners are engaged and when the learning environment offers opportunities for interactive experiences. Finally, the tasks within the learning environment should offer learners some degree of control, choice, and constructivistic experience. Students need to collect, filter, organize, and construct new knowledge in a learning community (Ward & Tiessen, 1997). They should also be collaborative, where possible, and help learners form a sense of learning community.

Task evaluation might take various forms. For instance, online survey instruments might determine the degree of relevance of the learning experience. Transcript analyses or interviews might document the individualization and depth of discussion within the course. Checklists or questionnaires could be used to note the forms of online collaboration or constructivism. Focus groups could address whether online learning communities were formed.

Technology Tool Measures

As the proliferation of collaborative tools brings new learning opportunities (Gray, 1999), it is important to measure the impact of these tools. First, the technology must have high utility. Technology that is not functional or contains flaws will negatively impact learner success rates and attitudes. Second, since online learners are often returning adult students with highly relevant work experiences, the technology must lend itself to learner-centered instruction (Wagner & McCombs, 1995). That is, the technology tools should allow for learner choice, meaningful tasks or problems, and higher-order thinking. Third, the technology must offer opportunities for learners that are unique and engaging. For instance, it might link outside mentors and guest experts into the class, or have features for peer mentoring and advice. Fourth, the technology should be ultra friendly. Ease of use is a key determiner of course satisfaction and success. Finally, the technology should be highly supportive of the learners as well as the instructors and course designers. There should be orientation features, tutorials, and other forms of assistance.

There are other ways in which the online technology can be assessed. Speed of delivery is usually vital. In addition, one might assess the types of reports the system or tool provides on e-learners as well as on a particular e-learning course or program. The different forms of learner assessment that the tool provides is also a key feature to consider. Of course, the cost effectiveness of the tool or system is usually a deciding factor. When the costs are indeterminable, however, the effectiveness can be measured in other ways suggested throughout this chapter.

Course Measures

Those concerned with evaluating at the course level will naturally be concerned with course quality. For instance, courses might be evaluated for coherence, interactivity, feedback mechanisms, uniqueness, ease of navigation, and forms of assessment. In terms of course quality, ASTD now evaluates course quality for corporate training (ASTD, 2001; Rosenberg, 2001). For those in higher education, a white paper detailing 24 key features or benchmarks for online learning quality is available (Institute for Higher Education Policy, 2000). These benchmarks address course development guidelines, instructional materials, student feedback and interaction, access to library resources, technical support, student advising procedures, and the evaluation of intended learning outcomes. In the future, it is conceivable that there will be a site or tool for automatic assessment of course quality and interactivity.

There are other course evaluation concerns. For instance, is more content covered in the online class? Furthermore, what are completion rates and enrollment trends for a specific course? What are the forms of online learner support and assistance? Importantly, does the course effectively replace one taught face-to-face or one taught by other forms of technology (Mantyla, 2001)?

A related area that might be measured is the time required for instructors or course designers to develop online courses (Bourne, 1998). Studies indicate that Web courses take a significant amount of time to create and coordinate compared to traditional delivery methods (Bonk, 2001; Gaud, 1999). An e-learning study by McIsaac, Blocher, Mahes, and Vrasidas (1999) revealed that instructor time is divided into such tasks as planning and preparation, online teaching, administration, and interactions with peers, students, and content. While more time might be spent on initial course development, the focus of assessment might also address the amount of time allocated to lecturing, mentoring, testing, sharing, and modifying online courses.

Program, Certificate, or Degree Measures

Evaluation measures at the program, certificate, or degree level might initially focus on the costs involved. Such evaluation must also consider whether it meets learner needs. According to Fellows and McGrew (2001), successful programs need high-quality learner services. Such services may include pre-advising services, call centers, help desk support, registration services, course tracking, virtual bookstores, and other administrative services.

It is also important to know the effectiveness of a given program before modifying it or introducing new ones. A key concern here is whether the online version of the course is as cost effective as the live version. A program budget might include both direct costs (e.g., course development, technical support, courseware, etc.) as well as indirect costs (e.g., technology training, supplies, orientation programs, learner disk space, accreditation, integration with other systems, etc.). A parallel concern is whether e-learning programs are as effective as traditional instruction (Yellen, 1997-1998). While some contend that comparing traditional and online environments poses significant challenges (Burbules & Callister, 2000), educators, politicians, administrators, and other stakeholders commonly request such evidence.

The effectiveness of an online certificate or degree program often hinges on decisions made related to delivery and assessment. For instance, decisions may be made regarding whether the program utilizes a blended approach (e.g., face-to-face with online instruction) or fully online courses, team projects or individualized work, lecture-based or problem-based learning content, instructor-led or self-paced courses, and objective tests or performance-based assessments. The impact and effectiveness of each of these types of decisions can and should, at some point, be evaluated. For instance, student problem-solving and problem-finding abilities could be analyzed after working in online teams or in a self-paced mode. In addition, the forms of online mentoring as well as the responsiveness of the mentoring might be evaluated using transcript analyses, focus groups, or interviews.

Institutional or Organizational Measures

An institution or organization must consider all of the above factors in its e-learning evaluation framework. On a quantitative level, it might analyze the number of learners served and online enrollment trends. If it is a higher education institution, it might explore whether the online learning population is coming from new students, alumni, or its existing student population. It might also want to know whether and to what extent online teaching or training is even recognized in annual promotion and tenure decisions. An institution might explore whether there are policies for such, and if so, whether these policies are widely known, accepted, and implemented (Bonk, 2001).

For corporate or military training situations, the focus will be different. For instance, one might explore the degree to which the online training contributes to the business objectives of the organization. Was there an increase in efficiency, quality, or productivity (Horton, 2001), and can this be measured in some way? Moreover, has there been an increase in sales volume or new customers (Bersin, 2002)? Other concerns will relate to fewer project recalls, defects, or complaints, as well as whether customer service center personnel can more efficiently handle customer complaints. Still others will ask for data on whether e-learning led to reduced accidents and safety violations. Across these situations, corporate stakeholders are concerned with the return on investment (ROI) for the e-learning technology or initiative.

Some e-learning concerns relate to communications and support structures provided in the organization. Recent research from the ASTD and Masie Center (2001) indicates that the most successful e-learning courses are those that are well advertised, have an internal champion or sponsor, allocate monies for learner and instructor support, and use testimonials and e-mail to promote the course. Evaluation here might focus on: (1) internal marketing efforts and promotion of e-learning courses and programs; (2) the extent to which management and employees are paying attention to e-learning course promotions; (3) trends in "visits" to a Web site detailing the program; (4) partnerships with other learning organizations; and (5) the availability of white papers that detail strategic plans for the program.

Naturally, a key evaluation concern for any organization or institution entering e-learning is how well it has incorporated interactive and collaborative technologies for teaching (Burbules & Callister, 2000). Both hardware accessibility and speed of access requirements must be considered. In addition, e-learning technologies should be interoperable with existing and planned systems. It is vital to know whether the e-learning technologies impact student satisfaction, course interaction, and learning authenticity. Is the reputation of the institution or organization enhanced by the e-learning technologies selected? Has it switched to different platforms or learning management systems in the past few years (Van Buren & Erskine, 2002)? Given the ramifications, both the decision-making process and the long-range planning must be evaluated. It is somewhat of a dilemma since the institution or organization must be skeptical of what the technologies can actually afford, while simultaneously taking risks in trying something new.

Legal issues also abound here. Institutions must be aware of their compliance with laws related to copyright, accessibility, and ownership. Are course and program Web sites ADA compliant? Are materials posted to the Web abiding by copyright laws? What are the ownership agreements with instructors and course designers regarding online courses and associated course materials? Each of these areas must be part of an evaluation plan at the institutional or organizational level.

Conclusion

These eight evaluation considerations can assist in understanding the impact and effectiveness of an e-learning effort. While most attention is typically focused at the learner, instructor, or course levels (Holland, 1996), there are a myriad of other concerns confronting program developers, training managers, administrators, and government officials. E-learning is effective not just because most students are satisfied with the course or achieved the course objectives. At the same time, high quality is not simply indicated by higher enrollments or more learners completing the course. And while interactive and engaging online tasks should be goals for most course designers, not every motivational task one can design will match the required content and needs.

In effect, evaluating e-learning, or any learning for that matter, is a difficult and highly complex endeavor. Few scholars have acknowledged this complexity, and even fewer studies have adequately addressed it. Hopefully, we have shed some light on the necessary considerations, acknowledged potential stakeholders and their needs, and identified the key components that might be considered in any such evaluation. Evaluations should be viewed as an opportunity to understand and improve upon any of the eight components outlined in this chapter and reward those who are making a difference.

References

Aldrich, C. (2002). Measuring success: In a post-Maslow/Kirkpatrick world, which metrics matter? *Online Learning, 6*(2), 30, 32.

American Society for Training & Development. (2001). *ASTD Institute e-learning courseware certification.* Retrieved January 1, 2002, from http://www.astd.org/ ecertification/

ASTD and the Masie Center. (2001). *E-learning: "If we build it, will they come?" Executive summary.* Alexandria, VA: American Society for Training & Development.

Bersin, J. (2002). Measuring e-learning: The third wave. *E-learning, 3*(2), 30-31, 33.

Bonk, C. J. (1998, April). Pedagogical activities on the "Smartweb": Electronically mentoring undergraduate educational psychology students. In *Proceedings of the American Educational Research Association* (AERA) *Annual Convention,* San Diego, CA.

Bonk, C. J. (2001, May). *Online teaching in an online world.* Bloomington, IN: CourseShare.com. Retrieved December 28, 2002, from http://PublicationShare.com

Bonk, C. J., Angeli, C., Malikowski, S., & Supplee, L. (2001, August). *Holy COW: Scaffolding case-based "Conferencing on the Web" with preservice teachers. Education at a distance, United States. Distance Learning Association.* Retrieved December 28, 2002, from http://www.usdla.org/html/journal/AUG01_Issue/ article01.html

Bourne, J. R. (1998). Net-learning: Strategies for on-campus and off-campus network-enabled learning. *Journal of Asynchronous Learning Networks, 2*(2), 70-88.

Burbules, N. C., & Callister, T. A. (2000). Universities in transition: The promise and the challenge of new technologies. *Teachers College Record, 102*(2), 271-293. Retrieved March 14, 2002, from http://www.tcrecord.org/abstracts/10362.htm

Champagne, M. V., & Wisher, R. A. (2000). Design considerations for distance learning evaluations. In K. Mantyla (Ed.), *The 2000-2001 ASTD distance learning yearbook: The newest trends and technologies.* New York: McGraw-Hill.

Chen, G. D., Liu, C. C., Ou, K. L., & Liu, B. J. (2000). Discovering decision knowledge from Web log portfolio for managing classroom processes by applying decision tree and data cube technology. *Journal of Educational Computing Research, 23*(3), 305-332.

CIO. (2001, October). E-learning: The secret to profitability in a stumbling economy. *CIO Advertising Supplement, 15*(1), S1-S4.

Docent, Inc. (2000, June). *Calculating the return on your e-learning investment.* White Paper, Docent, Inc., Mountain View, CA. Retrieved February 11, 2002, from http://www.docent.com/elearning/ROI_01.html

Duin, A. H., & Baer, L. L. (2002). *Developing a successful partnership investment portfolio.* Commissioned Monograph, National Learning Infrastructure Initiative, San Diego.

Fellows, P. J., & McGrew, K. (2001, August). Behind the scenes of an online program: Effectively serving students. In *Proceedings of the 17th Annual Conference on Distance Teaching and Learning,* Madison, WI (pp. 141-144).

Freitas, F. A., Myers, S. A., & Avtgis, T. A. (1998). Student perceptions of instructor immediacy in conventional and distributed learning classrooms. *Communication Education, 47,* 366-372.

Fulford, C. P., & Zhang, S. (1993). Perceptions of interaction: The critical predictor in distance education. *The American Journal of Distance Education, 7*(3), 8-21.

Gaud, W. S. (1999). Assessing the impact of Web courses. *Syllabus, 13*(4), 49-50.

Gray, S. (1999). Collaboration tools. *Syllabus, 12*(5), 48-52.

Holland, M. P. (1996). Collaborative technologies in inter-university instruction. *Journal of the American Society For Information Science, 47*(11), 857-862.

Horton, W. (2001). *Evaluating e-learning.* Alexandria, VA: American Society for Training & Development.

Institute for Higher Education Policy. (2000). *Quality on the line: Benchmarks for success in Internet-based distance education.* Washington, DC: The Institute for Higher Education Policy.

Khan, B. (2000). A framework for Web-based learning. *TechTrends, 44*(3), 51.

Lawrence, B. H. (1996-1997). Online course delivery: Issues of faculty development. *Journal of Educational Technology Systems, 25*(2), 127-131.

Mantyla, K. (2001). *Blended e-learning: The power is in the mix.* Alexandria, VA: American Society for Training & Development.

McIsaac, M. S., Blocher, J. M., Mahes, V., & Vrasidas, C. (1999). Student and teacher perceptions of interaction in online computer-mediated communication. *Educational Media International, 36*(2), 121-131.

Millar, S. B. (2001, February). How do you measure success? Lessons on assessment and evaluation from the LEAD Center. *Syllabus, 14*(7), 11-13.

Olson, T. M., & Wisher, R. A. (2002). The effectiveness of Web-based instruction: An initial inquiry. *International Review of Research in Open and Distance Learning, 3*(2). Retrieved December 28, 2002, from http://www.irrodl.org/content/v3.2/

Reddy, A. (2002, January). E-learning ROI calculations: Is a cost/benefit analysis a better approach? *E-learning, 3*(1), 30-32.

Rosenberg, M. (2001). Can ASTD certification standards ensure quality off-the-shelf courseware? *E-learning, 2*(7). Retrieved January 1, 2002, from http://www.elearningmag.com/elearning/article/articleDetail.jsp?id=3917

Rosenkrans, G. L. (2000). Assessment of the adult student's progress in an online environment. *The Internet and Higher Education, 2*(2-3), 145-160.

Spooner, F., Jordan, L., Algozzine, B., & Spooner, M. (1999). Student ratings on instruction distance learning and on-campus classes. *The Journal of Educational Research, 92*(3), 132-140.

Thach, L. (1993). Exploring the role of the deliverer in distance education. *International Journal of Instructional Media, 20*(4), 289-307.

Usip, E. E., & Bee, R. H. (1998). Economics: A discriminant analysis of students' perceptions of Web-based learning. *Social Science Computer Review, 16*(1), 16-29.

Van Buren, M. E., & Erskine, W. (2002). *State of the industry: ASTD's annual review of trends in employer-provided training in the United States.* Alexandria, VA: American Society for Training & Development.

Wagner, E. D., & McCombs, B. L. (1995). Learner centered psychological principles in practice: Designs for distance education. *Educational Technology, 35*(2), 32-35.

Ward, D. R., & Tiessen, E. T. (1997). Adding educational value to the Web: Active learning with AlivePages. *Educational Technology, 37*(5), 22-31.

Wisher, R. A., Curnow, C. K., & Drenth, D. J. (2001). From student reactions to job performance: A cross-sectional analysis of distance learning effectiveness. In *Proceedings of the 17th Annual Conference on Distance Teaching and Education,* Madison, WI.

Wisher, R. A., Curnow, C. K., & Seidel, R. J. (2001). Knowledge retention as a latent outcome measure in distance learning. *The American Journal of Distance Education, 15*(3), 20-35.

Worthen, B. (2001, February). Measuring the ROI of training. *CIO,* 128-130, 132, 134, 136. Retrieved February 10, 2002, from http://www.cio.com/archive/021501/roi.html

Yellen, R. E. (1997-98). Distant learning students: A comparison with traditional studies. *Journal of Educational Technology Systems, 26*(3), 215-224.

Chapter XXVI

Evaluating Flexible Learning in Terms of Course Quality

Betty Collis, University of Twente, The Netherlands

Anoush Margaryan, University of Twente, The Netherlands

Introduction

Learning becomes more flexible when options are offered to learners, not only about the time and place and pace of learning, but also relating to types and origins of study materials, to forms and quantity of learning activities and assignments, to ways of interacting with others within the course, and to forms of assessment. De Boer (2004) has analyzed flexible course delivery within universities and found that the most flexibility is found in logistic aspects of the course such as flexibility in dates by which assignments must be submitted or flexibility in the location of course meetings, whereas pedagogical flexibility in which the learner can tailor aspects of the learning process itself is still relatively little seen. Within companies, flexible learning is often described as e-learning or blended learning. In an analysis of literature about flexible learning in companies, Margaryan and Bianco (2002) found that e-learning typically involves logistic flexibility at the price of pedagogy: little or no options are available for social interaction, a direct relationship with an instructor, or for choice in types of learning activities and ways of carrying out those activities.

Because of the pedagogical weaknesses of such an approach to flexibility, blended learning involving ways to bring the social interaction of personal encounters into the learning mix rather than e-learning alone is becoming common in corporate education (Rossett, Douglis, & Frazee, 2003). However, just as in universities, the major choice in blends in corporate learning tends to relate to logistic flexibility rather than pedagogical renewal, with a typical model in the corporate setting being independent-study e-learning combined with a shorter but still traditionally run classroom session (Margaryan & Bianco, 2002). One way to enrich this type of blend pedagogically is to change the nature of the non-classroom component of a blended course, away from self-study e-learning to a pedagogically richer blend of higher-level activities such as problem solving around real workplace problems with different mixes of social interaction and collabora-tive learning. The instructor monitors these workplace activities via use of a Web-based course environment into which participants upload reports or examples of their work, give each other peer feedback, and have opportunities to discuss and learn from each other in a variety of ways. Such a mixture is both logistically and pedagogically flexible. As the pedagogical aspects become dominant in this type of workplace-oriented course, the question arises whether the logistic limitation of requiring a same-time, same-place classroom component remains necessary. Thus a consideration relating to logistical flexibility in course design for the corporate sector is whether a blended course should include a blend of participation from the workplace and classroom events, or if the course can run without the classroom events as long as it still includes forms of social interaction. As has been the case with the introduction of logistic flexibility via distance education in universities, there is a concern in the corporate sector that course quality will diminish without a classroom component to the course, in that participants may lack the chance to appropriately interact with each other and the instructor via only a Web environment, even if the environment is used to support pedagogically rich interaction. This concern is even stronger if the non-classroom component of a blended course lacks pedagogically rich interaction.

In order to assess if this concern about the value of a classroom component of a course is justified when blended learning involving work-based activities is being carried out in practice, a first step is to define criteria for course quality, a second step is to assess a company's blended learning courses against these criteria, and a third step is to compare the quality ratings of blended courses with and without classroom components. However, in order to stimulate pedagogical flexibility as well as logistic flexibility, the criteria for course quality and their application in the evaluation process should also reflect the desirability of aspects of pedagogical flexibility, not only location flexibility. Thus the questions we have been studying for a number of years is: *How can the quality of flexible learning be operationalized so that both logistic and pedagogic components are valued and measured? What are the results when the measurement process takes place?* While we have studied these questions over a four-year period in the university context (De Boer, 2004), this chapter focuses on our current work in the corporate sector.

Criteria and Procedures for Evaluating the Quality of a Flexible Course in the Corporate Context: Merrill+

In this section we present a set of criteria for expressing the quality of a blended course in the corporate setting and describe the measurement procedure to carry out this evaluation.

Criteria for Course Quality

Learning in the corporate context by definition involves a target group of adults with a work-based reason for participating in a course or other learning event. Thus fundamental principles of good learning for adult professionals should apply. Merrill (2002) has identified five "first principles" of instruction, which fit well with adult-learning situations. He argues "Learning is promoted when:

1.   Learners are engaged in solving real-world problems.
2.   Existing knowledge is activated as a foundation for new knowledge.
3.   New knowledge is demonstrated to the learner.
4.   New knowledge is applied by the learner.
5.   New knowledge is integrated into the learner's world." (Merrill, 2002, pp. 44-45)

Merrill's principles show that adult professional learning should extend past knowledge transfer. In the corporate-learning context, not only must the new knowledge be integrated into and make sense in the learner's world, but also must lead to changes in performance that impact business results. For this to occur corporate learning also should be characterized by creating and sharing knowledge, capturing and reusing experiences and the tacit knowledge and know-how within the organization, and being able to solve workplace problems in a process-oriented, collaborative manner (Collis, Margaryan, & Kennedy, 2004). The more realistic and workplace-focused the learning, the more flexibility is required in the learning environment. Flexibility also relates to tailoring for individual differences and needs, not only in the time, place, and pace of learning, but also in the individual and intellectual diversity of the learner (e.g., differences in backgrounds and preferred ways of interacting with others). This becomes critically important when participants are from a variety of regions and cultures, as is the case in multinational corporations (Hofstede, 1986). For all of this to occur, the participants need to have a common electronic learning environment which integrates their course materials and processes and which can be accessed from their workplaces. Web-based course management systems provide such environments, if designed to support knowledge sharing, collaboration, and shared access to resources and submissions from others for all involved in the learning process.

Combining these aspects leads to a response to the first research question: Courses for adult professionals should reflect the attributes shown in Figure 1 which extend Merrill's five First Principles with a number of features specific to the pedagogy of flexible learning in the corporate sector.

Figure 1 shows that, in addition to demonstrating Merrill's five First Principles (represented by the ovals in the figure), pedagogic flexibility as well as overall course quality is enhanced by the attributes represented by the arrows:

- Learning from others through collaboration and by comparing and contrasting different submissions to similar/different problems (Scardamalia, 2004; Young, 1993)

- Learning from the experiences of others, in the course, in the participant's own workplace, and in the company more broadly (Boud & Middleton, 2003; Wertsch, 1991)

- Use and reuse of resources from the business (Campbell & Dealtry, 2003)

- Leveraging the diversity and individual characteristics of the participants (Hofstede, 1986; Illeris, 2003)

- Supervisor involvement via coaching of work-based activities (Matthews, 1999)

- Appropriate design of Web tools and environment to support both logistic and pedagogical flexibility (Abbey, 2000)

Figure 1. Merrill+ criteria for evaluating the quality of blended courses in the corporate setting

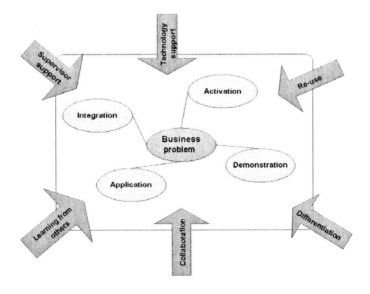

Thus, our proposition is that blended courses in the corporate sector should display the Merrill+ attributes. The attributes can serve as a framework for the evaluation of the design of blended courses. Work-based learning activities, if properly designed and managed, can be a tool for realizing these requirements. These activities, therefore, get particular attention in our evaluation approach. Particularly through the analysis of what the learners are doing, rather than the content they are receiving, can we best examine the degree of presence of each of the nodes in this Merrill+ model. This leads to a methodology for measuring course quality.

Measurement Procedures

After several rounds of piloting during 2002 and 2003, a course-scan procedure has been developed in which the Web-based environments of blended courses are studied in detail after the completion of the courses and coded on a set of items (n=62) reflecting each of the nodes shown in Figure 1. Other than demographic data about the course (including level, subject area, and type of location blend) which are coded as binary variables, the rest of the items are coded on a 1-5 Likert-type scale, where 1 indicates no evidence of the particular quality criteria, 5 indicates "best-practice" evidence of the criteria, and the values 2, 3, and 4 indicate qualitative and sometimes quantitative increases between these two endpoints. Some variables ask about the presence of a type of learning activity, with the coding ranging from 1 = this type of activity was not used, and 2 = was tried once, to 5 = was an important component of the course. In order to control for the subjectivity of such coding, two independent researchers coded a series of courses and compared their results, discussing any differences in interpretation until their coding became nearly identical. Examples of several of the items include:

- To what extent do the activities in the course relate to the participants' real workplace problems?

- To what extent do the activities provide opportunities for participants to learn from each other?

- To what extent are the study resources reused from the business?

- To what extent are there options for participants with various learning needs?

- Approximately how much individual feedback on learners' submissions is entered into the course site by the instructor?

- To what extent were supervisors of the participants involved in the course?

- To what extent do the activities involve collaboration with peers in the course?

- To what extent do the activities involve collaboration with others outside the course?

From these separate items, a total "Merrill+ score" was also calculated by summing the combination of items reflecting each of the attributes in Figure 1 and expressing the result per attribute as a number between 1-5. As there are 11 nodes, the overall Merrill+ score per course can range from 11 to 55. A total score of 33 (as well as a 3 on an individual attribute) can be taken as a satisfactory result for courses whose instructors and participants are going through the learning curve of a new approach to course participation. Over time, higher standards may come to be expected, and then a score of 44 could be a general target. The complete set of items for the course-scan procedure is described in Collis and Margaryan (2005) and is available from the authors on request. Once the researchers are familiar with the course-scan procedure, the scan takes approximately two hours per course. It should be noted that only aspects of the course that are evident in the course Web environment can be coded above a value of 1, because there is no systematic way to code interactions that are not captured in the environments. This is considered a reasonable restriction in that flexibility requires learners to be able to access course materials and procedures when needed, and thus records which are not traceable are not representative of support for flexible learning.

Validating the Methodology in Practice

Context

These steps have been carried out in practice within a multinational company, Shell Exploration and Production (Shell EP), where blended learning involving work-based activities and supported by a Web-based course management system has been evolving since 2001 (Margaryan, Collis, & Cooke, 2004). Over 40 different courses for technical professionals, petroleum engineers, and geologists have been redesigned to a blended form with work-based activities; and with some courses already occurring over several cycles, over 80 distinct blended events have occurred, mainly in 2003 and 2004. All blended courses share the same general approach of learning via activities carried out partially or fully in the workplace, with input and coaching from workplace colleagues and sharing of knowledge and experiences among the participants via the course Web environment. Approximately half of the blended events have chosen to do away with a classroom component altogether, while the other half blend the workplace portion with a shortened classroom portion. All blended courses make use of a Web-based course management system, *TeleTOP,* developed at the University of Twente (Collis & Moonen, 2001), to integrate all of their resources, activities, communications, and collaboration tools.

To carry out the course-scan procedure, the Web environments of 61 of the blended courses were coded using the 62 item course-scan instrument. After a pilot study which refined the methodology (Penning & Weiberg, 2004), scores for each of the 11 quality attributes were calculated and a total "Merrill+" score obtained for each course event. Then, the blended courses with a classroom component (n = 34) were compared to those without a classroom component (n = 27) on the quality criteria.

Table 1. Means of Merrill+ criteria for 61 blended courses from a corporate-learning setting

Merrill+ Component (range 1-5 except for total score)	Mean & SD, Blended with classroom component n=39	Mean & SD, Blended without classroom component n=29	Probability of t-test results (*p<.05)
Merrill+ total score (11-55)	33.5 (4.2)	34.0 (5.8)	.642
Business problem	3.8 (0.6)	4.0 (1.1)	.313
Activation of prior knowledge	3.0 (0.8)	2.3 (0.7)	.000*
Demonstration	2.8 (0.8)	2.4 (1.1)	.078
Application	3.7 (0.6)	4.5 (0.8)	.000*
Integration	3.1 (0.8)	3.7 (1.3)	.025*
Collaboration	4.1 (1.3)	3.4 (1.5)	.049*
Learning from others	2.7 (1.0)	2.4 (0.9)	.175
Supervisor support	2.5 (1.1)	2.1 (0.6)	.090
Technology support	2.9 (0.8)	3.5 (0.5)	.002*
Re-use	2.1 (1.0)	2.3 (0.6)	.380
Differentiation	2.7 (1.1)	3.5 (0.6)	.001*

Results

The total Merrill+ scores and the scores for each of the quality aspects that make up the Merrill+ score are shown in Table 1 for blended courses with and without a classroom component.

The results show that the blended courses are at an acceptable level of course quality, as expressed by the means of the Merrill+ total scores (33.5 and 34.0). One of the goals of striving to increase pedagogic flexibility was to tailor course activities to the actual *business problems* of the participants. The mean scores of 3.8 and 4.0 on this attribute are good results. Similarly, applying learning in the workplace, as indicated by the attribute *Application,* shows good results for the mean scores (3.7 and 4.5). A number of attributes have means below 3.0, for example *demonstration* of what is to be learned and *reuse* (of resources, experiences, and the contributions of previous participants). These are attributes that need further attention in the (re)design process of new learning events. Thus the results of the evaluation can be directly used to identify particular examples of good practice from individual courses (courses which score a 5 on an attribute) to highlight progress in terms of key quality attributes, and to focus attention on attributes that can benefit from increased attention in subsequent (re)design processes.

In terms of concerns about logistic flexibility, Table 1 shows the results when the Merrill+ mean scores are compared for blended courses with (n = 39) and without a classroom component (n = 29). Table 1 shows that there was no significant difference between the two groups in the Merrill+ total scores, but that there were significant differences on six of the eleven attributes, with four of the differences being in favor of the courses with no classroom component. Looking at these attributes more closely and then reviewing the courses led to the possible interpretation that courses with a classroom component had a tendency of positioning the work-based activities carried out in the workplace as preliminary to the classroom session, and thus the (traditional) classroom session was still seen as the heart of the course. For the blended courses with no classroom session, the work-based activities became the heart of the course, and consequently extra attention was given to the attributes relating directly to those work-based activities. In contrast, collaboration in activities during the workplace portions of the course seems easier to carry out when anticipating face-to-face collaboration in a classroom session than when such contact is not going to occur.

Conclusion

The Merrill+ model and methodology for course scanning and measurement of course quality have a number of implications in practice:

- First of all, the attributes in Merrill+ can be useful as a basis for a set of guidelines for course designers because they combine some of the key best practices in the field of instructional design with strategic practices related to learning in a corporate setting. The core of the criteria is Merrill's First Principles of Instruction, which represent some fundamental principles that were found to be shared by many major instructional design theories and models (Merrill, 2002).

- Second, the use of the model as the basis for a course scan shows how an evaluation approach can stimulate attention to aspects of pedagogical flexibility as well as logistic flexibility. Comparing scores on the different attributes can help steer collective discussions about which aspects of course quality should be priorities for attention in subsequent (re)design processes.

- Third, applying the method is a systematic way to provide each course with a single overall score. These overall scores can be used in comparisons of different groups of courses (as occurred with the comparison between the no-classroom and with-classroom blends in the Shell EP example). Trying to interpret the results of these comparisons within the local context can lead to further improvements in course quality or decisions to focus on one type of course rather than another.

There are many ways that the quality of a blended course can be evaluated; what is most important is that a set of attributes and a method for measuring those attributes that is systematic and sustainable in practice be found that fit the needs and culture of a particular learning context. The Merrill+ approach appears to be a good fit for the Shell EP context. To tailor it to another context, the five attributes that relate to Merrill's five "first principles of instruction" can be maintained, but the additional six attributes could be reviewed to see if some of them could be replaced by others more relevant to a different context. In the Shell EP context, the approach is being positively received by course instructors as well as the design team in that it steers focus on attributes that everyone tends to agree are important. Because capturing course quality in a single score is always going to be at best a simplification, other forms of input about course quality are also being used, such as the more traditional participant questionnaires (Collis & Margaryan, 2004). Together these different sources of input can provide a range of discussion points for the After Action Reviews that follow the completion of courses. This reduces the danger of a single score from the course scan being over interpreted.

References

Abbey, B. (Ed.). (2000). *Instructional and cognitive impacts of Web-based education.* Hershey, PA: Idea Group Publishing.

Boud, D., & Middleton, H. (2003). Learning from others at work: Communities of practice and informal learning. *Journal of Workplace Learning, 15*(5), 194-202.

Campbell, I., & Dealtry, R. (2003). The new generation of corporate universities: Co-creating sustainable enterprise and business development solutions. *Journal of Workplace Learning, 15*(7/8), 368-381.

Collis, B., & Margaryan, A. (2005). Design criteria for work-based learning: Merrill's First Principles of Instruction expanded. *British Journal of Educational Technology, 36*(5), 725-738.

Collis, B., & Margaryan, A. (2004, June). Criteria for evaluation of success of blended learning methodology. In *Proceedings of the 66th European Association of Engineers and Geoscientists (EAGE) Conference,* Paris, France.

Collis, B., Margaryan, A., & Kennedy, M. W. (2004, October). Blending formal and informal learning offers new competence development opportunities. In *Proceedings of the 11th Abu Dhabi International Petroleum Exhibition and Conference,* Abu Dhabi, UAE.

Collis, B., & Moonen, J. (2001). *Flexible learning in a digital world: Experiences and expectations.* London: Kogan Page.

De Boer, W. F. (2004). *Flexible learning in the changing university.* Doctoral dissertation, Faculty of Behavioral Sciences, University of Twente, The Netherlands.

Hofstede, G. (1986). Cultural differences in teaching and learning. *International Journal of Intercultural Relations, 10,* 301-320.

Illeris, K. (2003). Workplace learning and learning theory. *Journal of Workplace Learning, 15*(4), 167-178.

Margaryan, A., & Bianco, M. (2002). *An analysis of blended learning* (internal report). Noordwijkerhout, The Netherlands: Shell EP Learning & Leadership Development.

Margaryan, A., Collis, B., & Cooke, A. (2004). Activity-based blended learning. *Human Resource Development International, 7*(2), 265-274.

Matthews, P. (1999). Workplace learning: Developing a holistic model. *The Learning Organization, 6*(1), 18-29.

Merrill, M. D. (2002). First principles of instruction. *Educational Technology Research and Development, 50*(3), 43-59.

Penning, M., & Weiberg, M. (2004). *Comparative analyses of the design of Shell EP LLD blended-learning courses* (internal report). Enschede, The Netherlands: University of Twente, Faculty of Behavioral Sciences.

Rossett, A., Douglis, S., & Frazee, R. V. (2003). *Strategies for building blended learning.* Retrieved September 8, 2004, from http://www.learningcircuits.org/2003/jul2003/rossett.htm

Scardamalia, M. (2004). Instruction, learning, and knowledge building: Harnessing theory, design, and innovation dynamics. *Educational Technology, 44*(3), 30-33.

Wertsch, J. V. (1991). A socio-cultural approach to socially shared cognition. In L. Resnick, J. Levine, & S. Teasley (Eds.), *Perspectives on socially shared cognition* (pp. 85-100). Washington, DC: American Psychological Association.

Young, M. F. (1993). Instructional design for situated learning. *Educational Technology Research and Development, 41*(1), 43-58.

Chapter XXVII

Assessing Online Collaborative Learning:
A Theory, Methodology, and Toolset

Linda Harasim, Simon Fraser University, Canada

Introduction

This chapter considers the unique opportunities for assessing online collaborative learning (OCL) in both formal (primary, secondary, and tertiary) and non-formal (workplace) education contexts. The chapter provides a theoretical framework, a methodology, and a set of tools for understanding and assessing online collaborative learning and conceptual change. Online collaborative learning (OCL), it is argued, provides hitherto unprecedented qualities for implementing, supporting, and assessing individual and group intellectual progress.

The chapter focuses especially on the unique opportunities whereby instructors, educators, researchers, and students can analyze and assess learning (conceptual change) in OCL environments and applications: that is, online discussion that progresses from divergent (brainstorming) to convergent (conclusive statements) in such educational activities as group seminars, discussions, debates, case analyses, and/or team projects. Examples of OCL applications, such as the design of online student-led seminars, and ways to assess student moderators and student discussants, are included.

Context: Why Assess?
What to Assess? And How?

Traditionally, assessment is performed once a learning activity is completed in order to determine how accurately the student has retained and can recall the specific knowledge or skill contained in that activity. Conventional classroom approaches emphasize such educational measures as testing of content knowledge through quizzes, exams, and/or essays. The recent focus on educational IT (information technology) has led to development of educational assessment technology that is nonetheless largely a reformulation of traditional approaches based on pencil and paper tests—that is, online quizzes and online tests. Recent IT efforts are primarily aimed at automating conventional testing approaches. The technologies are new only in the sense of assisting educators in preparing and scoring tests by providing such online features as:

- easy-to-build multiple choice quizzes and tests;
- stored questions (or a database of questions) that could be remixed for each new class semester (either by the instructor or machine generated);
- multiple choice quizzes/tests that can be machine graded; and
- links from the test results to a class gradebook.

The assessment of individualized learning activities such as essays is addressed by such new technologies as plagiarism checkers and use of latent semantic-type engines to grade written essays.

Overall, however, these assessment tools are based on a traditional didactic view of learning that emphasizes retention of information and the evaluation of how well a student can recall and represent this information. The focus thus emphasizes learning as a product, at the expense of viewing learning as a process. This means that retention of information (memorizing and reproducing the 'right' answer) is highlighted over knowledge as a process (problem solving or generating new knowledge and solutions).

This traditional didactic approach to assessment is widespread and deeply ingrained in the culture of the classroom and is an integral part of the current "formal" system of education, based on a view of learning as retention and recall of information.

New Educational
Opportunities and Challenges

New educational pedagogies—particularly collaborative learning and constructivism— both challenge and enhance the didactic (retention) view of education and emphasize instead a process-oriented focus on collaborative learning and knowledge building, especially but not only online. Asynchronous online group discussions, debates, seminars, and team projects (employing Web-based forums, conferencing systems, or bulletin boards) provide teachers and students with powerful new OCL opportunities.

Learning in the collaborative constructivist models focuses on facilitating conceptual change (new perspectives and skills) utilizing knowledge building and problem solving, particularly through group discussion—processes viewed as underpinning work and community in the knowledge society. Testing, quizzes, and even individualized assignments, while widely used, are unable to provide (significant) insight into the level of student *understanding* of the subject matter, how to analyze or apply it, or how to construct new knowledge relevant to the subject.

Nonetheless, while the new field of OCL has focused particularly on new designs for learning, it has contributed little as to how to assess these new learning designs and practices. Instructors thus remain bereft of appropriate and relevant frameworks, methods, rubrics, and tools to assess online collaborative discourse, and moreover are hampered in generating guidelines and examples of best practice for their students since there is no accepted framework for judging what constitutes "best."

Thus, while the introduction of OCL in the 1980s enabled unprecedented new opportunities for the design and implementation of collaborative learning processes (Harasim, 2006), the field of assessment has lagged behind.

Theoretical Framework for OCL: Focus on Conceptual Change

New theoretical frameworks developed in recent decades contribute to our understanding of how collaborative discourse supports learning and under what circumstances, both in face-to-face and online environments. Researchers focusing on how collaborative learning contributes to educational effectiveness at the cognitive and social levels have found that collaboration facilitates higher developmental levels in learners than accomplished by the same individuals working alone. Bruffee (1999) argues that knowledge is a construct of the community's form of discourse, maintained by local consensus and subject to endless conversation. Learning is a social, negotiated, consensual process. Discourse is viewed as key. Bruffee presents a process in which students collaborate in small groups, then in larger or plenary groups, increasingly arrive at intellectual convergence (even if that means agreeing to disagree), and through this process with the support of an instructor or moderator begin to approximate the substantive and procedural language of the knowledge community towards which they aspire.

Roschelle (1996) posits a similar position that the "crux of learning by collaboration is convergence," a process of mutual construction of knowledge. Learning is defined as conceptual change. "Democratic participation, intellectual progress, and gradual convergence are base attributes of social inquiry practices that enable scientists to undergo conceptual change. A convergent account alone suggests the attractive possibility that students develop their concepts in the course of learning to participate in the practices of inquiry that scientists themselves use to develop scientific concepts" (p. 245). Bruffee's and Roschelle's theoretical developments were associated with face-to-face (f2f) learning environments, although Roschelle did focus on how students worked together in f2f environments such as computer labs.

Harasim (1990) focused on OCL, rather than traditional f2f classrooms or computer labs. The three processes Harasim identified (1990, p. 56) also emphasize collaboration as a key process in conceptual change; while Harasim's theoretical framework was conceptualized several years earlier (1990), these processes are theoretically supported by and resonate with Roschelle (1996), and Bruffee's (1999) position that intellectual convergence through collaborative discourse is key to learning and conceptual change.

Below is Harasim's revised framework for understanding OCL discourse in online seminars:

1. **Idea generating:** This phase is characterized by divergent thinking activities such as verbalization, brainstorming, generating input and information, and democratic participation. Idea generating typically occurs at the beginning of a seminar or topic. Analysis of the transcript demonstrates that participants are actively engaging and contributing to the discussion.

2. **Idea linking:** This phase occurs as students begin to organize and elaborate on the various ideas generated to date into intellectual positions or clusters. Idea linking represents intellectual progress as students, with the facilitation of instructor, begin to recognize multiple perspectives and relationships. Phase 2 also marks the beginning of convergence as new or different ideas become clarified, identified, and clustered into various positions (agreement/disagreement; questions/elaboration).

3. **Intellectual convergence:** This final phase involves idea structuring and conclusions reached as participants (engaging in ongoing discussion, debate, and access to knowledge community resources and expertise) gradually arrive at convergence, a level of intellectual synthesis, understanding, and consensus (including to agree to disagree). It is especially evident in co-production, whether as an assignment, a publication, a theory, a position statement, a work of art, or a similar output authored by the group or subgroup.

Figure 1 illustrates the three stages of collaborative discourse from idea generating to intellectual convergence. At the idea generating stage, individual participants, represented by squares, contribute their ideas and opinions, represented by circles, on the topics to the shared space, represented by an oval. Through the process of brainstorming, the participants begin to relate with each other's ideas. This leads to the second stage of the discourse—idea linking. At this stage, the participants begin to agree or to disagree, clarify and elaborate, and reflect and organize their own and others' ideas and positions. As a result, discrete ideas start to come together; many smaller ideas become a few large ones; individual understandings grow into group shared understanding. At this point, the discourse is ready to advance to the next higher level—intellectual convergence. At this third stage, the group actively engages the co-construction of knowledge based on shared understanding. The group members synthesize their ideas and knowledge into explicit points of view or products (such as theories, positions, publications, works of art, manifestos, scientific theories/hypotheses). They may also extend their ideas and understanding to new territories. The outcomes of this stage are a consolidated shared understanding and group convergence as evidenced by co-production.

OCL Assessment Methods and Rubrics

Figure 1 offers not only a theoretical framework for how OCL contributes to conceptual change, but also suggests a methodology for assessment and a rubric for studying OCL in analyses of the discussion transcripts.

Transcript Analysis of Student Discourse in OCL

A major feature of OCL using computer conferencing or bulletin board forums is that the online environment automatically generates and archives a verbatim, date-stamped chronological transcript of each student message. The availability of a verbatim tran-script of the online class discourse provides an unprecedented opportunity for instruc-tors and for researchers to assess and study student discourse. The archived text-based discussion enables detailed retrospective analysis of one seminar or of the discourse as it evolves over an entire course.

Moreover, the machine-generated transcript does not require instructors/researchers to record a transcript of the student discussion; the software accurately and automatically records verbatim the content, time, and date sent of each student message. Hence, issues of transcription bias, error, or omission are overcome.

Figure 1. Stages of collaborative learning and conceptual change

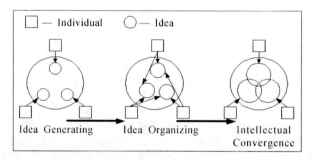

Another very significant attribute of OCL for assessment purposes is that participation in online seminars requires the input of written (text-based) messages. Students must comment (input messages) in order to be present. Written discourse is a form of "frozen thought". Written (or text-based) discourse represents student thought and understanding on the topic. The transcript of student input offers an opportunity for instructors to view how students understand the course materials, concepts, and theories.

The implications for assessment are significant: transcript analysis of social and intellectual development can arguably illuminate learning and understanding in a far more in-depth, comprehensive, and holistic manner than the use of final papers or examinations. Analysis of online discourse enables the study of the process of knowledge-building skills and understanding, rather than products which reflect potentially short-term retention and recitation of information.

Hence, the text-based, archival, group discussion space afforded by OCL environments (especially asynchronous systems) offers a powerful new opportunity for reviewing and studying the quality of student participation (in online discussions/discourse) over time, to assess whether learning and conceptual change are occurring. And if so, under what conditions?

A key obstacle has been the lack of a theoretical framework of online collaborative learning linked with a methodology to assess learning, conceptual change, and progressive discourse.

The availability of the archived text-based transcript has long been identified as a powerful source of qualitative data (i.e., Hiltz, 1986), but to date little progress has been made in the analysis of progressive discourse and learning, given the lack of a theoretical framework that can explain the role of discourse in collaborative learning and conceptual change. Earlier efforts were largely descriptive, describing what was happening, but without analysis of how and why or so what.

Figure 1 offers ways to frame, understand, and study the quality of student participation and student moderating in an online seminar, and to address such analytical questions as did conceptual change occur, how do we know, and under which conditions?

How to Assess Conceptual Change in Online Collaborative Learning Applications: An Example of a Course Design and Assessment Strategy

This final section of the chapter introduces an example of how to design and assess online student-led seminars. Among the designs that I feel most distinguish my work is that of OCL, and especially student-led moderating and weaving, especially in totally online seminars (which can be part of a totally online course or one taught in mixed mode). The issue of assessment is a critical component of successful design, and vice versa: assessment also drives design.

The approach described here is based on a flexible or mixed mode delivery approach, which I have used with undergraduate and graduate courses at Simon Fraser University since 1990. This particular approach employs an approximately 50/50 mix of f2f and online activity: of a 13 week semester, 7-8 weeks including Introduction and Final Class are held as f2f classes; 5-6 weeks are entirely online, based on student-led seminars.

This design works well for a class size of 12-25 (or for larger classes, subdivided into parallel streams of 12-25 students each). Online, like f2f, seminars are most effective in promoting progressive discourse (participation quality and quantity) with group sizes of 15-25 participants. Online seminars are presented consecutively.

In this example, the seminars are held entirely online, each topic is discussed for a period of one week, 24/7, and moderated by a group of students. Of the online seminar period, students will work in small groups to moderate a one-week seminar; for the remaining online seminars, they participate as individual discussants. Students, in both undergraduate and in graduate-level courses, thus have the task of undertaking two distinct and important roles:

1.   Moderators (for 1 online week)
2.   Discussants (for the remaining online weeks of seminars)

Moderating an Online Seminar: 30% of the Total Grade. This is a Group Grade.

Each week a small group of students (3-5) moderates a seminar topic online for seven days. Moderating an Online Seminar comprises three components (each worth 10%):

•   Seminar Introduction: 10%
•   Seminar Facilitation: 10%
•   Seminar Summary: 10%

The Introduction and Summary are presented as written/composed discourse; Facilitating supports group process and intellectual skills, hence conversational and informal comments. The unit of analysis for assessment purposes is the contribution of the student moderating team to each of three activities: Introduction, Facilitation, Summary (see Appendix A).

Online Participation as a Discussant

Online participation refers to participating in the weekly discussions online. During the online sessions, each student is expected to log on regularly, at least *two times per week:* (1) towards the beginning of the online week, to respond to the moderators' discussion questions; and then (2) towards the end of the online week, to respond to colleagues and to synthesize ideas on that topic (commenting about the readings, responding to or building upon other student's comments, and/or drawing from other sources to expand or illustrate some issue related to the topic).

For this course, four substantive comments per student each week are considered minimum participation. Students will be graded on quantity and especially quality of their comments, on posting at least twice per week, and also on reading all of the messages written in the seminar. Grading will especially assess the quality of the comment. Comments of two to three screens each are recommended, offering a thoughtful consideration of the issue or question, and an explication of the particular position being presented or a relevant new idea. References to the readings to add weight or to substantiate a point are important.

Conclusion

This chapter addressed the need for a methodology and rubric for assessing online collaborative learning by providing a theoretical framework which drives and contextualizes OCL. A methodology for transcript analysis and assessment of student discourse in student-led seminars, focusing on the two key roles (student discussants and student seminar moderators) is provided. Assessment based on the theoretical framework moves beyond merely describing what happens in OCL, to provide an analysis of the quality of learning (P1-3), and further study why and under what circumstances intellectual convergence can be supported.

Finally, two appendices provide specific examples of the design of a student-led online seminar, and rubrics to assess the roles of the student discussants and student moderators.

References

Bruffee, K. A. (1999). *Collaborative learning: Higher education, interdependence, and the authority of knowledge* (2nd ed.). Baltimore, MD: John Hopkins University Press.

Harasim, L. (1990). Online education: An environment for collaboration and intellectual amplification. In L. Harasim, (Ed.), *Online education: Perspectives on a new environment* (pp. 39-64). New York: Praeger Press.

Harasim, L. (2006). A history of e-learning: Shift happened. In J. Weiss et al. (Eds.), *The handbook of virtual learning environments* (pp. 25-60). The Netherlands: Springer Press.

Hiltz, S. R. (1990). Evaluating the virtual classroom. In L. Harasim (Ed.), *Online education: Perspectives on a new environment* (pp. 133-183). New York: Praeger Press.

Roschelle, J. (1996). Learning by collaborating: Convergent conceptual change. In T. Koschmann (Ed.), *CSCL: Theory and practice of an emerging paradigm* (pp. 209-248). Mahwah, NJ: Lawrence Erlbaum.

Appendix A:
Rubrics and Grade Sheets
for Student Moderators

Grade Sheet for Moderating: GROUP #1

Group Members:_____

_____

Topic: _____

Dates: _____

Final Grade: _____

Each of the following components (I-III) is worth 10%:

I. Introduction: Grade

☐   Posted in the conference space by NOON, Day 1.

☐   Site Quality: Easy to read and navigate; well organized and clearly presented.

☐   Well Written: No spelling errors, excellent grammar.

☐   No significant technical bugs re: tags, links, access, etc.

☐   Overview/Intro (Composed/Written discourse): Well articulated.

☐   Relevant, appropriate, comprehensive.

☐   Identified the design of the seminar (Discussion/Debate/Role Play, etc.).

☐   Agenda Setting: Provided adequate instructions to students on the process.

☐   Provided students with rationale for seminar design.

☐   Identified the expectations for student participation during seminar.

☐   Set the tone and the topic.

☐   Included a clear overview.

☐   Included samples or illustrations.

☐   Included definition of key terms.

☐   Provided three engaging, mindful, intellectually provocative Discussion Questions (DQs).

☐   Provided references for key readings.

☐   Provided hot Links to readings to support DQs.

☐   Included a bibliography with additional readings.

- ☐ Included three questions posed to the group that stimulated, focused, and worked to sustain the discussion (with links to appropriate readings).
- ☐ Quality of 3 Questions:

  DQ 1: 1 2 3 4 5

  DQ 2: 1 2 3 4 5

  DQ 3: 1 2 3 4 5

- ☐ Included team self-intros.

Comments: _____

_____

_____

II. Facilitating: Grade

- ☐ Logged on daily, monitoring.
- ☐ Kept the discussion flowing and focused, by stimulating the conversation and monitoring.
- ☐ Provided additional questions when/as needed for contextualizing.
- ☐ Reminded students about participation expectations during seminar.
- ☐ Weaving and summarizing were evident to facilitate idea organizing and convergence at strategic points in the seminar.
- ☐ Facilitated group process, encouraged progressive discourse (to advance and not repeat) also by introducing new questions, information.
- ☐ Responded to questions/requests for clarification.
- ☐ Provided feedback when appropriate.
- ☐ Guided messages, discouraged misinformation.
- ☐ Employed prompting, questioning, and probing to advance the discourse.
- ☐ Encouraged brainstorming, organizing, and intellectual convergence.
- ☐ Encouraged informed discussion: Reference to literature, evidence.
- ☐ Did discussants reach any convergence? Positions? Conclusions?

Comments: _____

_____

_____

III. Summary: Grade

- [ ] Posted within four days of end of respective seminar.
- [ ] Summary of the key issues raised on that topic.
- [ ] Summarized the design of the seminar.
- [ ] Provided reflections on moderating.
- [ ] Provided qualitative analyses of the discussion: How well were DQs discussed and analyzed?
- [ ] Provided quantitative analysis of the seminar, including graphics that employed usage statistics to display the volume of participation overall, by time of day, by gender, by DQ, etc; patterns of participation, change over time, etc. in the context of understanding the week's activity.
- [ ] Were summaries complete and accurate?

Comments: _____

_____

_____

_____

_____

Appendix B:
Rubrics and Grade Sheets
for Student Discussants

The unit of analysis for assessment purposes is the quality and quantity of messages by each student discussant in each seminar. My approach has always been to give more weight to the quality of the discussant input than to the quantity. Nonetheless, active participation by each student should also be recognized since this contributes to the overall quality of a seminar and student engagement in the online community.

Next, are included some considerations for assessment, but do not provide actual grading. This should be up to the instructor.

TOTAL per week: ?

Quantity of the Message Input: Some considerations:

1. **Active writing:** Posted at least four messages with substantive input.
2. **Replying:** Logged on at least 2x/week, to respond to DQ and to respond to other Discussants.
3. **Active Reading:** Read all messages.

Quality of the Message Input:

1. Addressed 3 DQ thoughtfully:
    - ☐   Referenced readings
    - ☐   Added new insights
    - ☐   Posed new ideas, questions
    - ☐   Built knowledge (moved from IG to IO to IC).

2. Built knowledge (moved from IG to IO to IC).

Table 1.

Participation	Week One			Week Two			Week Three			Week Four			Total	
	Qual.	Quan.	Total	Qual.	Quan.	Total	Qual.	Quan.	Total	Qual.	Quan.	Total		
Student 1														
Student 2														
Student 3														
Student 4														
Student 5														

Table 2.

	Quantitative			Qualitative A			Qualitative B			Total	
	WRE	RPLY	Read	DQ1	DQ2	DQ3	IG-IO	IO-IC		Qual.	Quan.
Student 1											
Student 2											
Student 3											
Student 4											

Chapter XXVIII

Evaluating the Flexibility of Learning Processes in E-Learning Environments

Maia T. Dimitrova, Joint Information Systems Committee (JISC), UK

Introduction

Flexible learning has many definitions, but it is typically used to describe the empowerment of the learner to choose when, how, and where to engage in learning in order to address their individual study needs. Collis and Moonen (2001) define a flexible learning approach as:

...a movement away from a situation in which key decisions about learning dimensions are made in advance by the instructor or institution, towards a situation where the learner has a range of options from which to choose with respect to these key dimensions. (p. 16)

A number of these key dimensions closely reflect the flexibility of the learning processes that students undertake, including the time and location of learning, the instructional approaches adopted, the variety of learning materials, and the course delivery model (Nikolova & Collis, 1998).

Flexible learning, however, has often been used inappropriately in regards to educational systems, notably those that employ online learning environments, due to the limited flexibility that a number of them embody. Roberts (2002) conducted a thorough analysis of allegedly flexible learning environments and concluded that "…in almost no cases can these environments be called truly flexible, as the flexibility built in them only relates to certain limited components of the learning process."

On the other hand, even if e-learning has been designed according to a flexible approach, this does not in itself guarantee improved student learning. Studies have revealed that students can find the concept unclear in the beginning, which can cause confusion and a difficult and unpleasant learning experience for students (Bofinger & Whateley, 2002). Such negative effects could be due to the lack of understanding of the diversity of the learners and their needs, and a failure to adopt a learner-centred approach to building e-learning environments (Bryant, Campell, & Kerr, 2003; Dimitrova, Sadler, Hatzipanagos, & Murphy, 2003).

Therefore, to ensure that e-learning environments effectively address students' learning needs, the extent to which they enable flexibility of the learning processes needs to be established. We then need to assess whether introducing flexibility has actually resulted in positive improvement to student learning.

To measure the flexibility of the learning processes of e-learning environments, a clear understanding of the dimensions of flexible learning is needed, together with well-defined evaluation criteria for each dimension.

Dimensions of Flexible Learning

Different attempts have been made to define the dimensions of flexible learning. One classification was proposed by Roberts (2002) in his Three by Three Model of flexible learning, which is shown in Figure 1.

Figure 1. Three by Three Model of flexible learning

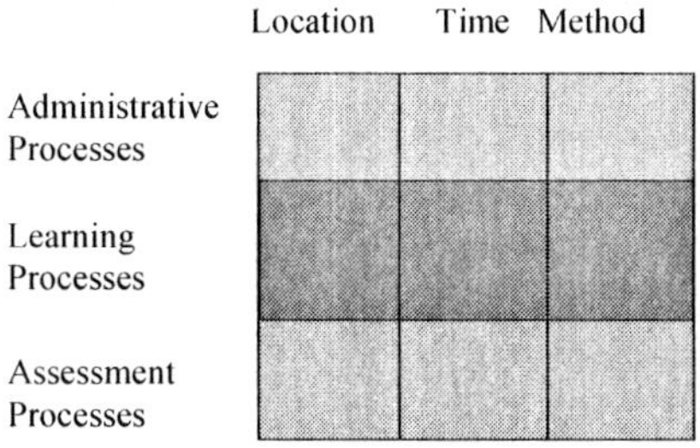

Along the vertical axis the flexibility is described in terms of three types of processes: administrative, learning, and assessment. These processes are then juxtaposed with the flexibility of each in terms of their location, time, and method of execution.

As the focus of this chapter is the evaluation of the learning processes of e-learning, we will consider the middle level of the above model. Each of its three dimensions—location, time, and method—is described below.

Location Flexibility of Learning Processes

Flexibility is increased when students can learn and conduct learning activities from various and remote locations and no longer have to attend scheduled classes. Firstly, this may be enabled by changing the ways in which students can access learning materials (Roberts, 2002). Learning materials can be presented in various forms, apart from the traditional paper format, to include multimedia representations in formats suitable for Web, wireless, or CD-ROM delivery. All students will require is a computer or a mobile device. Secondly, as engaging in learning activities is crucial for student learning, providing them with opportunities to undertake such activities off campus as well as on campus is vital. Finally, location flexibility can be enabled by providing alternative means for teacher-student and student-student interaction (Collis & Moonen, 2001). The place of study may, therefore, be either one of a number of alternatives provided by the institution (e.g., classroom, library, or learning centre) or a location chosen by the student (e.g., at home, work, local library, or community centre).

Time Flexibility of Learning Processes

This does not simply refer to whether students are able to choose when to begin and end their study at the programme or subject level. It can also refer to providing students with greater freedom to determine the pace at which they learn (Benjamin, 1994), as opposed to prescribed semesters and years of a course. Finally, it should involve students being able to choose the time of the day and the week when they are actually engaged in learning. For example, students may not be required to attend scheduled classes (or might attend a reduced number of classes), therefore providing them with the opportunity to study at times of their choice by accessing learning materials whenever they can. However, for this to be effective, it needs to be ensured that the relevant technology is operational at all times to enable easy 24/7 access (Roberts, 2002).

Method Flexibility of Learning Processes

For truly flexible learning courses, it is not sufficient to simply put the lecture notes online so that students can access them when and where they want. The student population of e-learning is becoming increasingly diverse in terms of language abilities, cultural and educational backgrounds, cognitive styles, and learning orientations. Addressing learner diversity in general and learning styles in particular has been shown to enhance students' academic achievement, as well as their attitude towards the course, interest, and motivation (Leneham, Dunn, Ingham, Murray, & Singer, 1994; Sharp, Harb, & Terry, 1997). In traditional classroom education, teachers were unable to effectively address diverse learning styles. Many course materials represented primarily paper-based resources arranged in a sequential order according to the teacher's perception. The advancement of information and communication technologies allows for the creation of different learning tools and resources, and for the representation of information in multiple formats which can address various learning styles and orientations.

Therefore, to meet the needs of the increasingly diverse student population, we need to ensure that students are given the opportunity to learn by a variety of methods. This can be enabled by building e-learning environments that achieve one or more of the following:

- Provide students with a selection of learning resources to choose from, including lecture notes, audio and video recordings of past lectures, PowerPoint presentations, worked examples, and practical case studies (Roberts, 2002; McKavanagh, Kanes, Beven, Cunningham, & Choy, 2002).

- Represent the learning content using a variety of media, such as still and moving images, audio and video clips, and simulations, apart from textual descriptions of the subject matter (Collis & Moonen, 2001; McKavanagh et al., 2002).

- Promote active, rather than passive, student participation in the learning process (Alexander & Boud, 2001). This can be ensured by providing a variety of learning tasks and activities which students can do either individually or as part of a group. Some examples can include reflective reading, essay and report writing, solving problems, analysing realistic case studies, role playing, and group projects and discussions.

- Provide a multiplicity of traversal paths within the learning materials (Leung & Chan, 2003). Levy (2003) criticises liner models of e-learning and advocates personalised learning paths where students are presented with the right amount of information in an order that suits their needs.

- Ensure that opportunities for teacher-student and student-student interaction are provided in a variety of ways (Jones, 2003). In addition to face-to-face communication, this can be enabled through e-mail, online synchronous and asynchronous conferencing tools, such as asynchronous forums and discussion boards, and synchronous chat rooms.

- Provide students with adequate and sufficient learner support to address the needs of all students in the e-learning environment (Mason, 2001; Tait & Mills, 2003). Different techniques for learner support can be employed including FAQs, use of asynchronous bulletin boards and synchronous chat with tutors, peer-moderation, and self-help groups.

Evaluation Criteria for the Flexibility of Learning Processes

Based on the three main dimensions described in the previous section, a set of evaluation criteria have been formulated in the form of a checklist. Each checklist criterion is presented as a question on a continuum from the least flexible to the most flexible option. Next, are 16 questions which can be used to evaluate the flexibility of learning processes across the three dimensions: location, time, and method.

A Case Study

The remainder of this chapter presents a case study in which the Global Campus e-learning environment was evaluated according to the above criteria to identify the extent to which it promotes flexible learning processes. We first present an overview of the learning environment, which is followed by a discussion of its flexibility in terms of the location, time, and method of learning.

Overview of the E-Learning Environment

The Global Campus (GC) project at Middlesex University in the United Kingdom (UK) has developed an e-learning environment for teaching Business Information Technology and Electronic Commerce to postgraduate students in four countries: the UK, Egypt, China, and Singapore. A combination of complementary learning materials was developed, including a learning environment within WebCT and CD-ROMs in addition to traditional textbooks and lecture notes. The WebCT learning environment contains the core course materials, self-assessment tools, and facilities for teacher-student and student-student interaction. The CD-ROMs contain all the course material except for the activities which the students have to complete online, such as online quizzes. All students use the same learning resources. The students in the UK follow the courses primarily in full-time classroom-based mode, where the face-to-face component is stronger. The students in Egypt, China, and Singapore follow the course in a part-time distance-blended learning mode, with limited face-to-face interaction with local tutors and peers during weekly seminar sessions in a local Learning Support Centre.

Each GC course comprises a number of modules, the content of which is divided into learning units which are individual sections of learning material, as shown in Figure 3. Each unit represents a pedagogically complete lesson that can be accomplished in about nine hours. The learning units were implemented according to the I CARE pedagogical system (Hoffman & Ritchie, 2001), which prescribes five steps of instruction including *Introduction, Connect, Apply, Reflect,* and *Extend.* A slight modification of the original I CARE model was introduced in that the *Connect* component was renamed to *Content,* as it was assumed that *Content* would have a more obvious meaning for students.

The *Introduction* section sets the learning objectives of the unit. The *Content* section presents a fairly linear development of the material in textual and graphical formats. At relevant places, hyperlinks to the *Apply* section offer the opportunity to move away from the narrative into activities with a wider, more exploratory scope. These may be computer based, such as programming or design exercises; paper based, such as examining an exemplary case study; or Web based, such as visiting relevant Web sites. Hyperlinks to the *Reflect* section present questions designed to reprise recently learned material in a reflective way. The hyperlinks between these sections enable a greater variety of learner-content interaction. The *Extend* section contains a review quiz to assist students in self-evaluation and to enable tutors in monitoring student progress. This section also contains additional material provided by the tutor to allow students who are more engaged to explore beyond the confines of the syllabus.

Figure 2. A checklist for evaluating the flexibility of learning processes of e-learning environments

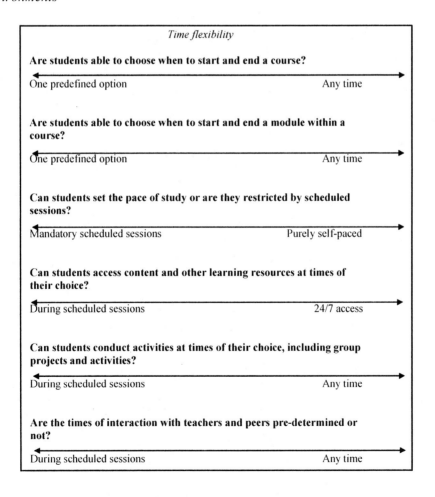

Figure 2. cont.

Location Flexibility

Are students able to access learning content from a place convenient to them or do they have to travel to study or access learning resources?

Single location on a campus   Multiple locations of student choice

Are students able to undertake learning activities from a place of their choice?

Single location on a campus   Multiple locations of student choice

Are students able to communicate with their teachers and peers from a variety of locations?

Face-to-face sessions on campus   Multiple locations of student choice

Learning Method Flexibility

Are students provided with a selection of learning resources?

Single resource   Multiple complementary resources

Is the content in the learning resources represented via alternative and complementary media?

Single medium   Multiple alternative media

Are students able to select from a variety of learning activities?

Single type   Multiple alternative types

Are different traversal paths allowed within the learning material?

Single   Totally self-directed

Are students provided with alternative ways for interacting with teachers?

Face-to-face   Multiple channels of communication

Are students provided with alternative ways for interacting with peers?

Face-to-face   Multiple channels of communication

Are students provided with diverse ways of learner support?

Basic   Context- and student-sensitive

Figure 3. The structure of GC courses

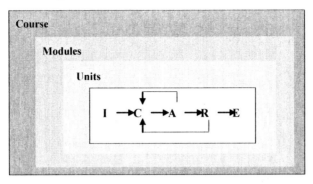

Flexibility Evaluation

To measure the flexibility of the learning processes of the GC e-learning environment, the students' learning behaviour with the technology and interaction styles with their peers and teachers were measured. A quantitative survey was conducted over the past two academic years (2002-2003 and 2003-2004) using a structured questionnaire, which was administered both online and in paper format to reach the maximum number of students. The questions covered different aspects of students' interaction with the e-learning environment, their tutors, and fellow students. In total 120 classroom and 57 distance students took part in the survey.

The sections below present the results from the survey in terms of the location, time, and method flexibility of the GC e-learning environment.

Location Flexibility

The WebCT learning environment can be accessed from any networked computer. When students do not have access to such, the CD-ROMs could be used instead from any other computer a student has access to. The questionnaire data revealed that the students have accessed the learning environment from different locations, as shown in Table 1.

Table 1. Location from which learning materials are accessed (multiple answers were possible)

Location	Classroom Students	Distance Students
Home	61%	87%
Work	20%	70%
Campus	76%	17%
Other	8%	4%

All students, however, need to attend compulsory face-to-face sessions either on campus in the UK or in a Learning Support Centre in their home country. In the latter case the sessions are limited to a couple of hours of seminars, during which students can engage in group discussions with fellow students. Therefore, group discussions take place primarily face to face; however, a limited number are also conducted in asynchronous discussion forums in WebCT. Students can also use the class bulletin board or e-mail to post questions and communicate with academics in the UK asynchronously. Occasionally, distance students can attend video conferencing sessions with their module leaders in the UK.

Time Flexibility

The classroom students can only start the Masters programmes in September of each year and are typically required to complete it in three semesters. A more flexible approach was adopted for the distance students who can choose to start the programme either in September, January, or June of each year. They also have up to four years or twelve semesters to complete their course. All students are expected to complete each module within a semester, although the number of modules studied in a semester varies for the classroom and distance students.

The students can access the WebCT learning environment and the CD-ROMs 24/7. The questionnaire data revealed that over two-thirds of the classroom students prefer to study during the day, and one-third during the evening or night. On the other hand, 74% of the distance students tend to access the materials in the evenings, 21% during the day, and 7% during the night.

The pace of study is determined by the scheduled weekly sessions for both modes, which are more frequent for the classroom students. In addition to this, students can complete the individual activities suggested in the *Apply* section in the e-learning environment at a time of their convenience. As mentioned in the previous sections, group discussions take place predominantly during the weekly face-to-face sessions, apart from a small number which are conducted asynchronously in WebCT. A considerable number of students also communicate with each other via e-mail and chat. Similarly, all students can contact their tutors and module leaders via e-mail if they need to.

Learning Method Flexibility

To identify whether students used different methods while engaging with the learning materials and interacting with their tutors and peers, hierarchical cluster analysis was used to identify patterns in the way the e-learning environment was used. The results have revealed distinct patterns identifying students' preferences in terms of delivery medium, usage of I CARE components, as well as tutor and peer communication. In particular, we found that five distinct types of learning behaviour were exhibited by the classroom students: Ideal Learners, Reflectors, Social Learners, Shallow Learners, and Strugglers. Four distinct types emerged amongst the distance students. They are Traditional Learners, Strategic Learners, Social Learners, and Strugglers. They are described in detail in Dimitrova, Belavkin, Milankovic-Atkinson, Sadler, and Murphy (2003).

All these types of learners prefer to use different kinds of learning resources, engage in different activities, browse the materials in a different sequence, and use different types of learning support to suit their individual needs. For example, the Social Learners tend to spend more time in group discussions and interacting with their tutors than reading and reflecting on subject content, whereas the Strategic Learners prefer to do the online quizzes in an attempt to maximise their exam marks.

While studying, the learners could communicate with their peers and tutors either face-to-face during their weekly seminar sessions or online in chatrooms and via bulletin boards and e-mail. The results indicated that most students preferred to communicate either face-to-face or using their personal e-mails, and the synchronous and asynchronous communication tools within WebCT were not widely used. From the studies, it also became clear that although some students seemed to have easily adapted to the learning environment, others did not. In particular, there were the Strugglers who persistently performed poorly in comparison to the other students and did not make the best use of the learning materials, which had an adverse effect on their learning.

Conclusion

Evaluating the flexibility of learning processes in electronic learning environments is an essential element of establishing how well they meet the needs of target students. The checklist criteria presented in this chapter proved very useful for the evaluation of the flexibility of the GC e-learning environment, which produced interesting results. The findings have provided us with evidence of the flexibility of the e-learning environment according to a number of criteria defined in each of the three dimensions: location, time, and method. Students seemed to have engaged in different learning tasks that may suit their learning needs better.

The results also highlighted two groups of students who might not have been well supported: the Social Learners and the Strugglers. The Social Learners seem to actively engage in collaborative learning, especially during the face-to-face seminars; however, this was outside the e-learning environment. These students particularly will benefit from more collaborative learning tasks, which need to be better integrated into the learning environment. Another category of student, the Strugglers, experienced problems adjusting to the novel mode of learning and therefore need to be provided with more support tailored to their specific needs and learning context.

References

Alexander, S., & Boud, D. (2001). Learners still learn from experience when online. In J. Stephenson (Ed.), *Teaching & learning online: Pedagogies for new technologies* (pp. 3-15). London: Kogan Page.

Benjamin, A. (1994, May). Affordable, restructured education: A solution through information technology. *RSA Journal, 43*-49.

Bofinger, I., & Whateley, G. (2002). The virtual conservatorium: A new emerging option for conservatoria. In B.A. Knight (Ed.), *Reconceptualising learning in the knowledge society* (pp. 134-149). Flaxton, Qld: Post Pressed.

Bryant, K., Campell, J., & Kerr, D. (2003). Impact of Web-based flexible learning on academic performance in information systems. *Journal of Information Systems Education, 14*(1), 41-50.

Collis, B. C., & Moonen, J. (2001). *Flexible learning in a digital world: Experiences and expectations*. London: Kogan Page.

Dimitrova, M., Belavkin, R., Milankovic-Atkinson, M., Sadler, C., & Murphy, A. (2003, December). Learning behaviour patterns of classroom and distance students using flexible learning resources. In *Proceedings of the International Conference on Computers in Education (ICCE03)*, Hong Kong (pp. 834-837).

Dimitrova, M., Sadler, C., Hatzipanagos, S., & Murphy, A. (2003, September). Addressing learner diversity by promoting flexibility in e-learning environments. In *Proceedings of the 14th International Workshop on Databases and Expert Systems Applications (DEXA)*, Prague, Czech Republic (pp. 287-291).

Hoffman, B., & Ritchie, D. C. (2001). An instructional design-based approach to developing online learning environments. In B. H. Khan (Ed.) *Web-based training* (pp. 213-218). Englewood Cliffs, NJ: Educational Technology Publications.

Jones, S. (2003, November). *Designing flexible learning opportunities through a nonlinear collaborative process*. Retrieved September 19, 2004, from http://ultibase.rmit.edu.au/Articles/nov03/jones2.htm

Leneham, M. C., Dunn, R., Ingham, J., Murray, W., & Singer, B. (1994). Learning style: Necessary know-how for academic success in college. *Journal of College Student Development, 35,* 461-466.

Leung, C., & Chan, Y. (2003, December). Perspective on electronic learning: Knowledge management and learning community. In *Proceedings of the International Conference on Computers in Education (ICCE03)*, Hong Kong (pp. 621-623).

Levy, J. (2003, November). A truck is not a horse: Releasing the innovation from e-learning invention for sustainable growth. In *Proceedings of the World Conference on E-Learning in Corporate, Government, Healthcare, & Higher Education (E-Learn) 2003*, Phoenix, AZ (pp. 586-592).

Mason, R. (2001). Effective facilitation of online learning: The Open University experience. In J. Stephenson (Ed.), *Teaching & learning online: Pedagogies for new technologies* (pp. 67-75). London: Kogan Page.

McKavanagh, C., Kanes, C., Beven, F., Cunningham, A., & Choy, S. (2002, February 25). *Evaluation of Web-based flexible learning.* Australian National Training Authority, Melbourne. Leabrook, Australia: National Centre for Vocational Education Research.

Nikolova, I., & Collis, B. (1998). Flexible learning and design of interaction. *British Journal of Educational Technology, 29*(1), 59-72.

Roberts, T. S. (2002, December). Flexible learning: How can we get there from here? In *Proceedings of ASCILITE 2002*, Auckland, New Zealand (pp. 553-560).

Sharp, J. E., Harb, J. N., & Terry, R. E. (1997). Combining Kolb learning styles and writing to learn in engineering classes. *Journal of Engineering Education, 86*(2), 93-101.

Tait, A., & Mills, R. (Eds.). (2003). *Rethinking learner support in distance education: Change and continuity in an international context.* London ; New York: Routledge Falme.

Chapter XXIX

Obstacles Encountered by Learners, Instructors, Technical Support, and Librarians

Badrul H. Khan, The George Washington University, USA

Laura J. Cataldo, National Louis University, USA

Ruth Bennett, National Credit Union Administration, USA

Salvatore Paratore, The George Washington University, USA

Introduction

To create a successful flexible learning system, one with a flexible learning environment where learning is actively fostered and supported, a systematic process of planning, design, development, evaluation, and implementation is needed. A flexible learning system should be meaningful not only to learners, but also to all stakeholder groups, including instructors and support services staff. For example, a flexible learning system is meaningful to learners when it is easily accessible, well designed, learner centered, affordable, and efficient and has a facilitated learning environment. When learners display a high level of participation and success in meeting a course's goals and objectives, this can make learning meaningful to instructors. In turn, when learners enjoy all available technical and library support services provided in the course without any interruptions, it makes technical and library support services staff happy as they strive to provide easy-to-use, reliable services.

In this chapter, we compiled major obstacles encountered by learners, instructors, technical support, and librarians during online learning. In compiling these lists, we communicated with learners, instructors, and technical and library support services staff involved in flexible learning all over the world. We researched flexible learning issues discussed in professional discussion forums, and reviewed literature on the topic.

The obstacles for each stakeholder group were compiled and selected after rigorous research efforts, including face-to-face and online discussions with subject matter experts (SMEs), and a thorough examination of the many responses obtained from posting an inquiry on the Distance Education Online Symposium (DEOS) Listserv and Instructional Technology (IT) Forum. The posting queried individuals about the many diverse issues that learners might encounter before, during, and after taking a course via an online format. Many of the obstacles fell into the dimensions and sub-dimensions of the Flexible Learning Framework by Khan (see Chapter I). The information was then compiled and arranged for each of the stakeholder groups (learners, instructors, technical and library support staff) and arranged in a format suitable for use as an evaluation tool.

Please note that these lists can serve as Obstacles Instruments; however, we would like to caution that none of these lists are empirically validated. Our future endeavor is to validate these obstacles for development of Obstacles Instruments (http://BadrulKhan.com/obstacles).

E-Learning Obstacles Survey

The purpose of this survey is to gather information from learners, instructors, technical support staff, and librarians about obstacles they have encountered while receiving, instructing, or supporting e-learning. Identification of various obstacles, as well as recognition of which obstacles are encountered most frequently, may assist organizations involved in e-learning as their staff members plan, design, and implement e-learning programs. In addition, individuals involved in e-learning may benefit knowing about various obstacles so they can plan accordingly before and during their e-learning experience.

We define e-learning as technology-delivered instruction presented in well designed, learner centered, interactive, and facilitated learning environments to anyone, anyplace, anytime. E-learning includes, but is not limited to, Web-based learning and computer-

based learning. Possible delivery technologies suited for the open, flexible and distributed nature of e-learning include the Internet, intranets/extranets (LAN/WAN), audio-
and videotapes, satellite broadcasts, interactive TV, CD-ROMs, etc.

The survey should take approximately 15 minutes to complete. Your input is vital for
ensuring the success of this study. Thanks for your help!

Demographics:
For statistical purposes, please supply the following information:

Age 18 - 25	26 - 35	36 - 45	46 - 55	66 and above	

Sex

Female	Male	

Country you live in _____

Highest level of education achieved

High School	Some college	College/University graduate	Advanced Degree	

Field of employment

Education – K-12___	Transportation/Utilities___
Higher education (colleges and tech schools)___	Retail___
Finance___	Manufacturing___
Consultant___	Hospitality___
Manufacturing___	Telecommunications___
Health care___	Information Technology___
Government (federal, state, and local)___	Other(Please indicate)_____

How do you connect to the Internet?

Dial-up	**Cable modem**	**DSL**	**ISDN**	**T1**	**T2**	**T3**	Don't know	Other

(Bold faced are broadband)

Choose the role that best represents you. Please respond to the appropriate survey based upon the role you have selected.

Learner ( )	Instructor( )	Tech Support ( )	Librarian ( )	

Table 1.

Obstacles Encountered by Learners						
Directions: Please indicate (✓) the extent to which you agree that the following obstacles have occurred in your e-learning experience.						
	Never	Seldom	Sometimes	Often	Always	Not Applicable
1. Did not understand what various buttons or labels on the course Web site meant						
2. Too long to download images						
3. Could not access links provided within the course						
4. Could not access media on the course Web site						
5. Difficulty navigating through course Web site						
6. Time management problems						
7. Insufficient communication with instructional staff						
8. Course Web site in a never-ending upgrade mode, leading to inconsistency with the user interface						
9. Limited hours of technical support						
10. Lack of necessary software						
11. Difficulty communicating with other learners due to diverse time zones						
12. Course Web site did not have adequate tools for use by those with disabilities						
13. Lack of necessary equipment (hardware)						
14. Difficulty keeping up with new technology						
15. Unsatisfactory communication with instructional staff						
16. Mismatch between stated course hardware requirements and actual course requirements						

Table 1. continued

17. Mismatch between stated course software requirements and actual course requirements						
18. Mismatch between stated course knowledge requirements and actual course requirements						
19. Insufficient course Web site support						
20. Course content outdated						
21. Course Web site design is complicated						
22. Could not get technical assistance						
23. Online format felt too stressful						
24. Took more time than expected						
25. Problem with course schedule						
26. Problem with course pace						
27. Learning materials arrived late						
28. Inadequate library support						
29. Numerous upgrades to the Web server resulting in reduced Web site availability for coursework						
30. Difficulty communicating with instructor due to diverse time zones						
31. Difficulty communicating with instructors due to conflicting hours of availability						
32. Difficulty finding course materials (i.e. syllabus)						
33. Course assignments not clear						
34. Course instruction not well presented						
35. Inflexible course structure						
36. Course goals were not clear						
37. Difficulty communicating with course instructor						
38. Course material was not sufficient to meet course objectives						

Table 1. continued

39. Prefer verbal communications in a face–to-face format						
40. Missed being in a true classroom environment						
41. Lack of free time						
42. Personal study problems						
43. Insufficient feedback on assignments						
44. Course focus not clear						
45. Course expectations not clear						
46. Confusing changes to course						
47. Unresponsive instructor						
48. Course content too difficult						
49. Collaborative group members (other students) not doing their share of work						
50. Low motivation level						
51. Lacked prerequisite knowledge						
52. Unable to figure out how to participate in online discussions and/or chats						
53. Disliked the solitary nature of online learning						
54. Did not like the expectation that work-related online learning was to be done outside of normal work hours						
55. Course did not meet my expectations						
56. Lack of (or insufficient) financial compensation for completing course						
57. Lack of (or insufficient) recognition for completing course (i.e., certificates, personal recognition)						
58. Deadlines not made clear						
59. Problems with my Internet service provider (ISP)						

Table 2.

Obstacles Encountered by Instructors

Directions: Please indicate (✓) the extent to which you agree that the following obstacles have occurred in your e-learning experience.

	Never	Seldom	Sometime	Often	Always	Not Applicable
1. Did not understand what various buttons or labels on the course Web site meant						
2. Too long to download images						
3. Could not access links provided within the course						
4. Could not access media on the course Web site						
5. Difficulty navigating through course Web site						
6. Time management problems						
7. Insufficient communication with instructional staff						
8. Web site in a never-ending upgrade mode, leading to inconsistency with the user interface						
9. Limited hours of technical support						
10. Lack of necessary software						
11. Difficulty communicating with learners due to diverse time zones						
12. Course Web site did not have adequate tools for use by those with disabilities						
13. Lack of necessary equipment (hardware)						

Table 2. continued

14. Difficulty keeping up with new technology						
15. Unsatisfactory communication with instructional staff						
16. Insufficient Web site support						
17. Course content outdated						
18. Too stressful to assist students utilizing an e-mail format						
19. Too stressful to assist students using telephone format						
20. Difficulty communicating with diverse learner group						
21. Students have outdated hardware						
22. Numerous course Web site design changes resulting in reduced Web site availability for coursework						
23. Numerous upgrades to the Web server resulting in reduced Web site availability for coursework						
24. Course Web site design is complicated						
25. Could not get technical assistance						
26. Difficulty communicating with learners due to technology problems						
27. Difficulty communicating with learners due to conflicting hours of availability						
28. Difficulty finding course materials (i.e., syllabus)						
29. Course instruction not well presented (when the course is designed by someone other than the instructor)						
30. Lack of time to assist students taking the course						
31. Lack of communication between course developer and librarian						

Table 2. continued

32. Lack of prerequisite knowledge noted in students taking the course						
33. Too time consuming to assist learners with their numerous questions						
34. Students unable to understand description of course assignments (when the course is designed by someone other than the instructor)						
35. Did not understand what various buttons or labels on the course Web site meant						
36. Learners seeking additional clarity in goals						
37. Prefer verbal/visual communication in a face-to-face format						
38. Missed being in a true classroom environment						
39. Lack of free time						
40. Learners requesting clarification about assignments						
41. Changes made throughout course were confusing for learners						
42. No training for instructors, specifically in Web-based instruction teaching methods						
43. Full features of Web not available to instructors due to IT staff decisions rather than pedagogical needs						
44. Collaborative group members (students) not doing their share of work						
45. Low student motivation level						
46. Low instructor motivation level						
47. Lacked prerequisite knowledge of Web-based instructional teaching methods and techniques						
48. Students were unable to figure out how to participate in online discussions and/or chats						

Table 3.

Obstacles Encountered by Librarians

Directions: Please indicate (✓)the extent to which you agree that the following obstacles have occurred in your e-learning experience.

	Never	Seldom	Sometime	Often	Always	Not Applicable
1. Did not understand what various buttons or labels on the course Web site meant						
2. Too long to download images						
3. Could not access links provided within the course						
4. Could not access media on the course Web site						
5. Difficulty navigating through course Web site						
6. Time management problems						
7. Insufficient communication with instructional staff						
8. Web site in a never-ending upgrade mode, leading to inconsistency with the user interface						
9. Limited hours of technical support						
10. Lack of necessary software						
11. Difficulty communicating with learners due to diverse time zones						
12. Course Web site did not have adequate tools for use by those with disabilities						
13. Lack of necessary equipment (hardware)						
14. Difficulty keeping up with new technology						

Table 3. continued

15. Unsatisfactory communication with instructional staff						
16. Insufficient Web site support						
17. Course content outdated						
18. Too stressful to assist students utilizing an e-mail format						
19. Too stressful to assist students using telephone format						
20. Difficulty communicating with diverse learner group						
21. Students have outdated hardware						
22. Numerous course Web site design changes resulting in reduced Web site availability for coursework						
23. Numerous upgrades to the Web server resulting in reduced Web site availability for coursework						
24. Course Web site design is complicated						
25. Could not get technical assistance						
26. Difficulty communicating with learners due to conflicting hours of availability						
27. Difficulty finding course materials (i.e., syllabus)						
28. Course instruction not well presented						
29. Unable to understand instructor's goals for the course						
30. Lack of time to assist students taking the course						
31. Lack of communication between course developer and librarian						
32. Lack of prerequisite knowledge noted in students taking the course						

Table 3. continued

	Never	Seldom	Sometime	Often	Always	Not Applicable
33. Too time consuming to assist learners with their numerous questions						
34. Students unable to understand instructor's description of course assignments						

Table 4.

Obstacles Encountered by Tech Support

Directions: Please indicate (✓)the extent to which you agree that the following obstacles have occurred in your e-learning experience.

	Never	Seldom	Sometime	Often	Always	Not Applicable
1. Did not understand what various buttons or labels on the course Web site meant						
2. Too long to download images						
3. Could not access links provided within the course						
4. Could not access media on the course Web site						
5. Difficulty navigating through course Web site						
6. Time management problems						
7. Insufficient communication with instructional staff						
8. Web site in a never-ending upgrade mode, leading to inconsistency with the user interface						
9. Limited hours of technical support						

Table 4. continued

10. Lack of necessary software						
11. Difficulty communicating with learners due to diverse time zones						
12. Course Web site did not have adequate tools for use by those with disabilities						
13. Lack of necessary equipment (hardware)						
14. Difficulty keeping up with new technology						
15. Unsatisfactory communication with instructional staff						
16. Mismatch between stated course hardware requirements and actual course requirements						
17. Mismatch between stated course software requirements and actual course requirements						
18. Mismatch between stated course knowledge requirements and actual course requirements						
19. Insufficient Web site support						
20. Course content outdated						
21. Too stressful to assist students utilizing an e-mail format						
22. Too stressful to assist students using telephone format						
23. Difficulty communicating with diverse learner group						
24. Students have outdated hardware						
25. Course Web site design is complicated						
26. Numerous upgrades to the Web server resulting in reduced Web site availability for coursework						
27. Numerous course Web site design changes resulting in reduced Web site availability for coursework						

Table 4. continued

28. Difficulty communicating with learners due to conflicting hours of availability						
29. Course instruction not well presented						
30. Unable to understand instructor's goals for the course						
31. Lack of time to assist students taking the course						
32. Lack of communication between course developer and librarian						
33. Lack of prerequisite knowledge noted in students taking the course						
34. Too time consuming to assist learners with their numerous questions						

Chapter XXX

A Program Satisfaction Survey Instrument for Online Students

Badrul H. Khan, The George Washington University, USA

Henry L. Smith, San Jose State University, USA

Introduction

With the advent of the Internet and online learning methodologies and technologies, online learning is becoming more and more accepted. Institutions are investing heavily in the development and deployment of online programs. To fulfill the demand of online education and training, academic institutions, corporations, and government agencies worldwide are increasingly using the Internet and digital technologies to deliver instruction and training. However, institutions must pay attention to the needs of learners. With the increasing use of a variety of approaches in learning in the information age, learners require rich learning environments supported by well designed resources. They expect on-demand, anytime/anywhere high-quality learning environments with good support services.

To cater to the needs of online learners, institutions should develop learning-focused educational and training systems where "the learner is the key entity and occupies the nucleus of the systems complex of education" (Banathy, 1991, p. 96). For Banathy, "when learning is in focus, arrangements are made in the environment of the learner that communicate the learning task, and learning resources are made available to learners so that they can explore and master learning tasks" (p. 101). Therefore, online learning environments that can effectively support learning-on-demand must be designed by placing the learners at the center. Learners' satisfaction becomes a major issue. In support of a learner-centered approach, Moore (1998) states:

Our aim as faculty should be to focus our attention on making courses and other learning experiences that will best empower our students to learn, to learn fully, effectively, efficiently, and with rewarding satisfaction. It is the responsibility of our profession to study ways of maximizing the potential of our environments to support their learning and to minimize those elements in their environments that may impede it. (p. 4)

An online program has the potential to satisfy learners' needs if it is meaningful to learners. A meaningful program involves a systematic process of planning, design, development, evaluation, and implementation to create a learning environment where learning is actively fostered and supported. When an online program is easily accessible, well designed, learner centered, affordable, efficient, flexible, and has a facilitated learning environment where learners display a high level of participation and success in meeting course goals and objectives, and enjoy all available support services provided in the program without debilitating interruptions—it is meaningful to learners. A meaningful program should then provide a moderate to high level of learner satisfaction with both the quality of instruction and all support services (Morrison & Khan, 2003).

Academic institutions ordinarily solicit student evaluations of courseware. Generally this is done on a course-by-course basis that focuses on traditional items such as course content and instruction. What seemed to be missing from the evaluation of online education was the determination of student satisfaction with online instruction as a delivery method or system. For us, concern was focused on satisfaction associated particularly with the emerging asynchronous online instruction method, in part because of its growing popularity among post-graduate educational agencies. Asynchronous instruction does not require the simultaneous participation of students and instructors, and students do not need to be gathered together in the same location at the same time (Ehrmann, 1995). It is critical for institutions to learn about learners' satisfaction with their online programs. It has been our interest to understand learner issues with electronically based education, and we began the process of understanding such issues with the idea of tapping student satisfaction with the implementations of online instruction programs.

A literature review was undertaken to look for an instrument that would measure student satisfaction with educational programs as a whole, and none was found. Additionally, the search focused on an instrument that would measure satisfaction specifically with the asynchronous online delivery method, and again, none was found. The search then turned to a listserv canvass of colleagues in the field of instructional technology and distance education for suggestions. The postings drew responses that generally pointed back to individual course evaluations.

After reflecting on various aspects of online learning, we have adopted the E-learning Framework (Khan, 2001) as a basis for a student satisfaction survey of online instruction. E-learning, nominally, is a modern type of distance education that is delivered via the use of computers, the Internet, and multimedia presentation. The seeds for the E-learning Framework began germinating with the question, "What does it take to provide the best and most meaningful flexible learning environments for learners worldwide" (Khan, 2001, p. 77). Khan (2001) found that numerous factors help to create a meaningful online learning environment, and many of these factors are systemically interrelated and interdependent. A systemic understanding of these factors can help us create meaningful learning environments. By clustering these factors into categories, Khan developed the *E-learning Framework* comprising eight dimensions of concern in the provision of electronically based education: institutional, management, ethical, pedagogical, technological, interface design, resource support, and evaluation. Using the E-learning Framework as a basis, complementary survey items were generated from a student/consumer perspective. The process involved the identification of factors in each of the eight dimensions of the E-learning Framework that influenced or impacted student satisfaction with the delivery method, the efficacy of the instructional strategies, and the quality of the educational experience.

Development of the Instrument

The list of factors was narrowed by using a rationale that looked at the factors' alignment with the focus defined in the dimensions of the E-learning Framework and whether they could be translated into consumer-side or student perspective items.

The student perspective constituted a lens created from the analysis of the focus and intent of a number of course evaluation instruments, such as the Student Instructional Report II (SIR II), created and offered by the Educational Testing Service (ETS, 2004). The idea was to include the most salient factors—referencing the E-learning Framework, affecting a student's online educational experience—as far as such could be determined by the analysis mentioned above. The generation of the lens was effected using the couse evaluation instrument analysis, the application of personal experience as an online student and instructor, and by reference to current texts and articles such as "Student Evaluation of College Teaching Effectiveness" (Wachtel, 1998), which reviewed research on student evaluations of college and university teaching; "Understanding Student Evaluations" (Hobson & Talbot, 2001), which offered an introduction to the scholarship of teaching evaluations with a specific emphasis on student evaluations of teaching effectiveness (SETEs); and "Student Perspectives on Teaching and its Evaluation" (Spencer & Schmelkin, 2002), which explored student perspectives on course and teacher ratings.

Generating factors in the *institutional* dimension, suitable for conversion into survey items from a student perspective, consisted primarily of determining which administrative, academic, and student service factors were accessible to student insight and evaluation, and had direct impact on online program implementation. *Management* factors, while at times hard to differentiate from institutional factors, were identified as those associated more with "hands-on" concerns such as content development and maintenance, staff administration, program evaluation strategies, and security. The identification of *ethical* factors included emphasis on the programs' sensitivity to cultural and diversity issues in the design of the interface, content, and environment of the instruction, as well as concerns such as etiquette, privacy, and copyright. Factors in the *technology* dimension presented the greatest challenge in terms of choice. There are myriad technological implementations for asynchronous instruction, so it was necessary to choose factors that represented generic issues rather than those associated with the employment of particular applications or products and then to provide a separate list of specific technologies that might be employed. As in separating the institutional and management factors, the identification of interface factors involved the difficulty of differentiating them from those in the technological dimension. The emphasis in the *interface design* dimension centered around navigation and usability issues, independent of the technology used. Also, like the technological dimension, the identification of *pedagogical* factors was challenged by volume. In this case emphasis was placed upon the program's incorporation of factors that seemed to be more aligned with asynchronous and online instruction rather than classroom instruction. Another dimension that presented a plethora of choices was *resource support.* In this dimension, factor choices were limited to those that, while not constrained to supporting just online courseware, were primarily accessed via the Internet. In the final dimension, *evaluation,* factors were chosen that addressed not only evaluative strategies for both student and instructional performance, but the ability of students to provide both formative (during the program) and summative evaluations of the program and courseware, and to have archival access to the evaluation outcomes.

From the resulting list of survey items, a Likert Scale-type questionnaire was generated for use as a survey instrument. In the questionnaire, respondents were initially asked to express their satisfaction on a scale from 'very satisfied' to 'very dissatisfied', with the implementation of factors in each of the eight dimensions, the impact of each of the factors on their perception of their learning experience in the program, and the influence their satisfaction with each factor had on their perception of the overall quality of the online program.

Instrument Refinement

The draft questionnaire was then distributed to a number of experts in educational technology, distance education, and online education for feedback. The feedback resulted in the removal of some items/factors seen as superfluous, esoteric, out of scope, and/or of too little significance. Subsequent to those adjustments, further refinement was undertaken to better focus each question toward soliciting responses that most accurately reflected student feelings about each factor. Each question was compared against others from the same dimension to eliminate duplication, and each question was scrutinized more closely against the definition of the dimension to ensure proper placement. As a result, some questions/factors were moved to other dimensions, and some questions required rewording to better reflect the intent of the investigation in a particular dimension.

Once the process of refinement progressed to a reasonable point with respect to the type, wording, and focus of the questions included in each dimension, the instrument was submitted, more formally, to a panel of experts for reaction. This panel was quite helpful in honing the dimension assignment of each item, the educational level appropriateness of the question wording, and the understandability of each question.

The survey was then implemented as a trial by administering it to the enrollees in a master's program in nutrition at a midsized international university on the east coast of the United States. The outcomes of that implementation resulted in several changes to the instrument, including the need to determine a student's previous experience with online education and the provision of the ability for a respondent to express a level of satisfaction with the existence/absence of a particular factor or component.

Conclusion

As more and more institutions offer online programs worldwide, learners will have more options in selecting their desired programs. Their selections of online academic programs may be greatly dependent on the level of satisfaction experienced by learners with program implementations and the quality of the educational experience. It is critical for institutions to understand student satisfaction levels with their program offerings by using a comprehensive satisfaction instrument. The instrument introduced here has the potential to facilitate student input about online programs and to inform the development of plans for program improvements.

Acknowledgments

There are many individuals who we should thank for their comments and suggestions that helped improve the instrument. These include student colleagues in the Educational Technology doctoral program at Pepperdine University, Dr. Decker Walker of Stanford University, Dr. Steve Zlotolow of San José State University, Dr. Owen Roberts of Lockheed Martin Corporation, Dr. LeeAnn Stone, and Dr. John McManus of Pepperdine University.

References

Banathy, B. H. (1991). *Systems designs of education: A journey to create the future.* Englewood Cliffs, NJ: Educational Technology Publications.

Ehrmann, S. C. (1995, July 7). Moving beyond campus-bound education. *The Chronicle of Higher Education.* Retrieved from http://chronicle.merit.edu/.external/.annenberg/.ehrmann1.html

ETS (Educational Testing Service). (2004). *Student instructional report II.* Retrieved October 1, 2004, from http://www.ets.org

Hobson, S., & Talbot, D. (2001). Understanding student evaluations. *College Teaching, 49*(1), 26.

Khan, B. H. (2001). A framework for Web-based learning. In B. H. Khan (Ed.), *Web-based training* (pp. 75-98). Englewood Cliffs, NJ: Educational Technology Publications.

Moore, M. G. (1998). Introduction. In C.C. Gibson (Ed.), *Distance learners in higher education.* Madison, WI: Atwood Publishing.

Morrison, J. L., & Khan, B. H. (2003). The global e-learning framework: An interview with Badrul Khan. *The Technology Source. A Publication of the Michigan Virtual University.* Retrieved May 18, 2003, from http://ts.mivu.org/default.asp?show=article&id=1019#options

Spencer, K., & Schmelkin, L. (2002). Student perspectives on teaching and its evaluation. *Assessment and Evaluation in Higher Education, 27*(5).

Wachtel, H. (1998). Student evaluation of college teaching effectiveness: A brief review. *Assessment and Evaluation in Higher Education, 23*(2).

Appendix

A Program Satisfaction Survey Instrument for Online Students

Participant,

Thank you for taking the time and making the effort to complete this satisfaction survey. The answers you provide will help inform and improve the provision of electronically-based education. To start, please respond to the following demographic inquiries.

Your Age:

Your Gender:

Marital Status:

Children in Your Household:

Distance You Live From Your Program's School:

Employment Status:

Have you participated in online education prior to this program?

The questionnaire contains eight sections with 10 questions each about factors associated with a specific dimension of your online experience. Each question requires a response to two separate aspects of your experience: (1) your satisfaction with the factor, and (2) the impact the factor has/had on your overall online learning experience. If a factor is listed that is not present or used in your program, use the satisfaction and impact columns to indicate your feelings about its absence.

Place an X in the spaces in the columns that most closely align with your feelings about the factor and its impact.

The *Institutional* section factors are associated with the efforts made by the institution to inform and support students in online learning.

The *Management* section factors are associated with the planning, policies, and implementation of the program.

The *Ethical* section factors are associated with social, cultural, and learner diversity as well as accessibility, etiquette, and legal issues.

The *Technological* section factors are associated with issues of technology infrastructure, standards, and guidelines.

The *Interface Design* section factors are associated with page and site design, navigation, and usability.

The *Pedagogical* section factors are associated with teaching and learning methods and strategies.

The *Resource Support* section factors are associated with the provision of adequate and accessible resources for learning and performance.

The *Evaluation* section factors are associated with the assessment of learners and of the instruction and learning environment.

Feel free to comment at the end of each section, especially about factors you think are missing.

Thank you for your time and effort in participating in this study.

Table 1. Institutional

FACTORS	Rate your satisfaction with these institutional factors associated with the provision of your distance education program by placing a checkmark in the appropriate box. Use the following scale: VS = Very Satisfied, SS = Somewhat Satisfied, N = Neutral, SD = Somewhat Dissatisfied, VD = Very Dissatisfied.					Rate the effect each of these institutional factors had/has on your overall learning experience in the program. Use the following scale: SE = Strongly Enhanced, E = Enhanced, N = Neutral, D = Degraded, SD = Strongly Degraded.				
	VS	SS	N	SD	VD	SE	E	N	D	SD
A1. Efforts in making you aware of pre-requisite skills and resources recommended for participation in asynchronous distance learning.										
A2. Information about the program faculty's experience in online or distance education instruction.										
A3. Provision of course material previews/demos before registration as a standard part of the program's offering.										
A4. If the program is offered in modules at different times, the ability for flexible choice of modules in which to enroll.										
A5. Information about program successful completion and dropout rates.										
A6. Institution's policy on class sizes with respect to their impact on the effectiveness of distance education programs.										
A7. Provision of adequate and effective guidelines on how to interact effectively at a distance.										
A8. Information about the preparation of instructors for teaching in distance education environments.										
A9. Comparison of degree content and requirements with traditional on-campus programs.										
A10. Accommodations for distance education students with physical disabilities or learning difficulties.										

Table 2. Management

FACTORS	Rate your satisfaction with these factors associated with the management of your distance education program by placing a checkmark in the appropriate box. Use the following scale: VS = Very Satisfied, SS = Somewhat Satisfied, N = Neutral, SD = Somewhat Dissatisfied, VD = Very Dissatisfied.					Rate the effect each of these management factors had/has on your overall learning experience in the program. Use the following scale: SE = Strongly Enhanced, E = Enhanced, N = Neutral, D = Degraded, SD = Strongly Degraded.				
	VS	SS	N	SD	VD	SE	E	N	D	SD
B1. Maintenance of the currency of the program's courseware.										
B2. Instructor training on software used in the program.										
B3. Monitoring program students to determine if they are comfortable using requisite technologies.										
B4. Handling/resolution of accessibility issues such as errors in different online functions.										
B5. Access to the right person with whom to discuss and resolve questions about grades or records in a timely hassle-free manner.										
B6. Ability to obtain replacements for missing program content distributed on transportable media such as disks, CDs, Tapes, DVDs, etc.										
B7. Ability to reach a person in a timely way to help with problems that don't fit the automated system.										
B8. Maintenance/ currency of connections to content material and resources.										
B9. Maintenance of the Knowledge Management (KM) site.										

Table 3. Ethical

FACTORS	Rate your satisfaction with these factors associated with the ethical provision and management of your distance education program by placing a checkmark in the appropriate box. Use the following scale: VS = Very Satisfied, SS = Somewhat Satisfied, N = Neutral, SD = Somewhat Dissatisfied, VD = Very Dissatisfied.					Rate the effect each of these ethical factors had/has on your overall learning experience in the program. Use the following scale: SE = Strongly Enhanced, E = Enhanced, N = Neutral, D = Degraded, SD = Strongly Degraded.				
	VS	SS	N	SD	VD	SE	E	N	D	SD
C1. Use of graphics and icons that are resistant to cultural misinterpretation and mistranslation.										
C2. Given global access, the program's efforts to address cultural diversity from a learning perspective, i.e., the minimizing of culture-bias-based educational dissonance.										
C3. Fostering of mutual respect, tolerance, and trust among distance education students and faculty.										
C4. Sensitivity about diverse student populations' accessibility to the Internet.										
C5. Provision of online etiquette guidelines on online message posting so that postings do not hurt others' feelings.										
C6. Provision of privacy policies and guidelines for online postings.										
C7. Provision of policies and guidelines regarding fraudulent activities in course-related testing, assignments, and projects.										
C8. Information about institutional/program policies and guidelines concerning copyright issues.										
C9. Information about policies and guidelines concerning intellectual property issues.										
C10. Accommodations for age-related differences in the student population.										

Table 4. Technological

FACTORS	Rate your satisfaction with these factors associated with the technology component of your distance education program by placing a checkmark in the appropriate box. Use the following scale: VS = Very Satisfied, SS = Somewhat Satisfied, N = Neutral, SD = Somewhat Dissatisfied, VD = Very Dissatisfied.					Rate the effect each of these technological factors had/has on your overall learning experience in the program. Use the following scale: SE = Strongly Enhanced, E = Enhanced, N = Neutral, D = Degraded, SD = Strongly Degraded.				
	VS	SS	N	SD	VD	SE	E	N	D	SD
D1. Provision of technical assistance in setting up and configuring student computers before program start.										
D2. Adequacy of the particular technology implementations used in your program to deliver distance education content.										
D3. Ease of use of the particular technology implementations employed in the program.										
D4. Modernity/currency of the technology implementations used in the program.										
D5. Provision of a "buddy system" that allows learners to have at least one person with whom they can do preliminary troubleshooting or from whom they can obtain technology advice.										
D6. Quality of the computer applications used for content presentation.										
D7. Provision of technical training or training references for students who need technical skill upgrades.										
D8. Adequacy of the communication channels used for delivering content and handing in assignments, such as bandwidth capacity and uplink/downlink speeds.										
D9. Provision of alternative processes or functions for instructional delivery or assignment completion if normal technology functions are not working.										

Table 5. Technology components

D10. TECHNOLOGY COMPONENTS	Rate your satisfaction with the program's use of these technology components for distance education students. Use the following scale: VS = Very Satisfied, SS = Somewhat Satisfied, N = Neutral, SD = Somewhat Dissatisfied, VD = Very Dissatisfied					Rate the effect your program's use of each of these technology components had/has on your overall learning experience in the program. Use the following scale: SE = Strongly Enhanced, E = Enhanced, N = Neutral, D = Degraded, SD = Strongly Degraded				
	VS	SS	N	SD	VD	SE	E	N	D	SD
Video/videotape										
E-mail										
Mailing lists										
Newsgroups										
Bulletin boards										
Chat										
Messaging										
Multi-user dialogues (MUDs)										
Computer conferencing										
CD-ROM										
DVD										
E-book										
Print (books/articles)										
Internet browsers and plug-ins										
Personal digital assistant (PDA)										
Other (write in)										
Other (write in)										
Other (write in)										

Table 6. Interface design

FACTORS	Rate your satisfaction with these factors associated with the interface design component of your distance education program by placing a checkmark in the appropriate box. Use the following scale: VS = Very Satisfied, SS = Somewhat Satisfied, N = Neutral, SD = Somewhat Dissatisfied, VD = Very Dissatisfied.					Rate the effect each of these interface design factors had/has on your overall learning experience in the program. Use the following scale: SE = Strongly Enhanced, E = Enhanced, N = Neutral, D = Degraded, SD = Strongly Degraded.				
	VS	SS	N	SD	VD	SE	E	N	D	SD
E1. Information about the program's distance education interface mechanisms and how to use them.										
E2. Content structural flexibility that allows multiple pathways through instructional media.										
E3. Ability to navigate program media in a user-friendly manner.										
E4. Ability for students to leave or broadcast messages for the entire class, cohort, group, or program.										
E5. Ease of instructional exchanges with instructors or teaching assistants compared to an on-campus program.										
E6. Efforts to improve communication and avoid misunderstanding by reducing/avoiding jargons, idioms, ambiguities, and acronyms outside of those that are clearly explained and unique to the subject area.										
E7. Coordination of instructional focus between different instructional media.										
E8. Ability to locate information and answers to the most frequently asked questions (FAQs) in a reasonable amount of time.										
E9. Provision of distance education communications' security that protected message content from tampering.										

Table 7. Interface components

E10. INTERFACE COMPONENTS	Rate your satisfaction with the program's use of these interface design components for distance education students. Use the following scale: VS = Very Satisfied, SS = Somewhat Satisfied, N = Neutral, SD = Somewhat Dissatisfied, VD = Very Dissatisfied.					Rate the effect the program's use of these interface design components had/has on your overall learning experience in the program. Use the following scale: SE = Strongly Enhanced, E = Enhanced, N = Neutral, D = Degraded, SD = Strongly Degraded.				
	VS	SS	N	SD	VD	SE	E	N	D	SD
Text										
Graphics										
Interactive Internet applications										
Audio										
Narration										
Animation										
Multi-user dialogues (MUDs)										
E-mail										
Listservs										
Online Chat										
Other (write in)										
Other (write in)										
Other (write in)										
Other (write in)										

Table 8. Petagogical

FACTORS	Rate your satisfaction with these factors associated with the pedagogy implementations of your distance education program by placing a checkmark in the appropriate box. Use the following scale: VS = Very Satisfied, SS = Somewhat Satisfied, N = Neutral, SD = Somewhat Dissatisfied, VD = Very Dissatisfied.					Rate the effect each of these pedagogy implementation factors had/has on your overall learning experience in the program. Use the following scale: SE = Strongly Enhanced, E = Enhanced, N = Neutral, D = Degraded, SD = Strongly Degraded.				
	VS	SS	N	SD	VD	SE	E	N	D	SD
F1. Comprehensiveness/completeness of the distance learning content.										
F2. Efforts in enabling students to learn according to preferred learning styles (e.g., visual/nonverbal, visual/verbal, auditory).										
F3. Use of multimedia attributes in creating a rich environment for active learning.										
F4. Encouragement of learner-learner interaction.										
F5. Use of instructional *facilitation* for distance learners, such as providing guidance, fostering discussion, suggesting resources, fielding questions, etc.										
F6. Promotion and enabling of collaboration with external personnel and resources (speakers, guest lecturers, Web sites, etc.).										
F7. Information about the recommended approximate number of hours per week that distance education students should spend on study and assignments.										
F8. Efforts in addressing learner dissonance or anxiety due to issues such as distance learner beginner role, lack of experience with distance learning technologies, and views of traditional learning systems.										
F9. Efforts of instructor/staff in contacting students who do not participate in distance learning activities to check for problems.										
F10. Promotion of, enabling, and supporting a community of learners environment.										

Table 9. Resource support

FACTORS	Rate your satisfaction with these resource support factors for distance education students by placing a checkmark in the appropriate box. Use the following scale: VS = Very Satisfied, SS = Somewhat Satisfied, N = Neutral, SD = Somewhat Dissatisfied, VD = Very Dissatisfied.					Rate the effect each of these resource support factors had/has on your overall learning experience in the program. Use the following scale: SE = Strongly Enhanced, E = Enhanced, N = Neutral, D = Degraded, SD = Strongly Degraded.				
	VS	SS	N	SD	VD	SE	E	N	D	SD
G1. Provision of someone other than the instructor who can help students with distance learning problems.										
G2. Provision of technical troubleshooting, expert support by specialized staff, or help line.										
G3. Provision of clear guidelines on what support learners can and cannot expect from a help line, e.g., things the student is responsible for and things the student can expect the help line to solve.										
G4. Provision of summaries and reviews of online discussions.										
G5. Use of examples of content-related professional work available online.										
G6. The institution's online library resources, including a librarian who is able to assist distance learners using electronically based informational and communications options.										
G7. Provision of easily accessible tutors or teaching assistants who are trained to assist distance education students.										
G8. Institution's use of e-learning partnerships with other institutions or programs.										
G9. Provision of archives of previous students' discussion forum transcripts on topical issues.										

Table 10. Resources

G10. RESOURCES	Rate your satisfaction with the program's use of these resources for distance education students. Use the following scale: VS = Very Satisfied, SS = Somewhat Satisfied, N = Neutral, SD = Somewhat Dissatisfied, VD = Very Dissatisfied.					Rate the effect the program's use of these resources had/has on your overall learning experience in the program. Use the following scale: SE = Strongly Enhanced, E = Enhanced, N = Neutral, D = Degraded, SD = Strongly Degraded.				
	VS	SS	N	SD	VD	SE	E	N	D	SD
Multimedia archives										
Mailing lists and their archives										
Outside Web site links										
FAQs										
Glossaries										
Online dictionaries										
Webliographies										
Databases										
Digital libraries										
Computer tutorials										
Experts online										
Journals										
Magazines										
Newsletters										
Personal journals (e.g., Weblogs/blogs)										
Knowledge management portal or site										
Borrow a laptop										
Borrow a PDA										
Borrow tech manuals										
Borrow a scanner										
Borrow a digital camera										
Borrow a video camera										
Borrow an e-book reader										
Borrow software										
Provide Web page space										
Other (write in)										
Other (write in)										
Other (write in)										

Table 11. Evaluation

FACTORS	Rate your satisfaction with these evaluation factors associated with your distance education program by placing a checkmark in the appropriate box. Use the following scale: VS = Very Satisfied, SS = Somewhat Satisfied, N = Neutral, SD = Somewhat Dissatisfied, VD = Very Dissatisfied.					Rate the effect each of these evaluation factors had/has on your overall learning experience in the program. Use the following scale: SE = Strongly Enhanced, E = Enhanced, N = Neutral, D = Degraded, SD = Strongly Degraded.				
	VS	SS	N	SD	VD	SE	E	N	D	SD
H1. Ability for student feedback to the institution about the quality, benefits, advantages, and disadvantages of the distance education program.										
H2. Appropriateness of the assessment strategies for the program content and alignment with program objectives.										
H3. Alignment of assignments and participation activities with program content and the distance education environment.										
H4. Provision of accessible distance education assessment mechanisms.										
H5. Use of assessment techniques and instruments that are aligned with real-world requirements.										
H6. Provision of a student accessible system for tracking student progress.										
H7. Ability for student feedback to the program about the quality, benefits, advantages, and disadvantages of the program content and environment while the program is in progress.										
H8. Ability for student feedback to the program about the quality of technical, resource, and administrative support while the program is in progress.										
H9. Ability for student feedback to the program about instructional quality while the program is in progress.										
H10. Accessibility of program evaluation results to students.										

About the Editor

Badrul H. Khan is an international speaker, author, educator, and consultant in the field of e-learning and educational technology. Dr. Khan authored the following books: *Web-Based Instruction* (1997), *Web-Based Training* (2001), *E-Learning Strategies* (2004), *E-Learning QUICK Checklist* (2005), *Managing E-Learning* (2005), and *Flexible Learning in an Information Society* (2006). As author of five books, more than 100 papers and a keynote speaker in more than 40 international learning conferences, he has become an international leading expert in blended learning design and implementation. His work addressing current and emerging technologies that revolutionize the way we learn and conduct training in open and distributed environments across diverse populations of learners has established him as a visionary in the field of e-learning. His 1997 *Web-Based Instruction* book defines the critical dimensions of e-learning and made him a pioneer in Web-based instruction. The book has become a bestseller and has been adopted by more than 350 colleges and universities worldwide. His *Managing E-Learning* book further matures e-learning processes and practices and has been translated into 14 languages.

A sought-after keynote speaker on e-learning, Dr. Khan is past president of the International Division of the Association for Educational and Communication Technology (AECT). He served as a consultant/advisor to distance education-related projects at the World Bank, various U.S. federal government departments, the ministry of education in several countries, and academic institutions and corporations in the United States and abroad. Dr. Khan served as founding director of the Educational Technology Leadership cohort program at The George Washington University and the educational technology graduate program at the University of Texas. He also served as instructional developer and evaluation specialist in the School of Medicine at Indiana University. He is founder of *BooksToRead.com*, a recommended readings site on the Internet. He is currently exploring the possibility of establishing the Asian Virtual University (www.BadrulKhan.com/AsianVU) as a hub for excellence in online education. For more information, visit his Web site at www.BadrulKhan.com/khan.

About the Authors

Edward Altman has spent the last decade developing media semantics as a senior scientist at the Institute for Infocomm Research (I2R), Singapore, and before that as a visiting researcher at ATR Media Integration & Communications Research Laboratories, Japan. He received a PhD in electrical and computer engineering at the University of Illinois, USA (1990) and performed post-doctoral research in a joint computer vision and cognitive science program at the Beckman Institute for Advanced Science and Technology.

Jason D. Baker is an associate professor of education at Regent University, USA, where he teaches and conducts research about online distance education. He has advised and trained faculty in the use of educational technology, consulted with institutions developing online learning programs, and has been an active online instructor for the past decade.

Kathleen Barclay, as director of academic affairs, is responsible for the implementation and delivery of student and faculty doctoral programs for the School of Advanced Studies, University of Phoenix Online, USA. Over the past 20 years, she has designed multiple global distance delivery programs involving satellite, computer-based, video, and Web-based approaches. A PhD in organizational systems psychology, her ground-breaking research in the field of online, live instruction is referenced internationally.

Ruth Bennett is a program manager and trainer at the National Credit Union Administration, USA. She has keen interest in educational technology and uses it regularly as a learner, instructor, and instructional designer. Her education consists of a BA in history from Pasadena College, an MA in history from the University of California at Riverside, and an MA in educational technology from George Washington University.

Jenny Bird is a lecturer and educational designer in the Teaching & Learning Center at Southern Cross University, Australia. She has researched and published widely on issues of flexible learning and assessment.

Curtis J. Bonk is a former accountant and CPA who is now professor of instructional systems technology at Indiana University, USA. Dr. Bonk is also a senior research fellow with the DOD s Advanced Distributed Learning Lab, and president of CourseShare and SurveyShare (see http://php.indiana.edu/~cjbonk/). He can be contacted at cjbonk@indiana.edu.

Richard Caladine coordinates the Learning, Innovation, and Future Technologies (LIFT) research unit at University of Wollongong, Australia. He regularly hosts staff development opportunities that involve the use of emerging learning technologies. Dr. Caladine has a background in video and audio performance and production, and has a range of qualifications including a PhD in information technology. In over 20 years at the University of Wollongong, he has helped staff and students acquire film and television production skills, produced educational videotapes, and trained staff in the use of educational technologies. He has also found time to build a television studio, edit a staff development journal, develop computer resources, and publish widely in the field. His spare time is spent riding bodyboards, painting, drawing, and taking photographs.

Laura J. Cataldo, RN, MA, MS, EdD, is a nurse, speaker, and educator. She has extensive medical experience as a nurse in both the emergency room and operating room arenas, administrative experience as a clinical systems analyst, and consultant experience as a medical advisor. In addition to the field of nursing, she has a background in business, educational technology, and program development. Ms. Cataldo is an adjunct faculty member teaching business and leadership courses to adult learners at National Louis University, USA. She is experienced in curriculum development and program design for both in-classroom and online environments. She also serves in a mentor role for prospective students of nursing. Ms. Cataldo received her doctorate in organizational leadership from Nova Southeastern University, USA.

Matthew V. Champagne is chief executive officer and senior evaluator for IOTA Solutions, USA. He has served as professor, consultant, researcher, and evaluator in the areas of learning assessment, feedback, and the integration of technology and education. He received an MS and PhD in industrial and organizational psychology from Purdue University, USA.

Lauren Cifuentes is associate professor in the educational technology program at Texas A&M University, USA, where she teaches integrating technology into the curriculum, computer graphics for learning, and instructional design. Her primary research interests are in design considerations for collaborative environments including distance partnerships and in the effects of shared multimedia.

Bonita Coleman is director of technology training and classroom integration at Valley Christian Schools, USA, a private school district in southern California. She has been involved with distance learning for more than 10 years, most recently working with National Geographic, Earthwatch, Global Friendship, and the NASA Distance Learning Network. She holds a master's degree in education technology.

Brian P. Collins is a former social studies teacher who is now working on a doctorate in learning, technology, and culture at Michigan State University, USA. His current research focuses on how new media can support flexible and adaptive thinking.

Betty Collis received her PhD in the measurement and evaluation of computer applications in education, but has focused on all aspects of technology support for learning over more than two decades of professional service. Her most recent appointments are professor of technology for strategy, learning, and change at the University of Twente in The Netherlands and also head of research for Shell Exploration & Production Learning & Leadership Development. She has been leader of more than 50 funded projects relating to technology and learning, and is a frequent author and presenter in the area (see http://users.gw.utwente.nl/collis/). As of 2005 she has taken early retirement from the University of Twente in order to focus on consulting work (http://bettycollisjefmoonen.nl).

Vanessa Paz Dennen is an assistant professor of instructional systems at Florida State University, USA. She researches how elements of activity design and facilitation impact social learning and interaction processes in online environments. She has been teaching online since 1998.

Maia T. Dimitrova has a number of years of experience in the design and evaluation of educational technology. She received a PhD in "Expert Evaluation of Educational Multimedia" from City University London. After that she worked on projects developing and evaluating the effectiveness of e-learning programs across a range of disciplines for City University London, Middlesex University, and Oxford University, UK. Dr. Dimitrova is currently leading a number of e-learning and e-science projects for the Joint Information Systems Committee (JISC), UK.

David A. Falvo is an assistant professor of instructional technology at the University of Northern Colorado, USA. He teaches graduate-level instructional design and authoring courses, as well as classes in classroom technologies. His research explores Web-based technologies for teaching and learning.

Mercedes Fisher is an associate professor in the Graduate School of Education and Psychology (GSEP) at Pepperdine University, USA. Dr. Fisher, a noted expert on educational technology, is best known for her research and development of collaborative learning models and e-learning communities. She has studied interactive learning environments with a focus on collaborative learning, facilitated, but not controlled, by technology. She is the author of *Designing Courses and Teaching on the Web: A How-To Guide to Proven, Innovative Strategies.* She teaches master's and doctoral courses in learning, technology, and design, as well as in action research methods. Dr. Fisher consults with school districts, museums, universities, and software developers, and she is also a distinguished research professor and Fulbright Scholar who is teaching and conducting research in the School of Informatics at the National College of Ireland, located in Dublin, Ireland, in the IFSC through 2006. She can be contacted at mercedes.fisher@gmail.com.

Diane M. Gayeski, PhD, is professor of strategic communication at Ithaca College, USA, and is CEO of Gayeski Analytics. Internationally recognized as a futurist in organizational communication and learning, she is one of the pioneers in interactive media. Her work builds and translates theories and best practices to practical applications; among her clients are the U.S. Centers for Medicare and Medicaid, Walgreens, Johnson & Wales University, Johnson Controls, and the Metropolitan New York City Library System.

Yakut Gazi is a PhD candidate in educational technology and a senior IT consultant with Instructional Technology Services at Texas A&M University, USA. Her research interests include collaboration and communication in online environments, and the impact of culture and technology on the way people interact.

Linda Harasim is a professor in the School of Communication at Simon Fraser University, Canada.

John G. Hedberg is millennium innovations chair in ICT and Education, and director of the Macquarie ICT Innovations Center at Macquarie University, Australia, a learning partnership with the NSW State Department of Education and Training to develop innovative programs in technology-enhanced learning for students and teachers. He is known for the constructivist learning environments he has designed culminating in a British Academy Award for an interactive theatre CD-ROM entitled *StageStruck*. His most recent book is *Evaluating Interactive Learning Systems* with Thomas C. Reeves.

Anthony Herrington is associate professor of both adult education and IT in education at the University of Wollongong, Australia. He has a long history of teaching in schools and universities, nationally and overseas. His initial teaching focus was mathematics education; however, with the impact of technology, his interests have broadened to include adult and ICT education. Professor Herrington has won national teacher development grants resulting in award-winning publications that have focused on the professional development of teachers using technologies such as video, CD-ROM-based multimedia, and the Internet. He is currently engaged in researching the benefits of online communities of practice for beginning teachers.

Jan Herrington is associate professor of IT in education at the University of Wollongong, Australia. She is a member of the Research Center for Interactive Learning Environments

(RILE) at the university. Her recent research and development interests have focused on the design of Web-based learning environments for higher education and the use of authentic tasks as a central focus for Web-based courses. She was awarded the Association of Educational Communications and Technology (AECT) Young Researcher of the Year Award in Houston, Texas, in 1999, and won a Fulbright Professional Award in 2002 to conduct research at the University of Georgia, USA.

Erin Hunt is an instructional designer with Colorado BOCES and a PhD candidate in educational technology at the University of Northern Colorado, USA. She can be contacted at Ehunt@boces.com.

Ben Johnson is the Poudre Valley School District technical coordinator and is a PhD candidate in educational technology at the University of Northern Colorado, USA. He can be contacted at Bjohnson@poudreschools.edu.

Esko Kähkönen works as director of research, heading the international PhD program in educational technology (IMPDET) at the University of Joensuu, Finland. His works include contributions in virtual university development, intercultural education, and issues of culturally contextualized use of educational technology. He is a co-founder of the International Conference on Educational Technology in a Cultural Context.

Gülsün Kurubacak is an assistant professor in distance education at the College of Open Education at Anadolu University, Turkey. She undertook graduate studies at Anadolu University (MA, educational technology) and the University of Cincinnati, USA (EdD, curriculum & instruction), and also has worked as a post-doctoral fellow at the College of Education at New Mexico State University, USA (2001-2002). She spent the last 20 years focusing on the democratic and multicultural aspects of distance online learning; finding new answers, viewpoints, and explanations for complex online educational problems; and improving learner critical thinking skills through Project-Based Online Learning (PBOL) in online asynchronous and synchronous learning milieus.

Linda L. Lohr is an associate professor of educational technology at the University of Northern Colorado, USA, and the author of *Creating Graphics for Learning and Performance.*

Anoush Margaryan is a research fellow and an associate director of the Institute of Learning Technology at the University of Dundee, Scotland. Her current research is focused on cultural and organizational aspects of the uptake and use of learning object repositories. She holds a master of science degree in education and training systems design from the University of Twente, The Netherlands. Her PhD research focused on the development and application of a technology-enhanced work-based learning model for international corporations, and was carried out at Shell Exploration and Production. She can be contacted at A.Margaryan@Dundee.ac.uk.

Joan D. McMahon has been teaching online since 1997. In her innovative work with the university system of Maryland's Web-Initiative-in-Teaching project, she saw the conflicts between intellectual property issues and curriculum transformation issues. This led to an analysis on ethics in course design. She has been involved with the FIPSE Quality Matters project as a faculty trainer and instructional designer.

Ankush Mittal earned BTech (computer science and engineering) and MS by research (computer science and engineering) degrees from the Indian Institute of Technology, Delhi, India, in 1996 and 1998 respectively. He obtained his PhD degree in electrical and computer engineering from the National University of Singapore. He was formerly a faculty member in the Department of Computer Science at the National University of Singapore. At present, he serves as assistant professor at IIT Roorkee, India.

M. G. Moore is professor of education at The Pennsylvania State University and the founder (1986) and editor of *The American Journal of Distance Education*. He is author of more than 100 books and articles about distance education, e-learning, and related subjects. He has been a speaker on educational technology issues in some 30 countries and as many American states. From 1996-1998 he was a visiting scholar at the World Bank, and continues as consultant to international agencies and national governments. In 2002 he was inducted into the United States Distance Learning Association Hall of Fame.

Chris Morgan is a lecturer and educational designer in the Teaching & Learning Center at Southern Cross University, Australia. He has written extensively on assessment and is the co-author of two books, *Assessing Open and Distance Learners* (Kogan Page, 1999) and *The Student Assessment Handbook* (Routledge, 2004).

Karen L. Murphy is associate professor *emeritus* in the educational technology program at Texas A&M University and faculty developer with the School of Education, Western New Mexico University, Silver City, USA. Her research interests include collaborative learning and the impact of culture in online learning environments.

Nick Nissley presently serves his alma mater, the Milton Hershey School, USA, as Vice President, Workforce & Organization Effectiveness. Formerly, he was an assistant professor at the University of St. Thomas, USA, in the Department of Organization Learning and Development. He earned his EdD in human resource development from the George Washington University's Graduate School of Education and Human Development. His teaching and research interests are in the field of workplace learning—specifically, arts-based learning (e.g., storytelling). Dr. Nissley continues to teach a doctoral course, "Organizational Storytelling," at the University of St. Thomas's doctoral program in organization development.

Ron Oliver is professor of interactive multimedia in the Faculty of Communications and Creative Industries at Edith Cowan University, Australia. He has a background in multimedia and learning technologies, and currently leads a research team at ECU in these fields. He has extensive experience in the design, development, implementation, and evaluation of technology-mediated and online learning materials. Current projects in which he is involved include investigations of authentic settings for online teaching and learning, the reusability of e-learning resources, and the modeling and specification of high-quality generic learning designs for online learning.

Krishnan V. Pagalthivarthi is an IIT Delhi graduate in mechanical engineering (1979) and is currently a professor in the Department of Applied Mechanics at IIT Delhi, India. He received his MS (1984) and PhD (1988) degrees from Georgia Institute of Technology, USA. He worked in reputed U.S. research organizations like the SWRI, GIW Hydraulic Lab, and Georgia Tech. He is well known for his excellent teaching both at IIT Delhi and at Georgia Tech.

Salvatore Paratore is professor of education at George Washington University, USA. He received his PhD from Syracuse University, USA. He is a research representative and has been involved with the GW Chapter of Phi Delta Kappa International for 15 years. He is also the president of the Epilepsy Foundation for the National Capital Area. Previous posts include Educational Leadership Department chair for six years; acting associate dean, School of Education; associate dean, Division of Continuing and Summer Sessions; assistant dean of Summer Sessions; high school mathematics teacher and coach; and an officer in the U.S. Navy. He is part of the executive committee, GW Faculty Senate.

Carla R. Payne is professor of graduate studies at Vermont College of Union Institute, USA and at the University in Montpelier, Vermont. Her BA is from Barnard College, and she earned MA and PhD degrees from SUNY/Buffalo. Her publications include "Good Practice and Motivation in Online Learning" (Virtual University Gazette) and "Teaching and Technology for Human Development," co-authored with A.W. Chickering and G. Poitras, in *Educational Technology,* and "Design for Success: Applying Progressive Educational Principles Online" in *Current Perspectives on Applied Information Technologies: Preparing Teachers to Teach with Technology.*

Cheryl Plett is an adjunct faculty member in the Computer Science Department at Cerro Coso Community College in Ridgecrest, California, USA.

Susan M. Powers is a professor of education technology in the College of Education at Indiana State University, USA. She works with undergraduate and graduate programs on innovative ways to infuse technology to enhance teaching and learning, and conducts research on distance learning, distance learning technologies, and online learning environments.

Aparna R. Ramchandran has a master's degree in telecommunication, information studies, and media from Michigan State University, USA. Her research has focused on multimedia development and emerging technologies in digital media with special interest in educational applications of digital media. She is the Flash/multimedia developer of EASE Projects.

Thomas C. Reeves is a professor of instructional technology at the University of Georgia, USA. His research interests include evaluation of instructional technology for education and training, socially responsible research goals and methods in education, mental models and cognitive tools, and instructional technology in developing countries.

Christine Salmon is coordinator of the Professional Support Center at Tomball College, USA. She has worked in faculty development for five years, assisting faculty in designing and developing distance learning courses. Ms. Salmon was assistant professor of French for 10 years in Indiana. She is currently pursuing a doctorate degree in education.

Henry L. Smith is an adjunct professor in the instructional technology master's program at San José State University, USA. Dr. Smith has also taught educational leadership as an adjunct professor in the educational technology master's program at Pepperdine University, USA.

Paul Sparks directs the online master's program in education technology at Pepperdine University, USA. He is past director of the EdTech doctoral program and guides courses in human-computer interaction, consulting, and constructivist leadership. Previously Dr. Sparks directed virtual collaboration at 3iNetworks, learning technologies for Rockwell International, and training for Epoch Internet.

Rand J. Spiro is a professor of learning, technology, and culture at Michigan State University, USA. Before coming to MSU, Dr. Spiro was a distinguished senior scholar in the College of Education at the University of Illinois at Urbana-Champaign, where he was professor of educational psychology, psychology, and the Beckman Institute for Advanced Science and Technology. He has been a visiting scientist in psychology and computer science at Yale University, where he worked in the Yale Artificial Intelligence Laboratory, and a visiting professor of education at Harvard University. Dr. Spiro is the originator of cognitive flexibility theory and its application to innovative approaches to hypermedia design.

R. Subramaniam holds a PhD in physical chemistry. He is an associate professor at the National Institute of Education in Nanyang Technological University, Singapore, and honorary secretary of the Singapore National Academy of Science. Prior to this, he was acting head of physical sciences at the Singapore Science Center. His research interests are in the fields of physical chemistry, science education, theoretical cosmophysics, museum science, telecommunications, and transportation. He has published several research papers in international refereed journals.

Erkki Sutinen, professor, holds a PhD in computer science. He is the director of the Educational Technology Research Group (http://www.cs.joensuu.fi/edtech) at the University of Joensuu, Finland. His research interests include ICT education in developing countries, learning tools like visualization and digital portfolios, cultural factors of educational technology, computer science education, and information retrieval/string algorithms.

Leo Tan Wee Hin has a PhD in marine biology. He holds the concurrent appointments of director of the National Institute of Education, professor of biological sciences at Nanyang Technological University, Singapore, and president of the Singapore National Academy of Science. Prior to this, he was director of the Singapore Science Center. His research interests are in the fields of marine biology, science education, museum science, telecommunications, and transportation. He has published numerous research papers in international refereed journals.

Steven R. Terrell is a professor at the Graduate School of Computer and Information Sciences at Nova Southeastern University, USA, where he teaches research methodology and learning theory. His publications focus on predictors of attrition and evaluation of online learning environments. Dr. Terrell also serves as chair of the American Educational Research Association's Education and WWW special interest groups.

Shauna Tonkin is a professor in the School of Education at Regent University, USA. She teaches and writes about instructional leadership, online education, and curriculum development. Previously, Dr. Tonkin launched and directed the activities of Regent's award-winning Center for Teaching and Learning, which provides comprehensive instructional support services for faculty and staff.

Lorna Uden teaches computing in the Faculty of Computing, Engineering, and Technology at Staffordshire University, UK. Her research interests include technology learning, HCI, activity theory, knowledge management, Web engineering, multimedia, e-business, and problem-based learning. She has published widely in conferences, journals, and chapters of books. Dr. Uden is also the founder and editor of the *International Journal of Web Engineering and Technology* (IJWET) and the *International Journal of Learning Technology* (IJLT), published by Inderscience.

Robert A. Wisher is director of the Advanced Distributed Learning Initiative within the U.S. Department of Defense. He specializes in research on the learning sciences and the effectiveness of training technologies. Dr. Wisher received a BS in mathematics from Purdue University and a PhD in cognitive psychology from the University of California, San Diego.

Claus Witfelt is a lecturer at the Danish University of Education, IT University of Copenhagen, Denmark, and BEC Education Center. He has worked for many years with flexible learning in many contexts, as a teacher, researcher, and evaluator. Professor Witfelt received his master's degree in computer science from the University of Roskilde in 1997.

Brian Yecies is a lecturer in the Department of Communication and Cultural Studies at the University of Wollongong, Australia. His research projects focus on the global popularity of South Korean Cinema, Hollywood™ negotiations with film import quotas, film policy in colonial Korea, and overcoming student attitudes of distance with interactive Web portals.

T. Volkan Yuzer is an assistant professor in the Department of Distance Education of the College of Open Education at Anadolu University, Turkey. He undertook graduate studies at Anadolu University, Turkey (MA and PhD, communication sciences). His research interests are new communicating technologies, synchronous online communications, and interactive communication milieus in distance education.

Index

contract assessment 251
Copenhagen, Denmark 110
course integrity 210, 211
course management system (CMS) 153, 205, 228
course transcripts 264
critical thinking 84, 136, 143, 252
cross-cultural differences 52
cross-cultural sites 219
CSCL 110, 153
CSCL systems 110
CSR 233
cultural contextualization 221
cultural heterogeneity 219
culturally sensitive learning content 220
CUPID 153, 154
customer service representative (CSR) 233

D

DAT 138
debates 70, 111, 248, 282, 284
delivery 248
dialogical learning 223
digital exhibits 108
digital gallery 157
Digital Storytelling Theater 91
digital text 150
digital video cases 22
Discussion Analysis Tool (DAT) 138
discussion board 204, 297
distance learning program 165
distributed learning 2, 4, 114, 227
diverse assessment schemes 252
dumping 205
dynamic HTML 103

E

EASE systems 22
EASE (Experience Acceleration Support Environment) 19, 22
eCollege™ 187
effectiveness evaluation 229
electronic portfolios 263
embedded audio 103
ethical awareness 252
ethical problem 210

ethics 117, 124, 142
ethnocomputing 223
evaluation 227
evaluation of the instruction and learning environment 227
experience acceleration 20
experience acceleration support environments 19

F

f2f 285, 288, 289
f2f learning environment 237, 285
face-to-face (f2f) 285, 288, 289
FirstClass 110
flexible assessment 247
flexible knowledge assembly 22
flexible learning 1, 6, 8, 13, 114, 248, 253, 275, 306, 307
flexible working schedule 159
formative assessment 250
formative evaluation 57, 228, 230
formative feedback 249
forum manager 138

G

GC 298, 301
geographically dispersed 255
Global Campus (GC) 298, 301
global positioning system (GPS) 149, 150
GPS 149, 150
graphical user interface (GUI) 176, 231
group-based activities 72
GUI 176, 231

H

habits of mind 19, 22, 23
helpdesk support 256
hot spot 165

I

ICDE 220
idea generating 285
idea linking 285
IHEP 127
ill-defined activities 27
immediate feedback 40

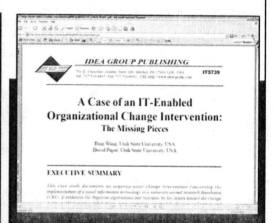

UNIVERSITY OF WOLVERHAMPTON
LEARNING & INFORMATION SERVICES